Law, Lawyers and Race

Critical Race Theory (CRT) is virtually unheard of in European scholarship, especially among legal scholars. *Law, Lawyers and Race: Critical Race Theory from the United States to Europe* endeavours to fill this gap by providing an overview of the definition and consequences of CRT developed in American scholarship and describing its transplantation and application in the continental European context.

The CRT approach adopted in this book illustrates the reasons why the relationship between race and law in European civil law jurisdictions is far from anodyne. Law plays a critical role in the construction, subordination and discrimination against racial minorities in Europe, making it comparable, albeit in slightly different ways, to the American experience of racial discrimination. Anti-Semitism, Islamophobia, anti-Roma and anti-Black racism constitute a fundamental factor, often tacitly accepted, in the relationship between law and race in Europe. Consequently, the broadly shared anti-race and anti-racist position is problematic because it acts to the detriment of victims of racism while privileging the White, Christian, male majority.

This book is an original exploration of the relationship between law and race. As such it crosses the disciplinary divide, furthering both legal scholarship and research in Race and Ethnicity Studies.

Mathias Möschel is a Postdoctoral Researcher based at the University of Paris Ouest Nanterre La Défense.

Law, Lawyers and Race

Critical Race Theory from the United States to Europe

Mathias Möschel

Routledge
Taylor & Francis Group
a GlassHouse Book

First published 2014
by Routledge
2 Park Square, Milton Park, Abingdon, Oxon, OX14 4RN

and by Routledge
711 Third Avenue, New York, NY 10017
a GlassHouse Book
Routledge is an imprint of the Taylor & Francis Group, an informa business

British Library Cataloguing in Publication Data
A catalogue record for this book is available from the British Library

Library of Congress Cataloging-in-Publication Data
Möschel, Mathias, author.
Law, lawyers and race : critical race theory from the US to Europe / Mathias Möschel.
pages cm
ISBN 978-0-415-73930-6 (hardback) -- ISBN 978-1-315-81673-9 (ebk) 1. Race discrimination--Law and legislation--Europe. 2. Minorities--Legal status, laws, etc.--Europe. 3. Critical legal studies. 4. Race discrimination--Law and legislation--United States. 5. Minorities--Legal status, laws, etc.--United States. 6. United States--Race relations--Philosophy. 7. Europe--Race relations--Philosophy. 8. Law--Philosophy. I. Title.
KJC5144.M56M67 2014
342.408'73--dc23
2014005760

ISBN: 978-0-415-73930-6 (hbk)
ISBN: 978-1-315-81673-9 (ebk)

Typeset in Baskerville by
Servis Filmsetting Ltd, Stockport, Cheshire

This publication is a revised version of an EUI Ph.D. thesis and has been published with a financial subsidy from the European University Institute.

MIX
Paper from responsible sources
FSC® C013604

Printed and bound by CPI Group (UK) Ltd, Croydon, CR0 4YY

To my family and Laurent whom I thank for their love and trust in me.

Acknowledgement

This book would not have seen the light of the day if it had not been for a number of people whom I would like to thank especially beyond my family and my friends.

First of all, Angela Harris who introduced me to Critical Race Theory, then also Ruth Rubio-Marín, Kendall Thomas, Wojciech Sadurski, and Gianfrancesco Zanetti who have all supported me during the time of my Ph.D. on which this book is based.

Second, a number of networks of scholars and activists have also contributed intellectually and inspirationally to this book. Special thanks go to the CRT Europe Group and in particular Kimberlé Crenshaw, Luke Harris and Cengiz Barskanmaz for creating this space in which to analyse issues relating to race and law in Europe; to the Black Europe Summer School in Amsterdam and in particular Philomena Essed, Stephen Small and Kwame Nimako for introducing a much needed academic visibility of Black European identities; and to REGINE and in particular Stéphanie Hennette-Vauchez, Diane Roman and Marc Pichard for offering me an academic home, support for this book and new intellectual and political adventures.

Last but not least, special thanks to Emma Nyhan and the (copy-)editors of Routledge who have turned this book from my terrible English and incoherent ramblings into something that reads like 'proper' English and that makes much more sense.

Parts of this book are loosely based on the below for which I have asked for/obtained authorisation to publish:

Race in mainland European legal analysis: Towards a European Critical Race Theory", *Ethnic and Racial Studies*, 2011, vol. 34, no. 10, pp. 1648–1664

Color Blindness or Total Blindness? The Absence of Critical Race Theory in Europe", *Rutgers Race & the Law Review*, 2007, vol. 9, no. 1, pp. 57–127

Contents

Table of Abbreviations

AALS	Association of American Law Schools
ABA	American Bar Association
AGG	Allgemeines Gleichbehandlungsgesetz
AGRIF	L'Alliance générale contre le racisme et pour le respect de l'identité française et chrétienne
AI	Amnesty International
BCDF	Boalt Coalition for a Diversified Faculty
BGBl	Bundesgesetzblatt
CC	Conseil Constitutionnel
CDP	Christian Democratic Party
CdS	Consiglio di Stato
CJEU	Court of Justice of the European Union
CLS	Critical Legal Studies
CNIL	Commission nationale de l'informatique et des libertés
COMEDD	Comité pour la mesure de la diversité et l'évaluation des discriminations
CRAN	Conseil Représentatif des Associations Noires
CRT	Critical Race Theory
DPCM	Decreto Presidente del Consiglio dei ministri
ECHR	European Convention on Human Rights
ECJ	European Court of Justice
ECommHR	European Commission of Human Rights
ECR	European Court Reports
ECRI	European Commission Against Racism and Intolerance
ECSR	European Committee of Social Rights
ECtHR	European Court of Human Rights
ERRC	European Roma Rights Centre
EU-MIDIS	European Union Minorities and Discrimination Survey
EU	European Union
FCPC	French Criminal Procedure Code
GA	Georgia
GED	Groupe d'études des discriminations

GU	Gazzetta Ufficiale
HRC	Human Rights Committee
HRW	Human Rights Watch
ICERD	United Nations' International Convention on the Elimination of All Forms of Racial Discrimination
INED	Institut national d'études démographiques
INSEE	Institut national de statistiques et études économiques
JORF	Journal Officiel de la République Française
KFN	Kriminologisches Forschungsinstitut Niedersachsen
LSAT	Law School Admission Test
MBE	minority business enterprise
NAACP	National Association for the Advancement of Colored People
NGO	non-governmental organisation
OJEU	Official Journal of the European Union
POPA	Public Order Protection Act
RED	Race Equality Directive
S CT	Supreme Court
SB	Senate Bill
TAR	Tribunale Amministrativo Regionale
TFEU	Treaty on the Functioning of the European Union
UCLA	University of California, Los Angeles
UC	University of California
UKSC	United Kingdom Supreme Court
UNESCO	United Nations Educational, Scientific and Cultural Organization
US Const	United States Constitution
ZAR	Zeitschrift für Ausländerrecht und Ausländerpolitik

Preface

Racism (and racial discrimination) is, to a certain extent, alive and well in every society, country, and region of the world. It can appear in a variety of forms depending on the culture or context in which it occurs and the period of history during which it rears its head. Nonetheless, one common thread that seems to be woven throughout almost every culture, country, and region is that people deny that racism even exists.

Ariel E. Dulitzky[1]

In the summer of 1989, when a small group of mostly young American law professors gathered outside Madison, Wisconsin for a workshop on the relevance of critical legal theory to studies of race, the conventional view was that the worst of the nation's racism was in the past. The movement born at that summer workshop – which its leaders named Critical Race Theory – was intended to challenge that view. The participants, myself included, took the position that racism was central, not peripheral, to American society. Indeed, we aimed at demonstrating that anti-discrimination jurisprudence itself, and all the legal actors and institutions charged with implementing guarantees of legal equality, would bend when necessary to accommodate White supremacy. Critical Race Theory was founded to investigate the peculiar fact that racism can pervade legal structures officially committed to anti-racism.

We all knew that American slavery was but one node in a transnational system of economic exploitation long justified by popular narratives about civilization, God, and savagery. Many of us were also steeped in the history of transnational anti-racist resistance – from the first pan-African conference in London in 1900, to the treason prosecution of Communist Party activist Angelo Herndon for advocating Black self-determination in the South in the 1930s, to the interconnections between the anti-colonial architects of Négritude in Paris and the writers and artists of the Harlem Renaissance in New York, down to the influence of Frantz Fanon's writings on the Black Panther Party in the 1960s. Our focus at the time,

1 Ariel E. Dulitzky, 'A Region in Denial: Racial Discrimination and Racism in Latin America', in Anani Dzidzienyo and Suzanne Oboler (eds), *Neither Enemies Nor Friends: Latinos, Blacks, Afro-Latinos* (New York: Palgrave Macmillan, 2005), p. 39.

however, was on American civil rights law, American culture, American constitutional theory, and the American legal academy. With a few notable exceptions, American critical race theorists left the international implications of our work unexplored.

Indeed, more than twenty years later, the relevance of Critical Race Theory beyond the borders of the United States remained underexplored. In an edited collection of essays published in 2002, Celina Romany asked some basic questions: 'Does "race-as-a-social-construct" adequately capture the multidimensionality of colonial/postcolonial exploitation? … How do we extrapolate a politics of difference and resistance located in the United States that, when carried to the world of international politics, wears a homogenous U.S. label?'[2] A handful of the scholars published in that volume used Critical Race Theory to examine human rights norms in international conventions such as the International Covenant on Civil and Political Rights, or to criticise the operation of international institutions such as the World Bank and the International Monetary Fund. Scholars in Canada and in England had begun to make use of the intellectual tools of American Critical Race Theory. Yet, no one had yet begun to forge a thoroughly comparative and transnational Critical Race Theory. And few had begun to recognise the significance of Critical Race Theory for Europe.

With the publication of this book, these long-overdue projects are at last well underway. Mathias Möschel is a scholar with deep roots both in American Critical Race Theory and in European law and legal theory. Since 2004, when he began to write his LL.M. thesis on this topic at the University of California Berkeley School of Law, Möschel has grasped the relevance – indeed, the urgency – of Critical Race Theory for contemporary Europe. As the epigraph to this Preface so astutely observes, wherever one travels in the world, racism is always somewhere else. Yet, despite a deeply engrained unwillingness to recognise it, in Europe today – just as in the United States – race and racism are central terms in political and social debates on equality, liberty, migration, and citizenship. Möschel's book brilliantly shows how in Europe, as in the United States, legal norms often collaborate with social norms to perpetuate racism in the name of anti-racism. Möschel persuasively argues that the reluctance of European states to speak of race is itself a symptom of the problem. Like the American discourse of 'colourblindness', European colourblindness leaves the state without adequate resources for challenging racism, and thus enables racism to persist. The paradox on which Critical Race Theory was founded – the persistence of racism in officially anti-racist societies – is therefore an international one.

The relationship between Critical Race Theory and European law and legal theory does not, however, move in only one direction. If Critical Race Theory is to be able to move across national borders, it must evolve and change. Möschel's

2 Celina Romany, 'Critical Race Theory in Global Context', in Francisco Valdes, Jerome McCristal Culp and Angela P. Harris (eds), *Crossroads, Directions, and a New Critical Race Theory* (Philadelphia: Temple University Press, 2002), p. 304.

careful case studies of racial discrimination against the Roma in several European countries, the French ideology of colourblindness, and the legal construction of White masculine privilege in Italy contribute to this project as well. Postcolonial history and theory, theories of migration and ethnicity, and race theory have long been oddly disconnected from one another. This book begins to close that gap. With its publication, Critical Race Theory is finally poised to fulfil its early promise as a rich comparative and international critical conversation on the links between race, religion, ethnicity, and nation.

Finally, this book is a bold intervention into European legal theory. As Möschel observes, in the terms of conventional European legal analysis his argument would be considered too 'sociological', too 'philosophical', and just plain 'not legal'. Critical Race Theory's relevance to Europe is not only in showing how legal, cultural, and social norms interact, but also in pointing the way toward a transformed and transformative continental legal theory – the birth of a distinctively European critical legal studies. Möschel's pioneering study thus enriches the language of European jurisprudence.

Möschel is well positioned to take on this important work. Not only is he an expert in both American and European equality law and legal theory, he is also a tireless convener of European conferences and workshops on feminist legal theory and Critical Race Theory, generating rich, cross-national conversations among scholars, legal actors, and activists. With the publication of this book, the promise of Critical Race Theory in 1989 is at last fulfilled for Europe. Race and racism are not American issues; they are global issues. *Law, Lawyers and Race: Critical Race Theory from the United States to Europe* is timely, insightful, and a must-read for all those interested in equality, discrimination, and the state.

Angela P. Harris
University of California, Davis School of Law (King Hall)

Introduction

> *I must also confess, Professor, I've been reading your stuff and that of your colleagues in the Critical Race Theory movement. It's fairly popular in Europe; many Italian law students read and discuss it.*[1]

> *And yet, being a problem is a strange experience – peculiar even for one who has never been anything else, save perhaps in babyhood and in Europe.*[2]

Critical Race Theory (CRT) has existed for more than twenty years in the United States, where it has given rise to an important range of scholarship analysing the relationship between race and law. In contrast to the American experience of CRT, such legal scholarship is virtually unheard of in mainland Europe. To date, however, American CRT scholars have focused primarily on their own domestic reality and have only recently started to look at other jurisdictions to understand the ways in which race and law are interrelated globally.

This book is therefore of interest to European scholars who are unfamiliar with CRT, its genealogy, its main tenets, and the developments and critiques it has been exposed to. And, in offering the first comprehensive attempt to look at continental European legal systems through the lens of CRT, it is also relevant to American scholars working critically, and increasingly also internationally and comparatively, on race and law who want to better understand the European legal, historical, and sociological context. In other words, this book undertakes comparative CRT by analysing continental European legal systems against the backdrop of the American experience of racism and law as witnessed and critiqued by critical race scholars.

At the same time, however, the main purpose of this book is not exclusively comparative but seeks to demonstrate how and in which ways law has shaped, and continues to shape and construct race in the continental European context, even if it differs from the American experience. Contrary to the orthodox vision and narrative, race and ethnicity do not play an exceptional role in the legislation,

1 Richard Delgado, 'Rodrigo's Chronicle', *Yale Law Journal* (1992), vol. 101, p. 1363.
2 W.E.B. Du Bois, *The Souls of Black Folk* [1903] (New York: The Modern Library, 2003), p. 4.

case law, and legal scholarship of mainland Europe. Rather, race and ethnicity constitute an underlying, unspoken but at times also open assumption, even after World War II. Thus, this book can be viewed as a broader exhortation to European legal academics to start critically analysing law and race and how they relate in this specific context.

The book's structure is designed to reflect and address these different, yet related, interests and goals. The first two chapters are situated in the United States. Chapter 1 sets the stage by describing the broader historical background in which CRT emerged. To this end, it is subdivided into two separate timelines: the first showing how law contributed to the construction and subordination of racial minorities in the United States, and the second providing a more traditional and better known account of American legal movements from legal formalism to postmodern legal scholarship. CRT, I posit, is to a large extent the result of the merging of these two timelines.

Chapter 2 contains a more detailed account of CRT itself, its emergence in the late 1980s, its main tenets, the internal and external critiques it has been exposed to, as well as its latest developments. Ultimately, these first two chapters will give the reader a clearer sense and overview of the context and the struggles from which CRT emerged. Yet, more importantly, these chapters also serve to detail the substantive aspects; the concepts and tools that will help with analysing the continental European systems in the last two chapters.

Chapter 3 represents the conceptual bridge between the American and the European legal systems. Drawing on the instruments of comparative law and cultural studies, such as travelling theory, the doctrine of legal transplants, and/or functional analogues, this part of the book will serve to explain the mechanisms, risks, the feasibility and the existence of CRT transplants in mainland Europe. This part will explain why CRT has received so little attention in this geographical setting until now.

The last two chapters are more directly concerned with an analysis of the continental European legal systems through the lens of CRT scholarship which will serve as a sort of methodological tool and roadmap to analyse and critique those legal systems.

Chapter 4 identifies the common features that in my opinion characterise the relationship between race and law in mainland European legal systems. This book posits that despite certain national differences one can identify common characteristics and positions in many of these countries. In contrast to the United States, there seems to be a common European narrative, whereby race has only played a marginal and exceptional role in each country's history and law, which disappeared and became discredited, especially in the period after World War II and due to the focus on anti-Semitism. Coupled with this narrative the anti-racist position from the early days contends that it is necessary to stop speaking about race and/or using the term in legislation because the on-going use of race perpetuates the idea that biological human races continue to exist thereby keeping racism alive. By defining this position and its consequences in the legal field as

'Continental European Colourblindness', this book will problematise not only its underlying assumptions but also the legal effects it produces.

Having set the overarching framework, the last chapter provides some nuances, which are specific to mainland Europe. Race, ethnicity, racism, and/or race discrimination are after all highly context dependent and shift over time, space, and groups involved, which makes these phenomena so difficult to grasp and to define. Chapter 5 contextualises the broader observations and analyses offered in the previous chapter. First of all, a more detailed analysis of how, in spite of the many recent non-discrimination and social justice initiatives at a European and national level, law adversely affects a specific minority – the Roma. Second, France and its model of Republican colourblindness provide an excellent ground of analysis for issues related to race and racism. Not only because it is almost the example *par excellence*, or the purest model, of 'Continental European Colourblindness' but also because it is one of the countries where the public debate on race has evolved most strongly in recent years and where legal decisions have started to surface at the constitutional level. Finally, the analysis of the situation in Italy provides an occasion to look at overlapping issues related to race, (im)migration, and religion and how these issues play out in a typically European way and get inscribed into legislation and case law. In terms of legal sources, the focus here will be on the local level, which is often overlooked by lawyers and where the popular/populist discourses mainly from Northern Italy become particularly visible.

Ultimately what emerges from this book is that in mainland Europe law has operated, and is still operating, in a similar, yet different, manner to American law in constructing and subordinating racial and ethnic minorities. In other words, this is not simply an attempt at highlighting racism's presence and rampancy in Europe, which is common knowledge and well-documented in various reports, surveys, and statistics by European human rights institutions.[3] Instead, this book reveals the White, Christian, male hegemony underlying seemingly neutral and objective laws and jurisprudence in the continental European context.

A number of clarifications are necessary at this point. First, this book does not advocate that race should occupy a central position in European legal analysis. Class, gender, religion, citizenship, and sexual orientation are just as important as race in terms of factors that determine social exclusion, discrimination, and vulnerability. However, there is a need to move away from the intellectual construction that race and class are mutually exclusive categories and that by adopting one type of analytical category the other category simply cannot co-exist or must disappear. The problem in mainland Europe is that class, citizenship, and religion have so far dominated the discourse in explaining structural and systemic

3 See e.g. the annual reports and the country reports by the European Commission Against Racism and Intolerance (ECRI) available at: www.coe.int/t/dghl/monitoring/ecri/default_en.asp or the data and information collected by the European Union Agency for Fundamental Rights. See e.g. 'EU-MIDIS, European Union Minorities and Discrimination Survey: Main Results Report' (Vienna: European Union Agency for Fundamental Rights, 2009) available at: http://fra.europa.eu/fraWebsite/attachments/eumidis_mainreport_conference-edition_en_.pdf.

disadvantage when, more often than not, race has also played a role. Nevertheless, the racial factor is often de-legitimised, silenced, and/or re-framed in weaker and cushier terms. Hence, this book is an attempt to carry out a race-conscious analysis of continental European legal systems against the backdrop of on-going widespread racism when talking and analysing in terms of race is almost taboo. While not every hostile and discriminatory act amounts to racism, at the same time, we need to be able to call it by its name instead of trying to cover it up.

Second, this book does not offer a strictly positivist and dogmatic legal analysis, which elegantly and doctrinally analyses and subsumes racial anti-discrimination law under some new or existing principle. Here one will uncover how law and the discourses surrounding or engrained in racism have a tendency to function in favour of the White, Christian majority both in the United States and in Europe. To this end, a broader framework of analysis, in which history, political sciences, and sociology play an important role, is indispensable. Nevertheless, the main concern remains with law in the broadest sense. Although law is only one aspect in combatting racial discrimination, it remains an important one. Therefore, assessing critically and honestly how and to whose benefit and detriment law operates when we are looking at the sensitive issue of race becomes crucial. This book argues that in spite of the legal instruments put into place in order to combat racial discrimination, it often reflects the position of the majority thus further legally marginalising those who are most often already socially, economically, and culturally vulnerable.

Third, at the risk of making hasty overgeneralisations and sweeping analyses at various points, this book adopts a broad comparative focus. For instance, to lump together most continental European countries when defining 'Continental European Colourblindness' or when portraying the common law/civil law dichotomy in such neat and absolute terms may seem bold, un-nuanced and de-contextualised. However, most mainland European countries are certainly closer to each other in their rejection of race compared with the United Kingdom and Ireland and their race-conscious statistics and legislation. Furthermore, in terms of legal structure, the academic traditions of the countries belonging to civil law systems share more with each other than with the United Kingdom and Ireland. This explains why those two countries are not included and only rarely referred to in the 'European' analysis to be found here. Ultimately, this book endeavours to strike a delicate balance between observing and/or discovering general trends while being aware that they vary at the national or local level, over time and space, and depending on the minority group involved. The local and contextualised analyses and differences or divergences can be and should be the object of future research and verification of the arguments presented here. In particular, Eastern European or Scandinavian countries that belong to the family of civil law systems but are not treated in-depth here may provide interesting and additional material and/or nuances.

Fourth, the reader may be surprised to find little or only marginal reference made to Jews and anti-Semitism in this book, even though this is the preferred lens to examine racism in the continental European context. However, I contend that this preferred reading of racism, in terms of anti-semitism, raises certain issues. Following the Shoah, anti-Semitism has almost become the only and paradigmatic prism through which to view race, race discrimination, and racism in Europe. Whereas it is probably correct to say that the era of state-sponsored anti-Semitism ended quite abruptly by the end of World War II and that legal protection against anti-Semitism functions relatively effectively, the same cannot be said for anti-Black racism, racism against the Roma and racism against Muslims (Islamophobia). Hence, without wanting to create racial hierarchies or inhibiting the creation of common anti-racist strategies between these different groups, one probably needs to distinguish them. True, the general matrix is one of racism and belief in the biological and cultural superiority of the White race. However, there are the more specific facets and racisms. Hence, the focus in this book will not be on anti-Semitism specifically because, at least in that case, the continental European legal systems seem to provide the necessary legal protection and have the necessary understanding of the structural issues related to this type of racism. The focus instead is on the fact that most of those systems do not adequately protect other racialised minorities, precisely because most equate racism with anti-Semitism, which has been adequately addressed with the necessary measures. Under this pretence, it is only a question of time and minor reforms within society and legal systems before the scourge of racism is eliminated.

Finally, some terminological clarifications and caveats need to be made here in order to clarify the choice of certain terms. First and foremost, the attention focuses on the key term race and the ways it is used throughout this book. It is a conscious choice not to put it in inverted commas as is often done in publications using the term. The reasons for using quotation marks for the word race are to draw attention to the fact the author is aware that it is a social construct and to signal its dangerousness and problematic nature. However, there are several terms that are social constructs, which can give rise to problems, misunderstandings and skewed readings. The majority of these, if not all, are written without quotation marks. For this reason, I avoid using quotation marks, which should not read that anything in this book is intended to suggest that I believe in the existence of different biological human races. Instead, race is seen as a social, historical, cultural, and legal construct and reality. Part of the effort of this book is precisely to demonstrate the role law plays in this construction. Therefore this is a conscious departure from the anti-racist strategy and policy of fighting racism by avoiding the race discourse in the hope that this will eventually lead to the elimination of racism. Both descriptively and normatively such strategy is ineffective at best and counterproductive at worst. Moreover, this book quite consciously does not provide a working or legal definition of race and/or ethnicity. One often sees that the insistence on providing such a definition leads to endless and fruitless discussions, which remain limited to the terminological and conceptual sphere. What this book intends to demonstrate is that race should be read as a thick concept which is not limited to biology and/or to anti-Semitism in the continental European context but incorporates culture, religion, and nationality when constructing such a definition. If race is read to encompass these elements and to apply conceptually to other racial minorities besides Jews, then it could function as a tool *against* any kind of subordination and discrimination. The thin concept and understanding of race and racism which is currently predominant in mainland Europe leads to a narrow legal definition of race and racism, and therefore vastly reduces one of the possible and available avenues to combat discrimination and to challenge White, Christian European supremacy and presumed cultural superiority.

The second terminological clarification concerns the terms 'visible minorities' and 'people of colour' and their interchangeable use throughout the book. Both terms have the advantage of avoiding the negative and stigmatising connotations, which arise when speaking of people with a 'migrant background' or 'second generation (im)migrants'. In particular, the latter term is erroneous with regards to children of immigrants born in Europe or to Roma who often have a European citizenship, but who are nevertheless continuously Othered by being referred to as 'second generation (im)migrants' instead of as 'first generation nationals'. This is also the case for similarly situated people in the United States. While the Canadian term 'visible minorities' might look out of place in a book, which mainly concerns the United States and Europe, it nevertheless best reflects the reality of the discrimination experienced by those belonging to such minorities. The fact of being *visibly* different either because of skin colour or because of a specific dress code adopted for religious or cultural reasons is often the cause for the most blatant forms of race discrimination in Europe, ranging from verbal aggression, to racial profiling, to violence up to murder. In those cases no one enquires into the nationality or the name of the victim but it is in fact the visible difference that literally makes all the difference. Similarly, 'people of colour' is being used from time to time, even though this term is more limited and raises questions about who is targeted and for what purpose an individual or group would identify with the term.

Third, when referring to American populations of African descent I will use the terms 'Black' or 'Blacks' with an uppercase 'B'. This is mostly in line with writings by other CRT scholars or academics writing on issues related to racial or other minorities and is based on the idea that 'Black' or 'Blacks' does not simply denote the skin colour but constitutes a specific heritage, history, experience, and personal identity and as such requires the use of a noun.[4] Similarly when referring to 'White' an uppercase 'W' will be used to show that there is more than simple appearance but that, as the burgeoning field of Whiteness Studies shows, Whiteness is also constructed, albeit as a default to other racial minorities.

Fourth, in the part of the book dedicated to the Roma, I broadly refer to groups and people that can be as different as the Roma, the Sinti, Gypsies, gitanos, Travellers, the Jenische, gens du voyage and the different names under which they might be known in various European countries (for example manouches or

4 See e.g. Catherine MacKinnon, 'Feminism, Marxism, Method, and the State: An Agenda for Theory', *Signs: Journal of Women in Culture and Society* (1982), vol. 7, no. 3, p. 516 in footnote.

Ashkali). While aware of the risk of essentialising through the use of this overarching term, it reflects the way in which these groups or individuals belonging to them are discriminated, positioned before and disadvantaged through the law in uncannily similar ways.

In conclusion, the outcome of this book cautiously contrasts and contradicts the two epithets at the beginning of this introduction. On the one hand, and more limitedly, it picks up on the idea that CRT is fairly popular in Europe, as stated by Rodrigo Crenshaw, a fictional half African American, half Italian character, who studied law at the University of Bologna. His statement is made in the first of a number of legal chronicles describing the meetings and discussions on race and law between him and an unnamed U.S. law professor – presumably Richard Delgado in person, one of CRT's main scholars and author of these chronicles that were published in various law journals.[5] Contrary to what Rodrigo Crenshaw states, CRT remains fairly unknown in Europe. On the other hand, this book also intends to break with the American and European myths that race does not count in Europe, only exceptionally emerging in certain time periods and countries, and that racial thought is part of a dark, unenlightened past. One of these myths was particularly widespread at the turn of last century by many African Americans. W.E.B. Du Bois' statement reproduced at the beginning of this introduction expresses a similar sentiment. Certainly, at a time in which segregation and lynchings were the order of the day in the United States, France and Europe must have felt like a free place. However, Europe was and remains a racialised space, if somewhat differently than the United States. Part of what this book attempts to demonstrate is how even today that ideology remains engrained in the DNA of European societies and therefore also in legal thought and reasoning.

5 Nine of those chronicles were republished: Richard Delgado, *The Rodrigo Chronicles: Conversations About America and Race* (New York, London: New York University Press, 1995).

Chapter 1

Critical Race Theory

The historical context

Critical Race Theory (CRT) is the product of a specific geographical history and context. In order to better understand some of its theoretical underpinnings, analyses, and critiques it is necessary to outline the broader historical framework in which CRT developed. In fact, one of the most important points raised by CRT scholars is that context matters, meaning that legal analysis must occur within a certain socio-historical context and should not be based exclusively on abstract, de-contextualised, formalised reasoning. Providing a picture of the broader context in which CRT developed not only serves as useful background information but helps explain the pre-conditions and underlying forces that made this theory and movement emerge.

To this end, two separate timelines are crucial in order to explain the intellectual genealogy of CRT. The first timeline will provide a brief overview of how law has historically constructed, affected, and subordinated (racial) minorities in the United States. More explicitly than in Europe, race in the United States has been robustly constructed by and through law. The description of how this occurred, nevertheless, will be positioned and critical, focusing on minority/critical scholars and judges who have interpreted this process. This is clearly not a glorious chapter in the history of American law but rather a dismal record of how law was, and according to CRT scholars continues to be, an actor or accomplice in racial subordination. It is not to say that other legal scholars are not aware and do not condemn cases like *Dred Scott*,[1] *Plessy*,[2] or *Korematsu*,[3] just to name a couple of the most disturbing ones. However, the first major difference between minority/critical scholars and mainstream liberal and conservative scholars lies in the assessment of how much influence and relevance those cases continue to have in the twenty-first century. One of CRT's main points is that the events and interpretations provided back then have managed to inform, shape, limit and influence legal arguments today. The second major difference between how those early decisions have been interpreted and read is that the liberal and conservative

1 *Dred Scott v. Sanford*, 60 U.S. (19 How.) 393 (1857).
2 *Plessy v. Ferguson*, 163 U.S. 537 (1896).
3 *Korematsu v. United States*, 323 U.S. 214 (1944).

narrative tends to portray American law as evolving positively, as correcting these shameful judicial errors by means of landmark cases such as *Brown v. Board of Education*[4] or through civil rights legislation. CRT scholars and other more critical academics are much less optimistic in their assessment of this history. They highlight the backlashes that followed after some emancipatory moments in the history of American racial minorities. For instance, the constitutional amendments and protective legislation in favour of former slaves, which passed into law after the Civil War, suffered significant setbacks due to a narrow interpretation by American courts. In the same way, modern civil rights legislation enacted in the 1960s has been voided of most of its transformative potential according to a similar dynamic.

The second timeline will briefly deal with the history of legal movements in the United States. It is impossible to understand the emergence of CRT without understanding the theoretical background of the legal movements and debates preceding it. Compared to the timeline, where a less conventional account of American case law is used to set the frame, the second timeline provides a somewhat more traditional account of modern American jurisprudence, which nevertheless provides an explanation of the broader legal–academic context in which CRT evolved.

1.1 Timeline 1 – history of American racial minorities

American law has dominated, shaped, and constructed the life of racial minorities in the United States. Arguably, law has played a pivotal role in the construction of races and is responsible for the introduction and maintenance of slavery, segregation, and other forms of subordination. Minorities are particularly aware of how law has shaped and, in most cases, negatively affected their lives.

Without pretending to provide an exhaustive history, the first timeline of this chapter will outline the most salient aspects of the racial subordination of minorities at the hands of the law in the American context. Indeed, as will be illustrated, law has played an instrumental role in creating, justifying, and perpetuating the subordination on the basis of the presumed racial superiority of those who identified as, or were themselves constructed as, the White majority. Nevertheless, the discrimination experienced by racial minorities has run along slightly different lines, depending on the way in which those groups were constructed and subordinated. In order to address such differences and to provide a more nuanced picture, separate sections are dedicated to the particular experience of African Americans, Native Americans, Asian Americans, and Latinos.

4 *Brown v. Board of Education*, 347 U.S. 483 (1954).

1.1.1 *African Americans*

The best known example of how law subordinated racial minorities is the fate of African Americans.[5] Slavery, lynching and segregation belong to America's darkest chapters. Beyond actual practice, law systematically created, legitimised and enforced these acts, starting from the very document which proclaimed that 'all men are created equal' and guaranteed 'liberty, life, and the pursuit of happiness' to everyone: the Constitution of the United States of America. Without entering into the details of how it came about that only Black people could become slaves whereas White people could become indentured servants at worst, the American Constitution based itself on and employed a social and legal reality, which had evolved and emerged from the arrival of the first slave ships on the East Coast.[6] While the word 'slavery' never explicitly appears in the American Constitution, the founding document nonetheless incorporates the institution of slavery into its architecture, leading some to contend that the Constitution was pro-slavery.[7] This occurred mostly pursuant to a political compromise between Southern and Northern states, where the former successfully maintained a racialised economic and social system, in which slavery played an important role. However, the North also had an interest in maintaining the slavery system. For example, a custom duty of up to ten dollars per slave was introduced to raise public revenues. Moreover, it was the Northern states that reaped economic gains and commercial interests in terms of revenue and goods generated from the plantations in the South. The compromise between the North and the South, which sacrificed moral arguments over economic and political reasons, already emerged prior to the entry into force of the American Constitution. An earlier draft of the Declaration of Independence, submitted by Thomas Jefferson to the Continental Congress, included among the charges against the King that he had enslaved people who had never offended him in violation of the principles of liberty and freedom. The Southern delegation pressed for the deletion of that specific charge since the colonists themselves were implicated in the slave trade. An inclusion of this claim might have made it more difficult to justify the continuation of slavery once ties to England were severed.[8]

The political compromise between North and South over slavery became entrenched in the Constitution itself; the so-called Apportionment Clause treated

5 See the dissenting opinion of Justice Thurgood Marshall, the first African American ever to serve on the U.S. Supreme Court: *Regents of the University of California v. Bakke* (438 U.S. 265 (1978) (Marshall, J. dissenting, pp. 387–396)). See also Derrick A. Bell, Jr., *Race, Racism, and American Law*, 5th edn (New York: Aspen Publishers, 2004), in particular pp. 16–50.

6 For a detailed historical account on how it came that only Black people could become slaves, see A. Leon Higginbotham, Jr., *In the Matter of Color: Race and the American Legal Process: The Colonial Period* (New York: Oxford University Press, 1978).

7 George William Van Cleve, *A Slaveholder's Union: Slavery, Politics and the Constitution in the Early American Republic* (Chicago, London: University of Chicago Press, 2010).

8 Thurgood Marshall, 'Reflections on the Bicentennial of the United States Constitution', *Harvard Law Review* (1987), vol. 101, pp. 1–5.

a slave as being equivalent to three-fifths of a person for purposes of apportioning representatives and taxes among the states.[9] By means of this clause the Southern states attempted to increase their power in Congress. Since the South had by that time a significant number of slaves, counting slaves to determine how many representatives a state could send to Congress would mean more power at the federal level. This led to a paradoxical result. Slaves, on the one hand, were treated like property, were considered inhuman, and did not count as citizens, which prohibited them from voting. On the other hand, when advantageous, slaves were counted as three-fifths of a person for apportionment purposes. A second aspect of the political compromise over slavery, which emerged from the American Constitution, is the Fugitive Slave Clause.[10] This clause ensured that when a slave escaped to another state, he must be returned if claimed by his master. The U.S. Supreme Court enforced this clause when Northern states tried to limit its applicability by criminalising the forcible removal of African Americans from the state for the purpose of enslaving them.[11] The effect of those decisions was pro-slavery. It extended the reach of this institution into the Northern states since slave owners were constitutionally granted the right to enforce their property claims in those states as well. Last but not least, the American Constitution also stated that the migration or importation of slaves into the existing states would be legal until at least 1808.[12] The combined effect of those constitutional provisions meant that the people who were supposed to be protected by the Constitution did not include those with skin of the wrong colour.

Slavery and legal subordination, which were enshrined in the American Constitution, were mostly enforced and perpetuated at the state level. The most efficient instruments established by individual states were the so-called Slave Codes. Slave Codes were designed primarily to defend the property interest of the owner in his slave. The statutory characterisation of African American slaves, commonly referred to as, in the language of the court at the time, 'Negro' slaves, as property was confirmed by one of the most heinous decisions of the U.S. Supreme Court: *Dred Scott v. Sandford*.[13] That case involved Dred Scott, a slave who had been taken to a free territory by his master and who attempted to sue for his freedom arguing that residence in a free state had made him free. In its decision ruling against the plaintiff, the Supreme Court held that the Missouri Compromise, which prohibited slavery in the portion of the Louisiana Purchase Territory north of Missouri, was unconstitutional because it deprived slave owners of their property without due process. The Court also held that under the Constitution a slave was property, equivalent to any ordinary article of merchandise, for which the

9 U.S. Const. Art. I, § 2.
10 U.S. Const. Art. IV, § 2.
11 See e.g. *Prigg v. Pennsylvania*, 41 U.S. (16 Pet.) 539 (1842).
12 U.S. Const. Art. I, § 9. However, slave boats landed on U.S. coasts until as late as 1859. See Anna Sylviane Diouf, *Dreams of Africa in Alabama: The Slave Ship Clotilda and the Story of the Last Africans Brought to America* (New York: Oxford University Press, 2007).
13 *Dred Scott v. Sanford*, 60 U.S. (19 How.) 393 (1857).

right to traffic was guaranteed to the citizens of the United States. The Court concluded that 'Negroes' were not intended to be included as citizens under the Constitution but were regarded as beings of an inferior order altogether unfit to associate with the White race, either in social or political relations; and so far inferior, that they had no rights which the White man was bound to respect.

Slavery was formally abolished after the American Civil War (1861–1865) with the introduction of the Thirteenth, Fourteenth, and Fifteenth Amendments to the U.S. Constitution. Nevertheless, in spite of these constitutional amendments and federal legislation granting former slaves citizenship, equality, and certain other rights[14] during the brief Reconstruction period, which spanned from approximately the end of the Civil War until 1877, their plight scarcely changed. This can be traced back to the resistance to this emancipation at the state level, which played out in several ways.[15] For instance, at the statutory level many States introduced the so-called 'Black Codes' which strongly resembled the pre-Civil War Slave Codes. Thus, Black Codes limited the rights of African Americans to own or rent property, to give testimony in court, and also permitted imprisonment for breach of employment contracts or for vagrancy. These laws were aimed at former slaves who, after acquiring freedom, started moving in search of a better life for their families and/or employment opportunities. Criminalising certain behaviour in order to literally get former slaves off the road or to force them to stay in an employment contract also had the added benefit of ensuring that there would be a continued supply of cheap African American workforce in the form of convict labour. In some ways this was worse than slavery, given that *de facto* the former slaves were doing exactly the same thing as before but without any of the limited protections that a slave master might grant as a property owner who wanted to maintain the value of his property. Additionally, it meant that sanctions, which under the old system had been administered directly by the slave owners, were now part of the state's competence, thus further increasing the law's involvement in perpetuating racial discrimination and subordination.[16] Another way in which freed slaves were denied their rights was through inaction from both the states and the federal government. The most visible example of this inaction is the so-called 'Hayes-Tilden Compromise' of 1877, which officially ended the short-lived Reconstruction period. In fact, during a very narrow presidential election, which almost sparked another civil war, a political compromise was reached. The compromise included the withdrawal of the remaining federal Northern troops from

14 These were e.g. the Civil Rights Act, 14 Stat. 27 (1866), the Enforcement Act, 16 Stat. 140 (1870) and the Ku Klux Clan Act, 17 Stat. 13 (1871). Congress also responded to the needs of freed slaves at the end of the Civil War by establishing the Bureau of Refugees, Freedmen, and Abandoned Lands, better known as the Freedmen's Bureau, to supply food, hospitals, land, and education to the newly freed slaves.

15 W. Haywood Burns, 'Law and Race in Early America', in David Kairys (ed.), *The Politics of Law: A Progressive Critique*, 3rd edn (New York: Basic Books, 1998), pp. 281–283.

16 See James W. Clarke, *The Lineaments of Wrath. Race, Violent Crime, and American Culture* (New Brunswick, London: Transaction Publishers, 1998), pp. 109–125.

the Southern states, which up to that point had appeared to be providing some sort of protection to former slaves. This gave the Southern states free rein and sacrificed African American interests in order to maintain peace in the country.

However, it was not only at the state or the legislative level that the emancipation of slaves was curtailed. Although the federal government enacted some protective legislative measures during the brief Reconstruction period, partly as a consequence of the Black Codes, they were subsequently undermined by the judiciary. Except for the few blatant cases of race discrimination such as the exclusion of African Americans from juries,[17] the U.S. Supreme Court mostly interpreted the Civil Rights Amendments and the federal protective legislation as not granting any, or very little, protection to former slaves. For example, in *The Slaughter-House Cases*,[18] the Supreme Court held that the Privileges and Immunities Clause of the Fourteenth Amendment protected and referred to only those very few privileges and immunities conferred by virtue of the federal U.S. citizenship but not those privileges and immunities contingent on state citizenship. Whereas this case did not involve African Americans but butchers in Louisiana, the fact that the U.S. Supreme Court reduced the protected privileges and immunities recognised under the Fourteenth Amendment to a very restricted number of scenarios, ultimately meant that former slaves could not have recourse to that legal avenue to judicially enforce their rights and were left with the Equal Protection Clause as the almost only constitutional avenue to seek protection against race discrimination.

In *Cruikshank*,[19] the U.S. Supreme Court invalidated indictments against White defendants for the Colfax massacre during which a White militia attacked freedmen following a controversial gubernatorial election. The indictments had been brought under the 1870 Enforcement Act which, *inter alia*, made it a felony for two or more people to conspire to deprive anyone of their constitutional rights. That legislation had been designed primarily to allow federal enforcement and prosecution of the Ku Klux Klan and other secret vigilante groups who prevented Blacks from voting by all means possible. The U.S. Supreme Court declared part of the Enforcement Act unconstitutional by holding that the Due Process and Equal Protection Clauses of the Fourteenth Amendment only applied to state action and not to individual actions. This decision left former slaves *de facto* at the mercy of the widespread terror and violence of paramilitary groups and corresponding inaction of hostile state governments, which did nothing or little to protect them.[20]

Similar reasoning distinguishing between state action and private action was the basis for an even more comprehensive judicial attack on the Reconstruction legislation in the *Civil Rights Cases*.[21] Deciding on a number of similar claims for discrimination from various corners of the United States, the U.S. Supreme Court

17 *Strauder v. West Virginia*, 100 U.S. (10 Otto) 303 (1880).

18 *The Slaughter House Cases*, 83 U.S. (16 Wall.) 36, 70 (1873).

19 *United States v. Cruikshank*, 92 U.S. 542 (1876).

20 See also *United States v. Harris*, 106 U.S. 629 (1882) where the U.S. Supreme Court reached a similar conclusion.

21 *The Civil Rights Cases*, 109 U.S. 3 (1883).

directly curbed Congress' efforts to use its power to promote racial equality. In those cases the U.S. Supreme Court invalidated sections of the Civil Rights Act of 1875 that made it a crime to deny equal access to inns, public conveyances, theatres, and other places for public amusement.[22] According to the U.S. Supreme Court, the Fourteenth Amendment gave Congress the power to proscribe only discriminatory action by the state. The Court ruled that Blacks, who were excluded from public places, merely suffered a violation of their social rights at the hands of private individuals, and Congress had no power to remedy that. The *Civil Rights Cases* are still deemed important and relevant today in as much as they determined that the Fourteenth Amendment only applies to state action as opposed to private action.

The best-known example of how little things changed for former slaves after they obtained their freedom is the Jim Crow legislation and the segregation regime between Whites and Blacks, which it introduced.[23] This system of racial segregation was legally imposed and went literally from the hospital where one was born to the cemetery where one was buried. Segregation was ultimately constitutionally upheld under the adage of 'separate but equal' in yet another of the U.S. Supreme Court's most infamous decisions, *Plessy v. Ferguson*.[24] Here the U.S. Supreme Court upheld a Louisiana statute that required railway companies to provide separate but equal accommodations for Whites and Negroes. The justices reasoned that the Fourteenth Amendment was not intended to abolish distinctions based upon colour, or to enforce social – as distinguished from political – equality, or to facilitate a commingling of the two races upon terms unsatisfactory to either. The U.S. Supreme Court rejected the plaintiff's claims and held that Plessy was wrong in assuming that the enforced separation of the two races violated the Constitution's Thirteenth and Fourteenth Amendment by marking African Americans with a badge of inferiority. Justice Harlan famously dissented. He understood that the real meaning of Jim Crow legislation was that African American citizens are so inferior and degraded that they could not sit in public coaches occupied by White citizens. He expressed his fear that if similar laws were enacted in other states, the effect would be in the highest degree mischievous because, in spite of the abolishment of slavery, states would retain the power to interfere on the basis of race and to place in a position of legal inferiority a large body of American citizens. Such distinction was contrary to the Constitution because in his words '[o]ur constitution is color-blind, and neither knows nor tolerates classes among citizens'.[25] Justice Harlan's dissent, however, is more famous than his degrading statements about Asians. Harlan opined that '[t]here is a race so different from our own that we do not permit those belonging to it to become citizens of the United States.

22 Civil Rights Act, 18 Stat. 335 (1875).

23 On Jim Crow, see C. Vann Woodward, *The Strange Career of Jim Crow* (New York: Oxford University Press, 1955).

24 *Plessy v. Ferguson*, 163 U.S. 537 (1896).

25 *Plessy v. Ferguson*, 163 U.S. 537 (1896) (Harlan, J. dissenting, p. 559).

Persons belonging to it are, with few exceptions, absolutely excluded from our country. I allude to the Chinese race.'[26] In spite of the seemingly progressive result advocated by Justice Harlan, it is clear he believes, just as much as his colleagues, in White superiority as the following statement from his dissenting opinion demonstrates: 'The white race deems itself to be the dominant race in this country. And so it is, in prestige, in achievements, in education, in wealth and in power. So, I doubt not, it will continue to be for all time, if it remains true to its great heritage and holds fast to the principles of constitutional liberty'.[27] From this perspective Justice Harlan's dissent, which is often hailed as an example of racial progressiveness, loses some of its appeal as a whole-hearted endorsement of racial minorities' rights and demonstrates that colourblindness is compatible with the belief in racial hierarchies.

Following *Plessy*, many states expanded their Jim Crow laws to include residential areas, parks, hospitals, theatres, waiting rooms, and lavatories. There were even statutes and ordinances authorising separate phone booths for African Americans and Whites, requiring that textbooks used by children of one race be kept separate from those used by the other, and requiring that African American and White prostitutes be kept in separate districts. It took another sixty years and some earlier strategic litigation[28] before *Plessy* was eventually overturned with the *Brown v. Board of Education*.[29] In other words, almost one hundred years had to pass before the effects of the Civil Rights Amendments made some impact, without however being able to address the continued violence, and social and economic disadvantage which had resulted from legislative emancipation.

The lessons that this history taught racial minorities are important and certainly contain little grounds for optimism. First, in spite of the formal changes, the system ultimately preserved its structure or in some instances even changed it for the worse. In a somewhat different context, this was aptly named 'preservation through transformation'; in the sense that even though a certain legal justification for certain institutions had become obsolete or no longer viable (here slavery), the new emerging institutions strongly resembled the previous ones and the legal system was able to justify them based on a new understanding, which seemed to be more in line with the changed conditions of segregation.[30] In fact, slavery was simply replaced by a system of law, which imposed new legal burdens on former slaves by curtailing their newly acquired rights and freedoms. Second, the two

26 *Ibid.* at p. 561.

27 *Ibid.* at p. 559.

28 See e.g. *Morgan v. Virginia*, 328 U.S. 373 (1946); *Sweatt v. Painter*, 339 U.S. 629 (1950); *McLaurin v. Oklahoma State Regents*, 339 U.S. 637 (1950).

29 *Brown v. Board of Education*, 347 U.S. 483 (1954).

30 Reva Siegel, 'The Rule of Love: Wife Beating as Prerogative and Privacy', *Yale Law Journal* (1996), vol. 105, pp. 2117–2207. The author here makes a similar argument with regards to wife beating, which was originally seen as the husbands' prerogative but when that legal justification was no longer considered feasible, privacy arguments emerged to ultimately prevent any sort of legal scrutiny of intra-marital (mis)behaviour.

most fundamental events in early American history, the American Revolution and the Civil War, were ultimately less concerned with African American suffering than with the advantages that White society would reap from these events. The political and legal compromises reached between Northern and Southern states both in the American Constitution as well as later in the 1877 *Hayes-Tilden Compromise* are perfect examples of this phenomenon. African American interests were not taken into consideration at all, and if they were, as soon as those interests no longer aligned with White interests, the former were easily and readily sacrificed or cast aside. The historical experience and knowledge therefore show how African Americans' and other racial minorities' interests were little more than a political bargaining chip and the legal system almost consistently validated such reality.

It is not difficult to imagine how this historical experience of a legally justified and authorised matrix of disenfranchisement of racial minorities has created a deep distrust towards liberatory moments. More importantly, for the purpose of better understanding the origins of CRT, it helps explain some of the critiques against modern equal protection jurisprudence by the U.S. Supreme Court, as well as CRT's general framework of analysis.

1.1.2 Native Americans

African Americans were certainly not alone in carrying the yoke of racial subordination and prejudice created, imposed and justified by laws and legal interpretations that ultimately benefited White European settlers and immigrants. In slightly different ways, Native Americans also became victims of racial prejudice and subordination through legal discourse, legislation, and adjudication. Native Americans were exterminated, expropriated, forcibly displaced, and discriminated against. This fact is not being questioned or denied. What is often less known or evident, at least to European readers and in spite of Alexis de Tocqueville's observations,[31] is the extent to which law played a fundamental role in justifying and rationalising the extermination of Native Americans. It was not 'simply' a question of conquest, expansion, and extermination – in and by itself already violent enough – but conquest, expansion, and extermination backed up by ideology translated into legislation and case law; hence also the very fitting expression of 'Genocide-At-Law'.[32] However, whereas in the case of African Americans the socio-legal subordination was heavily labour-related, in the case of Native

31 Already in the 1830s Alexis de Tocqueville stated that Americans succeeded in exterminating the Native Americans 'with wonderful ease; quietly, legally, and philanthropically, without spilling blood and without violating a single one of the great principles of morality in the eyes of the world. It is impossible to destroy men with more respect for the laws of humanity.' Alexis de Tocqueville, *Democracy in America*, [1835], George Lawrence (trans.), J.P. Mayer (ed.), 12th edn (London: Fontana Press, 1994), p. 339 (footnote omitted).

32 Rennard Strickland, 'Genocide-at-Law: An Historic and Contemporary View of the Native American Experience', *University of Kansas Law Review* (1986) vol. 34, pp. 713–756.

Americans the legal issues evolved along two different, yet linked axes; federal power over Native Americans and property rights over their land. This also led to different litigation and demands. Whereas African Americans pleaded equality of treatment under the Constitution and civil rights, Native Americans in contrast requested some sort of autonomy from federal power, a measured separatism and degree of control over their own laws, customs, and traditions.[33] The ultimate consequences and results nevertheless were more or less similar for both African Americans and Native Americans; the establishment of White supremacy, based on racial prejudice and alleged superiority of the White race, to the detriment of indigenous and/or minority populations. Another similarity is that the decisions and characterisations taken at a time of overt and blatant racism continue to shape and influence the policies and cases today. The following brief account tells how the legal system has subordinated Native Americans.

Resembling the legal position of African Americans, who were treated as chattels and counted as human beings for representational purposes, the legal characterisation of Native Americans with regard to federal powers was constitutionally as incoherent and anomalous from the start. The Constitution enumerates a power to regulate commerce with the Indian tribes.[34] In practice, Congress and the executive branch initially had treaty powers to deal with Native American tribes because the latter were viewed as sovereign nations. Regulation through treaties or legislation was designed to effectuate treaty protection promises that sanctioned individuals or states for infringing Native American land or punishing Native Americans in violation of treaty obligations. Historically and strategically speaking, in addition to the protection of tribal sovereignty, the submission of Native American affairs to federal powers was a move to limit states' powers and to prevent the escalation of further conflict as a result of states' eagerness to exploit natural resources on Native lands and the influx of European settlers, which gave rise to disputes between Natives and the settlers.

These issues emerged in the landmark case *Worcester v. Georgia*,[35] a case in which Georgia had attempted to assert ownership over gold-rich lands legally belonging to the Cherokee Nation. The U.S. Supreme Court invalidated the state law because the federal government had the exclusive power to deal with Native Americans. While recognising that Native American tribes possessed inherent sovereignty rights, this sovereignty could at the same time be diminished or eliminated by the United States but not by the individual states. As can be seen, *Worcester v. Georgia* was more a defence of federal over state power rather than a defence and recognition of Native American sovereignty rights. In fact, the Cherokees were not even a party to the litigation. Moreover, the decision was never enforced by the federal marshals due to fear of conflict on the issue between the U.S. Supreme Court

33 See Charles Wilkinson, *American Indians, Time, and the Law: Native Societies in a Modern Constitutional Democracy* (New Haven: Yale University Press, 1987), pp. 14–19.

34 U.S. Const. Art. I, §8, cl. 3.

35 *Worcester v. Georgia* 31 U.S. (6 Pet.) 515 (1832).

and then-President Jackson who favoured Indian removal to the West; neither Georgia nor the other states actually refrained from their policies of seizing Native American lands. Eventually, a few years later the Indian Removal Act[36] and the Treaty of New Echota forced the Cherokees to leave their land for Oklahoma on the infamous 'Trail of Tears', during which thousands of Cherokees died. The broader legacy of *Worcester* and placing Native American issues under federal control and into the realm of foreign affairs is that from then on the involvement of federal powers has rarely been questioned in this area. Two further consequences of this qualification to dealings with Native Americans as a federal foreign affairs question are: (i) that in this area the judiciary shows particular deference to political decisions, especially through the 'Political Question Doctrine' which is invoked by courts to decline justiciability of a case; and (ii) that treaties could be abrogated simply by a later conflicting statute adopted by Congress.[37] This allowed Congress to simply overrule earlier guarantees made by treaty when they were no longer convenient.

Stemming from the legal anomalies and inconsistencies arising out of the characterisation as a federal issue, Native American tribes were deemed to be sovereign, but their sovereignty could be suppressed by the federal government. Moreover, their sovereignty was only selectively recognised at the whim of Congress or the courts and usually the recognition or absence of it worked to the detriment of the Natives. In the Supreme Court's first Cherokee decision, *Cherokee Nation v. Georgia*,[38] the state of Georgia had enacted a series of state laws supposed to induce the Cherokee to leave their native lands. Following fruitless negotiations with the U.S. government and petitions to Congress, the case was taken to the U.S. Supreme Court, where the plaintiffs sought an injunction against Georgia, arguing that the Cherokee Nation was a foreign nation. The U.S. Supreme Court refused the injunction on jurisdictional grounds holding that the Cherokee Nation was neither a state of the union nor a foreign state like France or England, but a domestic dependent nation whose relation to the United States resembles that of a ward to his guardian. Since the Cherokee Nation was not a foreign nation the U.S. Supreme Court had no original jurisdiction over the case. The broad language used in this decision also created some doubts as to whether Native American tribes would have standing to sue in a federal court.

The picture sketched so far on the establishment of federal congressional and executive power over 'Indian affairs' might not be viewed as an outrageous anomaly. After all, there have been other areas in which Congress and the executive branch tried to affirm and establish their supremacy with regards to the states. What is different in this domain, however, is that most of the supposedly neutral and objective legal constructions relied on racial and cultural prejudice. Native

36 4 Stat. 411 (1830). This Act provided that Indians residing in any of the states or territories could exchange their ancestral lands with (mostly barren and fruitless) land west of the Mississippi River.

37 Bell, Jr., *Race, Racism and American Law*, pp. 66–67.

38 *Cherokee Nation v. Georgia* 30 U.S. (5 Pet.) 1 (1831).

Americans were viewed as culturally backwards and as savages who needed to be civilised and accustomed to American culture. Property law is where this attitude became most visible and which ultimately allowed for the justification of Congress' plenary powers over Native American affairs once the regulation by treaty ended under the Appropriations Act of 1871. At that point most of the land, which constitutes the United States today, had come under control of the American government. Hence, it became increasingly difficult to continue viewing Native Americans as foreign nations and thus justifying Congress' broad competence in this area with its Treaty Powers.

Eventually, the idea that federal government had some sort of property interest in Indian land became the cornerstone in establishing guardianship power over Native Americans. The source of that federal property interest derived from the 'Doctrine of Discovery', namely the medieval idea that land, which did not belong to Christians, was deemed to be empty and could be seized by the first Christians to arrive, even when the land was already inhabited by non-Christian natives. This rule of international law, on which most European discovery and colonisation were based, was confirmed in *Johnson v. M'Intosh.*[39] This Supreme Court decision involved a dispute between Native American property interests and the American government's property interests. The plaintiff, Thomas Johnson, had bought land from Piankeshaw Indian tribes in 1773 and 1775. The defendant William M'Intosh subsequently obtained a land patent to the same parcel of land from the U.S. federal government. An action for ejectment against defendant M'Intosh was brought and the legal issue at stake centred around who had a superior property title. The Supreme Court held that defendant M'Intosh's claim was superior on the grounds that the Piankeshaw were not able to actually convey the land because they never 'owned' it in the legal sense. Indians can only have a mere right to occupancy. The judges based their arguments on the 'Doctrine of Discovery'. Hence, this decision formally incorporated the medievally derived assumption of European cultural and religious superiority, to the detriment of Native Americans who were viewed as savages, unable to govern their land and thereby stripped of the possibility to convey an absolute property title to other private citizens.

The establishment of the superiority of the federal government's property title by legally granting the government the pre-emptive right to purchase Indian land or to confiscate it after a war, came to characterise the federal government's property interest as ownership and the Native American's title as a subordinate possessory interest. More importantly, however, it subsequently justified Congress' right to govern Indian affairs in the absence of any existing constitutional provision which might authorise such a solution. Once the treaty period was abolished in 1871, Congress could not rely on the characterisation of Native Americans as foreign nations. Another constitutional source justifying the continued federal authority over Native American affairs had to be found. By attributing the United States the

39 *Johnson v. McIntosh* 21 U.S. (8 Wheat.) 543 (1823).

ultimate title to land, including Indian land, federal government owned that land and with that ownership came the power to govern its inhabitants as well. This became known as the 'Plenary Power Doctrine' and was judicially established and confirmed in two U.S. Supreme Court decisions: *Ex parte Crow Dog*[40] and *United States v. Kagama*.[41] Both cases involved the application of federal criminal law over crimes committed by Native Americans against other Native Americans on tribal lands. In the former decision involving the murder of one Sioux by another which had been satisfactorily dealt with from the Sioux perspective, the U.S. Supreme Court refused to extend federal jurisdiction. The judgment, however, prompted a legislative response, which extended federal criminal jurisdiction to include eight enumerated felonies committed by Native Americans against other Native Americans on tribal lands. Thus, the decision in *Crow Dog* was legislatively overruled. The new statute was then applied in the murder committed by a California Native, Kagama, against another member of the same tribe on their reservation. Kagama challenged the statute as going beyond Congress' statutory powers under the Constitution's Indian Commerce Clause. The Constitution does not contain a provision granting Congress express authority to legislate on the matter. The U.S. Supreme Court did not find it necessary to express any textual reference. By linking their decision to the previous case law on property law and ownership title established by the Marshall Court, the U.S. Supreme Court recognised Congress' ability to ground its authority and plenary power over Indian affairs. The superior ownership title by the federal government recognised in *McIntosh* and the guardian-ward relationship described in *Cherokee Nation* were sufficiently convincing precedents for the justices to find that Congress did have considerable powers to legislate over Native American affairs. Thus, the link between racist prejudices and White racial supremacy over Native Americans written into property law and Plenary Power Doctrine was established.

At the same time period when the Supreme Court recognised the plenary powers of Congress over Native American affairs and the Treaty Period had been abandoned, the same court found that Native Americans were not citizens. This effectively put Native Americans under the control of the federal government for certain purposes without granting them citizens' rights. For example in *Elk v. Wilkins*[42] a Native American had renounced his tribal allegiance, became lawfully resident in a state and attempted to register to vote as a White citizen. The Supreme Court upheld the denial by the registrar of voters. The legal regime changed only in 1924 when the Citizenship Act extended citizenship to Native Americans. The legal characterisation of Native Americans as dependent subjects for some purposes and as non-citizens for others strongly resembles the inconsistency already observed with slaves, who counted as persons, albeit only three-fifths

40 *Ex parte Crow Dog*, 109 U.S. 556 (1883).

41 *United States v. Kagama*, 118 U.S. 375 (1886).

42 *Elk v. Wilkins*, 112 U.S. 94 (1884).

of a person, for apportionment purposes but were otherwise legally deemed to be mere chattels.

Even today, the earlier decisions involving and characterising Native Americans with all their questionable baggage still resonate in case law and legislation. Whereas since the 1930s a more restrictive view of the Plenary Power Doctrine has been adopted,[43] racist stereotypes contained and entrenched in those earlier cases have continued to exercise their influence in contemporary case law. This has been demonstrated in an analysis of some more recent decisions by the U.S. Supreme Court that continually refer to older decisions and legislative references which were based precisely on such beliefs.[44] Demonstrating how much the past is still present in modern jurisprudence and case law involving Native Americans is the objective of critical race scholars, who are engaged with specific issues that arose in connection with this minority group.

1.1.3 Asian Americans

Yet another story, distinct from African Americans and Native Americans, can be told for Asian Americans. Once again somewhat differing accounts of how law has constructed and affected another racial and racialised group emerge from America's history. Even within this grouping of 'Asian Americans' one can distinguish two separate narratives: the first concerns the Chinese, and the second the Japanese.[45]

As far as race discrimination and its legal justification against the Chinese are concerned, this mainly played out as an immigration and naturalisation issue. During the second half of the nineteenth century immigration from China to the United States and in particular to California increased dramatically. Chinese immigrants filled labour vacuums and provided a cheap and efficient labour force. Soon, however, animosity from within White labour groups arose and during a period in which racial ideas were at their height it was not difficult to introduce legislation which would specifically target the Chinese. California subsequently introduced special taxes and licenses, which either directly or indirectly affected Chinese immigrants.[46] However, the most blatant exclusionary practices towards the Chinese occurred through federal immigration and naturalisation legislation and the courts' interpretations of those enactments. In 1868, the Burlingame

43 See Bell, Jr., *Race, Racism, and American Law*, pp. 74–79.

44 See Robert A. Williams, Jr., *Like a Loaded Weapon: The Rehnquist Court, Indian Rights, and the Legal History of Racism in America* (Minneapolis, London: University of Minnesota Press, 2005), pp. 89–122.

45 For a more detailed account on the legal history of Asian Americans' racial subordination, see Bell, Jr., *Race, Racism, and American Law*, pp. 95–102.

46 The majority of these were actually declared unconstitutional. The most famous of these decisions is the U.S. Supreme Court case *Yick Wo v. Hopkins*, 118 U.S. 356 (1886). In this case, the justices held that a statute which imposed a license for operators of frame laundries that were mainly run by Chinese immigrants violated the Equal Protection Clause.

Treaty between the United States and China recognised the inalienable right of man to change his home and allegiance and the mutual advantage of free migration of their citizens from one country to another for purposes of trade, permanent residency or curiosity. Following a re-negotiation of the Burlingame Treaty in 1880, the United States was allowed to regulate, limit or suspend the entrance of Chinese labourers. Over the next years, Congress adopted legislation which suspended immigration and barred the re-entry of Chinese labourers.[47] In the *Chinese Exclusion Case*, the U.S. Supreme Court upheld the enactments even though admittedly they contravened the treaties with China.[48] As in the case of Native Americans where earlier treaties were simply overruled by subsequent legislation, the fact that treaties were deemed to be equal to acts by Congress and not superior sources of law, served as legal justification that the last expression of sovereign will could supersede earlier ones.

Even if Chinese migrants entered the United States legally, when it came to naturalisation, it was determined by a federal court in California that Chinese could not become citizens of the United States because they were not deemed to belong to the White race.[49] Also under the segregation system, the U.S. Supreme Court found no violation of the Equal Protection Clause, when a child with Chinese blood was excluded from a White school under state law.[50] Most of these exclusionary practices relied heavily on prejudices that Chinese were an inferior race[51] and could not be assimilated into American society. The tide changed with the outbreak of World War II when the United States became an ally of China against Japan. Slowly the restrictions on immigration and naturalisation legislation crumbled but it took until 1965 for the special immigration restrictions relating to Asians to be completely abolished.[52] Again one can observe how the convergence of political opportunity between White American interests and Chinese interests led to the elimination of formal discrimination. To what extent this led to the elimination of the actual prejudice remains another story.

The inclusion of the Chinese, however, went hand in hand with the exclusion of another group: the Japanese minority. Even before World War II and Pearl Harbor, the Japanese had not been treated particularly well. On the one hand, Alien Land Laws in various states were supposed to make it harder for people of Japanese descent to earn a living from agriculture by prohibiting them from owning land. The Supreme Court upheld these Alien Land Laws in a

47 Chinese Exclusion Act, 22 Stat. 58 (1882); Scott Act, 25 Stat. 476 (1888); Geary Act, 27 Stat. 25 (1892).

48 *Chae Chan Ping v. United States*, 130 U.S. 581 (1889).

49 *In re Ah Yup*, 1 F.Cas. 223 (C.C.D. Cal. 1878).

50 *Gong Lum v. Rice*, 275 U.S. 78 (1927).

51 See Justice Harlan's dissent: *Plessy v. Ferguson*, 163 U.S. 537 (1896) (Harlan, J. dissenting, p. 561).

52 Immigration and Nationality Act (a.k.a. Hart-Cellar Act), 79 Stat. 911 (1965).

number of cases.[53] On the other hand, the Immigration Quota Act of 1924 *de facto* made it impossible for Japanese aliens to obtain American citizenship.[54] However, the Japanese were to feel the full brunt of legal discrimination following the United States' declaration of war on Japan in 1941. Presidential executive orders[55] allowed for the establishment of military areas in which the removal and internment in prisoner camps of persons of Japanese ancestry was made possible. Prejudices by the local population who viewed the Japanese as an economic threat and competition further helped exert pressure and execute evacuations as well as confiscating, stealing or escheating the property of the interned Japanese.

The U.S. Supreme Court tested the constitutionality of the orders in three separate cases. In *Hirabayashi v. United States*[56] the legal issue was whether the curfew imposed by the military authorities on citizens of Japanese ancestry was an unconstitutional delegation by Congress of its legislative powers under the Fifth Amendment. The justices found no violation, holding that 'in time of war, residents having ethnic affiliations with an invading enemy may be a greater source of danger than those of a different ancestry.'[57] In another case, however, the U.S. Supreme Court upheld a writ of habeas corpus seeking release from an internment order because the detention was unauthorised by Congress, or the President.[58]

However, the most infamous case of the three was *Korematsu*.[59] In this decision Korematsu, a U.S. citizen of Japanese descent had refused to leave his home following an exclusion order and was tried and convicted for remaining in his home. The legal issue raised was whether the evacuation order contravened the Equal Protection Clause because the civil rights of a single racial group were violated by the order. The U.S. Supreme Court held that while restrictions curtailing the civil rights of a single racial group are immediately suspect and subject to the most rigid scrutiny, pressing public necessity may justify the existence of such restrictions. Even though *Korematsu* was the first time that the U.S. Supreme Court used heightened scrutiny in order to evaluate racial classifications, the justices found that the war efforts against Japan provided sufficient justification to uphold the exclusion order and the conviction, even though they were clearly based on racial prejudice. The injustice to those citizens of Japanese descent who survived the evacuation and internment was only slowly and reluctantly remedied.[60] On the

53 *Terrace v. Thompson*, 263 U.S. 197 (1923) and *Porterfield v. Webb*, 263 U.S. 225 (1923). Only in 1947 did that court overrule its own jurisprudence: *Oyama v. California*, 332 U.S. 633 (1947).

54 Immigration Quota Act, 43 Stat. 153 (1924).

55 *Executive Order* no. 9066, 7 Fed. Reg. 1407 (1942) and *Executive Order* no. 9102, 7 Fed. Reg. 2405 (1942).

56 *Hirabayashi v. United States*, 320 U.S. 81 (1943).

57 *Ibid.* at p. 101.

58 *Ex parte Endo*, 323 U.S. 283 (1944).

59 *Korematsu v. United States*, 323 U.S. 214 (1944).

60 See more in detail Eric K. Yamamoto, *et al.* (eds), *Race, Rights, and Reparation: Law of the Japanese-American Internment* (New York: Aspen Publishers, 2001).

one hand, legislation provided little compensation for the loss of freedom, property, education opportunities, businesses, and employment income,[61] as well as for late restitution to individuals forced to leave their homes.[62] On the other hand, courts also intervened by overturning Mr Korematsu's conviction in 1984 on the ground that the government had withheld information from the courts when assessing the question of military necessity.[63]

1.1.4 Latinos

Latinos can be broadly identified by different groups, which are loosely connected, because they come from a Spanish-speaking country or territory. It does not necessarily mean that they speak Spanish today however. Therefore the term Latinos includes Mexican Americans, Puerto Ricans, or more recent migrants from Middle and South America, whose history of legal discrimination in the United States takes slightly different trajectories depending on the group involved and their place of origin.

A slightly artificial starting point for the history of Latino discrimination is 2 February 1848 when the Republic of Mexico ceded some of its territories to the United States under the Treaty of Guadalupe Hidalgo. These territories correspond with parts of California, Nevada, Utah, Texas, Colorado, New Mexico, Arizona, and Wyoming. This treaty provided, *inter alia*, that the United States would grant U.S. citizenship to Mexicans who because of shifting territorial boundaries suddenly found themselves on American territory. Treaty provisions guaranteed property protection as well as civil and cultural rights. However, Mexican American's properties were confiscated, they were disenfranchised, discriminated against and lynched,[64] much like other racial minorities in the United States.[65]

Supreme Court cases illustrate the extent of discrimination perpetrated against the Mexican American community. In *Hernandez v. Texas*,[66] Pete Hernández was convicted of murder by a grand jury that consisted of all-White jurors. The challenge under the Equal Protection Clause was not about the conviction per se but about the practice of systematically excluding individuals of Mexican descent from jury service in criminal trials in many Texan counties. In this case, in the specific county where Hernández had been convicted, Mexican Americans constituted

61 Japanese-American Evacuation Claims Act, 62 Stat. 1231 (1948).

62 Civil Liberties Act, 102 Stat. 903 (1988).

63 *Korematsu v. United States*, 584 F. Supp. 1406 (N.D. Cal. 1984).

64 Richard Delgado, 'The Law of the Noose: A History of Latino Lynching', *Harvard Civil Rights – Civil Liberties Law Review* (2009), vol. 44, pp. 297–312.

65 See e.g. Ediberto Román, *Citizenship and Its Exclusions* (New York, London: New York University Press, 2010), pp. 131–132 and Christine A. Klein, 'Treaties of Conquest: Property Rights, Indian Treaties and the Treaty of Guadalupe Hidalgo', 26, *New Mexico Law Review* (1991), vol. 26, pp. 201–256.

66 *Hernanadez v. Texas*, 347 U.S. 475 (1954).

fifteen per cent of the population. The trial court and the court of appeal rejected the Fourteenth Amendment challenge, holding that this amendment only applied to Black and White Americans but not to Mexican Americans. The Supreme Court reversed the lower courts' decisions. Ignoring the race and colour distinction, the court found that the Fourteenth Amendment did in fact protect Hernández because he belonged to a class identifiable on a different basis and suffered from discrimination as a result.[67] It is interesting to note that this decision was handed down only two weeks before the famous *Brown* segregation decision by the same court. However, in spite of adopting a similar non-segregationist stance, the court differentiated Mexican-Americans and classified them as not racially separate but something else. The court refrained from defining what the something else was. In this sense, *Hernandez* not only shows how Mexican Americans were treated like other racial minorities but also highlights an unresolved tension when trying to determine whether Latinos are victims of racial discrimination or another form of discrimination based on ethnicity and/or national origins.[68]

Beyond the more specific history of Mexican Americans, a common thread amongst Latinos living in the United States is related to racially exclusive immigration and citizenship laws and practices. Here again, some of the past experiences and cases inform present day analyses. With regard to immigration legislation, from 1924 to 1965 the national origins quota system favoured immigration from Northern and Western Europe, in other words, White immigrants. Even today this facially neutral system, which is based on an annual numerical limit, continues to have a negative impact on racial and ethnic minorities through an in-built preference for White immigrants.[69] Besides the official immigration system, historically Mexicans were often 'imported' as labour into the United States when needed. For example, the Bracero Program facilitated immigration of Latinos, who were only to be deported or expelled again when the need expired. During such operations, including the infamous 'Operation Wetback' of 1954,[70] Mexican immigrants and American citizens with Mexican ancestry, together with other Hispanics and their U.S. born children, were rounded up and deported.[71]

It is against this backdrop, embedded within racially exclusionary practices and legislation, that contemporary issues relating to Latinos in the United States must be read and understood. California's Proposition 187 of 1994 that emerged out of general anti-Mexican American and anti-Latino sentiments and hostility demanded, *inter alia*, the expulsion of undocumented children from public

67 *Ibid.* at pp. 477–480.

68 Ian F. Haney López, 'Race, Ethnicity, Erasure: The Salience of Race to LatCrit Theory', *California Law Review* (1997), vol. 85, pp. 1143–1211.

69 Kevin R. Johnson, 'Race and the Immigration Laws: The Need for Critical Inquiry', in Valdes, McCristal Culp and Harris (eds), *Crossroads, Directions, and a New Critical Race Theory*, pp. 192–194.

70 Juan Ramón García, *Operation Wetback: The Mass Deportation of Mexican Undocumented Workers in 1954* (Westport, CT: Greenwood Press, 1980).

71 Román, *Citizenship and its Exclusions*, pp. 132–137.

schools.[72] More recently, a legislative initiative in the state of Arizona, better known as SB 1070,[73] would have made it a state crime for an irregular immigrant to be present in Arizona without carrying registration documents required by federal law. In addition to this, SB 1070 would have authorised state and local law to enforce federal immigration laws, and penalise those who shelter, hire or transport irregular immigrants. Other states such as Indiana, Georgia, South Carolina, and Alabama followed suit with similar legislation. Those in favour of such legislation saw it as a necessary measure to close the floodgates to irregular immigration. In stark contrast, the opponents saw it as opening the floodgates to racial discrimination, racial profiling and the criminalisation of immigrants and people of Latino ancestry. Not surprisingly, several legal challenges to such legislation were filed in court. The central argument in these petitions is that federal law pre-empts such state immigration laws. In a 5/3 opinion, the Supreme Court ruled that certain state provisions, such as those making it a state crime for an immigrant not to carry registration papers, those allowing for a warrantless arrest, and those prohibiting an undocumented migrant from working in Arizona, were pre-empted by federal law. However, some of the most controversial sections of the law, mainly pertaining to an officer's powers to determine the immigration status of any person stopped, detained, or arrested, were upheld.[74] In the Court's decision neither the civil rights issues in such immigration legislation, nor the disparate racial impact, in terms of the racial profiling and the facially neutral term 'alien', were at stake.[75]

Apart from the immigration laws and practices described above, race also plays a role in the citizenship status of Latinos. Despite the occasional legal recognition equating Mexicans with White citizens for naturalisation purposes,[76] Latinos are more often than not considered second-class citizens with fragile citizenship. This is because of the general distrust towards immigrants. Acknowledging the fact that Latinos with an American passport are always suspect and are at risk of deportation, the legal status of Puerto Rico and its inhabitants within the United States' system serves as a fitting example to unveil the paradox. Acquired through the Treaty of Paris pursuant to the Spanish–American War of 1898, this territory could be defined as an American colony. Puerto Ricans obtained American citizenship in 1917 but legally speaking it amounts to second-class

72 In this sense: Kevin R. Johnson, 'An Essay on Immigration Politics, Popular Democracy, and California's Proposition 187: The Political Relevance and Legal Irrelevance of Race', *Washington Law Review* (1995), vol. 70, pp. 629–674.

73 'Support Our Law Enforcement and Safe Neighborhoods Act', Senate Bill 1070, 49th Leg., 2d Reg. Sess. (Ariz. 2010).

74 *Arizona v. United States*, 132 S. Ct. 2492, 567 U.S. (2012).

75 Kevin R. Johnson, 'A Case Study of Color-Blindness: The Racially Disparate Impacts of Arizona's S.B. 1070 and the Failure of Comprehensive Immigration Reform', *U.C., Irvine Law Review* (2012), vol. 2, pp. 313–358.

76 *In re Rodriguez*, 81 F. 337 (W.D. Tex. 1897). On this issue of the requisite of Whiteness for naturalisation purposes, see *infra* Chapter 2.2.1.

citizenship. Despite having to pay all federal taxes, Puerto Ricans may not vote in U.S. Presidential elections and the full American Bill of Rights, most notably the Fourteenth Amendment, does not apply to them. This means that the U.S. citizenship can be unilaterally withdrawn at any time from people born in Puerto Rico by the U.S. Congress. This differential treatment is possible following a series of decisions by the U.S. Supreme Court that are known as the *Insular Cases*.[77] In these cases, the court defined the U.S. powers over the territories acquired at the end of the Spanish–American War. Like Guam and the Philippines (in the past), Puerto Rico is an unincorporated territory, where Congress nevertheless exercises plenary powers and Puerto Ricans enjoy second-class citizenship.[78]

The reason for telling these different narratives, albeit in a superficial manner, is to illustrate the fundamental role law played in establishing White male supremacy, while simultaneously racialising, and subordinating minorities in the United States. Without this historical backdrop it would be difficult to understand CRT's claims and how the past shapes the present normative baselines. It is these baselines that contemporary CRT theorists are challenging. Nevertheless, it is important to remember that CRT is not only a product or result of these specific legal-historical events. In order to better understand the broader contingencies leading to the emergence of CRT scholarship, it is necessary to analyse a second timeline that is related to the history of legal movements in American academia. Whereas CRT would not have developed without the backdrop of racial minorities, it is also a result of a very specific American history of legal scholarship generally, and legal movements in particular.

1.2 Timeline 2 – history of American legal movements

According to a generally shared account, American jurisprudence evolved in a pendulum swing motion, which saw legal formalism being substituted by legal realism, which in turn was supplanted by a return to formalism because of process jurisprudence, which again led to critical legal studies. While there is some disagreement over this way of presenting the history of American jurisprudential thought[79] for the sake of explanatory simplicity this somewhat mainstream narrative helps situate CRT in its jurisprudential context.

Modern academics have attempted to map the history of American legal thought in terms of historical periods. The classical tripartite subdivision was first proposed by Karl Llewellyn[80] and became better known thanks to Grant Gilmore who named those three periods 'The Age of Discovery', 'The Age of Faith' and 'The Age of Anxiety'.[81] The first of these ages, 'The Age of Discovery', runs

77 E.g. *De Lima v. Bidwell*, 182 U.S. 1 (1901); *Downes v. Bidwell*, 182 U.S. 244 (1901); *Dorr v. United States*, 195 U.S. 138 (1904); and *Balzac v. Porto Rico*, 258 U.S. 298 (1922).

78 Román, *Citizenship and its Exclusions*, pp. 99–112.

79 Neil Duxbury, *Patterns of American Jurisprudence* (Oxford: Clarendon Press, 1995), p. 2.

80 Karl N. Llewellyn, *The Common Law Tradition: Deciding Appeals* (Boston: Little, Brown and Co., 1960).

81 Grant Gilmore, *The Ages of American Law* (New Haven, London: Yale University Press, 1977).

roughly from American Independence in the 1780s to the American Civil War in the 1860s. During this time a distinct legal profession emerged, the first legal treatises on American law were published, universities established separate law faculties and courses, and judges started to conceive of common law not as a set of rules which needed to be discovered, but by consciously making rules in what has been called the 'Grand Style' of pre-Civil War cases,[82] and by taking their social and economic consequences into consideration.[83] This was the 'Golden Age'[84] during which the U.S. Supreme Court asserted its power of judicial review in the landmark decision *Marbury v. Madison*[85] and during which that same court interpreted the powers conferred by the Constitution to the federal government and federal courts expansively.[86] That seemingly glorious period appears under a slightly different light, taking into account that it coincides with some of the most disturbing decisions of the U.S. Supreme Court in which slavery and the appropriation of Native American lands were legally justified.

The second age, 'The Age of Faith', runs roughly from the end of the Civil War until the 1920s and is associated with formalism, namely the idea that law or legal rules, and other fields of knowledge, can be deducted from certain logical and interrelated principles. This led to the emergence of a specific legal science in universities. In the relatively young law schools, formalism became intimately associated with the name of Christopher Columbus Langdell, to the point that 'the beginnings of Langdellian legal science must, for any American lawyer, be an historical commonplace.'[87] As the Dean of Harvard Law School, Langdell managed to establish the idea of law as a science and that the case method, namely the study of case law from which to extrapolate legal principles, is the best pedagogical methodology in place of the traditional lecture. The assumptions of this new legal science were that law is a coherent, organised, objective system where rules logically derive from a small number of abstract principles and concepts. Hence, cases can be decided correctly by means of logic since they can be subsumed under a certain legal premise and a legal conclusion follows almost automatically. Moreover, in order to study these cases and to analyse them systematically, the law library with renewed casebooks became a fundamental component of this methodology. Langdell's method quickly established itself as the classic legal orthodoxy in the United States with many law schools following Harvard's example. The belief in science and reason clearly places his conceptualism and formalism into the spirit of the Enlightenment and the idea that the world is organised according to generally applicable truths, the reason why Gilmore also referred to this age as the 'Age of Faith'.

82 Llewellyn, *The Common Law Tradition*, p. 5 and p. 36.

83 Morton J. Horwitz, *The Transformation of American Law 1780–1860* (Cambridge, MA: Harvard University Press, 1977), p. 2.

84 Gilmore, *The Ages of American Law*, p. 12.

85 *Marbury v. Madison* 5 U.S. (1 Cranch) 137 (1803).

86 See e.g. *Swift v. Tyson*, 41 U.S. (16 Pet.) 1 (1842).

87 Gilmore, *The Ages of American Law*, p. 11.

At the court level formalism also found its entry, albeit in slightly different ways. Judges began to shy away from their more creative, policy-oriented predecessors and instead of making the law they contended that they merely discovered it. This was again possible because law was viewed as a closed, logical system, leading to a narrower, deductive approach of decision-making in which the underlying facts were of little importance as long as the coherence of the system was maintained.[88] Nevertheless, judicial formalism became more notorious for a different reason, almost by association with America's emerging capitalism and its underlying ideal of *laissez-faire*. This approach viewed economic freedom of the individual as a natural state. In a free society individuals should be free to contract, to trade, to make economic gains, and to bargain without any interference from the state.[89] Clearly aspects of Social Darwinism also played a role because ultimately *laissez-fairism* advantages the party that has more power to determine the terms of the contract or the bargain. Courts interpreted this vision as enshrined in and protected by common law and as what was assumed to be the natural order of things. Formalism helped them in doing so, for instance, by staunchly defending the principle of freedom of contract and striking down any perceived limitations of it. During this period social legislation, which had been introduced to protect weak parties from abuse, was struck down as unconstitutional. One of the most famous examples was *Lochner v. New York*.[90] In this case the U.S. Supreme Court declared that a New York statute which introduced a ten-hour workday for bakers violated the Fourteenth Amendment's Due Process Clause. Such a statute, according to the judges, interfered with the right to freely contract between employers and employees who must be free to determine the working hours. The right to make a contract is part of those liberties protected by the Due Process Clause of the Constitution, of which no state can deprive the individual. From a formal point of view this reasoning might make sense because it is based on the assumption of a complete symmetry in position between parties. It is clear, however, that freedom of contract, especially in the employment context, where the employer can impose conditions, is rarely based on equal bargaining powers. However, the spirit of that age and the judge's formalism did not permit such reasoning.[91]

Lochner also occupies a central position in the emergence of legal realism and to some extent ushered in the third age of American law, 'The Age of Anxiety'. While by admission of one of legal realism's main protagonists, Karl Llewellyn, it was questionable whether anything such as a Realist school or Realist movement

88 *Ibid.* at pp. 62–63.

89 For more details on *laissez-faire*, see Duxbury, *Patterns of American Jurisprudence*, pp. 25–32.

90 *Lochner v. New York*, 198 U.S. 45 (1905).

91 Another example of such formalistic reasoning is *Coppage v. Kansas*, 236 U.S. 1 (1915). Here the Supreme Court declared the unconstitutionality of Kansas state legislation, which outlawed employment contracts containing clauses prohibiting employees to engage in union activities, the so-called 'yellow dog contracts', because such legislation impaired the parties' freedom of contract.

ever existed,[92] one common thread of scholars associated *ex post* with this movement is the critique of the formalist and conceptualist jurisprudence in vogue at the time. In the first place, they questioned the idea of law as a formal, logical, self-sufficient, and coherent science. Rather than analysing law on the basis of abstract principles, social and economic reality should be taken into account. Social sciences instead of a separate and autonomous legal science would provide the necessary analytical and scientific framework from which to assess law and cases. At the same time, the case law methodology with its idea that from a small number of cases doctrinal and logical unity could be achieved or found was also under attack. Judges, as realists demonstrated, do not decide on the basis of some formal, logical criterion but their decisions are ultimately political and partisan. This demonstrates that realists not only managed to cast doubt over the Langdellian case law method, they also succeeded in directing their other main critique at formalism as it was practiced in courts. Based not only on *Lochner*, whose 'specter [...] has loomed over most important constitutional decisions, whether they uphold or invalidate governmental practices',[93] but also on numerous other cases, realists have shown how political arguments, much more than logic and reason played a role in judicial decisions even when politics were seemingly absent. The realist attack on the *Lochner* court was not that it was a logical mistake or an error in its systematic logical reasoning. Rather, they proceeded to show how the judges' assumption that the concept of liberty also included the *laissez-faire* vision of freedom of contract constituted a contested policy choice. More than a formal and corrective interpretation of the supposedly natural state of common law, this case was one of judicial activism, where the judges imposed their view of a normative baseline in striking down the New York legislation. Realists argued that instead of appealing to formal, abstract, and conceptual principles in adjudication, reality should be studied and taken into consideration. In the *Lochner* case, for instance, that would have been the unequal bargaining powers between the employers and the bakers. Hence, social sciences were crucial for realists, who highlighted the importance of studying law as it works in practice.[94]

Legal realism was possibly more a mood[95] than a unified school or a coordinated movement, which criticised formalism from a different angle and under different circumstances. Therefore, it is important to note how there were several identifiable strands,[96] not only because of the different effects those strands have had on later jurisprudence but also to look at legal realism's legacy in American

92 Gilmore, *The Ages of American Law*, p. 78.

93 Cass Sunstein, 'Lochner's Legacy', *Columbia Law Review* (1987), vol. 87, p. 873.

94 For a more detailed account on legal realism's emergence, see Duxbury, *Patterns of American Jurisprudence*.

95 In this way see *ibid.* in particular the chapter 'The Evolution of a Mood', pp. 65–159.

96 On this classification, see Gary Minda, *Postmodern Legal Movements* (New York, London: New York University Press, 1995), pp. 28–31.

jurisprudence. On the one hand, there were the progressive legal realists,[97] who developed out of a more pragmatic approach traceable to Oliver Wendell Holmes and Benjamin Cardozo and finding their ultimate representative in Karl Llewellyn who went on to develop the Uniform Commercial Code. They were responsible for rejecting the idea of law as a science, 'only' to substitute it with law as a social science. Law should be practiced and studied pragmatically and empirically by taking into account the findings of social sciences. This is the strand that Gilmore tends to refer to in his account of American legal jurisprudence.[98] On the other hand, there was the much less known strand of radical legal realists whose main proponents are Felix Cohen, Walter Wheeler Cook and Robert Hale.[99] Their critique of formalism came from a different perspective and emphasised the politics and power structures inherent in public and private law behind the cloak of legal objectivity. By unveiling the incoherence of some key legal categories they ultimately managed to unveil how judges relied more on politics and political judgments than on formal logic. In other words, judges decide a case based on what looks or feels fair to them when looking at the facts and based on their world views or political ideology. Legal reasoning and rules only come in at a second stage as a rationalisation or justification of the judges' primary intuition. Radical legal realists demonstrated the second prong of their thesis by exposing the incoherence of established patterns of reasoning in judicial decisions. Clearly, if the decisions were based on no logic and reason whatsoever, something else must explain their outcomes. Radical legal realists' political vision of law and adjudication was ultimately confirmed by the conflict between the U.S. Supreme Court and the President over New Deal legislation, in which it became clear how the courts declared the unconstitutionality of the majority of the President's legislation for political reasons.

Legal realism is generally said to have ended by the outbreak of World War II. The reasons for its demise are less than clear. On the one hand, there was the impression that its radical strand led to moral relativism, nihilism, and indeterminacy, which during a time of war was not an easy position to defend. On the other hand, empirical research did not really take place or had only marginal relevance. Another suggestion is that in the last instance the contrast between deconstructionist logic and the belief in objective social sciences may have brought about the fall of legal realism.[100] Regardless of legal realism's presumed failures and/or internal contradictions, its legacy is still visible today. First, in the United States very few today would doubt that judges' declarations of rules are policy

97 Referred to as the 'Sociological Wing of Realism' by Brian Leiter in 'American Legal Realism', in Martin P. Golding and William A. Edmundson (eds), *The Blackwell Guide to the Philosophy of Law and Legal Theory* (Malden: Blackwell Publishing, 2005) p. 54.

98 Gilmore, *The Ages of American Law*, pp. 68–98.

99 Referred to as the 'Idiosyncracy Wing of Legal Realism' by Leiter in 'American Legal Realism', p. 54.

100 G. Edward White, 'From Realism to Critical Legal Studies: A Truncated Intellectual History', *Southwestern Law Journal* (1986), vol. 40, pp. 821–825.

judgments rather than a logically necessary consequence of legal reasoning. The fact that most modern legal academic writing and court decisions contain policy considerations amounts to a lasting and direct consequence of legal realism.[101] Second, law is no longer viewed as a separate, static entity and science but it is seen as dynamic and dependent on the underlying society.[102] Third, the presence in American legal scholarship of social sciences, empirical analyses and the burgeoning of so-called 'law and … ' approaches are also a lasting legacy of legal realism. Social sciences, instead of natural sciences, had become the reference model, meaning that lawyers were still somehow anchored to the idea that there could be general 'good' law and 'right' decisions and policies. In that sense, to varying degrees, realists still remained entrenched in the traditional belief that some kind of universal truth was attainable.

This last point is precisely what separates modern jurisprudence from postmodern jurisprudence according to an updated classification of American jurisprudence introduced by Gary Minda.[103] According to this newer vision American legal thought had a pre-modern period coinciding with Gilmore's 'Age of Discovery', a modern period corresponding to the 'Age of Faith' and the 'Age of Anxiety', and then a postmodern period in which we are now.[104] The main idea behind this categorisation is that in spite of the differences and the contrasts which had occurred in some fundamental way, legal thought during the post-Civil War period up until the late 1970s remained imbued with the enlightened idea(l)s that some sort of universal truth, some kind of science – be it legal or social – reason and/or logic could help explain law and guide lawyers in their activities. However, these idea(l)s were fundamentally challenged, according to Minda's account by what he grouped together as 'postmodern legal movements'.

True, between the end of legal realism and the emergence and establishment of the first postmodern legal movements there were about thirty years and a resurgence of some sort of formalism thanks to Process Jurisprudence. Since legal realism emphasised policy and de-formalisation in decision-making, some other judicial constraint needed to be developed to prevent the nightmare of law equals politics. Principled adjudication[105] and institutional constraints through the reinforcement of democratic process and its inner morality[106] were the answers to that perceived necessity. However, the revolution sparked by the civil rights movement at the social, political, and legal level as well as the changes in the composition of legal academy which hired women and professors of colour at

101 Leiter, 'American Legal Realism', p. 60.

102 White, 'From Realism to Critical Legal Studies: A Truncated Intellectual History', p. 828.

103 See Minda, *Postmodern Legal Movements*.

104 See also Stephen M. Feldman, *American Legal Thought from Premodernism to Postmodernism* (New York: Oxford University Press, 2000).

105 Herbert Wechsler, 'Toward Neutral Principles of Constitutional Law', *Harvard Law Review* (1959) vol. 73, p. 1.

106 Lon Fuller, *The Morality of Law* (New Haven: Yale University Press, 1977), pp. 33–91.

unprecedented rates,[107] triggered the new swing of the pendulum away from Process Jurisprudence's formalism to the postmodern era.

Minda groups the following five intellectual currents under the heading of postmodern legal movements: (i) Law and Economics; (ii) Critical Legal Studies; (iii) Feminist Legal Theory; (iv) Law and Literature; and (v) Critical Race Theory. According to Minda, each of these schools went through generations where the first generation, albeit innovative, was still steeped in the modernist tradition and only in a second step moved to a more radical, postmodern stance. Clearly, this classification – as any classification – is not free from criticism: for instance, it is not clear why Law and Economics should figure as a postmodern legal movement when its aspirations are like the modern ones of assessing and analysing law from one universally true vantage point guaranteeing legal certainty and predictability through the lens of economics. Moreover Minda, who deems himself to be a postmodern legal scholar, and who as such should be wary of rigid categorisations and classifications, falls into the modernist trap.[108] However, for the purposes of providing a descriptive framework in which CRT developed, suffice to say here that there is a broad consensus that CRT is part of those movements that have challenged the modern orthodoxy.

Amongst the postmodern legal movements the most important for CRT's genealogy is undoubtedly Critical Legal Studies (CLS). Without entering into the details of this eclectic school of thought and only describing those aspects relevant to CRT here, it is necessary to mention that institutionally CLS appeared in 1976 when a group of legal scholars met at the University of Wisconsin Law School to form a network called *The Conference on Critical Legal Studies*.[109] The fact that CLS emerged as a network of scholars who also defined themselves as 'Crits', may also explain its open-endedness as to methodology or approach to law. Indeed, one of CLS' representatives doubted whether it makes sense to even talk about CLS as a 'movement' or as a 'school' and rather identified it as a political location.[110] However, this view is not shared unanimously. Martha Minow, for example, identifies shared commitments, assumptions and activities as the key characterisation of CLS scholars.[111]

As to those commitments and shared ideas, the mainstream narrative is that CLS springs directly from the radical strand of the legal realist movement.[112] In fact, in its core ideas CLS built on the indeterminacy analysis advanced by the

107 On this second point see Feldman, *American Legal Thought from Premodernism to Postmodernism*, pp. 158–159.

108 Christopher L. Sagers, 'Postmodern Legal Movements: Law and Jurisprudence at Century's End – Book Review', *Michigan Law Review* (1997), vol. 95, pp. 1938–1942.

109 For more details on the genealogy of CLS see Mark Tushnet, 'Critical Legal Studies: A Political History', *Yale Law Journal* (1991), vol. 100, p. 1515.

110 *Ibid.*

111 Martha Minow, 'Law Turning Outward', *Telos* (1986), vol. 73, pp. 83–85.

112 For a slightly different account see White, 'From Realism to Critical Legal Studies: A Truncated Intellectual History', p. 819.

radical realists by pushing it further. Like the radical realists, the Crits rejected the idea that law is a systematic and rational ensemble of principles and policies and rather saw it as the outcome of political/personal preferences, which are then disguised behind categories, formalism, disciplinary and doctrinal thematisation, and schematic thinking. The additional layer CLS added to this older analysis was the insight that law operates as a tool of domination cloaked behind abstract language and seeming objectivity and neutrality both in the legal process as well as in the actual outcome. Law, therefore, works as a justification for the status quo, which is presented as the politically neutral and objective position. In Western legal systems this corresponds to liberal ideology. Anything or anyone not fitting into the liberal framework is portrayed as, or implicitly and automatically becomes, a departure from that dominant political ideology and is necessarily viewed as the non-neutral subject or ideology, thus being marginalised precisely because of law's neutrality.

The novel domination aspect introduced into legal scholarship by CLS clearly refers to left-wing, Marxist doctrine and to Gramsci's idea of hegemony, whereby control by the dominant majority is maintained not just through violence and political and economic coercion, but also ideologically, through a hegemonic culture which helps maintain the status quo because minorities identify their own good with that of the majority instead of starting a revolution. The hegemonic culture and ideology also permeates academia; the reason why CLS started the tradition of counterhegemonic workshops, conferences, and summer schools, which later on became vital for CRT as well. With their broad reference to Marxist doctrine and domination CLS scholars also took a second novel step with regards to radical legal realism. They expressly and intentionally situated themselves politically in the legal arena. By doing so they also managed to unveil the underlying political, liberal ideology of many apparently neutral legal concepts and principles. Hence, even the 'invisible', implicit choice to work in the liberal legal framework becomes transformed into a political choice, just as the more visible one CLS scholars opted for. The common assumption for many CLS scholars therefore is that law is politics.[113]

The resulting political aspect in legal analysis and doctrine led CLS to another fundamental position, namely that legal categories are basically indeterminate and incoherent. In fact, once the political, ideological choices and currents underlying legal categories have been unmasked it becomes harder and even impossible to justify them on the basis of some allegedly neutral and objective principle. An example of such a CLS type of analysis is Duncan Kennedy's essay on Blackstone's *Commentaries*, the latter being one of the most influential law treatises in British and American law.[114] Instead of the usual portrait of this masterpiece as a presentation of common law challenging arbitrary royal power based on the rights of persons

113 See Tushnet, 'Critical Legal Studies: A Political History', p. 1517.

114 Duncan Kennedy, 'The Structure of Blackstone's *Commentaries*', *The Buffalo Law Review* (1979), vol. 28, pp. 209–321.

and the rule of law, Kennedy asks a set of political questions relating to the social and political ideologies informing the text of Blackstone's *Commentaries* as well as what Blackstone's treatise actually conceals.

Kennedy also analysed the ideological situatedness of law and legal actors at the judicial level and the potential conflict between a judge's ideological position and the legal outcome of a case.[115] By means of a hypothetical example involving a bus company that has applied to a federal judge to obtain an injunction against striking drivers, Kennedy establishes a critical phenomenology of judging. He analyses the judge's reasoning in a situation where the judge's personal politics and ethical position make him sympathetic to the striking drivers but where the law is against unions in similar cases. Conscious of the desired outcome, namely not granting the injunction, and the law, which favours the opposite result, a significant amount depends on how the judge frames the legal issue. If framed as a question of whether the workers can legitimately obstruct the means of production, then it would be hard to resist the injunction. However, if the issue is viewed as freedom of speech, then the injunction would become an illegitimate interference with the worker's right to free speech. While not completely unconstrained in his or her political choices because some considerations of the judgment's consequences – such as the institutional position of the judge, his or her future career, the long-term or short-term consequences for workers – and the traditional boundaries of freedom of speech law will have a bearing on the ultimate outcome, the judge nevertheless is able to use law to some extent as a means to further a certain political and ideological agenda. CLS' critique of law's indeterminacy was also decried as 'trashing'[116] because it led to the call to abandon traditional doctrinal categories used by lawyers, including the category of rights.

In order to better understand CRT's emergence, another important strand of CLS is related to the use of social construction and deconstruction to destabilise claims of neutrality and objectivity in legal reasoning.[117] For instance, Gary Peller demonstrated how the public/private dichotomy underlying the jurisprudence of freedom of contract by the U.S. Supreme Court in decisions such as *Lochner v. New York* was socially constructed.[118] He did so by showing how that divide essentially relied on the historical myth of the social contract. Such a contract assumes the existence of a group of autonomous individuals, who freely created and authorised a government or public sphere, with the understanding that this would be contrasted to the private sphere consisting of autonomous individual subjects freely entering into relationships with one another into which the government would not be authorised to intervene. Once the social construction of the seemingly neutral and natural order behind the social contract and thereby behind the public/

115 Duncan Kennedy, 'Freedom and Constraint in Adjudication: A Critical Phenomenology', *Journal of Legal Education* (1986), vol. 36, pp. 518–562.

116 Mark G. Kelman, 'Trashing', *Stanford Law Review* (1984), vol. 36, p. 293.

117 Minda, *Postmodern Legal Movements*, p. 120.

118 Gary Peller, 'The Metaphysics of American Law', *California Law Review* (1985), vol. 73, p. 1151.

private divide has been unmasked by means of deconstruction, Peller was also able to show how the judges in *Lochner* had not really made an objective decision but had privileged a certain interpretation of the law over another one. Including freedom of contract under due process analysis therefore was not a rational, neutral, and objective outcome but a politically contingent decision.

However, CLS was not the only, albeit the most important, intellectual predecessor to CRT amongst the postmodern legal movements. Feminists and Feminist Legal Theory especially in the form of its postmodern strand also played an important role in CRT's genesis and development. Without entering into the details of feminist jurisprudence,[119] it suffices to say that Black feminists like Patricia Williams, Kimberlé W. Crenshaw, and Angela P. Harris, to name the most important, were particularly active from CRT's inception in determining the agenda of CRT and feminist legal theory. Their particular position and experience at the intersection of race and gender helped highlight the shortcomings of more traditional anti-discrimination doctrine on the one hand and feminist jurisprudence on the other. In particular, CRT feminists built on or critiqued the universality and the essentialism underlying some aspects of modern liberal, cultural, and radical feminism. In fact, these feminist strands base their analysis on the assumption of one universal gender conception, which happens to coincide with the experience of White women. Women of colour are overlooked in this context and are forced to opt between predominantly male race politics, and predominantly White gender politics, without being able to draw the attention to the particular aspects of subordination of Black women. Their non-recognition creates serious shortcomings at the representative political and legal level.[120] This passage from a universal female subject to a number of different female subjects destabilises and decentres legal analysis, therefore opening up the legal discourse to diverse identity and cultural politics of postmodernism while distancing itself from the universalising aspects of modernism.[121] Hence, it should come as no surprise that feminist jurisprudence and CRT share a lot in common. In fact, many observations made by feminist legal scholars in connection with law's effects on women can be extended almost by analogy to law's effects on racial minorities. Both are concerned with the problematic normative baseline, which takes the White male as the neutral, objective, and therefore invisible assumption. However, as with CLS, Critical Race Feminists have taken the analysis further and in new directions, as will be shown in more detail in the next chapter.

In conclusion and summarising vastly what has been said in the first chapter of this book, CRT can be seen as the product of these two distinct timelines: one relating to the historical context of racial minorities as they have been constructed,

119 See for an overview of the history and developments of feminist legal theory, Nicola Lacey, 'Feminist Legal Theory and the Rights of Women', in Karen Knopp (ed.), *Gender and Human Rights* (Oxford: Oxford University Press, 2004), pp. 13–30.

120 Kimberlé W. Crenshaw, 'Mapping the Margins: Intersectionality, Identity Politics, and Violence Against Women of Color', *Stanford Law Review* (1991), vol. 43, pp. 1241–1299.

121 For more details, see Minda, *Postmodern Legal Movements*, pp. 141–148.

affected, and subordinated by law, and the other one relating to the more specific developments in American jurisprudence, from formalism over legal realism to the (post)modern critiques of legal liberalism, amongst which CLS and feminist jurisprudence played the main role. Only by taking this broader context into account is it possible to understand CRT as it emerged in the late 1980s and early 1990s.

Chapter 2

Critical Race Theory

Its genealogy and writings

2.1 Description of Critical Race Theory

2.1.1 Brief institutional history

In many ways, CRT can be described as a reaction to, or result of the historical developments discussed in Chapter 1. While the previous chapter provided the broader framework in order to locate the legal theory, here a detailed description is given of its more immediate genealogy, the main writings and critiques, and its current developments.

One of the most important factors to mention about the literature on the emergence of CRT is the growing frustration amongst minority scholars with the limitations of the liberal civil rights movement.[1] In their eyes, the traditional approaches – from demonstrations, to developing new litigation strategies and filing amicus briefs – did not yield the hoped for results of racial reform,[2] especially because American courts, most notably the U.S. Supreme Court, gradually dismantled some limited achievements of the civil rights movement. CRT's critical stance towards the civil rights movement and the embedded philosophy of anti-discrimination law can be traced back to the tensions and debates already existing within the African American community and the National Association for the Advancement of Colored People (NAACP) on how best to invest resources in order to end racial segregation. On the one hand, the integrationist strategists, who would ultimately prevail, argued for a litigation strategy. Whereas the separatist strategists, on the other hand, argued that it would be better to invest the funds directly into Black institutions, such as schools and hospitals, to ameliorate socio-economic conditions of the Black community as a whole.[3] Clearly both strategies relied on a different ideological basis and had different outcomes. The

1 Kimberlé W. Crenshaw, *et al.* (eds), *Critical Race Theory: The Key Writings that Formed the Movement* (New York: The New Press, 1995), pp. xiv–xvii.

2 See Richard Delgado and Jean Stefancic, 'Introduction', in Richard Delgado and Jean Stefancic (eds), *Critical Race Theory: The Cutting Edge* (Philadelphia: Temple University Press, 2000), p. xvi.

3 See Mark Tushnet, *The NAACP's Legal Strategy Against Segregated Education, 1925–1950*, 2nd edn (Chapel Hill: University of North Carolina Press, 2005).

former advocated for a world, in which race would be irrelevant and racism would represent an irrational vestige of the past. Under the integrationist approach, White supremacy and Black nationalism[4] would become symmetrical expressions of the same thing. The separatists were preoccupied with improving the actual living conditions in Black communities, ensuring the maintenance and continued existence of Black communities and preventing their assimilation into White society and its structures. Moreover, instead of relying on colourblindness or the idea(l) of a race-free or race-neutral society, which would nonetheless reflect White structures, this strategy actually proposed a race-conscious approach. Race-consciousness would lead to separate communities that would deal with each other on equal footing and with equal power structures. The Black nationalist critical position was fundamental to informing CRT's scepticism towards the anti-discrimination approach and CRT's advocacy for a race-conscious legal analysis.[5] Despite this legitimate scepticism, CRT scholars managed to mobilise the drive and protest from the civil rights movement in the 1950s and 1960s into legal academia.[6]

The second factor, referred to by several 'insiders' as contributing to the emergence of CRT, is the dissatisfaction of minority scholars with the predominantly White leftist movement of CLS' 'trashing' of rights and the failure to address the race factor in its analyses.[7] In other words, CRT brought 'a left intervention into race discourse and a race intervention into left discourse.'[8] A third factor that played a role in CRT's development was the student movements. However, here the views diverge somewhat. Kimberlé W. Crenshaw explains that a central element to the emergence of CRT were the student protests, boycotts and the organisation of an 'alternative course' on race and law at Harvard Law School in 1981 after Derrick Bell resigned and the law school decided to offer only a short course on civil rights instead of a full course on 'Constitutional Law and Minority Issues.'[9] Others argue that the student movements at the University of California, Berkeley in the 1960s, especially the law school's *Boalt Coalition for a Diversified Faculty* (BCDF), provided the necessary terrain for the emergence and the establishment of CRT in top law schools.[10] Last but not least, in recent times another potential factor was presented as an alternative narrative to explain

4 This term loosely identifies and unites people over differing time periods such as Marcus Garvey, Martin Delany, Stokely Carmichael, Malcolm X, just to name a few, who all in one way or the other promoted Black unity, self-determination and pride which clearly involved racial separatism.

5 For more details on this difference, see Gary Peller, 'Race – Consciousness', *Duke Law Journal* (1990), vol. 1990, pp. 758–847.

6 See e.g. Bernie D. Jones, 'Critical Race Theory: New Strategies for Civil Rights in the New Millennium', *Harvard Blackletter Journal* (2002), vol. 18, pp. 1–90.

7 Crenshaw, *et al.* (eds), *Critical Race Theory: The Key Writings that Formed the Movement*, pp. xxii–xxiii.

8 *Ibid.* at p. xix.

9 Kimberlé W. Crenshaw, 'The First Decade: Critical Reflections, or "A Foot in the Closing Door"', *UCLA Law Review* (2002), vol. 49, pp. 1344–1354.

10 Sumi Cho and Robert Westley, 'Critical Race Coalitions: Key Movements that Performed the Theory', *UC Davis Law Review* (2000), vol. 33, p. 1377.

the origins of CRT. Here, the emphasis is placed on the shift from the individual stories to broader structural factors: the influence of radical, White Marxist and socialist professors who were denied tenure during the 1970s under what is defined as 'Liberal McCarthyism'. During their unemployment or underemployment, these individuals were able to, and had time to, spread their radical ideas, thus contributing to the rise of both CLS and CRT.[11] Instead of presenting these factors as competing stories, the purpose here is to provide a picture of the more immediate causes and conditions leading up to CRT's beginning. There is possibly a grain of truth in each of these narratives, meaning that they all had an impact, which enabled the emergence of CRT. Even so, some factors were more influential in establishing CRT in one law school or geographic area and less in another.

There is little doubt, however, that one of the watershed moments for CRT occurred in 1987. Dissatisfied and frustrated with the attitude within CLS, which tended to silence voices of colour within the movement and in the legal academy more broadly, a number of scholars organised a panel discussion called 'The Minority Critique of CLS Scholarship (and Silence) on Race' as part of the tenth National Critical Legal Studies Conference, entitled 'Sounds of Silence: Racism and the Law'. This, in turn, led to the organisation of the first independent CRT workshop, whose attendants[12] gathered at the Benedict's Center in Madison, Wisconsin on 8 July, 1989, where Kimberlé W. Crenshaw coined the term 'Critical Race Theory'.[13] From then on there was no stopping the movement which had been set in motion. Following the CLS tradition of organising counterhegemonic meetings, where intellectual exchanges free of institutional and ideological constraints would be possible, annual workshops were organised,[14] a number of separate symposiums or conferences were held on different occasions resulting in additional publications and exchanges.[15] Even when the annual CRT workshops stopped taking place regularly, CRT's legacy continued, on account

11 Richard Delgado, 'Liberal McCarthyism and the Origins of Critical Race Theory', *Iowa Law Review* (2009), vol. 94, p. 1505.

12 For a list of those names, see Crenshaw, 'The First Decade: Critical Reflections, or "A Foot in the Closing Door"', p. 1361, at fn. 19.

13 For a more detailed account of this history see *ibid* at pp. 1354–1360 and Charles R. Lawrence III, 'Foreword. Who Are We? And Why Are We Here? Doing Critical Race Theory in Hard Times', in Francisco Valdes, Jerome McCristal Culp and Angela Harris (eds), *Crossroads, Directions, and a New Critical Race Theory* (Philadelphia: Temple University Press, 2002), p. xii.

14 Information on most of the early workshops can be found in Stephanie Phillips, 'The Convergence of the Critical Race Theory Workshop with LatCrit Theory: A History', *University of Miami Law Review* (1999), vol. 53, pp. 1247–1472.

15 See e.g. 'Theorizing the Connections Among Systems of Subordination', *UMKC Law Review* (2002), vol. 71, no. 2, pp. 227–527; 'Critical Race Theory: The Next Frontier', *Washington and Lee Law Review* (2004), vol. 61, no. 4, pp. 1485–1799; 'Going Back to Class? The Reemergence of Class in Critical Race Theory', *Michigan Journal of Race and Law* (2005), vol. 11, no. 1, pp. 1–273; and 'Re-defining Critical Race Theory: The Future of the Movement', *Iowa Law Journal* (2009), vol. 94, no. 5.

of LatCrit, which also organised annual conferences.[16] In other words, from an institutional point of view it can be said that CRT has been around for more than twenty-five years.

2.1.2 CRT's literature and main tenets

These workshops, conferences, symposia, and other meetings and exchanges between scholars have helped develop a vast and diverse body of literature on CRT. It is hard to pin down this doctrinally and methodologically eclectic legal scholarship to one canonical unity. Indeed, this open-ended approach reflects the necessity of prioritising identity over substance so as to create a safe space and platform for participation in racial struggle.[17] Hence, it can be said that the main aim of CRT is not to develop a coherent, methodologically flawless theoretical framework but it is rather an academic political enterprise. However, even political action necessitates some core ideas to develop its programme and CRT scholars have over the years defined such ideas, principles, and goals.

These have been identified, and later refined, during a workshop which discussed a seven-point description of CRT's core tenets, according to which CRT:

1. Holds that racism is endemic to, rather than a deviation from, American norms;
2. Bears scepticism towards the dominant claims of meritocracy, neutrality, objectivity and colourblindness;
3. Challenges ahistoricism, and insists on a contextual and historical analysis of the law;
4. Challenges the presumptive legitimacy of social institutions;
5. Insists on recognition of both the experiential knowledge and critical consciousness of people of colour in understanding law and society;
6. Is interdisciplinary and eclectic (drawing upon, *inter alia*, liberalism, post-structuralism, feminism, Marxism, critical legal theory, postmodernism, pragmatism), with the claim that the intersection of race and the law overruns disciplinary boundaries; and
7. Works toward the liberation of people of colour as it embraces the larger project of liberating oppressed people.[18]

Put differently, CRT seeks to challenge popular, mainstream beliefs about racial injustice, such as 'blindness to race will eliminate racism', 'racism is a matter of individuals, not systems', and 'one can fight racism without paying attention to

16 For a list of those conferences, see the following website: www.latcrit.org/content/conferences/.

17 Crenshaw, 'The First Decade: Critical Reflections, or "A Foot in the Closing Door"', pp. 1362–1363.

18 See Phillips, 'The Convergence of the Critical Race Theory Workshop with LatCrit Theory: A History', p. 1250.

sexism, homophobia, economic exploitation, and other forms of oppression and injustice'.[19] Methodologically, one of the main tools to achieve these goals is the use of legal narrative, which allows personal experiences to enter academic writing and legal analysis. The main idea is that academic legal writing and jargon tend to silence minorities' visions and experience. Through legal narrative and storytelling those voices can finally be heard and provide a sort of counterhegemonic account of law and its effects. For this reason, one will find that many CRT writings start with a personal narrative or else are completely written in a narrative-style .[20]

Even today, these principles and goals are integral to the CRT project, to which most CRT scholars continue to subscribe. Since it is impossible to give an account of all CRT publications, as a first step I will provide a more detailed picture of the principles and goals in the American law setting, by selecting and summarising seminal CRT writings. The selection is partly personal, and partly based on the work of CRT scholars, who have published a number of anthologies of key CRT publications. However, CRT literature, especially the earlier writings, can be grouped into two main categories, which represents the novelty of CRT in American jurisprudence. The first body of work focuses on the difference of opinion over the traditional civil rights scholarship. The second category can be described as a critique of CLS writings.

In a second step, I analyse the critiques both from within and outside the movement. This will allow me to describe some other central points CRT scholars have made, ranging from issue of legal narrative to its critique of merit. Finally, I intend to convey a somewhat comprehensive overview of the writings, the dynamics, and the ideas behind CRT. From this, it is hoped that the reader will have obtained a better idea of CRT's eclectic legal scholarship and the CRT movement.[21]

2.1.2.1 *Contesting liberal civil rights and freedom of speech case law and scholarship*

Some of CRT's most significant pieces were written before CRT was officially established in the workshops in the late 1980s. These writings were key because they functioned as path-breakers and catalysts for the movement's imminent

19 Francisco Valdes, Jerome McCristal Culp and Angela Harris, 'Battles Waged, Won, and Lost: Critical Race Theory at the Turn of the Millenium', in Valdes, McCristal Culp and Harris (eds), *Crossroads, Directions, and a New Critical Race Theory*, p. 1.

20 See e.g. Patricia Williams, *The Alchemy of Rights* (Cambridge, MA: Harvard University Press, 1991) and Derrick A. Bell Jr., *Faces at the Bottom of the Well. The Permanence of Racism* (New York: Basic Books, 1992).

21 For more complete bibliographical references to CRT literature (as well as Latino/a critical scholarship), see Richard Delgado and Jean Stefancic, 'Critical Race Theory, An Annotated Bibliography', *Virginia Law Review* (1993), vol. 79, p. 461; Richard Delgado and Jean Stefancic, 'Critical Race Theory, An Annotated Bibliography 1993, A Year of Transition', *University of Colorado Law Review* (1995), vol. 66, p. 159; and Jean Stefancic, 'Latino and Latina Critical Theory: An Annotated Bibliography', *California Law Review* (1997), vol. 85, p. 1509.

arrival. Their focus was mainly on traditional civil rights discourse in general, and the shortcomings of the civil rights movement and lack of judicial activism in particular.

The name that regularly crops up in this context is the late Derrick A. Bell Jr.[22] and his two essays dealing with *Brown v. Board of Education*, the landmark ruling that abolished racial segregation in American public schools.[23] In his first essay,[24] he criticised *Brown* because the focus was on integration and desegregation, and not the need for quality education. According to him, the first goal – integration and de-segregation – represented the ideals of elite, liberal public interest lawyers and only established formal equality. The second goal – quality education – was in fact pursued by the plaintiffs, African American parents, who wanted a better education for their children, irrespective of the school's system of segregation or desegregation. Bell therefore criticised how many civil rights lawyers directed their client's interests without, in fact, listening to them and their specific needs and wishes.

A few years later, Bell's second essay[25] adopted yet another unconventional view of *Brown*. Countering Herbert Wechsler's critique of the case because it lacked any principled reasoning,[26] Bell argued that most judicial cases involving race can be explained by the principle of 'interest convergence', meaning that 'the interest of blacks in achieving racial equality will be accommodated only when it converges with the interests of whites.'[27] Hence, the outcome of the *Brown* decision can only be understood by taking into account the interests of the White community. Bell offered three arguments to explain why it was possible for White interests to converge with Black ones at that period of time. First, by showing its commitment to equality, America made a strategic political move in the Cold War struggle with communist countries over its influence in the developing world. Second, an unspoken motivation behind the *Brown* decision could be linked to a growing fear of disillusionment and anger among Black people, especially Black soldiers who fought for freedom and equality during World War II but continued to face discrimination in their own country. Third, Whites realised that the rural South needed to be industrialised and segregation represented an obstacle in this process.[28]

22 Derrick A. Bell Jr., one of the first African Americans to become tenured at Harvard Law School, is considered by many the founding father of CRT. The importance of Derrick Bell's role also emerges from the tribute paid to him by Charles R. Lawrence III, 'Doing the "James Brown" at Harvard: Derrick Bell as Liberationist Teacher', *Harvard Blackletter Journal* (1991), vol. 8, p. 263.

23 *Brown v. Board of Education (Brown I)*, 347 U.S. 483 (1954) and *Brown v. Board of Education (Brown II)*, 349 U.S. 294 (1955).

24 Derrick A. Bell Jr., 'Serving Two Masters: Integration Ideals and Client Interests in School Desegregation Litigation', *Yale Law Journal* (1976), vol. 85, p. 470.

25 Derrick A. Bell Jr., '*Brown v. Board of Education* and the Interest Convergence Dilemma', *Harvard Law Review* (1980), vol. 93, p. 518.

26 Wechsler, 'Toward Neutral Principles of Constitutional Law', pp. 1–35.

27 Bell, '*Brown v. Board of Education* and the Interest Convergence Dilemma', p. 523.

28 *Ibid.* at pp. 524–525.

At the time Derrick Bell's articles were published, criticising *Brown* and viewing the civil rights movement under a less friendly or more pessimistic light, especially as a Black professor, came close to 'being branded, at best, an apologist for segregated education, and at worst, an accomplice to racist resistance to integration.'[29] Bell's observations and misgivings were confirmed, nevertheless, by both the later developments of civil rights litigation and the gradual dismantlement of rights acquired during a first period of liberalisation and by subsequent studies based on his observations.[30] Moreover, he set the tone for a number of young scholars, inspired by his analysis, which started to question the basic assumptions concerning the treatment of minorities, thus making him one of the founders of CRT.

Derrick Bell was not the only influential writer in the embryonic stages of CRT. A seminal piece by Alan Freeman,[31] an exponent of CLS, is also viewed as a building block in the foundations of CRT. His analysis focused more specifically on the development of anti-discrimination case law by the U.S. Supreme Court in the aftermath of *Brown*. He argued that anti-discrimination law can be viewed from two perspectives; either from the perpetrator's point of view or the victim's point of view. For Freeman, the victim's perspective of discrimination is influenced by a number factors grounded in history and the social fabric. These include objective conditions of life such as job, housing, and financial difficulties as well as the victim's consciousness about these conditions. In contrast, according to Freeman, the perpetrator's perspective has prevailed in anti-discrimination law. This perspective is premised on a worldview, which considers only individual actions, or a series of actions, inflicted by the perpetrator as relevant. Racial discrimination is therefore not the result of broader social phenomena but only the wrongful conduct of one particular actor, the perpetrator. Legal concepts such as 'fault' or 'causation' further manage to successfully separate the innocent mass of society from the handful of guilty racists. On the one hand, the concept of fault establishes the idea that only intentional discrimination is legally relevant under anti-discrimination law. This in turn leads to complacency amongst the members of society, who need not feel any responsibility for broader structural and societal discrimination. On the other hand, causation limits conditions, which law deems to be necessary to establish if discrimination took place.

These analyses have been further elaborated upon and partially countered by Kimberlé W. Crenshaw. In one of her most notable works,[32] she challenges critiques of the civil rights movement, which had been created by what she defines

29 Crenshaw, *et al.* (eds), *Critical Race Theory: The Key Writings that Formed the Movement*, p. 2.

30 Mary L. Dudziak, 'Desegregation as a Cold War Imperative', *Stanford Law Review* (1988), vol. 41, p. 61 and Mary L. Dudziak, *Cold War Civil Rights: Race and the Image of American Democracy* (Princeton: Princeton University Press, 2001), confirming the hypothesis that the Cold War had an influence in determining the outcome in *Brown*.

31 Alan David Freeman, 'Legitimizing Racial Discrimination Through Anti-Discrimination Law: A Critical Review of Supreme Court Doctrine', *Minnesota Law Review* (1978), vol. 62, pp. 1049–1119.

32 Kimberlé W. Crenshaw, 'Race, Reform, and Retrenchment: Transformation and Legitimation in Anti-Discrimination Law', *Harvard Law Review* (1988), vol. 101, pp. 1331–1387.

as the 'New Left' and the 'New Right', thus making clear where CRT positions itself. The critique of the 'New Right' is described here and her response to the 'New Left' critique is addressed below in the analysis of CRT's objections to CLS. Regarding the position of the 'New Right,' personified by Thomas Sowell,[33] she responds in CLS-like fashion, arguing that anti-discrimination law contains both an expansive view as well as a restrictive view. The former stresses equality as an outcome and the latter equality as a process. However, since both views are contained in anti-discrimination law there is a certain inherent indeterminacy in civil rights law and the interpretation mostly depends on views of the interpreter. Consequently, Sowell's and the neo-conservatives' contentions that 'color-conscious, result-oriented remedies are political perversions of the law, but that his preference, color-blind, process-oriented remedies are not'[34] has no foundation because the colourblind view is as much a political interpretation of anti-discrimination law as colour-consciousness.

Another path-breaking CRT critique of anti-discrimination law comes from Charles R. Lawrence III,[35] who specifically addresses the problem of discriminatory intent as introduced by the U.S. Supreme Court in *Washington v. Davis*.[36] In that case the court imposed a requirement on the plaintiffs, who challenged the constitutionality of a facially neutral law, to prove that the lawmaker or administration acted with a racially discriminatory intent. This judgment considerably limited the applicability of disparate impact cases in constitutional law. It has been criticised by CRT scholars and others, because it imposed an excessive burden of proof on the plaintiff to prove racial discrimination and that the injury and loss as a result of racial discrimination exists irrespective of the decision-maker's motives. However, what Charles Lawrence showed, as opposed to others, is that deliberate intent cannot adequately explain racial discrimination. Indeed, in his view racial bias is endemic in American society, its social practices, and the interaction of culture, psychology, and context. It is so endemic that people are not even aware of it, and for that reason it is called 'unconscious racism'. This leaves the problem of whether and how law can intervene in those instances when racism is dissimulated unconsciously or hidden behind other justifications. He therefore suggests replacing discriminatory motive with a cultural approach. The U.S. Supreme Court should analyse the cultural meaning of laws in order to uncover instances of collective, unconscious racism. This 'cultural meaning test' would require the court to evaluate almost like a cultural anthropologist, whether racial significance is attached to the government's behaviour. It would require an examination of the historical and social context, in which legislation or regulation was promulgated, and if the evidence suggests that a portion of the population views

33 Thomas Sowell, *Civil Rights: Rhetoric or Reality* (New York: William Morrow and Co., 1984).

34 Crenshaw, 'Race, Reform, and Retrenchment: Transformation and Legitimation in Anti-Discrimination Law', p. 1346.

35 Charles R. Lawrence III, 'The Id, the Ego, and Equal Protection: Reckoning with Unconscious Racism', *Stanford Law Review* (1987), vol. 39, pp. 317–388.

36 *Washington v. Davis* 426 U.S. 229 (1976).

the government's action in racial terms, then heightened scrutiny is required, even to legislation that is facially neutral.[37] The lasting influence of Charles Lawrence's article was confirmed twenty years later, when an anniversary issue was published which incorporated the main tenets of the original essay and its legacy.[38]

As the last example shows, in some ways the failures and obstacles encountered by anti-discrimination law within the American constitutional framework have led to innovative, alternative proposals for judicial reasoning, legal analysis, and ways to remedy the plight of racial minorities. The Equal Protection Clause contained in the Fourteenth Amendment clearly demonstrates this phenomenon.

To avoid the pitfalls of colourblind jurisprudence in equal protection cases, Neil Gotanda suggested to frame race issues under the Free Exercise and Establishment Clause of the U.S. Constitution's First Amendment,[39] and to apply its case law. According to Neil Gotanda, the Supreme Court's case law on religion better accommodates a race-conscious analysis due to a more historically contextualised analysis of social issues in the Court's judgments. Moreover, it would have the advantage of shifting the focus of the discussion from issues concerning proper standard of review to a more policy-driven one, which would allow the introduction of other considerations such as cultural references and the free exercise of positive aspects of race.[40]

Angela Harris sees openings in the Privilege or Immunities Clause of the U.S. Constitution's Fourteenth Amendment.[41] This clause provides that '[n]o state shall make or enforce any law which shall abridge the privileges or immunities of citizens of the United States.'[42] As already mentioned, the Fourteenth Amendment was introduced following the American Civil War. Its main purpose was to ensure that each individual's natural, civil, and political rights, which are guaranteed by the federal government, were protected from state intervention. Read in this context, the objective was to help freed slaves, who were entitled to enjoy citizenship rights and equal protection from the federal government, especially when the (Southern) states were unwilling or unable to intervene.[43] Nevertheless, in 1873, less than ten years after its enactment, the U.S. Supreme Court in the *Slaughter House Cases*[44] muted this amendment. The court held that it was the responsibility of the states to protect the natural and civil rights of the individual. The court further held that citizenship privileges and immunities consisted of special

37 In this sense: Lawrence, 'The Id, the Ego, and Equal Protection': vol. 39, pp. 355–356.

38 See 'Unconscious Discrimination Twenty Years Later: Application and Evolution', *Connecticut Law Review* (2007–2008), vol. 40, no. 4, pp. 927–1235.

39 U.S. Const., amend. I.

40 Neil Gotanda, 'A Critique of "Our Constitution Is Colorblind"', *Stanford Law Review* (1991), vol. 44, pp. 64–69.

41 See Angela P. Harris, 'Beyond Equality: Power and the Possibility of Freedom in the Republic of Choice', *Cornell Law Review* (2000), vol. 85, p. 1181.

42 U.S. Const., amend. XIV, § 1.

43 Harris, 'Beyond Equality: Power and the Possibility of Freedom in the Republic of Choice', p. 1183.

44 *Slaughter House Cases* 83 U.S. (16 Wall.) 36 (1873).

federal rights, such as interstate freedom of movement or the right to petition the federal government.[45] In practice terms, it was the law of equal protection, and not privileges and immunities, which served as the main legal instrument to resist oppression.[46] Interestingly, in 1999, more than hundred years later, the U.S. Supreme Court resurrected the Privileges and Immunities Clause in *Saenz v. Roe.*[47] The court declared the unconstitutionality of a Californian statute, which limited the maximum welfare benefits of new residents to the amount they received in the state where they previously resided. It justified its decision on the basis of the Privileges or Immunities Clause. Hence, this clause could be used, albeit with some reservations, to avoid some of the pitfalls of equality, and its related discourse and jurisprudence. This reversal means the equal protection and privileges and immunities of national citizenship can work side by side in helping protect racial minorities.[48]

Other authors have suggested abandoning the notion that the courts are the right venue to best serve and advance minority interests.[49] Girardeau Spann, for instance, argues that the disappointing and unreliable track record of American courts as well as their veiled majoritarianism and politics have badly served minorities. In his proposal, he suggests taking action at the legislative level in the open political arena. This arena, he argues, is where most progressive action has taken place, as demonstrated by the Thirteenth and Fourteenth Amendments, and the Civil Rights and Voting Rights Acts.

CRT scholars' critique of civil rights court decisions, specifically their handling of the issues of equal protection and race, was subsequently confirmed by the U.S. Supreme Court. Reflecting this judicial trend, CRT scholars' search for an alternative solution to the Fourteenth Amendment to combat race discrimination was appropriate and timely. The U.S. Supreme Court employed the ideological and dogmatic tool of colourblindness to slowly but surely dismantle the use of race and race-conscious remedies by the legislator and public authorities. A number of cases illustrate this slow but continuous erosion, which started with *Bakke.*[50] In that case, the U.S. Supreme Court declared the unconstitutionality of a quota system, which reserved a number of placements at the medical school of University of California, Davis to minorities, including racial minorities. Racial classifications were deemed unconstitutional because they treated people as members of a group, and not as individuals. Moreover, the justices invalidated a main justification for affirmative action, namely that of seeking to remedy general societal and systemic discrimination, because it was too broad and burdensome on

45 *Ibid.* at p. 77–78.

46 Harris, 'Beyond Equality: Power and the Possibility of Freedom in the Republic of Choice', p. 1184.

47 *Saenz v. Roe* 526 U.S. 489 (1999).

48 Harris, 'Beyond Equality: Power and the Possibility of Freedom in the Republic of Choice', p. 1192.

49 Girardeau A. Spann, 'Pure Politics', *Michigan Law Review* (1990), vol. 88, pp. 1971–2033.

50 *Regents of the University of California v. Bakke*, 438 U.S. 265 (1978).

innocent Whites. Race-based affirmative action in higher education was capable of withstanding constitutional scrutiny under the Equal Protection Clause only when it furthers diversity and does not use rigid quotas.

The justices then continued down the path of dismantling race-conscious measures under equal protection case law. In *Croson*,[51] they applied the strict scrutiny test to the city of Richmond's set-aside programme for minorities, which gave preference to minority business enterprises (MBE) when awarding municipal contracts. The programme was found to be too broad and not sufficiently tailored to further a compelling governmental interest and was therefore declared unconstitutional under the Equal Protection Clause. Two aspects of this case are worth mentioning. First, the set-aside programme only concerned prime contractors. The city granted them construction contracts to subcontract at least 30 per cent of the dollar amount of the contract to one or more MBEs. Second, the U.S. Supreme Court ruled that the City of Richmond was previously guilty of race discrimination, which could easily justify the programme on grounds of remedying specific past racial discrimination.[52] Nevertheless, the justices ignored this perspective and further developed the idea that racial equality equals racial neutrality.

In *Adarand*, the Supreme Court emphasised this point further by declaring the racial classifications used by the federal government must be reviewed under the strict scrutiny test.[53] Before, the standard of strict scrutiny only applied to local and state governments as illustrated in *Croson*, while racial classifications used by the federal government would only be subject to intermediate scrutiny.[54] *Adarand* changed this situation and the stricter test was said to apply to all levels of government. Given the language employed by the majority of the Supreme Court in *Adarand*, it made it seem almost impossible to uphold the constitutionality of racial classification of any kind in the future.

However, in an interesting turn of events, the justices in *Grutter v. Bollinger* confirmed the *Bakke* decision and held that universities were permitted to use race in their admissions procedures,[55] while simultaneously deciding in its twin case *Gratz v. Bollinger* that the use of race cannot be automatic in admissions procedures, and categorically excluding quotas.[56] Whereas liberal scholars hailed the former decision as an important victory, CRT scholars were less enthusiastic. According to one CRT critique, the Michigan Law School programme was held constitutional within extremely narrow limits, and was far from addressing and redressing the on-going societal discrimination. Moreover, the distinction between *Grutter* and

51 *City of Richmond v. J.A. Croson Co.*, 488 U.S. 469 (1989).

52 See e.g. *Bradley et al. v. School Board of City of Richmond*, 382 U.S. 103 (1965) (*per curiam*) (holding that the proposed school desegregation plans were unconstitutional because they did not consider, at a full evidentiary hearing, the impact on those plans of faculty allocation on an alleged racial basis).

53 *Adarand Constructors, Inc. v. Peña*, 515 U.S. 200 (1995).

54 *Metro Broadcasting, Inc. v. FCC*, 497 U.S. 547 (1990).

55 *Grutter v. Bollinger*, 539 U.S. 306 (2003).

56 *Gratz v. Bollinger*, 539 U.S. 244 (2003).

Gratz is constitutionally irrelevant as both would likely lead to the same numerical results. What is interesting is that the programme that was more open about its objectives was held unconstitutional, whereas the one that was less obvious was upheld. In this way, affirmative action was artificially kept alive, preventing racial minorities from becoming too unruly while striking down effective affirmative action programmes.[57] Moreover, in *Grutter*'s majority opinion, Justice O'Connor stated that although affirmative action programmes like the one by Michigan Law School were permissible, they would be unnecessary in twenty-five years. Besides the fact that calculating the number of years is arbitrary, it is unclear why such justification should disappear within that specific time range, especially if the justification for affirmative action is to enhance the diversity among the student body, and not to remedy specific past discrimination or societal discrimination.[58]

The issue of affirmative action in higher education came under scrutiny more recently in one of the latest U.S. Supreme Court cases on race. In *Fisher v. University of Texas*,[59] the per cent plans introduced by the public University of Texas system were challenged. These plans provided that the top 10 per cent of each Texas high school's graduating class would be accepted at the University of Texas at Austin, regardless of their race. While race neutral, this ensured that a number of students from public schools, who would otherwise not have been able to access higher education, gained access to public universities. Due to historical reasons, the system often coincided with mainly Black or Latino schools, therefore, it functioned to a certain extent like a race-based affirmative action programme. The two plaintiffs, both White women, had been denied admission and filed suit against the university, for violation of the Equal Protection Clause of the Fourteenth Amendment. However, the Court avoided addressing the issue of whether such plans were constitutional because it remanded the case on the grounds that the lower court had not applied the standard of strict scrutiny. It is interesting to point out that over the past thirty years the court has intervened on four separate occasions in affirmative action programmes relating to racial discrimination in higher education.

However, the criticisms and concerns raised about the U.S. Supreme Court's path towards an increasingly colourblind interpretation of the Fourteenth Amendment's Equal Protection Clause were confirmed in decisions outside the domain of higher education. Quickly and unabated, the U.S. Supreme Court continued to dismantle race-conscious measures with its equal protection doctrine of colourblindness. In the decision of the newly appointed Chief Justice Roberts,[60] it was held that a plan assigning students to public schools solely for the purpose of achieving racial integration and balance did not amount to a

57 In this sense: Girardeau A. Spann, 'The Dark Side of Grutter', *Constitutional Commentary* (2004), vol. 21, pp. 221–250.

58 See Kevin R. Johnson, 'The Last Twenty Five Years of Affirmative Action?', *Constitutional Commentary* (2004), vol. 21, pp. 171–190.

59 *Fisher v. University of Texas*, 133 S.Ct. 2411, 570 U.S. __ (2013).

60 *Parents Involved in Community Schools v. Seattle School District No. 1*, 551 U.S. 701 (2007).

compelling state interest and that the plan was not narrowly tailored. Moreover, the diversity argument from *Bakke* and *Grutter* was rejected and distinguished as applying to higher education only.

The decision in *Ricci v. DeStefano* confirmed that race neutrality and colour-blindness were the constitutional way towards equality.[61] That case involved a charge of racial discrimination by a Latino and several White fire-fighters against the city of New Haven, Connecticut for declining to certify promotional test results. If the promotional results were certified, then no African American and only two Latino applicants would have succeeded in obtaining a job promotion. New Haven justified its decision not to certify promotional test because it was concerned that it might not be able to successfully defend itself against a disparate impact claim from the African American and Latino candidates under Title VII of the Civil Rights Act of 1964. In a somewhat twisted turn of events, New Haven was sued for disparate racial treatment because the city's decision to annul the promotional tests was seen as being race-based and a pretext to discriminate against White fire-fighters. The District Court[62] and Court of Appeals[63] rejected those arguments. However, the Supreme Court reversed the lower courts' decisions. The Supreme Court re-framed the question. Instead of asking whether New Haven's conduct was discriminatory, which it presumed it was, it asked if the city had a lawful justification for its race-based action. Moreover, the majority imported a stricter standard of evidence, namely the 'strong basis in evidence' from equal protection case law, in order to interpret this statutory Title VII claim. In other words, whereas under the more lenient test an employer could take race-conscious action based on good faith, under *Ricci* an employer must do so only if they have a strong basis in evidence that they will be subject to disparate-impact liability if they fail to take such action. Thus, the Supreme Court was able to reverse the lower courts' decision because it held that New Haven was not able to satisfy that standard.

The case has been heavily criticised by CRT scholars.[64] Such scholars argue that this latest decision Whitens discrimination conceptually. By adopting the more stringent standard of evidence, the Supreme Court enforced an employer's defence against disparate impact claims by minorities, while simultaneously reducing the evidentiary burden on White plaintiffs alleging disparate treatment. This was possible because the highest court framed Whites as the paradigmatic victims of race discrimination and focused on their experience of anti-discrimination

61 *Ricci v. DeStefano*, 557 U.S. 557 (2009).

62 *Ricci v. DeStefano*, 554 F. Supp. 2d 142 (D. Conn. 2006).

63 *Ricci v. DeStefano*, 530 F.3d 87 (2d Cir. 2008) (*per curiam*). This decision was taken by three judges amongst whom the future Supreme Court justice, Sonia Sotomayor, who was attacked heavily during her Senate confirmation hearings for precisely this decision.

64 Cheryl I. Harris and Kimberly West-Faulcon, 'Reading *Ricci*: Whitening Discrimination, Racing Test Fairness', *UCLA Law Review* (2010), vol. 58, pp. 73–165.

law.[65] Whites are portrayed as hardworking and meritorious individuals, whose efforts are being thwarted by racially-rigid procedures and city officials, who are under the control or influence of politically powerful minorities. These powerful groups are accused of furthering members of their own race at the expense of others. At the same time, the commentators of *Ricci* suggest that test fairness has been racialised because it equates the city's attempt at preventing an unfair test result with a racial preference for non-Whites. Rather than assessing if the test actually related to job performance, or if the test was conducted fairly or if a less discriminatory selection criteria were available – all issues that could have been raised to challenge the result – the Supreme Court interpreted New Haven's attempt at avoiding the discriminatory impact of these test results as a racial agenda.

The last case in the Supreme Court's path towards a colourblind society and jurisprudence involved the Voting Rights Act. Introduced in 1965, as a reaction to the continued obstacles Black voters faced in Southern states, this legislation was an attempt by the federal government to force local governments to respect the law and ensure equal voting rights for every American citizen, irrespective of the voter's skin colour. One of the central provisions of this act required that certain states and local governments with a history of racial discrimination in voting matters obtain pre-clearance from the federal government before implementing any changes to their voting laws or practices. In particular, Section 4(b) established a coverage formula to help determine which jurisdictions are subject to pre-clearance. In *Shelby County v. Holder*,[66] in a narrow 5–4 decision, the U.S. Supreme Court declared Section 4(b) unconstitutional because the coverage formula was established on outdated data, and thus constituted a violation of the constitutional principles of federalism and equal sovereignty among states. Clearly this decision did not directly involve the Equal Protection Clause or discussions about the legitimacy and use of race in remedying racial gerrymandering. However, it cast a long shadow over the constitutionality of the only remaining Civil Rights Act, which had withstood legal challenges until this point.

The case law described here has left little in place of what was designed in the 1960s to combat race discrimination. Diversity justifications in higher education continued to be valid, albeit for a limited timeframe if Justice O'Connor's dictum in *Grutter* was to be followed. Some provisions of the Civil Rights Act, such as the disparate impact ones, also allow for race-based action. However, Justice Scalia's concurring opinion in *Ricci* ominously hang over such provisions since he explicitly framed the Equal Protection Clause against the backdrop of colourblindness, a principle previously inscribed by the Supreme Court.[67] In addition to this, the

65 During the past two decades all cases accepted by the U.S. Supreme Court on race discrimination except for one (*Johnson v. California*, 543 U.S. 499 (2005)) were brought by White plaintiffs.

66 *Shelby County v. Holder*, 133 S.Ct. 2612, 570 U.S. (2013).

67 *Ricci v. DeStefano*, 557 U.S. 557 (2009), (Scalia, J., concurring).

Voting Rights Act itself has a similar sword dangling over its head. In an ironic parallel to what happened during the Reconstruction Period following the Civil War, the Supreme Court has gradually hollowed out civil rights legislation, emptying it of legal substance and weight. The highest court of the land managed to do so by holding that racial classification is discriminatory regardless of its purpose. It established a symmetrical correspondence between the normative use of race to exclude, marginalise, and discriminate, and the use of race as an instrument to combat racial discrimination. In its most extreme version, it failed to make any distinction between race used in a benign way and race used in a discriminatory and stigmatising way. In other words, colourblindness in American law views 'treat[ing] a Dixiecrat Senator's decision to vote against Thurgood Marshall's confirmation in order to keep African Americans off the Supreme Court as on a par with President Johnson's evaluation of his nominee's race as a positive factor.'[68] As a consequence of the U.S. Supreme Court's ideology, besides a couple of exceptions, race today is normatively off limits and viewed with great suspicion.

However, it is not only the courts' restrictive and increasingly colourblind interpretation of civil rights legislation and the constitutionally protected Equal Protection Clause which CRT scholars have criticised. In other areas affecting racial minorities a similar trend has been under CRT's scrutiny. This is the area of hate speech or racial slurs as interpreted in connection with the freedom of speech in the American Constitution. Again, from a minority point of view, in the early 1950s the U.S. Supreme Court upheld, albeit by a narrow 5–4 majority, a conviction for hate speech of a White supremacist who had distributed leaflets accusing Blacks of various crimes, including rape, robbery, and other violent acts.[69] However, since the *Beauharnais* decision, the U.S. Supreme Court has consistently interpreted freedom of speech as able to authorise hate speech, unless it poses a clear and present threat of violence.[70] For example, in *R.A.V.*,[71] the Supreme Court reversed a conviction of a young White extremist, who had set alight a cross inside the fenced garden of a Black family. The perpetrator was convicted under a local criminal ordinance, which was subsequently declared unconstitutional. The local ordinance targeted speech not leading to incitement to violence but an impermissible viewpoint. The majority opinion written by Justice Antonin Scalia was extremely controversial. CRT scholars view the court's decision as an ahistorical and decontextualised legal analysis that ignores the significance of the practice of cross burning for African Americans.[72]

68 *Adarand Constructors, Inc. v. Peña*, 515 U.S. 245 (1995), (Stevens, J., dissenting).

69 *Beauharnais v. Illinois*, 343 U.S. 250 (1952).

70 *Brandenburg v. Ohio*, 395 U.S. 444 (1969) and *National Socialist Party of America v. Village of Skokie*, 432 U.S. 43 (1977).

71 *R.A.V. v. City of St. Paul*, 505 U.S. 377 (1992).

72 Mari J. Matsuda and Charles R. Lawrence III, 'Epilogue: Burning Crosses and the *R.A.V.* Case', in Mari J. Matsuda, *et al.* (eds), *Words That Wound: Critical Race Theory, Assaultive Speech and the First Amendment* (Boulder: Westview Press, 1993), pp. 133–136.

According to CRT, this expansive interpretation of free speech has a particularly pernicious effect on racial minorities and tends to favour the position of the White, male majority. CRT scholars have argued that hate speech can cause direct harm in the form of psychological and emotional distress, which often ends up affecting children and can lead to pecuniary loss and physical damage to the victims.[73] As a result, they have proposed some alternative approaches and solutions to show how the 'marketplace of ideas' doctrine negatively affects minorities. Richard Delgado, for instance, suggests introducing a separate tort for racial slurs, which would avoid the shortcomings and limitations of other traditional torts, such as assault and battery, intentional infliction of emotional distress, defamation, or other constitutional or statutory provisions, which have until now insufficiently protected the victims of hate speech and racial insults.[74] Matsuda, on the other hand, attempts to throw light on the victim's experience. She argues that the legal response to racist propaganda is insufficient because it offers no redress to the actual real harm inflicted, which then goes on to perpetuate racism. She proposes that the victim's experience should be taken into account. Some other of her suggestions include reading an anti-subordination interpretation of the First Amendment, criminalising a narrowly defined class of hate speech, and redressing other minor forms of such speech through private law remedies.[75]

2.1.2.2 *Contesting Critical Legal Studies*

The novelty of CRT does not reside exclusively in the criticism of traditional, liberal civil rights and freedom of speech scholarship. In fact, colourblindness and civil rights critiques had already been advanced by other academics who are not necessarily affiliated with CRT. Here, CLS plays an important role. One of the early 'founding' writings, discussed above, is authored by Alan Freeman, who is a follower of the CLS tradition and not CRT. But, CRT has distanced itself from CLS and arguably has succeeded in overshadowing it.[76]

CRT scholars disagree with the rights-critical approach of CLS, also referred to as 'rights-trashing', which they connect with the indeterminacy of law. On the one hand, CRT scholars share the Crits' scepticism towards a liberal vision of the rule of law. They agree that rights discourses are indeterminate and that legal ideals are easy to manipulate, and tend to legitimate racial hierarchy and the status quo based on inequalities of wealth and power through seemingly neutrally structured legal argumentation. On the other hand, they disagree with CLS scholars' critiques of rights. Some CLS scholars argue that rights are unstable

73 See for all Richard Delgado, 'Words That Wound: A Tort Action For Racial Insults, Epithets and Name Calling', *Harvard Civil Rights – Civil Liberties Law Review* (1982), Vol. 17, pp. 133–181.

74 *Ibid.* at pp. 150–165.

75 Mari J. Matsuda, 'Public Response to Racist Speech: Considering the Victim's Story', *Michigan Law Review* (1989), Vol. 87, pp. 2320–2381.

76 Paul Brest, 'Plus Ça Change', *Michigan Law Review*, (1993), Vol. 91, p. 1945.

because they are highly dependent on their social setting and they do not produce determinate outcomes. According to this group of CLS academics, they transform real experiences into empty abstractions. In effect, the use of rights discourse prevents real social transformation.[77] Such transformation cannot occur because law is the expression of the ruling class' domination. Rights and rights discourse help legitimise hegemony, thereby inducing people to accept domination. Due to the underlying ideology, rights cannot function as a means towards radical social transformation.

According to CRT scholars, this rights-critical position disregards the potential value of the rights discourse for people of colour. In fact, for the underprivileged and oppressed, rights are a powerful instrument as a means to protect themselves. Discarding rights as a hegemonic tool not only deprives minorities of an instrument against oppression but also of 'a symbol too deeply enmeshed in the psyche of the oppressed to lose without trauma and much resistance'.[78] Therefore, CRT scholars highlight how rights are not simply an external instrument, but are deeply engrained and even constitutive of identities and the human psyche. In this sense, liberal theory and CLS share a similar position. CRT scholars, however, contend that Crits are mostly White, male university professors teaching at some of the top law schools. This elite group cannot fully grasp the internal and symbolic relevance of rights for racial minorities, or the role of others in shaping the individual self and the recognition granted in the form of rights by the community.[79] Moreover, discarding rights deprives racial minorities of their only tool to respond to White domination and oppression. CRT scholars are quite aware that – to use Audre Lorde's essay title – '[t]he Master's Tools Will Never Dismantle the Master's House'.[80] Substituting rights with an alternative can also worsen the situation of racial minorities. By 'trashing rights', one ultimately runs the risks of disempowering the racially oppressed, without addressing or even touching on the issue of White supremacy.

This first critique leads to and is to a degree constitutive of CRT's second objection to CLS. According to CRT scholars, CLS literature fails to adequately address the role of racism as hegemony or as a tool to establish racial domination and White supremacy in American history. Consequently it neglects the fact that this form of racial hegemony was established by means of coercion and not by consent. While the Crits' analysis is helpful in understanding the limited transformative potential law can have in a hegemonic context, particularly concerning anti-discrimination law, it bypasses the issue of racial hegemony. CRT scholars and CLS scholars have different understandings of domination and hegemony. While the latter posits an ideologically induced consent to establish hegemony,

77 Mark Tushnet, 'An Essay on Rights', *Texas Law Review* (1984), vol. 62, pp. 1363–1403.

78 Williams, *The Alchemy of Rights*, p. 165.

79 See Costas Douzinas and Adam Geary, *Critical Jurisprudence* (Oxford and Portland, Oregon: Hart Publishing 2005), pp. 179–202.

80 Audre Lorde, 'The Master's Tools Will Never Dismantle the Master's House', in *Sister Outsider* [1984], (Berkeley, California: Ten Speed Press, 2007), pp. 110–113.

CRT scholars argue that racial hegemony has never been about consenting to or accepting domination. It has been mostly about coercion. Moreover, CLS scholarship on rare occasions analyses racism as hegemony. Even when it does, it tends to exaggerate the role of liberal ideology as a hegemonic force but omits the role racism plays in White domination. Given that CLS and CRT speak of two different types of hegemony, the Crits' analysis is not in sync with the view that some aspects in liberalism and rights appeal to racial minorities because of their liberationist and transformative potential.[81] This, in turn, reinforces CRT's critique of CLS' rights-critical approach.

However, it is not only the awareness of the role of racial domination, or its absence, in CLS literature that CRT scholars highlight. It is also a certain intellectual and racially determined divide within CLS that is addressed. The traditional Crit is a White, male professor more concerned with a deconstructive critique of law and the theoretical underpinnings of the intellectual endeavour. Academics of colour associated with CLS cannot remain indifferent or forget their respective communities of belonging. Moreover, Black CLS scholars cannot be oblivious to the practical, everyday implications of their work. This ultimately leads to a divide, or a cleavage along the colour-line, where the theoretical side of CLS is White and the practical side is predominantly coloured. To make matters worse, there is a sense that the theoretical, White side attempts to silence and use the practical, coloured side by forcing minority scholars to speak in a certain language. This language is unable to communicate their own experiences, which may cause them to exclude their personal accounts or lead to the appropriation of the cultural references in their writings.[82]

Resulting from the objections directed towards CLS, CRT scholars have introduced a reconstructive minority perspective, which takes on board rights and race. As a substitute to the Crits' negative, de-constructive theoretical project, CRT scholars suggest that the study of race and rights must be followed, accompanied, and integrated by a positive, re-constructive, practical programme. CRT's founding writings, mentioned above under the critique of anti-discrimination law and alternative constitutional analyses, provide details of this programme while demonstrating how CRT scholars shaped this school of thought and distinguished it from its predecessor.

Another example comes from Mari Matsuda, who uses Japanese American reparation claims resulting from the internment suffered during World War II, to answer the Crits' dilemma concerning alternative normative sources once the more traditional sources – the market system, the pluralist tradition, and classical liberalism – have been deconstructed or dismissed as useless.[83] In line with a

81 Crenshaw, 'Race, Reform, and Retrenchment: Transformation and Legitimation in Anti-Discrimination Law', pp. 1356–1369.

82 See Harlon L. Dalton, 'The Clouded Prism', *Harvard Civil Rights – Civil Liberties Law Review* (1987), vol. 22, pp. 435–445.

83 Mari J. Matsuda, 'Looking to the Bottom: Critical Legal Studies and Reparations', *Harvard Civil Rights – Civil Liberties Law Review* (1987), vol. 22, pp. 323–399.

bottom-up approach, her proposed solution is to look to the actual experiences, history, and intellectual tradition of people of colour. While legal philosophy has wrongly overlooked victims of racial oppression, they are able to bring unique and distinct normative insights to the table.[84] She illustrates what such an analysis may look like by referring to the concrete example of reparations and the traditional standard objections to such reparations: the problematic identification of the victim, the causal link between past injustices and present claims, and the calculation of damages. By taking the victim's perspective into account, these objections can be refuted. More than that, the legal concept of reparations itself 'avoids the traps of individualism, neutrality, and indeterminacy' because its sole and direct addressees and beneficiaries are the powerless and minority group members and therefore cannot be interpreted in any other way, unlike the concepts of free speech or due process.[85]

To sum up, instead of 'mere' critical deconstruction of traditional civil rights and hate speech, CRT has come up with original solutions and alternatives to counter some of the problems which arise in the traditional, liberal approach to anti-discrimination and freedom of speech law, and in CLS writings. In many ways, the novelty of CRT resides precisely in the fact that it uses CLS tools to unmask some of the underlying inconsistencies, indeterminacies, and politics of traditional civil rights law and how those have negatively affected racial minorities. However, instead of an outright rejection of rights and law as politics, CRT proposes a broader framework, which includes the view of different groups – including minorities, and the disenfranchised or marginalised – more generally. As Patricia Williams puts it, '"[r]ights" feels so new in the mouths of most black people. It is still so deliciously empowering to say. It is a sign for and a gift of selfhood that is very hard to contemplate reconstructing (deconstruction is too awful to think about!) at this point of history.'[86]

2.2 Critiques of Critical Race Theory

Presenting the story and the content of CRT as a unanimous success would be misleading. CRT was, and to some extent remains, a minority scholarship which itself arose from a highly contested legal movement, CLS. Most, if not all, CRT scholars consider their work to be academic activism and do not view it as mainstream jurisprudence. Moreover, CRT scholars and CLS scholars share the view that their academic writing plays a highly political role. Hence, it should come as no surprise that some of the reactions to CRT have been highly critical. In this section, I first look at the internal critiques, which have helped CRT to mature

84 *Ibid.* at pp. 324–326.

85 *Ibid.* at pp. 393–394.

86 Patricia Williams, 'Minority Critique of CLS: Alchemical Notes: Reconstructing Ideals from Deconstructed Rights', *Harvard Civil Rights – Civil Liberties Law Review* (1987), vol. 22, p. 431.

into a broader, more diversified movement. Then I move on to the external critiques.

2.2.1 Internal critiques

The early writings described above provide the intellectual foundation of CRT. At the same time, since its inception and during the various workshops organised over the years, a number of internal critiques emerged. These can be broadly grouped into two different groups.[87]

The first major internal critique was voiced by a number of scholars who reacted against what was perceived to be CRT's essentialist strand. According to them, this favoured one version of persons of colour, while excluding or marginalising the voices of women, gays, lesbians and/or bisexuals of colour or other racial minorities. These views, mostly of Critical Race Feminists, posited that racial subordination cannot be fully understood if it does not consider other types of subordination and if it does not move away from essentialist positions that have the effect of marginalising rather than helping to build coalitions.[88] For instance, anti-racist and feminist discourses focus on either anti-racism or feminism and do not analyse how they interact or intersect with one another. Nowadays CRT scholars speak of 'intersectionality', which Kimberlé W. Crenshaw came up with in one of her path-breaking works.[89] In two articles, she highlights how feminist and anti-racist movements have marginalised the experience of women of colour because both operate as if women's experiences and the experiences of people of colour are mutually exclusive without ever intersecting. This attitude has led to two problems. The first issue concerns the legal arena and anti-discrimination legislation. Anti-discrimination law has been structured on similarly mutually exclusive terms. One can either sue for race discrimination or gender discrimination, *tertium non datur*. Hence, a dual claim for overlapping race *and* gender discrimination is not possible. Kimberlé W. Crenshaw exemplifies this by analysing a number of Title VII claims brought by Black women under the Civil Rights Act.[90] In these cases she shows how courts failed to recognise their interests and needs because law frames their claims as either sex discrimination or race discrimination but is unable to address both together.[91] For example, an employer who does not hire Black women may show that on the claim of sex discrimination they hire women and that on the claim of race discrimination they hire Blacks. Under this

87 Darren Lenard Hutchinson, 'Foreword: Critical Race Histories: In and Out', *American University Law Review* (2004), vol. 53, pp. 1196–1203.

88 In this sense, the most powerful piece remains that of Angela P. Harris, 'Race and Essentialism in Feminist Legal Theory', *Stanford Law Review* (1992), vol. 42, pp. 581–616.

89 Kimberlé W. Crenshaw, 'Demarginalizing the Intersection of Race and Sex', *University of Chicago Legal Forum* (1989), vol. 1989, pp. 139–167 and Crenshaw, 'Mapping the Margins: Intersectionality, Identity Politics, and Violence Against Women of Color', pp. 1241–1299.

90 Civil Rights Act, 78 Stat. 241 (1964).

91 Crenshaw, 'Demarginalizing the Intersection of Race and Sex', pp. 141–150.

framework, it turns out that Black women are unable to assert their claims for discrimination, which further entrenches their marginalisation and subordination.

The second aspect, which intersectionality problematises, relates to the political arena.[92] When subordinated groups organise politically in order to make their claims heard, it frequently happens that there are conflicting claims. In this case, belonging to two opposing subordinated groups can have a disempowering effect. Kimberlé W. Crenshaw illustrates this by looking at the politicisation of domestic violence. In feminist campaigns and politics against domestic violence, the fact that this occurs in minority communities predominantly is downplayed or hidden from the public eye, which potentially diverts funds and attention from domestic violence in those communities and ignores Black women's suffering.[93] In contrast, in anti-racist campaigns and politics, the collective values of the community prevail over feminism, which is presented as a divisive and White women's concern, at the expense of Black women's empowerment and development.[94] Hence, belonging to two subordinated groups leads to both legal and political marginalisation. The challenge this presents to conventional ways of thinking about anti-discrimination law and political movements is that intersectionality requires a complete overhaul of the entire framework. Only then can we seriously talk about a simultaneous incorporation of women's experiences and Blacks' experiences, which will ultimately lead to recognition of Black women's experiences.[95]

Intersectionality theory has been taken a step further and has given rise to 'multidimensionality analysis'.[96] As opposed to intersectionality theory, which is limited to those facing multiple elements of subordination, multidimensionality includes all members of subordinated groups. This provides a better understanding of how privilege and subordination play out differently in different contexts, whereas intersectionality only looks at cumulative elements of subordination. Multidimensionality for instance, provides insight into the interaction between Whiteness and gayness, whereas intersectionality would not. What is relevant in both theoretical approaches is that they counter essentialising people of colour and recognise the necessity to move beyond a one-dimensional analysis of race, racism and racial subordination.

A second major critique concerning the writings of CRT scholars, especially the initial works, is that they centred on the so-called 'Black/White Binary',[97] which encouraged an excessive focus on Black/White racial issues. This has left

92 Indeed, she calls this aspect 'political intersectionality'. Crenshaw, 'Mapping the Margins: Intersectionality, Identity Politics, and Violence Against Women of Color', pp. 1251 *et seq.*

93 *Ibid.* at pp. 1252–1253 and pp. 1258–1262.

94 *Ibid.* at pp. 1253–1258.

95 Crenshaw, 'Demarginalizing the Intersection of Race and Sex', pp. 140.

96 Darren Lenard Hutchinson, 'Identity Crisis: "Intersectionality", "Multidimensionality", and the Development of an Adequate Theory of Subordination', *Michigan Journal of Race and Law* (2001), vol. 6, pp. 285–317.

97 Juan F. Perea, 'The Black/White Binary Paradigm of Race: The "Normal Science" of American Racial Thought', *California Law Review* (1997), vol. 85, pp. 1213–1258.

other experiences such as those faced by Native Americans, Asian Americans, or Latinos marginalised within CRT. According to this critique, not only does such a narrow approach prevent coalition building in addressing racial injustice as well as inhibit a broad analysis of the pervasiveness of American racism but it also leads to ranking racial oppression along a continuum of suffering. As a result of this internal contestation, the focus has shifted slightly to a multiracial discourse. It is important to note that a certain 'Black exceptionalism'[98] is acknowledged, which provides an analytical framework for CRT scholars to analyse the experiences of other persons of colour and ethnic groups. The shift has been to an inclusive analysis, which has encouraged the formation of a number of separate branches within CRT, ranging from LatCrit, to AsianCrit, to NativeCrit and TribalCrit.[99] This inclusive approach also takes into account overlapping issues, such as sexual orientation, queer theory and race,[100] which focus on the specific aspects of subordination and marginalisation occurring within these respective communities. Only by expanding anti-racist theories beyond the narrow limits of Black/White can adequate and effective remedies against racial injustice be developed.

Partially related to the Black/White binary critique, which emphasises the African American experience over other minority groups' racialisation and oppression, another important development of CRT is the theoretical analysis of 'Whiteness', more broadly referred to as 'Whiteness Studies'.[101] Instead of focusing on how law and society has constructed and subordinated Blacks and other races in the United States, the focus of attention is shifted to the White majority. Such studies determine whether Whiteness is an on-going legal and historical construction, which has continuously evolved and continued to benefit from the subordination of other groups and races. CRT's contribution in this domain is to analyse the ways in which law was enabled to contribute to the construction of Whiteness and determine who is White. It also examines the structural ways employed to preserve Whiteness not only socially but also legally through rights protection and law enforcement.

Two publications illustrate this important strand of CRT scholarship. In the first instance, Haney López demonstrates how being White was the result of a long historical development, in which law played an essential role.[102] By looking at

98 Leslie Espinoza and Angela P. Harris, 'Embracing the Tar-Baby – LatCrit Theory and the Sticky Mess of Race', *California Law Review* (1997), vol. 85, p. 1596.

99 See e.g. Robert A. Williams, Jr., *Like a Loaded Weapon: The Rehnquist Court, Indian Rights, and the Legal History of Racism in America* (Minneapolis, London: University of Minnesota Press, 2005).

100 See e.g. Francisco Valdes, 'Sex and Race in Queer Legal Culture: Ruminations on Identities and Inter-Connectivities', *Southern California Review of Law and Women's Studies* (1995), vol. 5, pp. 25–71; Darren Lenard Hutchinson, 'Ignoring the Sexualization of Race: Heteronormativity, Critical Race Theory, and Anti-Racist Politics', *Buffalo Law Review* (1999), vol. 47, pp. 1–116.

101 For a collection of essays and pieces on Whiteness, see Richard Delgado and Jean Stefancic (eds), *Critical White Studies: Looking Behind the Mirror* (Philadelphia: Temple University Press, 1997).

102 Ian F. Haney López, *White by Law*, revised 10th anniversary edition (New York: New York University Press, 2006).

early case law concerning U.S. citizenship and Congress' restriction of naturalisation to White persons only, which officially ended in 1952, the author was able to show how judges and law were deeply intertwined in creating and constructing 'the White race'. Asked to decide whether applicants from China, Burma, India, Japan, Mexico, Syria, or Arabia, to name some of the most common and tricky cases, could or should be deemed to be White for naturalisation purposes, the courts struggled to determine the justifications for defining Whiteness. The main arguments put forward referred to scientific classifications of human beings or common knowledge.[103] The U.S. Supreme Court used both arguments in two infamous decisions. In *Ozawa v. United States*,[104] the judges denied American naturalisation to a Japanese applicant because it was popularly known that Asians were not part of the Caucasian race, combining common knowledge and scientific arguments. In *United States v. Thind*,[105] however, the same court denied an Indian applicant naturalisation on grounds of common knowledge. Interestingly, Indians were 'scientifically' classified as Caucasian but the court found it counterintuitive from a common knowledge point of view that people as dark as Indians could be legally White.[106] For Haney López these cases are particularly revealing because they expose the construction and definition of Whiteness in ways that would otherwise remain invisible. Unmasking the creation of a White nation through law contains an important lesson that continues to be relevant today. In fact, only if Whites – a socially contingent and changing category like other race categories – become critically conscious of their own race, and acknowledge the benefits they have reaped from this construction, is a meaningful deconstruction and elimination of systems supporting racial superiority and inferiority achievable. A critical theoretical analysis of White race-consciousness would also help uncover how the ideology of colourblindness operates and perpetuates the system of White dominance. In fact, colourblindness acts to curtail race-conscious efforts addressing race discrimination, while at the same time denying the existence of structural racial subordination. Through an understanding of how Whiteness is critically relevant in allocating legal, material, and status benefits, is it possible to appreciate how colourblindness undermines any serious and substantive effort at changing this status quo.[107]

By expanding their angle of analysis from the Black/White binary to Whiteness and its legal construction, CRT scholars have demonstrated how law has been an actor and accomplice in defining and answering the question of who is White. However, CRT scholarship has gone one step further and analysed the benefits and legal entitlements that accrue as a result of Whiteness. In a path-breaking article, Cheryl Harris argues that Whiteness functions like a property right, which

103 *Ibid.* at pp. 3–7.

104 *Ozawa v. United States* 261 U.S. 204 (1922).

105 *United States v. Thind* 260 U.S. 178 (1922).

106 For more details, see Haney López, *White by Law*, pp. 27–77.

107 *Ibid.* at pp. 143–162.

the legal system created and continues to protect.[108] The link between race/racial domination and property law originates in American history and runs along two axes. Regarding Native Americans, this fatal interaction between property law and racial domination is illustrated in the inferior recognition of the Native Americans' land possession and occupation, against the full recognition of White settlers' property titles. Original Native American ownership over their lands was delegitimised.[109] In the case of the African American population, property law transformed Blacks into legal objects, in the form of slaves, who could be sold, traded, or exchanged like chattel. Hence, in both cases White recognition became crucial to determine not only one's property rights but also one's societal and legal status. It should come as no surprise that the legal system protected and promoted Whiteness. If White in law, the individual could vote, freely move, become a citizen, attend schools, obtain work and own property.

Harris argues that the legal legacy of this interaction between racial domination and property is still visible; the White property interest is maintained and protected by the legal system. First, Harris shows how far Whiteness, as a piece of property, conforms to the traditional and modern forms of property. Second, Harris demonstrates how Whiteness fulfils the functional criteria of property. Third, Harris analyses how the legal doctrine of property interest in Whiteness has played out in the most famous U.S. Supreme Court decisions on race discrimination, *Plessy*,[110] *Brown I*[111] and *Brown II*.[112] Ultimately, Harris argues that the legal system serves the White interest only, which remains unchanged even though the most visible discriminatory provisions of the race and property arrangement have been removed. Moreover, there is also a social dimension at work. In society, Whiteness is a valued reputational identity, which is key to maintaining Whiteness. For example, until 1957, calling a White person Black amounted to defamation and it was possible for the White victim to petition the courts. It is also important to note that White preservation occurs on the collective level by legally denying group identity and by applying colourblindness in affirmative action cases. Understood in this way, affirmative action would be an important tool to addressing and undoing the unequal distribution of property and power which resulted from the establishment of property law.[113]

Far from being destructive, these internal critiques and developments have helped expand CRT beyond its initial reach, develop new vocabulary, and ultimately establish itself in American law schools. This was not an obvious feat, especially when looking at the external resistance from established scholars. Obviously, not everyone viewed CRT in the same critical manner. However, an

108 Cheryl I. Harris, 'Whiteness as Property', *Harvard Law Review* (1993), vol. 106, pp. 1707–1791.
109 *Ibid.* at pp. 1721–1724.
110 *Plessy v. Ferguson*, 163 U.S. 537 (1896).
111 *Brown v. Board of Education (Brown I)*, 347 U.S. 483 (1954).
112 *Brown v. Board of Education (Brown II)*, 349 U.S. 294 (1955).
113 Harris, 'Whiteness as Property', pp. 1757–1791.

overview of the external critiques provides an idea of the substance and the severity of the reactions.

2.2.2 External critiques

Somewhat unusual in the external reactions from scholars outside the CRT circle was the harshness of the criticism. However, such criticism was to be expected. If one's scholarship is explicitly positioned as political activism, which means abandoning the safe harbour of civil academic discourse and tolerance, then it should come as no surprise if the responses correspond with the political, and not the legal-academic, domain. One should equally be prepared that those responses can transcend the relatively secluded world of law journals and be picked up by the popular press, where political and ideological battles openly take place.[114] Some of the most virulent attacks were published in daily newspapers. Ironically, the most outspoken responses originate from those who would otherwise pride themselves on their rational, objective, and enlightened civic academic discourse and legal analysis. Some viewed the representatives of CRT as 'extremists', 'radical multiculturalists', a 'motley group',[115] the 'lunatic core' of 'radical legal egalitarianism',[116] 'narcissists',[117] who attack traditional concepts of objective truth, reason, merit, and the rule of law, having in common the 'abandonment of moderation and a dearth of common sense.'[118] According to others, the rhetoric of the CRT movement, which 'lurked only a few years ago at the fringes of the academy', is 'already reverberating beyond the lecture halls and seminar room', 'finding echoes in the court room, too, and in popular culture' with '[g]angsta rappers call[ing] openly for race war'.[119] Last but not least, a handful of critics considered 'their theories are anti-Semitic and racist in implication.'[120]

The wording of these comments targeting CRT scholars is explicit and virulent. According to another author they share a 'tendency to caricature feminist, gay, and critical race theory, and to pre-empt the possibility of public dialogue.'[121] However, it is necessary to try to understand the objective and the substance of these criticisms. I will present only some of the most heated discussions and criticisms. More specific debates on CRT's proposals have been analysed above.

114 For a more sympathetic review of early CRT scholarship, see Jon Wiener, 'Law Profs Fight the Power', *The Nation*, September 4/11, 1989, pp. 246–248.

115 Daniel A. Farber and Suzanna Sherry, *Beyond All Reason. The Radical Assault on Truth in American Law* (New York: Oxford University Press, 1997), pp. 3 and 5 respectively.

116 Richard A. Posner, 'The Skin Trade', *The New Republic*, 13 October 1997, p. 40.

117 Douglas E. Litowitz, 'Some Critical Thoughts on Critical Race Theory', *Notre Dame Law Review* (1996–1997), vol. 72, p. 516.

118 Farber and Sherry, *Beyond All Reason. The Radical Assault on Truth in American Law*, p. 3.

119 Jeffery Rosen, 'The Bloods and the Crits', *The New Republic*, December 9, 1996, p. 27.

120 Farber and Sherry, *Beyond All Reason. The Radical Assault on Truth in American Law*, p. 9.

121 Nancy Levit, 'Critical of Race Theory: Race, Reason, Merit, and Civility', *Georgetown Law Journal* (1999), vol. 87, p. 796.

One of the main objections against CRT is the perceived attack on legal liberalism and the values of truth, reason, objectivity, neutrality, universalism, and the Enlightenment-inspired foundations of legal academia, which go hand in hand with this view of law. The critiques are not solely directed against CRT, but include all movements and ideologies, such as CLS, radical feminism, and queer theory, which question the objectivity and neutrality of the law, legal reasoning, and argument. The biggest fear has been that CRT, and similar scholarship, could lead to 'balkanization, a splintering effect in which each racial, ethnic, or gender category becomes a unitary focus, to the neglect of the fragile overlapping consensus which binds us.'[122] In other words, enlightened universality in legal scholarship is under threat by a piecemeal approach to law and legal scholarship. Instead of looking for principles and analyses which might apply uniformly to everyone from a universal perspective, CRT scholarship adopts and promotes a race specific perspective that can undermine the very essence of a liberal, democratic state. Somewhat ironic is that CRT's critique towards liberalism is not explicit and neither liberalism as a theory nor the names of any classic or contemporary liberals such as Rawls, Dworkin, Kant, or Locke are explicitly mentioned in any of the CRT publications.[123]

The most comprehensive charge from this 'enlightened' perspective has come from Daniel A. Farber and Suzanna Sherry, who direct their criticism at CLS generally but it can be applied to CRT alike.[124] In their opinion, the dangers of radical multiculturalism arose when it spread into law schools, where these ideas could be transformed into effective policies. According to them, CLS' indeterminacy hypothesis questions the existence of rational thought and logical argument in legal rules and the legal system as a whole. In particular, it questions the unconscious mind-set of lawyers and judges, who are responsible for providing predictability in legal outcomes. CLS scholars counter the power of rational legal argument with narrative power, which is a type of storytelling that brings those mind-sets to the surface. Moreover, narrativism rejects analytical or empirical scientific methods designed to approach objective truth. Radical multiculturalists question precisely the possibility of such objective truth ever existing because in their view even truth is socially constructed. Throughout their book, Farber and Sherry hold that these views represent a direct challenge to Enlightenment's reliance on reason, and the danger of such an approach would be the rise of authoritarianism and implicit anti-Semitism. For Farber and Sherry, this would result in scholarship becoming a question of power, a substitution of politics for truth without any recourse to a standard of truth independent of politics, and therefore ultimately a reduction of human freedom.[125]

122 Litowitz, 'Some Critical Thoughts on Critical Race Theory', p. 519.

123 *Ibid.* at pp. 513–514. He uses his review of the CRT by Richard Delgado and Jean Stefancic, *Critical Race Theory: The Cutting Edge* (Philadelphia: Temple University Press, 2000) as a starting point for a more general assessment of the movement. *Ibid.* at p. 503.

124 Farber and Sherry, *Beyond All Reason. The Radical Assault on Truth in American Law.*

125 *Ibid.* at pp. 34–49.

A second major objection directed specifically against CRT concerns the explicit call for race-conscious scholarship and for a stronger representation of the voice of colour in legal academia. In an article, Randall L. Kennedy,[126] an African American professor at Harvard Law School, created what became known as the 'Racial Critiques'.[127] Kennedy was critical of academic advocates for a race-based scholarship who denounce the whiteness of some, if not all, legal academic writing and teaching and who believed this leads to a blunted and skewed literature on race, racism, and American law.[128] Kennedy argued that by advocating for such race-based scholarship, it would do a disservice to minority scholars and to scholars in general for numerous reasons. First, it would place a preference on the identity of scholars over the merit of their ideas. Second, it could risk silencing the important contribution of White scholars, thus alienating them from the field, which might end up being perceived as 'soft' by other academics. Third, and finally, it could lead to the exclusion of Black scholars from 'hard' areas such as antitrust, corporate finance, or securities regulation.[129] The debate became the subject of a special colloquy published in the *Harvard Law Review*,[130] which reached the *New York Times*.[131] Similar doubts have been voiced by Stephen L. Carter, an African American professor, whose concern is that this kind of alignment with the voice of colour could lead to the introduction of loyalty tests in academia and therefore impede academic freedom.[132] However, his critique intentionally avoids 'the debate over the existence or the worth of a voice of color' and he directs his attention to developing a proper standard for academic tenure in law schools.[133] This argument leads to the third main area of criticism mounted against CRT: the role and construction of merit.

CRT scholars working on the question of merit in American society generally, and at the academic or professional level in particular, are preoccupied with how the concept is socially constructed to serve the dominant group and

126 Randall L. Kennedy, 'Racial Critiques of Legal Academia', *Harvard Law Review* (1989), vol. 102, p. 1745.

127 Scott Brewer, 'Introduction: Choosing Sides in the Racial Critiques Debate', *Harvard Law Review* (1990), vol. 103, p. 1844. A summary of this debate can also be found in Minda, *Postmodern Legal Movements*, pp. 175–176.

128 Examples of this literature are: Richard Delgado, 'The Imperial Scholar: Reflections on a Review of Civil Rights Literature', *University of Pennsylvania Law Review* (1984), vol. 132, pp. 561–578; Richard Delgado, 'The Imperial Scholar Revisited: How to Marginalize Outside Writing, Ten Years Later', *University of Pennsylvania Law Review* (1992), vol. 140, pp. 1349–1372; and Mari J. Matsuda, 'Affirmative Action and Legal Knowledge: Planting Seeds in Plowed-Up Ground', *Harvard Women's Law Journal* (1988), vol. 11, p. 1.

129 Kennedy, 'Racial Critiques of Legal Academia', pp. 1795–1796.

130 See 'Colloquy – Responses to Randall Kennedy's Racial Critiques of Legal Academia', *Harvard Law Review* (1990), vol. 103, no. 8, pp. 1844–1886.

131 See Derrick A. Bell Jr., 'Letter to the Editor', *New York Times*, 26 January 1990, p. A30, col. 6.

132 Stephen L. Carter, 'Academic Tenure and "White Male" Standards: Some Lessons from the Patent Law', *Yale Law Journal* (1991), vol. 100, p. 2065.

133 *Ibid.* at p. 2068.

maintain power structures, while relegating minority groups to subordinate positions. CRT's work on merit has been quite controversial. For CRT scholars, merit ends up becoming 'white people's affirmative action'.[134] However, CRT's argument is not to abolish merit altogether but to demonstrate how allegedly neutral standards of merit are determined by elites in order to guarantee ongoing promotion and privileged position in society, at the expense of minority groups.[135] CRT's proposals to remedy the backlash of merit are extensive and include strengthening the voices of colour in academia,[136] developing alternative curricula, abandoning standardised tests for educational access and introducing selection criteria to benefit minorities, and granting them better access to power and elite positions.[137]

One of the strongest counterarguments against CRT's analysis of merit centres on the question of why certain minorities, particularly members of the Jewish community but also Asians, have been so successful in American law schools.[138] If merit is excluded in order to explain their success, according to these commentators, it must have been obtained unjustly or illegitimately. To further this thesis, four hypotheses are advanced, including: '(i) that a Jewish conspiracy exists; (ii) that Jews are parasitic on American culture; (iii) that American culture is essentially Jewish; or (iv) that there is no such thing as a distinct Jewish culture or identity'.[139] While the authors do not accuse critical theorists of explicit anti-Semitism, they reject the socially-constructed notion of merit because of the inherently anti-Semitic implications.

It is important to note that the criticism is not only directed at the epistemological insights of CRT. The methodological instruments, and in particular legal storytelling, have provoked some of the most widespread resistance, which ranges from sympathetic critique to outright opposition.[140] On the sympathetic level, one can find scholars who see the epistemological and methodological challenges and concerns raised by legal narrativism. They find that the stories should, nonetheless, connect to some normative position in order to be deemed legal scholarship.[141] Others hold that the rejection of a meritocratic system is impractical because of

134 Richard Delgado, 'Rodrigo's Tenth Chronicle: Merit and Affirmative Action', *Georgetown Law Journal* (1995), vol. 83, p. 1723.

135 *Ibid.* at pp. 1720–1745.

136 Alex Johnson, 'The New Voice of Color', *Yale Law Journal* (1991), vol. 100, p. 2007.

137 Richard Delgado, 'Official Elitism or Institutional Self-Interest? 10 Reasons Why UC Davis Should Abandon the LSAT (and Why Other Good Law Schools Should Follow Suit)', *UC Davis Law Review* (2001), vol. 34, p. 593.

138 Daniel A. Farber and Suzanna Sherry, 'Is the Radical Critique of Merit Anti-Semitic?', *California Law Review* (1995), vol. 83, p. 853.

139 *Ibid.* at p. 871.

140 See Eleanor Marie Brown, 'The Tower of Babel: Bridging the Divide Between Critical Race Theory and "Mainstream" Civil Rights Scholarship', *Yale Law Journal* (1995), vol. 105, p. 520.

141 Kathryn Abrams, 'Hearing the Call of Stories', *California Law Review* (1991), vol. 79, pp. 971–1052.

academia's reliance on some sort of evaluation.[142] Staunch representatives of the outright opposition include Daniel Farber and Suzanna Sherry, who, in their article critiquing legal narrative, find no evidence that a distinct voice of colour exists in the first place. Because of the lack, or little, description about the content of such a voice, they query the evaluation standards to measure such narrative scholarship, and fail to see a clear connection between the voice of colour and storytelling. Moreover, they question the validity of stories because of difficulties with the verification of the narrator's honesty and truthfulness, and by extension their story. Finally, they are suspicious of the story's individuality and its representative value, especially for individuals who face a similar situation to the storytellers.[143] The broader implication of such criticism is that these stories may simply amount to fabrication, or outright lies.[144]

Other more general arguments are levied against legal narratives and the inherent dangers in the story-telling approach. The autobiographical elements often contained in legal narratives are considered problematic.[145] Even if a critic does not question the accuracy of the autobiographic story or find that the autobiographer has been conscientious and honest, adopting any critical stance towards the story is also a critical stance towards the writer.[146] Others have highlighted the problems of one-sidedness,[147] and the tendency towards essentialism in some CRT writings.[148] Moreover, the risk of using stories instrumentally and emotionally is high, especially when the filter and constraints of legal doctrine and methodology are absent. When a narrative is used for instrumental purposes or is emotionally-overloaded, it can inadvertently reinforce prejudices and stereotypes,[149] making us less sensitive to minorities' perspectives.[150] A last general critique involves the risk of losing an already fragile credibility within the legal-academic arena if the stories

142 Edward L. Rubin, 'On Beyond Truth: A Theory Evaluating Legal Scholarship', *California Law Review* (1992), vol. 80, p. 929.

143 Daniel A. Farber and Suzanna Sherry, 'Telling Stories Out of School: An Essay on Legal Narratives', *Stanford Law Review* (1993), vol. 45, pp. 807–840.

144 David A. Hyman, 'Lies, Damned Lies, and Narrative', *Indiana Law Journal* (1998), vol. 73 p. 797.

145 Anne M. Coughlin, 'Regulating the Self: Autobiographical Performances in Outsider Scholarship', *Virginia Law Review* (1995), vol. 81, p. 1229. This article in turn provoked a critical reaction by Richard Delgado, 'Coughlin's Complaint: How to Disparage Outsider Writing, One Year Later', *Virginia Law Review* (1996), vol. 82, p. 95.

146 Coughlin, 'Regulating the Self: Autobiographical Performances in Outsider Scholarship', p. 1234.

147 Richard A. Posner, *Overcoming Law* (Cambridge, MA: Harvard University Press, 1995), pp. 380–384.

148 Jean-François Gaudreault-DesBiens, 'La *Critical Race Theory* ou le droit étatique comme outil utile, mais imparfait, de changement social', *Droit et Société* (2001), vol. 48, pp. 586–588.

149 Ioannis S. Papadopoulos, 'Guerre et paix en droit et littérature', *Revue interdisciplinaire d'études juridiques* (1999), no. 42, p. 194.

150 These dangers are highlighted by Douglas E. Litowitz, 'Some Critical Thoughts on Critical Race Theory', *Notre Dame Law Review* (1996–1997), vol. 72, pp. 520–523.

remain anecdotal, without stimulating any socio-legal academic discourse.[151] A similar risk of credibility in legal narrativism is raised at a more strategic level. By insisting on a specific voice of colour and, ultimately, a legal scholarship of colour, the political battle of minorities in academia and politics may hamper the CRT scholars' opportunities for making alliances.[152]

Finally, legal storytelling has garnered negative attention in specific areas. For example Mark Tushnet, a leading CLS scholar, criticised new forms of narrative jurisprudence in the constitutional context specifically. In his opinion, 'constitutional adjudication is the vehicle we use to mediate particular cases and general rules'.[153] Such mediation has to occur according to narrative integrity and judgment. By means of a number of stories, he exemplifies how they are flawed due to issues of narrative integrity and literary style, thus failing to perform the necessary mediation between the particular case and the general rule.[154] Another academic describes the consequences of adopting legal narrative in the legislative arena and compares it to the use of statistical evidence in empirical scholarship.[155] He concludes that narrative or anecdotal evidence can be extremely successful in influencing legislative change but that one should be extremely wary of it because of its source. He contends that it must be backed up with non-anecdotal, empirical evidence when trying to make a general statement. The reason for this distrust in narrative is that if conflicts around data arise, there is always some way to solve them, whereas for narratives there is no similar alternative solution.[156]

Eleanor Marie Brown has raised methodological critique in a constructive, almost friendly manner.[157] While recognising that CRT has made a massive contribution, she highlights that the main charges levied against CRT revolve around peripheral issues. Moreover, the author makes the observation that there has been a lack of communication between CRT and its peers. She compares this to a 'Tower of Babel' in academia. Her idea is that the miscommunication, or absence of communication, cannot be blamed on legal narrative but is caused by the one-sided portrayal of racism, which ignores how White attitudes towards race have become more sophisticated. This sophisticated shift can be explained by a move away from the 'dominative' racism to an attitude that ignores White

151 Gaudreault-DesBiens, 'La *Critical Race Theory* ou le droit étatique comme outil utile, mais imparfait, de changement social', p. 592.

152 Papadopoulos, 'Guerre et paix en droit et littérature', p. 195.

153 Mark Tushnet, 'The Degradation of Constitutional Discourse', *Georgetown Law Journal* (1992), vol. 81, p. 251.

154 This article, published in the same law journal, has provoked its own small controversy: Gary Peller, 'The Discourse of Constitutional Degradation', *Georgetown Law Journal* (1992), vol. 81, p. 313; which prompted a reaction from Tushnet: Mark Tushnet, 'Reply', *Georgetown Law Journal* (1992), vol. 81, p. 343.

155 Hyman, 'Lies, Damned Lies, and Narrative', pp. 797–865.

156 *Ibid.* at pp. 849–851.

157 See Brown, 'The Tower of Babel: Bridging the Divide Between Critical Race Theory and "Mainstream" Civil Rights Scholarship', pp. 513–547.

contribution to discourse on racial privilege and superiority. By taking these changes into account, which have been proven by empirical research in social science, it opens up the possibility to create a platform for communication and engagement between CRT scholars and White scholars, who otherwise feel alienated and remain unconvinced by CRT scholarship because they simply do not feel these narratives speak to them.[158]

The richness of these critiques and the debates which they have grounded have made one thing clear: CRT has managed to touch upon important issues concerning legal scholarship and legal analysis. CRT questions the ontological and epistemological foundations of legal scholarship, thus broadening and deepening its own development and circles of legal academia. Even some of the most critical voices admit there is truth to be found in CRT's propositions. For instance, Farber and Sherry believe that 'although storytelling has no necessary gender-based, racial, or ideological connection, some special benefits may flow from stories "from the bottom".[159] Richard Posner, in discussing Patricia Williams' 'The Alchemy of Rights', concedes that 'maybe one has to learn to see through her eyes as well as one's own before one can fully evaluate the arguments pro and con various racial policies' and that the 'very one-sidedness of her presentation, however questionable by the conventional standards of scholarship [...] has value in providing insight into the psychology and rhetoric of many blacks'.[160] Similarly, another critic highlights CRT's consciousness raising function,[161] and concedes that CRT demonstrates the pervasiveness of racism, the difficulty to regulate everyday acts of racism by law and the necessity to incorporate silent or marginalised voices into legal scholarship.[162]

Regardless of these critiques surrounding CRT scholarship, CRT scholars are seated in most of the important American law schools. They have the potential to influence future generations of legal scholars not only in their own law schools but further afield. This leads to the question of what developments can we expect, and what is the future of CRT.

2.3 Developments of Critical Race Theory

After a first period of intense debate around CRT during the late 1980s and the 1990s, there was a sense that things had calmed down with the turn of the new millennium. This led to interesting questions about CRT. Had CRT exhausted its potential, or dispersed it too much, or failed to establish itself in American legal thought? Had this theory become engrained in legal scholarship, which chimed with the 'acceptable' liberalist view? Is CRT still able to generate new knowledge

158 *Ibid.* at p. 513.

159 Farber and Sherry, 'Telling Stories Out of School: An Essay on Legal Narratives', pp. 807–855.

160 Posner, *Overcoming Law*, p. 384.

161 Litowitz, 'Some Critical Thoughts on Critical Race Theory', pp. 528–529.

162 *Ibid.* at pp. 510–512.

and provide additional insight into the mechanisms of law and society vis-à-vis racism and racial subordination?

One of the first points to make, as mentioned earlier, is that CRT has become an established field throughout most American law schools with a number of CRT professors succeeding to teach in some of the most renowned law schools in the United States. They have also published their articles in top law journals. Some of them are ranked amongst the most-cited law review articles.[163] From a strategic point of view this is extremely important because it guarantees the continuity and development of the movement, facilitates communication with their peers, creates role models for their respective communities and future generations of lawyers, and advances the international reputation and visibility of American law schools on a global scale.

A second point, considered one of CRT's most notable features from a substantive point of view, is CRT's expansive mode, which has been evident since its very inception. We have seen that this expansion has run along anti-essentialist strands and so-called 'communitarian' or identity politics lines, with the development of separate branches like LatCrit, AsianCrit, TribalCrit, and QueerCrit. This has come as a natural progression of CRT's teachings, which seek to situate law in its history and proper context. Such historical context has played out differently, depending on the minority group involved, which in turn has led to more tailored analyses. This has also stimulated the discourse on whether this expansion will cause the dissolution or fragmentation of CRT's forceful message, leading to its oblivion at worse, or being labelled a fad of the 1990s in legal scholarship. In response, many CRT scholars argue that the separate branches, like LatCrit, have 'actually deepened and broadened the Critical Race Theory project by providing the necessary intellectual expansion and theoretical bridges between identity politics and a politics of solidarity based on difference.'[164]

At the same time, the expansion of CRT has taken place along different lines outside legal academia. On the one hand, CRT has enabled the incorporation of insights from other disciplines and has created bridges between different fields beyond the strictly legal context, ranging from psychology,[165] economics,[166] and

163 See Fred Shapiro and Michelle Pearse, 'The Most Cited Law Review Articles of All Time', *Michigan Law Review* (2012), vol. 110, pp. 1483–1520. Articles of Charles R. Lawrence III, Angela P. Harris, Kimberlé W. Crenshaw, Mari Matsuda, Richard Delgado, Neil Gotanda, and Alan Freeman are on that list.

164 Athena D. Mutua, 'The Rise, Development and Future Directions of Critical Race Theory and Related Scholarship', *Denver University Law Review* (2006), vol. 84, p. 369.

165 Gary Blasi, 'Advocacy against the Stereotype: Lessons from Cognitive Social Psychology', *UCLA Law Review* (2002), vol. 49, p. 1241 and Gregory S. Parks, Shayne Jones and W. Jonathan Cardi (eds), *Critical Race Realism* (New York: The New Press, 2008).

166 Devon Carbado and Mitu Gulati, 'The Law and Economics of Critical Race Theory', *Yale Law Journal* (2003), vol. 112, p. 1757.

literature,[167] to music,[168] sports,[169] or the educational-pedagogical field, where a whole body of new literature is currently developing.[170] This may be the result of a broader tendency towards interdisciplinarity in the American legal context, where since legal realism the incorporation of findings from other social sciences has become part of legal analysis. On the other hand, CRT's analysis has continuously expanded within law towards less evident legal fields, such as business law and bankruptcy law.[171]

The expansion has also taken place geographically. CRT has moved beyond the American context and beyond a presumed 'American parochialism'.[172] Critiques of international law from a CRT perspective,[173] and analyses of foreign legal systems through a CRT lens,[174] are on the rise. This trend may be explained

167 Toni Morrison, 'Playing in the Dark: Whiteness and the Literary Imagination', in Richard Delgado and Jean Stefancic (eds), *Critical White Studies: Looking Behind the Mirror* (Philadelphia: Temple University Press, 1997), pp. 79–84.

168 John O. Calmore, 'Critical Race Theory, Archie Shepp, and Fire Music: Securing an Authentic Intellectual Life in a Multicultural World', *Southern California Law Review* (1992) vol. 65, p. 2129 and Jonathan A. Beyer, 'Second Line: Reconstructing the Jazz Metaphor in Critical Race Theory', *Georgetown Law Journal* (2000), vol. 88, p. 537.

169 Kevin Hylton, *'Race' and Sport. Critical race theory* (New York, London: Routledge, 2009) and by the same author 'How a Turn to Critical Race Theory can Contribute to our Understanding of "Race", Racism and Anti-Racism in Sports', *International Review for the Sociology of Sport* (2010), vol. 45, no. 3, pp. 335–354.

170 Gloria Ladson-Billings and William F. Tate IV, 'Toward a Critical Race Theory of Education', *Teachers College Record* (1995), vol. 97, no. 1, pp. 47–68; Daniel G. Solorzano, 'Images and Words that Wound: Critical Race Theory, Racial Stereotyping, and Teacher Education', *Teacher Education Quarterly* (1997), vol. 24, no. 3, pp. 5–20; Laurence Parker, Donna Deyhle and Sofia Villenas (eds), *Race Is … Race Isn't: Critical Race Theory and Qualitative Studies in Education* (Boulder: Westview Press, 1999); Adrienne D. Dixson and Celia K. Rousseau, *Critical Race Theory in Education* (New York, London: Routledge, 2006); and Ed Taylor, David Gillborn, and Gloria Ladson-Billings (eds), *Foundations of Critical Race Theory in Education* (New York, London: Routledge, 2009).

171 David A. Skeel Jr., 'Racial Dimensions of Credit and Bankruptcy', *Washington and Lee Law Review* (2004), vol. 61, pp. 1695–1724; A. Mechele Dickerson, 'Race Matters in Bankruptcy', *Washington and Lee Law Review* (2004), vol. 61, pp. 1725–1776; Dorothy A. Brown, 'Pensions, Risk, and Race', *Washington and Lee Law Review* (2004), vol. 61, pp. 1501–1539; and Steven A. Ramirez, 'Games CEOs Play and Interest Convergence Theory: Why Diversity Lags in America's Boardrooms and What To Do About It', *Washington and Lee Law Review* (2004), vol. 61, pp. 1583–1613.

172 See on this expression as applied to CRT, David Theo Goldberg and Philomena Essed, 'Introduction: From Racial Demarcations to Multiple Identifications', in David Theo Goldberg and Philomena Essed (eds), *Race Critical Theories* (Oxford: Blackwell, 2002), p. 4.

173 See e.g. the Symposium entitled 'Critical Race Theory and International Law' whose proceeds were published in the *Villanova Law Review* (2000), vol. 45, no. 5, pp. 827–1220.

174 Adrien Katherine Wing, 'A Critical Race Feminist Conceptualization of Violence: South African and Palestinian Women', *Albany Law Review* (1997), vol. 60, pp. 943–976; Adrien Katherine Wing (ed.), *Global Critical Race Feminism* (New York: New York University Press, 2000); Adrien Katherine Wing and Monica Nigh Smith, 'Critical Race Feminism Lifts the Veil?: Muslim Women, France, and the Headscarf Ban', *UC Davis Law Review* (2006), vol. 39, pp. 743–785; Mathias Möschel, 'Color Blindness or Total Blindness? The Absence of Critical Race Theory in Europe', *Rutgers Race and Law Review* (2007), vol. 9, pp. 57–128; Eddie Bruce-Jones, 'Race, Space

because of the necessity to analyse racial injustice on a global scale. Colonialism, globalisation, international trade, and Western thought paradigm, which have (forcibly) replaced other kinds of epistemology, have contributed to the need to broaden CRT's horizons beyond the strictly American context. In some ways this book can be seen as part of this development in CRT's internationalisation and globalisation.

The expansion of CRT's theoretical and geographical remit has not brought about a dilution or dispersion within CRT scholarship itself. If anything, certain areas of CRT inquiry have deepened and raised interesting contradictions and conundrums for CRT scholars. One of those areas is the renewed call by scholars for a stronger focus on CRT and class in order to show how race intersects with material factors within society.[175] A number of earlier writings by commentators associated with CRT had already looked at the interaction between race and class.[176] In 1994, Angela Harris indicated that 'it might be useful for race-crits to return to the vexed question of the relationship between race and class.'[177] This return was harder than expected, possibly because the older debate on race and class has become marginalised due to its Marxist origins.[178] Additional explanations for the relative absence of class in CRT analysis is that idealist approaches and discourse analysis studying the social construction of race have become prominent nowadays, to the detriment of materialist, realist, grassroots legal analyses, which were at the basis of CRT when it first evolved.[179] In the nascent days of CRT, the focus shifted to discourse on its epistemology and cultural origins rather than economic elements.

and the Nation–State: Racial Recognition and the Prospects for Substantive Equality Under Anti-Discrimination Law in France and Germany', *Columbia Human Rights Law Review* (2008), vol. 39, pp. 423–470; Smita Narula, 'Equal By Law, Unequal By Caste: The "Untouchable" Condition in Critical Race Perspective', *Wisconsin International Law Journal* (2008), vol. 26, pp. 255–343; Tanya Katerì Hernandez, 'The Value of Intersectional Comparative Analysis to the "Post-Racial" Future of Critical Race Theory: A Brazil–U.S. Comparative Study', *Connecticut Law Review* (2011), vol. 43, pp. 1407–1438; and Angela P. Harris, *Race and Equality Law* (Farnham, Burlington: Ashgate, 2013).

175 See in particular Richard Delgado, 'Crossroads and Blind Alleys: A Critical Examination of Recent Writings About Race, Crossroads, Directions, and a New Critical Race Theory', *Texas Law Review* (2003), vol. 82, pp. 125–128 and p. 151; Mutua, 'The Rise, Development and Future Directions of Critical Race Theory and Related Scholarship', pp. 377–394; and the contributions made during the Symposium entitled 'Going Back to Class? The Reemergence of Class in Critical Race Theory', published in *Michigan Journal of Race and Law* (2005), vol. 11, pp. 1–273.

176 John O. Calmore, 'Exploring The Significance of Race and Class in Representing the Black Poor', *Oregon Law Review* (1982), vol. 61, p. 201; Lisa C. Ikemoto, 'The Code of Perfect Pregnancy: At the Intersection of the Ideology of Motherhood, the Practice of Defaulting to Science, and the Interventionist Mindset of Law', *Ohio State Law Journal* (1992), vol. 53, p. 1205; and Regina Austin, 'Sapphire Bound!', *Wisconsin Law Review* (1989), p. 539.

177 Angela P. Harris, 'Foreword: The Jurisprudence of Reconstruction', *California Law Review* (1994), vol. 82, p. 777.

178 *Ibid.*

179 See Delgado, 'Crossroads and Blind Alleys: A Critical Examination of Recent Writing About Race', pp. 126–127.

Moreover, psychological arguments – why CRT may have abandoned or forgotten about class analysis – may have played a role as well. CRT scholars may have a 'fear of analysing and critiquing capitalism, the reigning economic order', where the current economic framework is almost unchallengeable or taken for granted. Moreover, they may simply not want to look at class because a lot of them have become members of the educated elite that is less affected by class oppression. Whatever the reasons for this absence may be, there seems to be a need to re-examine the relationship between race and class on a new basis, leading to what has been called ClassCrit. These new ClassCrits focus on the material and economic foundations of race to help better understand how class feeds into the systems of subordination related to race, gender and sexuality. A CRT analysis of class and economy, encompassing the associated vocabulary and ideology, can provide insight into power relations running along economic lines. It can also uncover practical ways to eliminate racialised economic allocations of material resources by addressing the fundamental issue of class. In the aftermath of Hurricane Katrina, those African Americans stranded in the flooded city of New Orleans who were victims of racism, would serve asn an apt example to undertake a ClassCrit analysis. An overlap or integration of traditional CRT with class can provide a more exact picture of what actually happened and how class can compound race-related problems.[180]

The move towards class is only one indicator towards a more materialist, realist CRT in the future. In fact, there is at the same time a tendency towards a more concrete grounding of CRT in the practice of law, a real anti-subordination praxis, and a suggestion to return to the grassroots struggle which was described in CRT's founding documents.[181] Part of the move towards activism for oppressed communities, and for grounding critical race theorising in practice and active engagement against racial injustice, is already underway.[182] The CRT conference that took place in February 2013 at Yale Law School, which was entitled 'Critical Race Theory: From the Academy to the Community', is also indicative of this bottom-up trend.

However, the most important latest development in CRT was triggered by Barack Obama's election as the first Black President of the United States. Hailed by many as the moment in which America had finally overcome its racial issues and in which America allegedly became post-racial, CRT scholars are more wary of the event and its implications. While clearly welcoming the election, they have

180 On this reasoning see Mutua, 'The Rise, Development and Future Directions of Critical Race Theory and Related Scholarship', pp. 329–394.

181 See Delgado, 'Crossroads and Blind Alleys: A Critical Examination of Recent Writing About Race', pp. 150–152.

182 See e.g. Eric Yamamoto, 'Critical Race Praxis: Race Theory and Political Lawyering Practice in Post-Civil Rights America', *Michigan Law Review* (1997), vol. 95, pp. 821–900; Carol A. Aylward, *Canadian Critical Race Theory* (Halifax: Fernwood Publishing, 1999); and the different contributions of the Symposium entitled 'Nanook of the Nomos: A Symposium on Critical Race Praxis' published in the *Michigan Journal of Race and Law*, (1999), vol. 5, pp. 31–237.

certain misgivings about the meaning of this post-racial turn at the intellectual, political, and judicial levels. One of the main concerns of CRT scholars is that it enables a new alignment of the conservative colourblind discourse with White liberal progressive positions that had always been ambivalent about race-conscious measures. In other words, the latter, who had objected to colourblind ideology but are plagued by 'racial exhaustion',[183] could be persuaded to rally behind the new 'cool' position of post-racialism, which promotes the idea that race in the United States is over. The question that arises is whether this is colourblindness, albeit in a different camouflage.[184]

Beyond the ideological and political consequences of President Obama's election and re-election and the so-called post-racial turn, it is necessary to ask what elements distinguish post-racialism from colourblind ideology, given that there is a significant overlap between the two? In her seminal article, Sumi Cho identifies four central features of post-racialism. The first feature is racial progress, which holds that racial thinking and racial solutions are no longer seen as necessary because society has transcended the past racial divisions. The second concerns race-neutral universalism, which views racial remedies as partial and divisive. The third deals with the moral equivalence whereby racism under Jim Crow is viewed as reprehensible as race-conscious measures of the civil rights era seeking to remedy minority subordination. The fourth, and last, consists of a distancing move which allows mainly White liberals, who have so far been sympathetic to Black claims, to defend a post-racial stance. In other words, while distancing themselves from plain old school racism, they embrace new school colourblindness by invoking a distinctive and sophisticated stance.[185]

Sumi Cho easily identified the post-racial turn at the intellectual and political level by referring to some recent publications which moved away from race and focused on President Obama's campaign itself. Empirically assessing the *actual* and not just the discursive effect of post-racial ideology on case law was still too early at the time of publication. As the years passed and President Obama was re-elected, the post-racial turn has also been analysed with regard to its effects on case law. One recent article looks at how the election of President Obama has influenced employment discrimination litigation and concludes that far from decreasing such litigation, one observes that negative references and racial slurs about President Obama have become a tool to perpetuate race discrimination at the workplace. Hence, at this level the post-racial turn does not necessarily imply the end of anti-discrimination litigation but rather proves the reality of racism at the workplace under shifting forms and shapes.[186] Others have analysed two

183 On this term, see Darren Lenard Hutchinson, 'Racial Exhaustion', *Washington University Law Review* (2009), vol. 86, pp. 917–974.

184 See in this sense Kimberlé W. Crenshaw, 'Twenty Years of Critical Race Theory. Looking Back to Move Forward', *Connecticut Law Review* (2011), vol. 43, pp. 1310–1336.

185 Sumi Cho, 'Post-Racialism', *Iowa Law Review* (2009), vol. 94, pp. 1589–1650.

186 See Angela Onwuachi-Willig and Mario L. Barnes, 'The Obama Effect: Understanding

of the U.S. Supreme Court's recent cases on racial issues[187] from a post-racial perspective and argue that the elections have provided the Supreme Court with additional arguments to support the opinion that there is little discrimination left to be remedied in the United States today.[188]

This argument was deployed in 2013 with the Supreme Court's decision to invalidate parts of the 1965 Voting Rights Act, which had been left untouched and unchallenged until recently.[189] As already described more in detail above, the Supreme Court justices invalidated the preclearance procedure precisely on the grounds that race discrimination belongs to the past. What is relevant for the purposes of this book is that the post-racial argument is emerging. The majority opinion, handed down by Chief Justice Roberts, held that in a time when African Americans have attained political office in record numbers, it can be said that race is behind us. In his concurring opinion, Justice Thomas was even willing to go one step further and declare the whole preclearance procedure unconstitutional.[190]

To conclude, CRT is significantly contributing to analysing and critiquing the latest post-racial turn in American politics, as illustrated in the consistent body of writing which is emerging.[191] CRT is far from silent and many of its analyses remain at the cutting edge of legal research in the United States. It is also highly relevant in the European and indeed the global context, as this book will attempt to show.

Emerging Meanings of "Obama" in Anti-Discrimination Law', *Indiana Law Journal* (2012), vol. 87, pp. 325–348.

187 *Parents Involved in Community Schools v. Seattle School District No. 1*, 551 U.S. 701 (2007), and *Ricci v. DeStefano*, 557 U.S. 557 (2009).

188 Girardeau Spann, 'Disparate Impact', *Georgetown Law Journal* (2010), vol. 98, pp. 1133–1164.

189 *Shelby County v. Holder*, 133 S.Ct. 2612, 570 U.S. (2013).

190 *Ibid.* Thomas, J., dissenting.

191 Beyond the articles already referred to, see e.g. Mario L. Barnes, Erwin Chemerinsky and Trina Jones, 'A Post-Race Equal Protection?', *Georgetown Law Journal* (2010), vol. 98, pp. 967–1004; Ian F. Haney Lopez, 'Post-Racial Racism: Racial Stratification and Mass Incarceration in the Age of Obama', *California Law Review* (2010), vol. 98, pp. 1023–1073; and Devon Carbado and Mitu Gulati, *Acting White? Rethinking Race in Post-Racial America* (New York: Oxford University Press, 2013).

Chapter 3

Transplanting Critical Race Theory to Europe

3.1 Travelling legal scholarship or theory

The vast body of scholarship, ideas, and critiques developed over the last two decades has gone practically unnoticed and unheeded in European legal literature.[1] To date there is little legal literature describing CRT in a non-English, European language. Most of the few publications are in Italian,[2] some are in French,[3] and a handful in German.[4] Spain has experienced limited exposure to CRT, which was facilitated by LatCrit Theory. For instance, in 1999 and in 2000 the Universidad de Málaga hosted the First and Second Annual LatCrit Summer Colloquium. The proceeds of the first event were published in an American law review.[5] Even fewer publications of these foreign language publications apply CRT analysis to

1 'Legal literature' here includes journals and publications that have a political theory background as well.

2 The most important are: Kendall Thomas, 'Legge, Razza e Diritti: "Critical Race Theory" e politica del diritto negli Stati Uniti', *Filosofia politica* (2003), no. 3, pp. 447–466; Kendall Thomas and Gianfrancesco Zanetti (eds), *Legge, razza e diritti. La* Critical Race Theory *negli Stati Uniti* (Reggio Emilia: Diabasis, 2005); Marco Goldoni, 'Costituzionalismo americano e razza. La lezione della *Critical Race Theory*', *Politica del diritto* (2006), no. 3, pp. 475–495; Thomas Casadei and Lucia Re (eds), *Differenza razziale, discriminazione e razzismo nelle società multiculturali*, vols. I and II (Reggio Emilia: Diabasis, 2007); Mathias Möschel, 'L'assenza della *Critical Race Theory* nei paesi di civil law', *Rivista trimestrale di scienza dell'amministrazione* (2007), no. 4, pp. 109–123; Nicola Riva, 'Differenza "razziale" ed eguaglianza di opportunità', *Materiali per una storia della cultura giuridica* (2008), Year 38, no. 2, pp. 553–560. Also see the Italian translation of Minda's *Postmodern Legal Movements*: Gary Minda, *Teorie postmoderne del diritto* [1995], Mauro Barberis (trans.), (Bologna: il Mulino, 2001).

3 Papadopoulos, 'Guerre et paix en droit et littérature', pp. 181–196; Gaudreault-DesBiens, 'La *Critical Race Theory* ou le droit étatique comme outil utile, mais imparfait, de changement social', pp. 581–612; Hourya Bentouhami, '*Critical Race Theory* ou comment la "race" compte', in Hourya Bentouhami, *et al.* (eds), *Le souci du droit: Où en est la théorie critique?* (Paris: Sens & Tonka, 2010), pp. 1–16.

4 Cengiz Barskanmaz, 'Rassismus, Postkolonialismus und Recht – Zu einer deutschen *Critical Race Theory*?', *Kritische Justiz* (2008), vol. 41, pp. 296–301; Johanna Künne, 'Critical Race Theory. Eine andere Sichtweise im Deutschen Recht', *ForumRecht* (2008), no. 3, pp. 92–94.

5 'The First Annual LatCrit Summer Colloquium: Spain, the Americas and Latino/as: International and Comparative Law in Triangular Perspective', *University of Miami International and Comparative Law Review* (2001–2001), vol. 9, pp. 1–224.

national or European law.[6] The few such studies available which use the CRT lens to examine the continental European context are in English, and are usually authored by lawyers trained in the United States.[7] This absence is even more surprising given that racism and xenophobia have been high on the political and legal agenda in many European countries and at the wider EU level. Given that anti-discrimination law originated in the American legal system and that the United States have become the reference point for European legal scholars ever since the post-war period,[8] one would expect CRT to become part of the exported vocabulary and instrumental toolkit. However, with the exception of intersectionality, the absence of CRT in Europe begs the question as to what prevented if not the successful reception then at least more attention to this body of scholarship.

In order to answer this question and to gain a better grasp of CRT in the European context, one needs to look more generally at how legal theories, scholarship or knowledge are transferred from one system to another or travel from one academic and socio-historical context to another. What are the mechanisms favouring or impeding such a transplant, reception, or travel? In reality, this issue has not been comprehensively applied or analysed in legal scholarship. There are some isolated articles describing the influence of some legal movement or theory in other legal systems;[9] however, none of these provide a theoretical framework, which would allow an analysis of the mechanisms that may come into play during such processes. Elements of this type of framework are found in Edward Said's concept of 'travelling theory' and in Alan Watson's 'doctrine of legal transplants', which have become influential in cultural studies and amongst comparative lawyers and sociologists. Because of these trends, in the first part of this chapter the transfer/transplant of CRT to Europe is critically assessed through the lens of these two theoretical frameworks. In the second part, the

6 See Casadei and Re (eds), *Differenza razziale, discriminazione e razzismo nelle società multiculturali*, vol. II, pp. 19–79 applying a CRT driven analysis to European prisons; and Alessandro Simoni, 'Appunti per una "lettura romani" del "pacchetto sicurezza"', *Diritto, immigrazione e cittadinanza* (2009), no. 4, pp. 217–230 using CRT as a theoretical framework to look at Roma discrimination in Italy.

7 Damian Chalmers, 'The Mistakes of the Good European?', in Sandra Fredman (ed.) *Discrimination and Human Rights* (Oxford: Oxford University Press, 2001), pp. 193–249; Bruce-Jones, 'Race, Space and the Nation-State: Racial Recognition and the Prospects for Substantive Equality Under Anti-Discrimination Law in France and Germany'; Marco Goldoni, 'Profiles of Discrimination: A Critical Argument Against Racial Profiling', *Sortuz. Oñati Journal of Emergent Socio-Legal Studies* (2013), vol. 5, no. 1, pp. 19–35; and Uladzislau Belavusau, *Freedom of Speech. Importing European and US Constitutional Models in Transitional Democracies* (London, New York: Routledge, 2013).

8 Ugo Mattei, 'Why the Wind Changed: Intellectual Leadership in Western Law', *American Journal of Comparative Law* (1994), vol. 42, p. 195–218.

9 Mario G. Losano, 'La legge e la zappa. Origini e sviluppo del diritto alternativo in Europa e in Sudamerica', *Materiali per una storia della cultura giuridica* (2000), Year 30, no. 1, p. 109. See also Toni Malminen, 'The Effects of Scandinavian Legal Realism on Finnish Legal Studies, 1929–1965', in Vanessa Duss, *et al.* (eds), *Rechtstransfer in der Geschichte* (München: Martin Meidenbauer, 2006), p. 298 and p. 306.

centrality of the methodologies and theories of comparative law is examined and then applied in order to explain CRT's absence or non-influence in mainland European academia.

3.1.1 *Travelling theory*

An apt starting point in understanding which mechanisms are at play when theories, concepts and ideas are either transferred or travel from one system or context to another comes from Edward Said's concept of 'travelling theory', introduced in the early 1980s.[10] In his essay, he investigates how ideas or theories travel and what happens during the journey. He starts out by subdividing the travelling theories or ideas into four recurring stages. The first stage concerns the point of origin and the initial circumstances that give rise to the idea. The second stage is the distance traversed by the idea or theory as it moves from its point of origin to a different time and place. The third stage concerns the conditions of acceptance or resistance that confront the transplanted theory or idea, which allow its introduction or toleration. The last stage concerns the accommodation or incorporation of the idea or theory and how it is transformed by its new uses and adapted to the new time and place. By using the specific example of Georg Lukács' theory of 'reification', Said argues that theories develop in response to specific historical and social events but when they move from their original context to a new location some of their power and rebelliousness can dissipate, become assimilated into academic orthodoxy, or else become domesticated and dehistoricised. In a subsequent essay, Said revisited his earlier analysis on how certain ideas or theories are degraded and subdued into a tame academic substitute during transfer because later versions cannot replicate the original power of the theory or idea in different spaces and time. Remaining with the example of Lukácsian thought, Said states that under certain circumstances theories and ideas can be invigorated, ignited by the conditions and context encountered in their destination or time of arrival.[11] Thus, he analyses how Adorno uses Lukács to understand Schoenberg's place in the history of music and how Frantz Fanon probably applied Lukács' subject/object dialectic to the colonial context in one of the former's most famous pieces, *Les damnés de la terre* (*The Wretched of the Earth*).[12]

Edward Said's two essays have been influential in cultural, postcolonial, and literary studies, due also to his position as an outstanding cultural critic and postcolonial scholar.[13] His metaphor of travelling theory introduced the new perspective in the humanities by shifting the focus from travelling subjects or

10 Edward W. Said, 'Travelling Theory', *Raritan: A Quarterly Review* (1982), vol. 1, no. 3, pp. 41–67.

11 Edward W. Said, *Reflections on Exile* (Cambridge, MA: Harvard University Press, 2001), pp. 436–452.

12 Frantz Fanon, *Les damnés de la terre* [1961] (Paris: La Découverte, 2002).

13 See e.g. James Clifford, 'Travelling Cultures' in Lawrence Grossberg, Cary Nelson and Paula Treichler (eds), *Cultural Studies* (New York, London: Routledge, 1992), pp. 96–116; Mieke Bal, *Travelling Concepts in the Humanities: A Rough Guide* (Toronto: Toronto University Press, 2002).

agents to travelling theories and ideas and the way they are embedded in cultural practices and power struggles. Said is a particularly interesting starting point to frame the travel of CRT from one context to another for multiple reasons. First of all, it is clear that Said's interests and examples are situated in a politically engaged type of theorising, which is also the case in CRT scholarship. Second, the reference to Fanon also resonates within CRT circles because his writings are a cultural and political orientation in CRT literature. Indeed, Said's position as a critical postcolonial scholar and thinker ensures a certain ideological and intellectual closeness to CRT scholars and to scholars working on race, class or gender. It should therefore come as no surprise that his lens of travelling theory has been used by CRT scholars to analyse the travel of CRT to other scientific domains in the American reality,[14] as well as in sociology to analyse the transfer of the triad of 'race, class, gender' from the American context to the European one.[15]

With regard to the potential transfer or travel of CRT to Europe, while also bearing in mind Said's observations, it is necessary to understand the original cultural, historical, political, and legal context that determined CRT's initial emergence and subsequent struggles. This context has been described in the previous two chapters. A myriad of questions about CRT and its travel and transfer crop up. What then happens if a theory is transferred or travels outside of a particular context? What are the conditions for acceptance or resistance in the European arena and which discipline will be most open to CRT arguments? Will CRT become absorbed into academic orthodoxy or will it acquire a force of its own, finding fertile ground on which to thrive because it speaks to a certain group of persons or academics? What are the specific differences that will emerge in a European CRT?

Whereas Said's travelling theory stems from an extra-legal domain, it has some bearing on how to think about and how to conceptualise the transfer of CRT to continental European legal academia and jurisprudence. Moreover, similar, although more limited, observations have been made in comparative law with reference to the theory of legal transplants. What is interesting to note here is that although Said highlights the cultural context of a theory's origins, legal transplant theory contends that the circulation of legal institutions and ideas seems to be more detached from the underlying social context.

3.1.2 *Legal transplants*

The phenomenon relating to how legal rules are received or borrowed by a specific legal system has for some time been at the centre of discussion among comparative lawyers, sociologists, and legal historians, owing to Alan Watson's

14 Devon Carbado, 'Afterword. Critical What What?', *Connecticut Law Review* (2011), vol. 43, pp. 1619–1623.

15 See Gudrun-Axeli Knapp, 'Race, Class, Gender: Reclaiming Baggage in Fast Travelling Theories', *European Journal of Women's Studies* (2005), vol. 12, No. 3, pp. 249–265.

influential doctrine of legal transplants.[16] His main ideas relevant for the purposes of this book are:[17] (i) that law is not a perfect mirror of society and that there is no necessary correlation between social, economic, or political circumstances of a legal system and rules of private law;[18] (ii) that the relative autonomy of law is due to the central role of the legal profession in its development;[19] (iii) that law develops primarily on the level of ideas;[20] and (iv) that law develops mainly by borrowing and that legal transplants occur regularly and with much more ease than expected.[21] These observations have not remained unchallenged. While some simply try to modify and hone some of the most extreme elements of legal transplants theory by claiming that law's autonomy from the underlying society depends on the branch of law one is looking at,[22] others are much more outspoken and argue that the doctrine of legal transplants does not take into account the fact that law and legal institutions developed and evolved historically[23] and that it ignores the specific cultural and social aspects inherent in every legal system.[24] Nonetheless, the idea of legal transplants has been influential, with comparative lawyers building upon this doctrine by trying to understand why and how legal transplants occur. Apart from Watson's conclusions that most of it is due to chance, some commentators have indicated that it may be the most economically efficient way to bring about legal change in a given system,[25] or that legal borrowing occurs because of the prestige and intellectual leadership of a legal system.[26]

What needs to be asked in relation to the doctrine of legal transplants and CRT is whether the arguments developed in favour or against the doctrine of legal transplants may extend to the transfer of a whole school of thought or a theoretical legal approach. At first glance, it seems that Watson focused mainly

16 Alan Watson, *Legal Transplants: An Approach to Comparative Law*, 2nd edn (Athens, Ga.: University of Georgia Press, 1993).

17 This classification of Watson's doctrine is borrowed from Edward M. Wise, 'The Transplant of Legal Patterns', *American Journal of Comparative Law Supplement* (1990), vol. 38, pp. 2–7.

18 Alan Watson, *Society and Legal Change* (Edinburgh: Scottish Academic Press, 1977).

19 Alan Watson, *The Nature of Law* (Edinburgh: Edinburgh University Press, 1977), pp. 91–113.

20 Alan Watson, 'Legal Change: Sources of Law and Legal Culture', *University of Pennsylvania Law Review* (1983), vol. 131, p. 1152.

21 In his Afterword to the second edition, Watson states that he 'gravely underestimated the extent and impact of legal borrowing'. Watson, *Legal Transplants: An Approach to Comparative Law*, p. 108.

22 William Ewald, 'American Revolution and the Evolution of Law', *American Journal of Comparative Law Supplement* (1994), vol. 42, p. 1, claiming that public law is much less independent from underlying society and culture than private law.

23 Martin de Jong, Virginie Mamadouh and Konstantinos Lalenis, 'Drawing Lessons About Lesson Drawing. What the Case Reports Tell Us about Institutional Transplantations', in Martin de Jong, Konstantinos Lalenis and Virginie Mamadouh (eds), *The Theory and Practice of Institutional Transplantation* (Dordrecht, Boston, London: Kluwer Academic Publishers, 2002), pp. 283–299.

24 See on the cultural relativist approach Pierre Legrand, 'What "Legal Transplants"?', in David Nelken and Johannes Feest (eds), *Adapting Legal Cultures* (Oxford: Hart Publishing, 2001), pp. 55–68.

25 Ugo Mattei, 'Efficiency in Legal Transplants. An Essay in Comparative Law and Economics', *International Review of Law and Economics* (1994), vol. 14, p. 3.

26 Mattei, 'Why the Wind Changed: Intellectual Leadership in Western Law', p. 195.

on the transplant of specific rules or areas of law. However, his demonstration of how the Scottish legal order adapted to categorisations of Roman law[27] seems to speak in favour of including legal theory, or legal knowledge, as a potential subject of transplantation.[28] Moreover, due to the important role attributed to the legal profession, particularly legal elites, Watson argues that legal borrowing must necessarily include the transfer of legal academics' thoughts from one system to another. It would be counterintuitive and hard to justify why the doctrine of legal transplants should only apply to more technical aspects while excluding the philosophical basis and grounds of legal rules from this type of analysis, especially if one considers that one of Watson's own tenets holds that law develops primarily at the level of ideas. Therefore, assuming that legal theory and jurisprudence can be included as subject of legal transplants, a couple of things should be applicable to CRT's spread into Europe.

In the first place, since the doctrine of legal transplants can only work on the assumption that law is to a large extent independent of its socio-historical underpinnings, a transfer from the United States to Europe should occur easily. Second, based on the prestige that the U.S. legal system has acquired over the years, European academics should have been eager to describe, analyse and adapt the writings of CRT and use its tools to critique European legal systems. Why then did neither happen, especially when racism and xenophobia are at the centre of on-going public debate today? The example of CRT's non-existent reception would be a black mark against the doctrine of legal transplants, at least in its purest form. In fact, the almost complete absence of CRT from European analysis seems to be a strong indication that borrowing is not wholly independent from underlying socio-historical factors. Alternatively, it could suggest that a transplant of legal theory, and not of single rules or areas of law, functions according to different mechanisms in which historical, political, cultural, economic, or academic factors play an important role. Hence, I will try to identify the impeding underlying 'external' factors that determine the resistance to CRT's reception and then combine them with 'internal' resistance of the legal profession and legal academia in order to obtain the bigger picture of CRT's absence from the continental European analysis. Even though this example proves that law does in fact react to underlying societal and historical factors, which means that the relationship between law and society is to some extent a causal one, I do not draw the conclusion that transplants cannot or should not happen. In this book, I will try to provide theoretical arguments and practical examples showing what, with certain provisos and adaptations, CRT might look like in the European context. Moreover, this will substantiate my position that such an analysis could and should be introduced into mainland European legal thought.

27 Watson, *Legal Transplants: An Approach to Comparative Law*, pp. 44–56.

28 In this sense also Kaspar Näf, 'Die nationale Autonomie Karl Renners als Vorbild für die jüdische Kulturautonomie in Litauen und Lettland während der Zwischenkriegszeit', in Vanessa Duss, *et al.* (eds), *Rechtstransfer in der Geschichte* (München: Martin Meidenbauer, 2006), p. 66.

3.1.3 Existing CRT transplants

Prior to addressing the absence of CRT, a slightly more nuanced picture needs to be sketched. In fact, some limited elements of CRT have already crossed the Atlantic and help us visualise what a CRT transplant looks like in the continental European legal context and which aspects of travelling theory and/or legal transplants may actually become relevant.

The first example concerns the exception and describes the very limited presence of CRT in the continental European legal analysis: intersectionality.[29] Indeed, this is the only CRT concept which has effectively become established, mainly in European feminist jurisprudence and anti-discrimination law, both in English[30] and in other European languages.[31] Moreover, its success has not been limited to the academic arena but has extended to the political domain, especially thanks to the engagement of European institutions[32] and discussions on its institutionalisation.[33] Referred to as a 'buzzword', the success of intersectionality as a social theory has been attributed to the fact that it tackles a fundamental concern of feminist theory and appeals to the postmodern ideal of moving away from static to shifting, multiple identities. In addition to this, it provides a novel twist to an old problem. It also appeals to both generalists and specialists in the area. Finally, intersectionality's ambiguity and open-endedness allows successive scholars to fill in the blanks and to open up further discussion.[34]

By today's standards, there is general consensus that feminist legal research needs to be intersectional. However, parts of intersectionality's success in Europe stems from the fact that it has been read and received outside of CRT context.

29 For more details on intersectionality, see Chapter 2, part 2.2.1, 'Internal critiques'.

30 See e.g. Iyiola Solanke, 'Putting Race and Gender Together: A New Approach to Intersectionality', *Modern Law Review* (2009), vol. 72, no. 5, pp. 723–749; Dagmar Schiek and Victoria Chege (eds), *European Union Non-Discrimination Law – Comparative Perspectives on Multidimensional Equality Law* (London, New York: Routledge-Cavendish, 2009); and Dagmar Schiek and Anna Lawson (eds), *European Non-Discrimination Law and Intersectionality: Investigating the Triangle of Racial, Gender and Disability Discrimination* (Farnham: Ashgate, 2011).

31 In French: Alexandre Jaunait and Sébastien Chauvin, 'Les théories de l'intersectionnalité à l'épreuve des sciences sociales', *Revue française des sciences politiques* (2012), vol. 62, no. 1, pp. 5–20; in German: Nora Markhard, 'Die andere Frage stellen: Intersektionalität als Analysekategorie im Recht', *Kritische Justiz* (2009), vol. 42, pp. 353–364; in Italian: Sabrina Marchetti, 'Intersezionalità. Pensare la differenza', in Caterina Botti (ed.), *Etiche della diversità culturale* (Firenze: Le Lettere, 2013), pp. 133–148; in Swedish: Maria Carbin and Sofie Tornhill, 'Intersektionalitet – ett oanvändbart begrepp?', *Kvinnovetenskaplig Tidskrift* (2004), vol. 25, no. 3, pp. 111–114.

32 See e.g. European Commission, 'Tackling Multiple Discriminations – Practices, Policies and Law' (Luxembourg: Office of the Official Publications of the European Communities, 2007).

33 Johanna Kantola and Kevät Nousiainen (eds), 'Institutionalizing Intersectionality', *International Feminist Journal of Politics* (2009), vol. 11, no. 4; and Andrea Kriszan, Hege Skjeie and Judith Squires (eds), *Institutionalizing Intersectionality. The Changing Nature of European Equality Regimes* (Basingstoke: Palgrave Macmillan, 2012).

34 Kathy Davis, 'Intersectionality as Buzzword: A Sociology of Science Perspective on What Makes a Feminist Theory Successful', *Feminist Theory* (2008), vol. 9, pp. 70–77.

Indeed, the enthusiastic appropriation of the concept by mainly White feminists and European institutions has highlighted the feminist prong of intersectionality, while its race-conscious prong has been omitted or side-tracked. Due to this, intersectionality has been 'e-raced' and risks becoming a meaningless, formal exercise in which one simply adds overlapping grounds of discrimination. By taking the second prong more seriously, it would enhance the debates taking place within European feminism, addressing whether European feminist movements actually exclude, or include, migrant women and how far the experience of sex discrimination is based on the experiences of White, European, Christian women.[35] Moreover, it may allow better communication with American feminists, who are at odds with the reluctance of European feminists to acknowledge race and to fully embrace race conscious views and analyses.[36]

The second example concerns the transplant, or the potential transplant, of CRT into the United Kingdom. The lower linguistic and legal hurdles between the two systems – both use English and belong to the common law tradition – make the United Kingdom an ideal candidate and testing ground for such a transfer. What is interesting is that most of the academic debates and discussions occur in the educational domain, without any significant involvement of lawyers or legal analysis. In fact, two of the first seminars/conferences to be organised on CRT in the United Kingdom took place in education departments of British universities.[37] Moreover, most academic publications on CRT in the United Kingdom are about the heated debates and disputes on the alleged contrast between Marxism and CRT and the question whether racism/White Supremacy or class are the better theoretical frameworks to explain and analyse disadvantage, discrimination and subordination in modern societies.[38] This also leads to divergent opinions on whether race trumps class in explaining under-achievement in education and what concrete consequences need to be drawn in this domain. While the debate is quite intense, it is reminiscent of the differences between CLS and CRT. It may

35 See Maria Carbin and Sara Edenheim, 'The Intersectional Turn in Feminist Theory: A Dream of a Common Language', *European Journal of Women's Studies* (2013), vol. 20, no. 3, pp. 233–248.

36 See on the emergence of such a gulf: Gail Lewis, 'Celebrating Intersectionality? Debates on a Multi-Faceted Concept in Gender Studies: Themes from a Conference', *European Journal of Women's Studies* (2009), vol. 16, pp. 203–210.

37 20 November 2006 at the Education and Social Research Institute at Manchester Metropolitan University and 25–26 June 2009 at the Institute of Education, University of London.

38 See Mike Cole, 'Critical Race Theory Comes to the UK: A Marxist Response', *Ethnicities* (2009), vol. 9, pp. 246–269; Charles W. Mills, 'Critical Race Theory: A Reply to Mike Cole', *Ethnicities* (2009), vol. 9, pp. 270–281; Mike Cole, 'A Response to Charles Mills', *Ethnicities* (2009), vol. 9, pp. 281–284; Mike Cole, 'The Color-Line and the Class Struggle: A Marxist Response to Critical Race Theory in Education as it Arrives in the United Kingdom', *Power and Education* (2009), vol. 1, pp. 111–124; David Gillborn, 'Who's Afraid of Critical Race Theory in Education? A Reply to Mike Cole's "The Color-Line and the Class Struggle"', *Power and Education* (2009), vol. 1, pp. 125–131; and Mike Cole, 'On "White Supremacy" and Caricaturing, Misrepresenting and Dismissing Marx and Marxism: A Response to David Gillborn's "Who's Afraid of Critical Race Theory in Education"', *Journal for Critical Education Policy Studies* (2009), vol. 7, pp. 29–49.

also come across like a revival of a long-existing tendency of pitting race against class. It is interesting to note that the law does not feature in these specific analyses concerning CRT. As illustrated above, law's role and complicity in creating and subordinating racial minorities is one of the central tenets in CRT scholarship. By bracketing law during the transfer to the United Kingdom, one risks trivialising CRT and watering down some of its more powerful and persuasive analytical tools to show the role of the law and the state in racial subordination. Simply focusing on the race aspect, or the White Supremacy aspect, without linking it to the legal aspect gives rise to a situation whereby CRT, as transplanted, resembles debates that have been doing the rounds in British Cultural Studies for many years now.

These two examples confirm Said's observations about travelling theory and the possible consequences following the domestication of a theory's radical aspects in a new context. Despite broadening their scope beyond CRT's initial domains, at the same time this has blunted the edges and flattened its critique upon arrival and reception in the different context(s), which makes it a milder, watered down version of the original CRT. What these two examples also confirm is that the argument put forward that legal concepts or theories travel independently from the underlying society is wrong and inapplicable. The social, historical and academic context is relevant when determining the success or failure of a legal theory transplant. Hence, understanding this context will help in understanding what has impeded a broader reception of CRT in mainland Europe.

3.2 Underlying factors impeding a successful transfer of CRT

Despite instances of a CRT transplant to the European context, the question of CRT is silent around this type of scholarship, especially in the legal arena. Besides legal transplants, comparative law teaches us that the absence of a legal institution or instrument in a given system can be explained by the presence of a functionally similar, but differently named, mechanism. Because an alternative exists, albeit under a different title, it is therefore not necessary to introduce an external institution or instrument. In light of this fact, before analysing the factors contributing to the absence of CRT in Europe, it is helpful to gain a better sense of European and non-European scholarship which addresses similar CRT concerns, and therefore functionally occupies CRT's place. This will also help explain why a transplant has been avoided or prevented.

3.2.1 *The presence or absence of functional analogues*

That CRT in the continental European context is absent so far could be attributed to the fact that there are other kinds of scholarship in practice. While these other scholarly enterprises can fulfil the same task and share the same perspective, it may not be necessary to adopt the exact same measure or name, or refer explicitly to CRT and its concepts, which may have inspired the model in the first place. Moreover, this scholarship does not necessarily have to be found within legal academia. Again, similar to legal transplants, this idea stems from one of the fundamental methodological principles of all comparative law, namely functionality.[39] The basic idea of this principle is that every society faces similar problems and solves them by different means that lead to similar results. Instead of looking at Europe and saying that there is very little on CRT, it might make more sense to first find out whether there are any functional analogues in mainland European systems that are located in the law or outside the law, given the different disciplinary boundaries existing in legal scholarship between continental European legal systems and the United States. Only once, or if, it has been determined that nothing exists, does it become interesting to understand, why in fact CRT has not travelled across the Atlantic. From this perspective, it would come as a surprise if someone were to say that Europe does not face a problem of racism either because of or through law under the functional comparative analysis. It would come as an even bigger surprise if some were to say that there is no problem to solve.

I will first examine the potential of legal analogues. In doing so I will try to understand which areas of the law or which types of legal analysis and scholarship can provide similar solutions or critiques to CRT in the European context, or at least try to locate where the seeds for such approaches can be found. The analysis will then move on to determine whether there are any analogues in the non-legal domain. Again, this is a very broad sketch but it is necessary in order to assess CRT's relevance and potential added value to continental European legal scholarship.

3.2.1.1 Legal analogues

One of the first domains in which to look for a functional legal analogue to CRT in the European context is feminist theory, specifically feminist legal theory. As was mentioned earlier, one of the few CRT transplants to successfully enter mainland Europe is intersectionality, which did so through the vehicle of feminist legal theory. However, the European intersectionality is a domesticated, e-raced version where a central aspect of CRT, namely its race-conscious prong, is essentially missing.

The second area where one could find the seeds for a European analogue to CRT is in scholarship on equality and racial anti-discrimination. In fact, race discrimination is usually framed in terms of equality or emerges in equality scholarship in European law debates. Although the debates on discrimination, including gender discrimination, are preoccupied with labour law issues from a conceptual perspective, they are the consequence of a broader sense of justice and equality.

39 See Konrad Zweigert and Hein Kötz, *An Introduction to Comparative Law*, 3rd edn (Oxford, New York: Oxford University Press, 1998), p. 34. This has also been identified as the functional method of comparative law.

In contrast to the United States, where the constitutional debate on equal protection is often framed in terms of standards of review,[40] in Europe one of the most fundamental distinctions and aspects in equality law is between formal and substantive equality. Traditionally, this dichotomy has been presented in terms of mutual exclusivity or distinctive conceptions of the equality principle. Therefore, it has been represented by alternative juxtapositions, such as *de jure* equality and *de facto* equality, or prescriptive and descriptive equality. Against this vision, which often interprets substantive equality as derogation to formal equality, thereby creating different standards of treatment, some scholars have attempted to show that the equality principle consists of both components and that moving beyond this dichotomy is the best possible solution.[41] However, even in this context we see scholars, such as Susanne Baer, who ardently support a substantive vision of equality, while at the same time arguing for the elimination of the term race from the German *Grundgesetz*.[42] It becomes clear that as much as the proponents of substantive equality share some of the main concerns and goals of CRT scholars, their problems with the term race and with the ways in which European societies have engaged in racial domination and discrimination prevent a deeper engagement with CRT. Moreover, from many perspectives, this legal scholarship remains steeped in a more positivistic or analytical legal approach, which undoubtedly has merits of its own and can pursue a progressive agenda[43] but sometimes is not enough to demonstrate or explain the racial impact of law on people's lives or the way institutions and law perpetuate a White, Christian, male point of view. CRT scholars, on the other hand, adopt a more historical and sociological approach and critique to the law of equal protection. As has been explained in the previous chapter, they highlight and critique the U.S. Supreme Court's restrictive interpretation of the Equal Protection Clause, which serves to benefit the White majority, unless the interests of that majority converge with those of racial minorities. Such a point of view and analysis, for example, is wholly absent from European analysis of equality law and policies. For instance, one could read the adoption of the Race Equality Directive (the RED)[44] as one of those moments where interests between the White, European majority converged with those of European racial minorities. Indeed, one of the elements arguably prompting EU Member States to adopt this progressive and race-conscious non-discrimination legislation so

40 See e.g. Suzanne B. Goldberg, 'Equality without Tiers', *Southern California Law Review* (2003–2004), vol. 77, pp. 481–582.

41 See Sandra Fredman, 'Beyond the Dichotomy of Formal and Substantive Equality: Towards a New Definition of Equal Rights', in Ineke Boerefijn *et al.* (eds), *Temporary Special Measures: Accelerating De Facto Equality of Women under Article 4(1) UN Convention on the Elimination of All Forms of Discrimination Against Women* (Antwerp: Intersentia, 2005), pp. 111–118.

42 Susanne Baer, 'The Basic Law at 60 – Equality and Difference: A Proposal for the Guest List to the Birthday Party', *German Law Journal* (2010), vol. 11, no. 1, pp. 67–87.

43 E.g. Davide Strazzari, *Discriminazione razziale e diritto* (Padova: CEDAM, 2008).

44 Directive 2000/43/EC of 29 June 2000 implementing the principle of equal treatment between persons irrespective of racial or ethnic origin, *Official Journal (OJ) L 180* of 19 July 2000, pp. 22–26.

swiftly and almost unexpectedly was the rise of the extreme right party of Jörg Haider in Austria.[45] Today, this convergence of interests has disappeared which may help explain why a Commission proposal to expand and harmonise EU non-discrimination directives has stalled for years now.[46]

This brief example of European interest convergence comes from a third legal area in which some seeds of CRT-like scholarship can be identified: European Union law or EU law. The reasons here are twofold and somewhat different from what was identified in the legal debate around formal and substantive equality scholarship. On the one hand, as we have just seen, one of the most race-conscious and progressive anti-discrimination instruments in the European context, namely the RED, introduced broad civil remedies against direct and indirect racial and ethnic discrimination as well as harassment in the private sector. This means that legal scholars not belonging to the Anglo Saxon race-conscious approach are somehow forced to interpret the RED's provisions and to openly acknowledge and address the issue of race and racism in areas which were left impenetrable. The introduction of the RED also means that some of the scholars or practitioners applying the instrument automatically look at the United States or to the United Kingdom. Hence, it should not come as a surprise that one of the first commentaries written on the RED refers to CRT scholarship and reasoning.[47] A more recent piece critiquing the European anti-discrimination framework explicitly refers to the discriminatory character of applicable European anti-discrimination legislation because it creates a hierarchy of equalities and a hierarchy of people.[48] In some ways the increased reference to intersectionality in EU policies and policy documents, discussed in the previous chapter, is also an indication of the easier establishment that CRT might find in EU law.

On the other hand, there is a broader reason why EU law is potentially more open to the legal realist or political reasoning contained in CRT and CLS than national legislation and legal scholarship. The political character in EU legislation is much more visible than in national legislation. Very often the regulations, directives, or decisions adopted by the EU institutions are so evidently the result of political compromises between Member States that it becomes much harder to sustain the objectivity and neutrality of EU law as well as its autonomy. This also explains why in EU law and EU legal writing it is easier to move away from the dominance of the doctrinal paradigm to a more critical and contextual legal scholarship which openly addresses law's political character and makes more

45 Mark Bell, *Anti-Discrimination Law and the European Union* (Oxford: Oxford University Press, 2002), p. 74.

46 See the European Commission proposal for a Council Directive on implementing the principle of equal treatment between persons irrespective of religion or belief, disability, age or sexual orientation, 2 July 2008, COM(2008) 426 final.

47 Damian Chalmers, 'The Mistakes of the Good European?', in Sandra Fredman (ed.), *Discrimination and Human Rights. The Case of Racism* (Oxford: Oxford University Press, 2001).

48 Sara Benedí Lahuerta, 'Race Equality and TCNs, or How to Fight Discrimination with A Discriminatory Law', *European Law Journal* (2009), vol. 15, no. 6, pp. 738–756.

use of political science literature than could be expected in national, continental European legal scholarship.[49] Nevertheless, the dogmatic tradition remains strong and as much as EU law presents some characteristics of legal realism and of contextual analysis, it remains steeped in mainland European legal analysis and scholarship.

Fourth, there are a handful of continentally educated scholars, who write from a critical and/or identitarian perspective in the area of race, gender, or sexual orientation discrimination and human rights. In particular, and without any of the cited authors explicitly self-identifying in such categorisation, the work of Marie-Bénédicte Dembour,[50] Dagmar Schiek[51] or Thomas Spijkerboer spring to mind.[52] However, they work and publish in and from the United Kingdom, which means they are situated in a context where their more race critical analysis is not uncomfortable, side-lined, or relegated to the more theoretical/philosophical domains that are often invisible in mainstream legal literature. Moreover, none of these scholars is bound by a common, overarching ideal or framework, which might mobilise them in the same way that CRT mobilised minority scholars in American law schools.

A last undoubtedly important and new area in legal studies in which one could expect to find a legal analogue to CRT is migration law. With the ever-increasing harshness of immigration laws, coupled with the criminalisation of migrants and the fundamental repressive role that law plays in these processes, there is an ideal ground for critical thought to develop.[53] Moreover, the previously existing theoretical work by Foucault and Bourdieu further facilitates critical academic analyses as well as dialogues with sociologists, anthropologists and historians in this domain. However, even here there is a notable absence of the word race and a reading of these phenomena in terms of racial formation, racial domination or racialisation. Despite the parallels and obvious connections, the racial and ethnic implications of citizenship and migration policies, laws, and decisions are rarely invoked, let alone analysed.

The brief glance at the potential legal analogues of CRT in the European context shows that it is not particularly helpful. Whereas one could argue that some CRT-like traces or seeds could be found and identified here and there, they are

49 Anthony Arnull, 'The Americanization of EU Law Scholarship', in Anthony Arnull, Piet Eeckhout and Takis Tridimas (eds), *Continuity and Change in EU Law* (Oxford: Oxford University Press, 2007), pp. 415–431.

50 See e.g. Marie-Bénédicte Dembour, *Who Believes in Human Rights: Reflections on the European Convention* (Cambridge, New York: Cambridge University Press, 2006).

51 See e.g. Schiek and Chege (eds), *European Union Non-Discrimination Law*, and Schiek and Lawson (eds), *European Non-Discrimination Law and Intersectionality*.

52 See Thomas Spijkerboer, *Gender and Refugee Status* (Aldershot: Ashgate, 2000), and Thomas Spijkerboer and Sarah van Walsum (eds), *Women and Immigration Law: New Variations on Classical Feminist Themes* (Abingdon, New York: Routledge-Cavendish, 2007).

53 One can refer to a number of legal journals which publish in the area of migration law from a critical perspective, such as: *Diritto, immigrazione e cittadinanza* in Italy; *Plein droit* in France; and the *Zeitschrift für Ausländerrecht und Ausländerpolitik* (ZAR) in Germany.

a far cry from being identifiable as a functional analogue. Hence, due to the different disciplinary boundaries running between law and social sciences in Europe and the United States, it proves necessary to look beyond the legal domain and see whether frameworks of analysis outside of jurisprudence may potentially provide an answer to this question.

3.2.1.2 Non-legal analogues

One of the first and most obvious places where one could look for a functional analogue of CRT outside legal scholarship is in the philosophical field, because of some common philosophical roots that they share. Indeed, while CRT scholars have predominantly focused their analysis on the American reality, their inspiration is partly based on the philosophy of European thinkers, especially Antonio Gramsci, Frantz Fanon, Michel Foucault, and Jacques Derrida.

The reference to Gramsci's terminology is twofold. On the one hand, law, and more specifically the failed civil rights movement, is being analysed by using Gramsci's concept of 'hegemony', to show how the reforms introduced in the 1960s and 1970s only served to maintain and legitimise the existing dominant order.[54] On the other hand, the notion of the 'organic intellectual' is also being invoked to highlight the importance that intellectuals at the basis of the movement may have, in as much as they are especially able to relate the theory with the experience of racial oppression through narratives and individual experiences from below.[55]

The influence of Foucault and Derrida on CRT scholarship comes into play on two separate levels. On the one hand, there is a strong trend to focus on discourse analysis and how legal texts have participated in constructing, developing, and entrenching race in the American legal and societal context. This trend, although criticised, has become highly influential in CRT scholarship.[56] On the other hand, these writings, in particular Foucault's work, have been important for the feminist and queer theoretical strands contained in CRT scholarship. His analyses on sexuality, identity, power and subject formation have certainly inspired, if not directly left their mark on, CRT's writings dealing with these issues.

The question at this point becomes whether and how far the common philosophical ground, which helped create CRT in the United States, might have led to a similar development in mainland Europe, albeit in another field or discipline outside the law. While undoubtedly Gramsci, Foucault, and Derrida are influential philosophers none of them, except for possibly Foucault, is really directly or exclusively concerned with law itself. Law is one of the mechanisms or tools

54 Crenshaw, 'Race, Reform, and Retrenchment: Transformation and Legitimation in Anti-Discrimination Law', pp. 1350–1352.

55 Matsuda, 'Looking to the Bottom: Critical Legal Studies and Reparations', p. 324.

56 Delgado, 'Crossroads and Blind Alleys: A Critical Examination of Recent Writing About Race', pp. 124–125.

through which power, oppression, or hegemony are exercised but there are few, if any, indications that in the domain of European philosophy a parallel type of scholarship to CRT emerged.[57]

Similar points could be raised with regard to other non-legal areas and in particular 'Postcolonial Studies', which could be potentially seen and conceived in the European setting as an analogue performing some of CRT's functions. While there is wide disagreement as to what exactly postcolonial theory encompasses in the field of scientific research and analysis,[58] it is clear that CRT shares more than just nuances with the postcolonial approach. This is especially the case if the postcolonial is conceived as a set of discursive practices where the resistance to colonialism, colonialist ideologies, and their contemporary forms and legacies of subordination are considered. A similar strand of discourse analysis has also been developing and criticised in CRT.[59] And indeed, two influential thinkers of and for postcolonialism, Frantz Fanon and W.E.B. Du Bois, are considered as having exerted a major influence on CRT.[60] The latter's influence is directly visible in CRT writings, either through explicit reference by using, referring, and alluding to his concepts, metaphors, or images of 'double consciousness'[61] and the 'color line',[62] and the idea of the 'gift'.[63] The former's influence on CRT scholars is mediated through Black activism and conceptualisation.[64] Moreover, his explanation of the construction of a person of colour in a White world with its existing tension between structural identities and lived identities,[65] as well as his liberationist essay[66] have impacted the views of CRT writers, who found his writings inspirational and helpful to develop their own views on the combined workings of law, politics, and psychology on Black identities in the United States.

Despite these common roots, postcolonial studies have developed in the domain of cultural studies and are more concerned with literary discourse and historical

57 One could argue that Marxism might have provided an alternative in the philosophical domain but especially in the European context class is pitted against race.

58 See e.g. Peter Childs and Patrick Williams, *An Introduction to Post-Colonial Theory* (Essex: Pearson Education Limited, 1997), pp. 1–25.

59 Delgado, 'Crossroads and Blind Alleys: A Critical Examination of Recent Writing About Race', pp. 124–125.

60 Lewis B. Gordon, 'A Short History of the "Critical" in Critical Race Theory', *The APA Newsletter on Philosophy and the Black Experience* (Spring 1999), vol. 98, no. 2, pp. 23–26.

61 See e.g. Matsuda, 'Looking to the Bottom: Critical Legal Studies and Reparations', pp. 333–335.

62 See e.g. Angela P. Harris, 'From Color Line to Color Chart? Racism and Colorism in the New Century', *Berkeley Journal of African-American Law & Policy* (2008), vol. 10, pp. 52–69.

63 See e.g. Charles R. Lawrence, III, 'The Word and the River: Pedagogy as Scholarship as Struggle', *Southern California Law Review* (1992), vol. 65, p. 2276.

64 Indeed, the treatment of African Americans (and Native Americans) has been framed by Black activists and future members of the Black Panther Party in terms of 'internal colonisation'. See Eldridge Cleaver, 'The Land Question', *Ramparts* (May 1968), no. 6, p. 51. Shortly thereafter 'internal colonialism' was translated into academic parlance by sociologists. See e.g. Eric Blauner, 'Internal Colonialism and Ghetto Revolt', *Social Problems* (1969), vol. 16, pp. 393–408.

65 Frantz Fanon, *Peau noire, masques blancs* [1952] (Paris: Seuil, 1971).

66 Fanon, *Les damnés de la terre.*

analysis. While it is true that law is a very specific type of discourse, at the same time postcolonial studies and their exponents did not necessarily place law at the centre of their analysis. Because of this, they failed to examine the way colonial law or the existence of colonies used to influence the continental legal systems and the consequences in the postcolonial era.[67] Nevertheless, even if there had been more 'legal analysis' in postcolonial studies, it is doubtful whether continental European legal scholarship would have paid much attention to it. The concern is that too much attention to what is considered outside scholarship and non-legal analysis might threaten the autonomy of legal scholarship and may not be deemed legal scholarship.

One other area where some of CRT's work could be performed is sociology. Some of the sociological findings, analyses, and studies in the European context come close to what CRT does, or at least sociology explores things in a direction that challenges and questions certain assumptions, albeit with a reservation due to the problematic use of the term race. However, there is one major difference, namely the normative claims. Whereas U.S. lawyers, including CRT scholars, view their position very much as one of social engineer, whose job it is precisely to make normative claims, European sociology is still influenced by the Weberian view that sociological analyses must be neutral and only describe and unveil certain processes within society. These analyses do not purport to take any specific position nor do they make explicit suggestions for legal or societal change.

There is another domain in which some aspects of CRT could emerge in the European context: Whiteness Studies. As we have seen, this is one part of CRT's analyses and interest in this kind of scholarship is evidenced by the fact that there is an entire reader dedicated to the subject matter. In some continental European countries, especially in Germany,[68] Whiteness Studies is developing and a whole body of literature is emerging. However, European lawyers remain uninvolved in this kind of research so it ends up being left to the sociology or literature departments. Therefore, law's role in constructing Whiteness, as analysed by Haney López,[69] is left undone or ignored because non-legal scholars shy away from a field that is viewed as difficult and subject to its own reasoning, constraints, and methodologies.

As a conclusion to this section, in my opinion, none of the above-mentioned types of scholarship or disciplines really provide a substantial overlap with CRT in the European context. Therefore, they cannot be identified as a functional analogue to CRT in mainland European academia. As a result of this trend, I will go on to propose some factors which, based on my observations, have determined this absence. I group these factors into two broad categories. The first belongs to

67 There are obviously exceptions. See e.g. Sandro Mezzadra and Enrica Rigo, 'Diritti d'Europa. Una prospettiva postcoloniale sul diritto coloniale', in Aldo Mazzacane (ed.), *Oltremare. Diritto e istituzioni dal Colonialismo all'età postcoloniale* (Napoli: CUEN, 2006), pp. 175–204.

68 See e.g. Maureen Maisha Eggers, *et al.* (eds), *Mythen, Masken und Subjekte: kritische Weissseinsforschung in Deutschland* (Münster: Unrast, 2005); Martina Tissberger, *et al.* (eds), *Weiss, Weisssein, whiteness: kritische Studien zu Gender und Rassismus* (Frankfurt am Main, New York: P. Lang, 2006).

69 Haney López, *White by Law*.

the broad 'external' conceptual-historical plane and the second, more specifically, to the 'internal' legal-academic one.

3.2.2 *'External' conceptual-historical factors*

Historical contingencies have played a major role in shaping our perceptions of race and racism, influencing their conceptualisation, and directing the development at the legal level. These factors are identified as external, because they tend to influence legal and normative debates with elements that are not inherent to the legal profession, legal academia, or legal reasoning. As such they belong more to the historical, cultural, and political arenas.

3.2.2.1 *Differing history and conceptualisation of race and racism*

One of the major factors preventing CRT's expansion to continental European legal analysis is the perception that the United States and Europe have had a different historical, and by consequence conceptual, track record with regard to race and racism. This should not be surprising given that race, racism, and the connected processes of racialisation are nowadays seen as a historical,[70] social,[71] and legal[72] construction and take on different shapes according to the time and place in which they occur. With the rise of the nation-state, these concepts have developed along separate paths and assumed particular forms according to the 'local' conditions. Nevertheless, it is possible to broadly distinguish between United States and European racism.[73]

As we have seen in the first chapter of this book, in the United States the history of race and racism can be described as one involving people of African, Native, Asian, and Latino descent enforced by means such as slavery, segregation, miscegenation, deportation, and the infamous 'one-drop rule', to name the most obvious. In that context, '[a]ll the mechanisms of oppression, exclusion, and disadvantage, therefore are designed to distinguish between people by their color, rather than on some other basis such as class or religion.'[74] Law has played an important role in American history. In the United States race continues to function as a general framework of analysis, which allows many social and societal

70 Ivan Hannaford, *Race. The History of an Idea in the West* (Washington, D.C.: Woodrow Wilson Center Press, 1996) and his analysis of how the idea of 'race' has been developed and constructed from the Ancient world until today. See also Christian Geulen, *Geschichte des Rassismus* (München: C.H. Beck, 2007).

71 Ian F. Haney López, 'The Social Construction of Race: Some Observations on Illusion, Fabrication, and Choice', *Harvard Civil Rights – Civil Liberties Law Review* (1994), vol. 29, p. 1.

72 Haney López, *White by Law*, pp. 9–10.

73 Maykel Verkuyten and Jessica ter Wal, 'Introduction: Racism in a Comparative Perspective', in Maykel Verkuyten and Jessica ter Wal (eds), *Comparative Perspectives on Racism* (Aldershot: Ashgate, 2000), pp. 13 –14.

74 Edward L. Rubin, 'Book Review: Jews, Truth, and Critical Race Theory', *Northwestern University Law Review* (1999), vol. 93, p. 531.

phenomena to be looked at through the lens of race. It is not surprising, therefore, that anti-discrimination legislation in the United States started out from the need to combat racial discrimination and only afterwards shifted its conceptual focus towards other groups, such as women.[75]

In Europe, however, the history of race and racism is primarily associated with the horrors of the Holocaust and anti-Semitism, and with the state-sponsored and organised campaigns of segregation, miscegenation, and physical suppression as the ultimate step to eliminate Jews. Racial laws certainly played an important part in this context. A different type of racism in European history is linked to colonialism and to racial hierarchies, which places White Europeans and their civilisation above those of the colonised populations that were often identified as subordinate colonial subjects. Here as well, law played an important role in colonial legislation based on the application of racial criteria in the occupied territories. A third type of racism involves the Roma people, of which more will be said in the last chapter of this book. Another type of racism involves Muslims and the historical fear of Christian Europe falling victim to Islamic conquest. While there have certainly been times during which Islamic culture was seen as more advanced than European culture, this has more recently given way to Islam being framed as backward, misogynistic, and dangerous.[76]

For the purposes of this brief explanation, one can see that these different histories can lead to a different perception of what constitutes race and racism on both sides of the Atlantic. One big difference is that in Europe the 'social fault lines and mechanisms of oppression were often defined in religious terms.'[77] Europe's history in fact is filled with religious wars, pogroms, and persecutions. Jews, Protestants, Catholics, Muslims, and other religious minorities have to some extent and at some point all been or become victims of this reality. As opposed to the United States, skin colour was perceived to be less prominent, giving rise to the feeling that the 'American type' of racism is viewed as a less entrenched and rather exceptional phenomenon, which has little importance or relevance in the current continental European reality. The concept of race seems rather inextricably entangled with the contemporary discourses relating to anti-Semitism, immigration, Islam, and the Roma, something which relates more to the discourse of culture or the political-religious domain and seemingly leaves little space for a racial (re)interpretation and conceptualisation.[78] This may explain why in the

75 Serena Mayeri, *Reasoning from Race: Feminism, Law, and the Civil Rights Revolution* (Cambridge, MA: Harvard University Press, 2011).

76 See also Etienne Balibar, who besides the European anti-Semitism and the American/South African type of 'colour prejudice', identifies 'colonial racism' as a third type of racism in which human beings are divided into superior and inferior, civilized and barbaric races. Etienne Balibar, 'La costruzione del razzismo', in Casadei and Re (eds), *Differenza razziale, discriminazione e razzismo nelle società multiculturali*, vol. I, p. 55.

77 Rubin, 'Book Review: Jews, Truth, and Critical Race Theory', p. 531.

78 Leonardo Marchettoni, '*Razza* e cultura. Un confronto', in Casadei and Re (eds), *Differenza razziale, discriminazione e razzismo nelle società multiculturali*, vol. I, p. 44.

European racist discourse, terms such as prejudice, intolerance, anti-Semitism, or xenophobia are substitutes for the word racism, while ethnicity is a substitute for the word race.

The historical differences described above are also reflected in the conceptualisation of what constitutes race and racism. Indeed, because of the differing histories this can also lead to differing and ambiguous definitions of race and racism. The versatility and adaptability of both terms to ever-changing and new conditions can make it difficult and controversial to use them either as a normative category or as a strategy for anti-discrimination, anti-subordination and empowerment. Somewhat surprising is the observation that lawyers, for the most part, have been inactive in defining race and racism. Therefore, attempts to define these concepts are more easily and readily found in historical, sociological, or political works. This paradox also helps explain why purely lexical, linguistic definitions of race and racism are not particularly helpful, as they tend to blend out the context in which these terms originally developed.

In its most neutral and scientific definition, race is seen as a group of persons, animals or plants connected by a common descent or origin.[79] However, this scientific version of race used by Enlightenment botanists (Carl Linnaeus), zoologists (George-Louis Leclerc, Comte de Buffon), and doctors (Johann Friedrich Blumenbach) combined with value judgments is a means to determine the superior groups and the inferior groups.[80] In conjunction with Social Darwinism, these ideas soon became instrumentalised in other areas, assuming a central, value-laden position in history, politics, and law. The spread of these ideas was essential to the nation-state project and was employed as 'the main ideological weapon of imperialistic politics'[81] for the exercise of power over other nations, which justified colonisation. This sketch is extremely reductive[82] and certainly does not reflect the complexity of the issue.

Nowadays, social scientists tend to distinguish between two main forms of racism. The first category – 'scientific or biological' racism – has been described above and has been widely discredited and rejected both in the United States and Europe, even though the reasons for this rejection are somewhat different. In the European context, UNESCO played a key role in refuting the biological and scientific foundations of race on four separate occasions during the 1950s and 1960s.[83] In the American context, it was the advance of genetics and modern

79 See e.g. John Simpson and Edmund Weiner (prepared by), *The Oxford English Dictionary*, 2nd edn (Oxford: Clarendon Press, 1989), vol. XIII, Quemadero – Roaver, p. 69.

80 See Neil MacMaster, *Racism in Europe* (Basingstoke: Palgrave, 2001), pp. 12–20 and Alana Lentin, *Racism and Anti-Racism in Europe* (London, Ann Arbor: Pluto Press, 2004), pp. 38–49.

81 Indeed, it has been authoritatively argued that imperialism and not nationalism was the main reason for the success of racism. See Hannah Arendt, 'Race-Thinking before Racism', *The Review of Politics* (1944), vol. 6, p. 41.

82 For more details, see Werner Conze, 'Rasse', in Otto Brunner, Werner Conze and Reinhart Koselleck, *Geschichtliche Grundbegriffe* (Stuttgart: Klett-Cotta, 1984), Band 5, Pro – Soz, pp. 135–178.

83 These are: 'Statement on Race' (Paris, July 1950), 'Statement on the Nature of Race and Race

molecular biology research, and the discovery of non-existent variation between racially identified populations, which seems to have tilted the scales towards such a rejection of scientific racism.[84] Nonetheless, this type of racism continues to be viewed as representative of the American paradigm, given that religion and culture were less present and prominent in the American history of racial discrimination.

The second category of racism is cultural racism.[85] The abandonment of the scientific or biological foundation of race and racism in the aftermath of the atrocities of World War II has led to the emergence and the success of the concept of ethnicity as its semantic substitute.[86] In cultural racism, more than in biological and physical hierarchies between groups of people, culture explains differences and radical incompatibilities between groups of people. For these reasons this new form of racism has also been referred to as 'differential racism'.[87] Under 'old racism', certain exterior traits were genetically attributed to one defined group of people, who were then classified hierarchically. Today a similar thing is done but using cultural heritage, language, traditions, and religion instead. It should be stressed however that some forms of cultural racism have always been present even in scientific or biological racism. In cultural racism, culture amounts to a supposedly fixed attribute that cannot be assimilated by an outsider. In turn, this justifies the exclusion and segregation of immigration groups with different cultural backgrounds, even after a long period of stay in the host country.[88] In some ways this new form of racism is even more insidious than the old 'scientific' racism because it is less explicit and diminishes the possibility of expressing and labelling what is racism or who is racist, even though the targets of cultural racism have previously been the object of biologically-based discrimination. The emergence of this paradoxical discursive overlap should not obscure the use of history and culture for anti-subordination and emancipatory potential by a community which has been disadvantaged and discriminated against, and the use of a similar discourse as an instrument to perpetuate subordination, albeit along lines which try to consciously avoid any racist reference.

Some examples of what this new form of cultural racism looks like, and how close it actually lies to the older idea of biological racism will be provided in order

Differences (Paris, June 1951), 'Proposals on the Biological Aspects of Race (Moscow, August 1964) and 'Statement on Race and Racial Prejudice' (Paris, September 1967). For additional details, see Anthony Q. Hazard Jr., *Postwar Anti-Racism. The United States, UNESCO and 'Race', 1945–1968* (New York: Palgrave Macmillan 2012).

84 Ron Mallon, '"Race": Normative, Not Metaphysical or Semantic', *Ethics*, (2006), vol. 116, p. 529.

85 In this sense also: Philomena Essed and Sandra Trienekens, 'Who Wants to Feel White? Race, Dutch Culture and Contested Identities', *Ethnic and Racial Studies* (2008), vol. 31, no. 1, p. 55.

86 Chris Lorenz, 'An Introduction to Conceptual History', in Stefan Berger and Chris Lorenz (eds), *The Contested Nation: Ethnicity, Class, Religion and Gender in National Histories* (London: Palgrave, 2008), p. 37.

87 Pierre-André Taguieff, *La force du préjugé. Essai sur le racisme et ses doubles* (Paris: La Decouverte, 1988).

88 See more in detail: Neil MacMaster, *Racism in Europe* (Basingstoke: Palgrave, 2001), pp. 193–198 and Nora Räthzel, 'Developments in Theories of Racism', in The Evens Foundation (ed.), *Europe's New Racism. Causes, Manifestations, and Solutions* (New York: Berghahn Books, 2002), pp. 6–10.

to clarify this point. The first example comes from the Netherlands where the distinction between *allochtoon* – the identification of the 'real Dutch', including the offspring of a White Dutch diplomat born and partially raised in Brazil, or White colonists and their offspring from the Dutch Indies – and *autochtoon* – the 'not-quite-Dutch' including persons born for example in Suriname, Aruba, Turkey, or any African or Asian country and their offspring even if born in the Netherlands – emerged as a new ethnic/racial labelling and was formalised by policymakers to increase labour participation of non-Western immigrants. What seems to be relevant in this categorisation is that *allochtoon* assumes a clearly negative connotation. It is not expressed as a racist category, even though skin colour plays a role and allows for criticism concerning the cultural vices of *allochtoonen*.[89] A similar informal classification has emerged in Italy with the definition of *extra-comunitari*, a pejorative reference to non-EU citizens or third country nationals. This 'category', however, does not include or apply to Americans, Canadians, Australians, New Zealanders, or Japanese. The *real* foreigner or *extra-comunitario* is understood to be someone from a developing country with non-White skin.

The second example illustrating how cultural racism plays out in Europe concerns the election of Miss Italia in 1996. The winner, Denny Méndez, was the daughter of an immigrant family who came from the Dominican Republic. The 'problem' related to her dark skin. Two members of the jury were suspended because they questioned whether she should be allowed to represent the typical Mediterranean Italian beauty. Those who raised that argument denied being racist and alleged pseudo-cultural grounds to justify their arguments. Eventually, Méndez won the competition, because the rules for the Miss Italia contest clearly stated that in order to be eligible to participate in the contest, only Italian citizenship was required. Since Méndez carried an Italian passport, she could not be excluded from the competition.[90]

The terminological difficulties with race and racism are not limited to their biological and cultural definitions or old and new forms of racism. Along with other terms such as nation, ethnicity, gender, class, and religion, race is an 'essentially contested concept'.[91] These are concepts, characterised by their conflicting interpretations and the lack of consensus over their meaning, guarantee infinite debates in order to come up with a proper definition. More specifically, in relation to race one can identify opposing conceptual approaches such as: (i) 'racial scepticism', which maintains the view that races do not exist and therefore race should be simply eliminated on the normative level; (ii) 'racial constructionism',

89 For a more detailed account on this, see Philomena Essed and Sandra Trienekens, 'Who Wants to Feel White? Race, Dutch Culture and Contested Identities', *Ethnic and Racial Studies* (2008), vol. 31, no. 1, pp. 57–63.

90 For more details, see Celestine Bohlen, 'Italians Contemplate Beauty in a Caribbean Brow', *New York Times*, 10 September, 1996, p. A3.

91 Chris Lorenz, 'An Introduction to Conceptual History' in Stefan Berger and Chris Lorenz (eds), *The Contested Nation: Ethnicity, Class, Religion and Gender in National Histories* (London: Palgrave, 2008), pp. 30–33.

which holds that races do not naturally exist but are partially socially constructed; and (iii) 'racial population naturalism', which is of the view that biologically based races may exist, but with a different social significance than the one attributed to them. The two latter approaches believe that on the normative level race picks out something real and should therefore not simply be ignored.[92]

Most of continental Europe can be characterised by racial scepticism. The concepts of race and racism have become taboo since the horrors of the Holocaust, which was when the expression of 'scientific' or 'biological' racism was most virulent. It was during this dark chapter in European history that one 'dominant' group, primarily the White majority, targeted other groups which they considered biologically inferior from an ideological perspective. This ideology was subsequently consolidated by legal, social, and political rules.[93] This version of racism was officially rejected with the end of World War II and the collapse of the Third Reich.[94] The images arising in connection with the term race conjured up pictures of millions of gassed, burnt Jews and the Nazi atrocities, and did not evoke Martin Luther King or the civil rights movement. While the Holocaust forms a key part of European history and the history of racism in particular, the United Kingdom and Ireland did not have direct experience or exposure to these events. Similarly, the United States was not directly impacted. This can in some ways help explain race scepticism in mainland Europe, where, for understandable reasons, those images are considered too strong to be acceptable for societies that regard themselves as modern liberal democracies, especially in France, Germany, and the Netherlands.[95] Hence, the idea of actively employing the terms race and racism in legislation or legal analysis has an odious connotation because they had been employed to eliminate Europe's Jewish community. As a result, it raises difficult questions and memories, particularly in those countries under Nazi control and influence during the mid-twentieth century. This may help explain the divergent use of the terms race and racism in the Anglo Saxon and continental European systems. For example, in the United Kingdom the 'literature assumes, and sometimes argues, that the only or most important racism is that which treats Blacks as object',[96] whereas '[i]n France and Germany, for instance, the term "race" is hardly ever used in public discourse today [...].'[97] This racial position provides additional arguments in explaining why, in contrast to the United States,

92 Mallon, '"Race": Normative, Not Metaphysical or Semantic', pp. 525–526.

93 Neil MacMaster, *Racism in Europe* (Basingstoke: Palgrave, 2001), p. 2.

94 Asbjørn Eide, 'Racial and Ethnic Discrimination in Europe: Past, Present and Future', in Danièle Joly (ed.), *Scapegoats and Social Actors: The Exclusion and Integration of Minorities in Western and Eastern Europe* (Basingstoke: Macmillan, 1998), p. 13.

95 Teun A. van Dijk, 'Denying Racism: Elite Discourse and Racism', in John Wrench and John Solomos (eds), *Racism and Migration in Western Europe* (Oxford, Providence: Berg Publishers, 1993), p. 191.

96 Robert Miles, 'The Articulation of Racism and Nationalism: Reflections on European History', in Wrench and Solomos (eds), *Racism and Migration in Western Europe*, p. 41.

97 Nora Räthzel, 'Developments in Theories of Racism', in The Evens Foundation (ed.), *Europe's New Racism. Causes, Manifestations, and Solutions* (New York: Berghahn Books, 2002), p. 5.

anti-discrimination policies in Europe started from the traditionally disadvantaged position of women in employment and then expanded into other categories. It was only later on that specifically racial discrimination entered the scene.[98]

Clearly, such historical contingencies and resistance represent a seemingly insurmountable obstacle for the penetration of CRT, which has placed the term race at the heart of its programme, into the legal realm of many continental European countries. Both the terms race and racism are extremely controversial, almost normatively taboo in many European countries, and for this reason these concepts do not travel across legal traditions and cultures.[99]

What this discussion clearly shows is how different histories and different conceptual and metaphysical debates on race and racism in Europe and the United States have caused CRT to be seen and perceived as an American phenomenon that is less pertinent or relevant to the European reality. Moreover, the taboo surrounding race in many continental European countries, the conceptual difficulties, and the emergence of 'cultural racism' as the European form of racism certainly play a major role in hampering CRT's success in mainland European legal analysis. In addition to this, these cumulative factors have created resistance against using or proposing a colour or race-conscious approach in Europe.

3.2.2.2 *The absence of a socio-academic movement*

Moving from the historical and conceptual level to a more sociological explanation, the failure of a CRT transplant could be traced to the fact that CRT minority scholars have only recently started to slowly emerge in Europe. As demonstrated in Chapter 2, CRT was born as an academic movement and theory thanks mostly to African American professors at American universities. A shared history of oppression, a shared presence of discrimination within and outside academia, as well as a common language and cultural references constituted the basis from which such a movement could spring.

The situation presents itself slightly differently in Europe. There is still not a sufficient number of minority scholars to generate a similar movement and analysis. This book is not the place to provide an in-depth analysis of the reasons for this absence. Nevertheless, it is arguably a combination of class and racial discrimination that can explain the absence of a racial justice movement in Europe. In the case of class, many of those who could constitute such an academic movement have a migrant background which often, albeit not always, goes hand in hand with

98 Thomas Trelogan, Steve Mazurana and Paul Hodapp, 'Can't We Enlarge the Blanket and the Bed? A Comparative Analysis of Positive Action in the European Court of Justice and the United States Supreme Court', *Hastings International and Comparative Law Review* (2004), vol. 28, pp. 73–74. See also more specifically for Germany: Kendall Thomas, 'The Political Economy of Recognition: Affirmative Action Discourse and Constitutional Equality in Germany and the U.S.A.', *Columbia Journal of European Law* (1998–1999), vol. 5, p. 329.

99 For more on traveling concepts, see William Twining, 'Have Concepts, Will Travel: Analytical Jurisprudence in a Global Context', *International Journal of Law in Context* (2005), vol. 1, p. 5.

economic hardship and with a lower-level educational background of the parents. Regarding racial discrimination, students from different racial backgrounds are possibly not encouraged to pursue further education and are directed towards other areas of occupation. Moreover, even if a person of colour or belonging to a visible minority does make it, they then have to operate in an environment which reflects the majority's power structures, values, views, and professional background, irrespective of an appearance of openness. This is discouraging and can persuade those from Europe to seek 'refuge' in the American or in the British university system, where at least issues related to race can be addressed openly.[100] Hence, it should come as no surprise that the first analyses to examine European anti-discrimination law including a social movements perspective,[101] and the European Court of Justice and minorities,[102] are authored by Iyiola Solanke, who is a British legal scholar of colour. Rather than focusing solely on the role played by the White elites in drafting the legal instruments on race discrimination, she analyses the influence of non-governmental actors and their contribution in the evolution of anti-discrimination law in Germany and the United Kingdom. By doing so, Solanke highlights the otherwise understated, if not ignored, role that people of colour have played in this important development.

However, beyond the narrower issue of the absence of visible minorities within the legal academic community who might have picked up on the message of CRT, the broader question is what unifying elements such an imagined community could be based upon. That some sort of transnational European association for victims of racism is possible is demonstrated by Romani people and the European Roma Rights Centre (ERRC), which is a powerful actor on the legal-political scene. In the case of Blacks, however, it seems more difficult to contextualise and theorise the very existence of a 'Black Europe'. Two somewhat rhetorical questions to ask are whether it is possible to speak about such a thing as a 'Black Europe'? And what are the main challenges in developing a Black European collective identity and agency? Indeed, as opposed to the United States, where African Americans share the same citizenship, language, and history, developing something like a common ground in Europe amongst visible minorities, and by consequence a Black European identity, a Black European constituency, and Black European agency, encounters a number of almost insurmountable obstacles. First of all, there is no such thing as a European citizenship. Black Europeans live in different states with different political and legal perspectives of migration, asylum, citizenship, and discrimination, as well as speak different languages. Ironically,

100 See on this point Philomena Essed, 'Foreword', in Darlene Clark Hine, Trica Danielle Keaton and Stephen Small (eds), *Black Europe and the African Diaspora* (Urbana, Chicago: University of Illinois Press, 2009), pp. xiii–xiv.

101 Iyiola Solanke, *Making Anti-Racial Discrimination Law. A Comparative History of Social Action and Anti-Racial Discrimination Law* (London, New York: Routledge, 2009).

102 Iyiola Solanke, 'Diversity and Independence in the European Court of Justice', *Columbia Journal of European Law* (2008), vol. 15, pp. 89–121.

the common policies on asylum, immigration,[103] and anti-discrimination[104] at the European level may actually create an incentive for identity formation or at least act as a sort of unifying dynamic to rally together in some form or other.

This leads to the second problematic aspect in theorising on a 'Black Europe', namely how the Black community is defined or defines itself, including who its members are and who identifies as a member of the community. External official government classifications may contribute as much as internal self-identification processes. In Britain, a so-called Black politics has emerged. Interestingly, at some stage Asians were considered Black for the benefit of building a collective pride and fighting against discrimination, which this common reference and identity supposedly created.[105] This, however, is not the case in most continental European countries. The self-identification process with an imagined Black European community is made harder due to the differing status of those individuals who might be counted or include themselves in such a category. Some families and individuals have been here for generations, are classified as European citizens, and never knew any other country outside Europe. Others were adopted by White Europeans. Others are cultural migrants who came for educational purposes, economic migrants who came for work purposes, social migrants who came to join their families, or political migrants who were forced to leave for political reasons. These widely differing personal experiences and statuses can also influence how one might or might not relate to a Black European identity.[106] For instance in France, Blacks could have been French citizens for a very long-time, like individuals from Guadeloupe, Martinique, and Guyana, or could have just arrived from Africa. These different histories and experiences lead to different legal claims or strategies, and represent a major hurdle in a common identification process.[107]

Nothing here intends to suggest that political agency around the idea or imagined community of Black Europeans is impossible. What needs to be established is the actual type of identity formation, whether it amounts to a thick or a thin identity. According to some, a thick concept of Black identity based on a common culture, history, and/or language, which prevails in the United States, cannot and should not be reproduced in the European context.[108] Instead, a thin version,

103 See e.g. Treaty on the Functioning of the European Union (TFEU), Part 3 ('Union Policies and Internal Actions'), Title V ('Area of Freedom, Security and Justice'), Chapter 2 ('Policies on Border Checks, Asylum and Immigration', Articles 77–80).

104 See e.g. Articles 10 and 19 TFEU.

105 See critically on this process: Tariq Modood, '"Black", Racial Equality and Asian Identity', in Marco Martiniello and Jan Rath (eds), *Selected Studies in International Migration and Immigrant Incorporation* (Amsterdam: Amsterdam University Press, 2010), pp. 201–215.

106 For more details on Black Europe and how it relates to the African Diaspora, see Kwame Nimako and Stephen Small, 'Theorizing Black Europe and the African Diaspora: Implications for Citizenship, Nativism, and Xenophobia', in Darlene Clark Hine, Trica Danielle Keaton and Stephen Small (eds), *Black Europe and the African Diaspora* (Urbana, Chicago: University of Illinois Press, 2009), pp. 212–237.

107 See more in detail: Pap Ndiaye, *La condition noire* (Paris: Calmann-Lévy, 2008), pp. 39–47.

108 *Ibid.* at p. 352.

which is based on a 'pragmatic Black conscience', proposes to recognise a group of Blacks not because of some presumed common identity but because of the common experience of injustice, which can best be addressed through collective action.[109] The advantage of framing a Black European identity more in terms of an interest group rather than a cultural one is because it allows for a sort of over-broad, colour-determined generalisation, thereby facilitating the formation of coalitions and alliances when interests overlap and coincide with issues of other interest groups, such as workers' issues.[110]

Some timid signals in the direction of scholarly work, as well as national and transnational political agency on the basis of criteria of discriminatory characteristics, are slowly emerging. Resulting from the increased presence of visible minorities on the European continent and their day-to-day experience of discrimination, academic publications are addressing the phenomenon of an emerging Black, European, or national, identity.[111] Recent concrete indicators of a budding academic debate and possible change are evident, for example, at the inauguration of the Study Centre 'Black Europe' at the Johannes Gutenberg University of Mainz, Germany in 2004. The centre's aim is to conduct empirical studies focused on the often-neglected history and present of Black people in Europe.[112] Similarly, in June 2008 the National Institute for the Study of Dutch Slavery (NiNsee) and the University of Amsterdam hosted their first Summer School, entitled 'Black Europe: Exploring Dimensions of Citizenship, Race, and Ethnic Relations', which has continued annually.

At the political level, some sort of changing social reality is slowly starting to show. In 2005, France witnessed the birth of the Representative Council of Black Associations (*Conseil Représentatif des Associations Noires (CRAN)*). This umbrella organisation joins a number of Black associations in fighting against discrimination and condemning France for its colonial and postcolonial past. Interestingly, the CRAN unites French, Arab, and Afro-French associations under the heading of Black as a racial-political constituency. Last but not least, it is necessary to mention that the First Black European Women's Congress took place in Vienna,

109 See Tommy Shelby, 'Foundations of Black Solidarity: Collective Identity or Common Oppression?', *Ethics* (2002), Vol. 112, pp. 231–266.

110 In this sense again for France: Ndiaye, *La condition noire*, pp. 352–353.

111 Beyond the already cited work by Pap Ndiaye, which could be seen as the founding piece of Black French Studies, see also Trica Danielle Keaton, T. Denean Sharpley Whiting and Tyler Stovall (eds), *Black France/France Noire: The History and Politics of Blackness* (Durham: Duke University Press, 2012); for Germany: Katarina Oguntoye, May Opitz and Dagmar Schultz (eds), *Farbe Bekennen: Afro-deutsche Frauen auf den Spuren ihrer Geschichte* (Berlin: Orlanda Verlag, 1986); Rose-Marie Huber-Koller, 'Schwarze Deutsche: Zwischen "Ethnos" und "Demos" im historischen Spannungsfeld unterschiedlicher Legitimationsgrundlagen und Techniken politischer Herrschaft', in Franz F. Müller *et al.* (eds), *Vom Ausländer zum Bürger: Problemanzeigen im Ausländer-, Asyl-, und Staatsangehörigkeitsrecht* (Baden Baden: Nomos, 1994), pp. 126–180; and Fatima El Tayeb, *Schwarze Deutsche: der Diskurs um "Rasse" und nationale Identität 1890–1933* (Frankfurt a. Main/New York: Campus-Verlag, 2001).

112 www.best.uni-mainz.de/modules/Informationen/index.php?id=13.

Austria, in September 2007, which brought about the establishment of a Black European Women's Network.[113]

Without wanting to marginalise these important initiatives, these examples of Black European or national Black movements and/or frameworks of analysis remain very limited. While possibly constituting the seed for a brighter future, they are still not sufficiently robust and numerous in order to rise to a coherently organised social and/or academic movement. Due to the absence of a strong presence of minority faculty, who could have been attracted by CRT's perspectives and analyses, this scholarship has not drawn the attention of many academics in the European context.

3.2.3 'Internal' legal-academic factors

As opposed to the 'external' factors described above, this section is more concerned with the 'internal' obstacles to CRT, generated from within the ideological and structural realities of the legal profession – legal reasoning and legal academia more specifically.

3.2.3.1 *Different object of critique*

Arguably, one of the main reasons for CRT's invisibility in Europe is due to philosophical differences. Broadly speaking, the United States has a tradition of favouring individual rights, enhanced by non-discrimination provisions, over collective goals. This approach has been elaborated and defended by John Rawls, Ronald Dworkin, and Bruce Akerman.[114] CRT has been critical of this philosophy and its constitutional consequences for minorities, specifically in its manifestations before the U.S. Supreme Court. Collective rights rarely prevail over individual rights; group identifications by the legislator are subject to strict scrutiny. In Europe, the liberal individual rights philosophy has not followed the same trajectory. It goes beyond the scope of this book to explain the reasons for this, but it may in part be related to the different role that judges play on both sides of the Atlantic and how this has influenced judicial review. On the one hand, in the United States, following the decision in *Marbury v. Madison*,[115] ordinary judges were quick to assert their competence to exercise judicial review, leading to what is known as the American model of decentralised judicial review. On the other hand, according to the European tradition, ordinary judges are not supposed to review laws enacted by parliament. To do so would be deemed a usurpation of power to exercise judicial review over acts of the 'natural' lawmaker. This explains how Hans Kelsen came

113 For more detailed information on this event and in general of the Black European's Women Network, see www.bewnet.eu/.

114 See Charles Taylor, 'The Politics of Recognition', in Charles Taylor and Amy Gutman (eds), *Multiculturalism: Examining the Politics of Recognition* (Princeton, NJ: Princeton University Press, 1994), p. 56.

115 *Marbury v. Madison* 5 U.S. (1 Cranch) 137 (1803).

up with the European model of centralised judicial review, in which specific constitutional courts exercise this function.[116] Kelsen played a major role in creating the first centralised constitutional court in Austria in 1920.[117] From a systematic point of view this structural difference also has had another consequence; for the most part, European constitutional courts exercise their function of judicial review to maintain the abstract hierarchy of norms within a legal system rather than to guarantee the protection of individual rights. Hence, the 'abstract review' of laws, which is entirely dissociated from concrete cases and as such forbidden in the United States, has traditionally been more relevant in Europe. For example, the Austrian constitutional court initially allowed the examination *in abstracto* of a statute's constitutionality only. Until recently, the French Constitutional Council only reviewed the constitutionality of a statute prior to its entry into force; in other words, review in a preventive and abstract way.[118] Kelsen's positivist vision of law and legal systems was seriously put in doubt after the atrocities of the Holocaust.[119] This explains why the role of the individual rights protection in judicial review increased after World War II.[120] This can be seen in Germany, with the introduction of direct constitutional complaints (*Verfassungsbeschwerden*) by any person claiming the German government violated his or her rights under the German Constitution.[121] Such a complaint is the only one that really corresponds to the individual rights logic defended by Rawls or Dworkin. Moreover, it accounts for 95 per cent of the German Constitutional Court's docketed caseload even though many of the most important decisions are still ultimately taken by abstract review.[122] Italy did not go so far, and only allows a system of 'collateral review'.[123] An individual cannot commence legal proceedings by claiming the unconstitutionality of a statute. The only time it is permissible to raise the question of the validity of a statute is during the course of a trial before an Italian court.[124] Lastly, the European Court of Justice, or today Court of Justice of the European Union (ECJ or CJEU), and the European Court of Human Rights (ECtHR) play

116 Mauro Cappelletti, *Judicial Review in the Contemporary World* (Indianapolis: Bobbs-Merrill, 1971), pp. 69–84.

117 Hans Kelsen, 'Judicial Review of Legislation, A Comparative Study of the Austrian and the American Constitution', *Journal of Politics* (1942), vol. 4, p. 183.

118 See *Loi constitutionnelle* no. 2008–724, 23 July 2008, *Journal Officiel de la Republique Française (JORF)*, 24 July 2008.

119 Mauro Cappelletti, '"Constitutional Justice" and the Overcoming of the Antithesis "Equity-Law" and "Natural-Positive Law"', in *Conflict and Integration: Comparative Law in the World Today* (Tokyo: Chuo University Press, 1988), pp. 18–19.

120 Constance Grewe and Hélène Ruiz Fabri, *Droits constitutionnels européens* (Paris: Presses Universitaires de France, 1995), pp. 74–75.

121 Article 93, para. (1), 4a. of the German Basic Law (*Grundgesetz*).

122 Vicki C. Jackson and Mark Tushnet, *Comparative Constitutional Law*, 1st edn (New York: Foundation Press, 1999), pp. 521–522.

123 For this term, see *ibid.*

124 Article 23 of *Legge* no. 87, 11 March 1953, *Gazzetta Ufficiale (GU)* 14 March 1953, no. 62.

a big role in the increased individual rights protection. Their judicial review function, for this reason, must not be underestimated.

Nonetheless, the main point to take away from this section is that Kelsen's vision continues to exercise some influence in European constitutional doctrine as can be shown from the new constitutions adopted in Eastern Europe in the early 1990s.[125] Europe is not a place with a liberal individual rights vision comparable to the United States. By consequence, CRT's critique of the liberal individual rights model is slightly impaired due to Europe's different tradition, leaving the deconstructionist critique without any real bite because there is not enough to deconstruct.[126]

3.2.3.2 *Scientific and systematic approach to law*

The second major internal obstacle to the spread of CRT in Europe, and more specifically in those states belonging to the civil law tradition, consists in the scientific understanding of law. The idea of law as a *scientia iuris* is deeply rooted in this legal tradition and plays a fundamental role at different levels. More than the superficial distinction between statutory and judge-made law, the vision of law as a science might be one of the most profound differences between the common law tradition and the civil law tradition.[127]

The common law was born and has developed through the political will of the Norman kings during the Middle Ages, who created a centralised state and court system. As a result, lawyers were trained and educated by practicing before the courts. The civil law tradition, on the contrary, did not have that kind of central political aid by a sovereign when it first began. It developed in a historical moment, during which continental Europe was highly fragmented.[128] Its origins are generally traced back to the birth of universities in Italy, especially Bologna, during the Middle Ages, where law was taught along with other sciences, such as medicine and theology. Most important for the legal field was the 'discovery' of the *Corpus Juris Civilis* of the Roman Emperor Justinian, which became the object of legal studies and triggered its development in the early legal academic world. However, this body of law that slowly started to emerge in these universities and spread throughout Europe lacked the political force and legitimacy of a sovereign. This lack of legitimacy was compensated by the affirmation of the scientific nature of the law. This vision of the law as a neutral, rational science, which has helped it overcome the political fragmentation in medieval Europe and persuaded

125 Bojan Bugaric, 'Courts as Policy Makers: Lessons from Transition', *Harvard International Law Journal* (2001), vol. 42, p. 260.

126 In this sense, see also Leonardo Marchettoni, '*Razza* e cultura. Un confronto', in Casadei and Re (eds), *Differenza razziale, discriminazione e razzismo nelle società multiculturali*, vol. I, p. 44.

127 Antonio Gambaro and Rodolfo Sacco, *Sistemi giuridici comparati*, 1st edn (Torino: UTET, 1996), p. 242.

128 René David and Camille Jauffret-Spinosi, *Les grands systémes de droit contemporains*, 11th edn (Paris: Dalloz, 2002), p. 31.

sovereigns of its validity, is still pervasive in modern Europe[129] and has only been further enhanced by the Enlightenment's aspirations of universalism and objectivity. This historical development equally explains why civil lawyers are almost exclusively educated in an academic setting.

The United States had approached this European educational academic model, and in particular the German one, through the efforts of Christopher Columbus Langdell, Dean of Harvard Law School from 1870 to 1895.[130] Nevertheless, the underlying common law structure quickly exposed the model to serious critique by the legal realists, who 'attacked the formalist notion that law embodies neutral, general principles derivable from cases.'[131] Empirical social sciences were supposed to substitute the formalists' approach, thus opening the way to empirical legal research,[132] and more importantly fostering the development of legal scholarship which would analyse law according to external criteria and not internal systematic or coherence-based ones.[133] As already mentioned, CLS and CRT built on this critique. They rejected the realist assumption that social legal empiricism is objective,[134] thus breaking away from the last connection to a scientific idea of the law. Instead, they emphasised the fact that law is a purely social construction and that it is constructed so as to benefit those who are in power, particularly White, heterosexual males.[135]

On the Old Continent, on the contrary, legal realism or schools of thought having similar anti-formalistic approaches have never really taken root.[136] For instance, in Germany, the '*Freirechtsbewegung*' ('Free Law Movement') at the beginning of the twentieth century came close to some of the critical stances taken by legal realists but never really managed to 'go mainstream'. A similar fate was destined for another critical legal movement, also in Germany, whose efforts even led to the founding of the law review *Kritische Justiz*. Moreover, this movement kept its distance from the American model and has always been oriented to theoretical debates, whether in political science or legal philosophy and much

129 Gambaro and Sacco, *Sistemi Giuridici Comparati*, p. 242.

130 On the influence of German legal scholarship on the United States legal educational system, see Laura I. Appleman, 'The Rise of the Modern American Law School: How Professionalization, German Scholarship, and Legal Reform Shaped Our System of Legal Education', *New England Law Review* (2005), vol. 39, pp. 274–283.

131 Farber and Sherry, *Beyond All Reason. The Radical Assault on Truth in American Law*, p. 17.

132 *Ibid.* at p. 18.

133 Kristoffel R. Grechenig and Martin Gelter, 'The Transatlantic Divergence in Legal Thought: American Law and Economics vs. German Doctrinalism', *Hastings International and Comparative Law Review* (2008), vol. 31, pp. 295–360.

134 Farber and Sherry, *Beyond All Reason. The Radical Assault on Truth in American Law*, p. 19.

135 *Ibid.* at p. 24.

136 However, see on Scandinavian realism Michael Martin, *Legal Realism. American and Scandinavian* (New York: Peter Lang, 1997), pp. 123–205. See also Carla Faralli, 'La ricezione del realismo giuridico nei paesi latini', *Materiali per una storia della cultura giuridica* (2000), Year 30, No. 2, p. 427. For a more detailed account on the realist movement in Italy, see Domenico Coccopalmerio *Francesco Carnelutti. Il 'realismo giuridico italiano'* (Napoli: Edizioni Scientifiche Italiane, 1989).

less to empirical studies in the more positivistic tradition of the sociology of law. Critical legal thinking in Germany is also strongly attached to issues of reason and rationality in social philosophy. This explains why French post-modernist theory, while having a great impact on Anglo-American critical legal thinking, was met with great reservation in Germany.[137]

In other continental European countries, different critical movements also encountered only limited success. This is the case of Italy's '*uso alternativo del diritto*' ('alternative use of law') movement[138] and the French anti-formalist movement, the '*juristes inquiets*'. The latter critiqued the legal classicist vision of the Civil Code, which had created a purely and profoundly formalistic and positivist system. As a consequence, the *juristes inquiets* helped promote the development of French law. However, their motivation was a fear of socialism rather than to create a link with it. Indeed, they were mainly afraid that if the legal system did not adopt a more pragmatic interpretation of law a conflict between the old individualism and the new social reality might arise.[139] Regardless of the political leanings or motivations for these different continental European critical, anti-formalist schools, a first and more limited reason why none of these movements were able to provoke the paradigmatic fundamental changes which legal realism introduced into American jurisprudence is the historical-political context. For example, with regards to the *Freirechtsbewegung* in Germany, World War I and eventually the arrival of the Nazi regime seem to have dealt a deadly blow to the exponents of this school, such as Hermann Kantorowicz.[140] Moreover, during World War II the Nazi regime attacked and destroyed legal formalism, which explains why after World War II lawyers in Germany were wary of going down a similar road and preferred to develop a style of legal doctrine, the *Rechtsdogmatik*, which is still prevalent in Germany today.[141]

137 Willem de Haan, Jos Silvis and Philip A. Thomas, 'Democracy, Rule of Law and Critical Legal Theory in Germany', *Journal of Law and Society* (1991), vol. 18, pp. 348–349. Also note that the BritCrits set themselves apart from their American colleagues by retracing their origins to Marxism, Freud and Lacan, feminism, Foucault, and Derrida rather than legal realism or CLS. Tim Murphy, 'BritCrits: Subversion and Submission, Past, Present and Future', *Law and Critique* (1999), vol. 10, p. 237 and pp. 242–243.

138 Mario G. Losano, 'La legge e la zappa. Origini e sviluppo del diritto alternativo in Europa e in Sudamerica', *Materiali per una storia della cultura giuridica* (2000), Year 30, No.1, p. 109; and Mario Barcellona, 'La scienza giuridica italiana e il marxismo (prima e dopo l' "uso alternativo del diritto")', *Rivista critica di diritto privato* (2000), vol. 18, no. 4, pp. 715–739.

139 Marie-Claire Belleau, 'The "Juristes Inquiets": Legal Classicism and Criticism in Early Twentieth-Century France', *Utah Law Review* (1997), vol. 1997, p. 382.

140 See Grechenig and Gelter, 'The Transatlantic Divergence in Legal Thought: American Law and Economics vs. German Doctrinalism', p. 351. See also Christian Joerges, 'On the Context of German-American Debates on Sociological Jurisprudence and Legal Criticism: A History of Transatlantic Misunderstandings and Missed Opportunities', in Alberto Febbrajo and David Nelken (eds), *European Yearbook in the Sociology of Law 1993* (Milano: Giuffrè, 1994), p. 403.

141 See Alexander Somek, 'From Kennedy to Balkin: Introducing Critical Legal Studies from a Continental Perspective', *University of Kansas Law Review* (1994), vol. 42, pp. 763–764.

A second, broader reason might be the different relationship between law and political power, which emerged in the divergent historical paths between common law and civil law jurisdictions described above. Without going into the details, the main idea here is that in civil law countries law functions as a justification for the state. Whereas in common law jurisdictions, law is conceived as a social engineering tool and is closer to the market and/or the economy than to political power.[142] This would explain why socio-legal critique of the state's institutions and their actions comes from within legal scholarship in common law jurisdictions, and why legal realism was ultimately more successful there. In contrast, in civil law jurisdictions socio-legal critique comes from outside the legal field. Legal scholars in mainland Europe are thus much closer to the state and often limit their critique to flaws in legal reasoning. As a counter-balance to that closer relationship with the state, the autonomy of legal doctrine is often stressed, facilitated also by the fact that law was taught as a separate subject at universities for centuries in mainland Europe. In turn this leads to a greater separation between law and other social sciences and to a different drawing of boundaries between those epistemological fields.

Against this backdrop, it becomes easier to understand why or how CRT has such a hard time penetrating civil law legal analysis. In this context, legal scholars perform a different function and operate at different levels than in America and the United Kingdom and Ireland. Moreover, in mainland Europe the dogmatic model of law is as a rational, objective, coherent science; in other words, classical legal thought still goes relatively unchallenged. Law continues to be analysed from within and according to standards pertaining to legal dogmatism. Any approach using external methods or analysing law as an object is relegated to the fields of philosophy and sociology, or at most of comparative law, which do not occupy a central position in the standard legal curriculum and have only a limited or less visible impact on 'mainstream' legislation, jurisprudence, and case law. It should be mentioned that for similar reasons the Law and Economics approach has had limited success, at least in the German-speaking countries, and arguably throughout the rest of continental Europe.[143]

In addition to this, the persistence of a scientific, formalistic vision of law in civil law countries also clarifies why legal storytelling, one of CRT's major strands, and its radical rejection of legal formalism and stress on empathy as opposed to 'objective legal reasoning' are particularly incomprehensible and almost repulsive to European legal scholars.[144] Yet, another feature of the common law might have facilitated this innovative way of formulating legal scholarship. In fact, the

142 Mauricio García-Villegas, 'Comparative Sociology of Law: Legal Fields, Legal Scholarships, and Social Sciences in Europe and the United States', *Law & Social Inquiry* (2006), vol. 31, no. 2, pp. 343–382.

143 The authors add as an additional reason the positive influence of Bentham's utilitarianism on American legal thought. Grechenig and Gelter, 'The Transatlantic Divergence in Legal Thought: American Law and Economics vs. German Doctrinalism', pp. 296–302.

144 See Papadopoulos, 'Guerre et paix en droit et littérature', pp. 192–196.

common law system is based on case law, and therefore on individual stories. Hence, the leap towards 'legal storytelling' was not as huge, compared to continental European law, where statutes and codes dominate the scene when studying law. Cases are only important for the abstract legal principles they establish but rarely do facts, and in this sense the story of the case, really matter. In a certain way, one could therefore not imagine a greater difference than between formal, dogmatic European law and informal storytelling.

A corollary to the idea of a legal science is the view that the law is a state-sponsored system, which is coherent in itself and all-embracing and unitary. This idea, present again in civil law systems, is best demonstrated by the existence of various statutory codifications, which aspire to be the exclusive and systematic regulator of an entire subject matter, even though in reality this aspiration belongs to the field of rhetoric rather than reality. The state stands at the centre of creation in this rational system of norms, where the existence of one basic norm guarantees a unitary approach. This vision has been metaphorically described as a pyramid.[145] Now, this whole image construction and idea of the legal system that is being taught to most European law students is under assault. In place of a pyramid, postmodernists have highlighted how the legal system bears a stronger resemblance to a rhizome, with multiple centres of law production instead of a unitary systematic state-originated law.[146] This automatically reverses, or at least challenges, the sense of legal production from a top-down logic to a bottom-up one.[147] Interests of differing groups or individuals become increasingly relevant in the battle for legal recognition and creation of legal rules, thus replacing the objective law, which had a more unitary, 'egalitarian' view of the human being. One of France's most influential lawyers has even spoken of the 'pulverization of the law into subjective rights'.[148] Civil law systems have had a much harder time coming to terms with this change of legal approach compared to the common law, because CRT, and its various expressions and different groups, is perceived as a non-unitary, partial approach to the law without the ambition of pursuing a single vision.[149] This clearly stands in stark contrast with the unitary, systematic idea of legal systems that still dominate mainland Europe today.

In general, the systematic, scientific, top-down view of the law continues to exist in most parts of continental Europe, which is possibly one of the most important internal reasons why CRT has found it particularly hard to cross the Atlantic and into European legal analysis.

145 For the origins and the functioning of a legal system under this rationale, see Hans Kelsen, *Pure Theory of Law* [1960, 2nd edn], Max Knight (trans.), (Gloucester, MA: Peter Smith, 1989), pp. 193–278.

146 Gilles Deleuze and Felix Guattari, *A Thousand Plateaus: Capitalism and Schizophrenia* [1980], Brian Massumi (trans.), 1st edn (Minneapolis: University of Minnesota Press, 1987), pp. 3–25.

147 See e.g. Denys de Béchillon, 'La structure des normes juridiques à l'épreuve de la postmodernité', *Revue interdisciplinaire d'études juridiques* (1999), no. 43, p. 2.

148 Jean Carbonnier, *Droit et passion du droit sous la Ve République* (Paris: Flammarion, 1996), p. 121.

149 Gambaro and Sacco, *Sistemi giuridici comparati*, 1st edn (Torino: UTET, 1996), p. 219.

3.2.3.3 *Rigid and conservative approach of academic setting*

A more rapid spread of CRT at the academic level is also hindered by the rigid and conservative approach of academic settings in general. In the first place one should mention the rigid structure of university curricula. In fact, legal education at universities in Europe is under the influence of the government as far the content and format of the curriculum is concerned. As a result, changes in the legal curriculum require approval by the state and it becomes difficult to introduce any sort of change.[150] This 'government controlled' model stands in sharp contrast to the United States model which is 'profession controlled' in as far as the American Bar Association, American Association of Law Schools and the state Supreme Courts have a bearing over legal education.[151] The bureaucratic structure of most public European universities makes it comparatively harder to introduce new courses in conventional law study programmes, and professors cannot simply propose a new course within their academic structure but have to go through cumbersome bureaucratic procedures. Alternatively, they can organise a more informal, small-scale seminar-type instruction method.

Second, the differing procedure for selecting law review articles in the United States and in Europe may influence the speed at which new ideas are spreading. In the United States students are heavily involved in the article selection process. On the contrary, in Europe it is mostly professors who are involved in this kind of activity. Whereas the former do not have any vested interest or approach to defend, the latter may oppose an approach strongly contrary to their own view, thus tending to reject potentially innovative articles and preventing a faster spread of new and critical ideas.[152] One last factor could also have to do with the more conservative appointment procedure of professors within European countries preferring more traditional approaches over more innovative ones.[153]

Even though it is not directly related to the absence of CRT from legal academic analysis, one should also mention that in certain civil law systems another important forum for the development of legal ideas, namely courts, is also less open to new influences and theories than in common law jurisdictions. This is astonishing, to a degree, given the excellent reputation professors enjoy in the civil law tradition and their proximity to the state and courts. The spectrum of impenetrability ranges from Italy where citations of the opinions of professors is outright forbidden, to France where the *Cour de cassation* and the *Conseil d'Etat*

150 Juergen R. Ostertag, 'Legal Education in Germany and the United States – A Structural Comparison', *Vanderbildt Journal of Transnational Law* (1993), vol. 26, p. 320. Even though this article focuses on the German system, the structural approach is similar to other continental European law faculties.

151 *Ibid.*

152 On this argument, Grechenig and Gelter, 'The Transatlantic Divergence in Legal Thought: American Law and Economics vs. German Doctrinalism', p. 306.

153 Ugo Mattei, *Comparative Law and Economics* (Ann Arbor: University of Michigan Press, 1997), p. 88.

refrain from revealing the opinions of writers in their judgments,[154] and finally to Germany where, on the contrary, judges often make references to works by professors in their decisions. Under these conditions, even if CRT has already started to move across the Atlantic in the doctrinal domain, it would still take a considerably longer amount of time than in the United States before it could show some lasting effect on legal systems, specifically in judicial decisions, and in particular in Italy and France. In the eyes of a European scholar it may appear surprising how CRT has actually managed to find ways into some recent judicial decisions at an unprecedented speed.[155] Interestingly enough, for the same reasons as CLS and CRT, also Law and Economics has not managed to penetrate deeply into the European legal practice[156] as has happened, on the contrary, in the United States.

In conclusion, before attempting to transfer or transplant CRT or proposing a CRT driven analysis of the continental European context, it is important to understand the mechanisms involved in such a process. Comparative law can help explain the problems that may arise in such a transplant or transfer. At the same time, this has also helped provide an explanation and a brief introduction of the European context, especially with regards to the academic 'climate', the various scientific disciplinary boundaries, as well as the differing attitudes towards race, which are crucial in order to understand the move towards a European CRT.

154 See on these two countries René David, 'Sources of Law', in René David (ed.), *International Encyclopedia of Comparative Law* (Tübingen: Mohr and The Hague, Boston, London: Martinus Nijhoff Publishers, 1984), vol. II, chapter 3, p. 277.

155 See e.g. *State v. Buggs*, 581 N.W.2d 329, (Minn. 1998); *America v. Leviner*, 31 F. Supp. 2d 23 (D. Mass. 1998); and *Taylor v. Metzger*, 706 A.2d 685 (N.J. 1998) cited in Richard Delgado and Jean Stefancic, *Critical Race Theory: An Introduction* (New York: New York University Press, 2001), pp. 42, 115, 118; or *Lam v. Univ. of Haw.*, 40 F.3d 1551, 1562 (9th Cir. 1994) where the court referred to Kimberlé W. Crenshaw's intersectionality theory.

156 See e.g. for Italy: Roberto Pardolesi and Bruno Tassone, *I giudici e l'analisi economica del diritto privato* (Bologna: il Mulino, 2003), p. 195; for France: Horatia Muir Watt, 'La fonction subversive du droit comparé', *Revue internationale de droit comparé* (2000), vol. 52, no. 3, p. 519.

Chapter 4

Towards a European Critical Race Theory

The previous chapter attempted to explain the absence of CRT in the continental European context due to challenging obstacles which have prevented CRT from penetrating the legal systems in Europe. Against such a backdrop, this chapter argues for a European CRT by identifying some factors that could favour a transplant of CRT to Europe, by deconstructing narratives around race and the objections to its use in that context, by contrasting them with the emergence of the idea of 'anti-White racism', and finally by identifying the legal elements that would or could constitute the building blocks of a European CRT and which I call 'Continental European Colourblindness'.

4.1 Constructing a European CRT

This section provides some of the constructive and deconstructive arguments necessary to build a European CRT. In a first step, I briefly identify the factors which speak in favour of a transplant of CRT into Europe. This shows the absence of CRT was not a necessary and unavoidable consequence. In a second step, I look at the objections levied against the use of race in the European context, many of which overlap with issues about citizenship and religion. In the previous chapter, we were exposed to the historical reasons why race is considered so problematic in Europe. Here, I take a deeper look at the rhetorical arguments and narratives underpinning such resistance. At the same time, I also highlight the counterarguments, which not only provide the basis for undermining them but also unveil the way in which way race can and should be used in Europe and sets the framework for a European CRT. The third step contrasts the difficulties to use race and racial interpretations of social and legal reality with the ease in which 'anti-White racism' is invoked in Germany and France, where attacks against members of the White, Christian majority by visible minorities are immediately and almost exclusively read in racial terms.

4.1.1 Theoretical factors favouring a CRT transplant to Europe

As has been shown in the previous chapter, in mainland European scholarship, especially legal scholarship, there exists nothing similar to CRT. A number of arguments have been presented to explain this absence; however, many of these speak in favour of a transplant of CRT scholarship, or at least a more favourable reception. Besides the shared common philosophical roots that could have facilitated an understanding and application of CRT in Europe, some other points speak for a European CRT.

First of all, it is necessary to mention CRT's rejection of indeterminacy, which is a central characteristic of CLS scholarship. CRT scholars fervently believe in rights, although they admit that they do not lend themselves to optimism and results. However, CRT scholars' belief in and commitment to rights stems from a deep distrust in the legal system. In a rather bleak way of thinking, CRT scholars argue that if rights and law have no meaning, they remain the lesser evil to a system which has no rights at all and where the same White majority wield all the power. Even though the CRT motives for such a legalistic, rights-based approach may differ from that adopted by European scholars, at least it comes closer to a continental European understanding of legal analysis than the deconstructionist, indeterminate approach of CLS scholars. It is important to note that CLS has experienced success abroad and has gained notoriety in European systems, albeit limited.[1] Nevertheless, it cannot be denied that the heavy accusations against CLS in the United States, which ranged from rights trashing to nihilism, must have resounded more forcefully in Europe where legal realism was never established. For this reason, it is especially important that CRT should not become tainted by these accusations and critiques. CRT makes a better fit in the European analytical framework than CLS.

A second aspect of CRT which, despite the above-mentioned obstacles, could have facilitated or echoed positively in the European context is LatCrit theory. This is not only due to the linguistic proximity with Spain,[2] but also because of the structural and conceptual commonalities between LatCrit scholarship and continental Europe: immigration and ethnicity respectively.

In immigration questions, when trying to compare American racism to European racism an argument often raised is that the racism suffered by African Americans and Native Americans is qualitatively different from racism suffered by European immigrants or their descendants. The former did not come of their own free will or were already there before the settlers arrived, whereas the latter supposedly willingly migrated to Europe. Based on this difference, racism against

1 See e.g. the special issue of the European Review of Private Law dedicated to Critical Legal Theory: 'Special Issue on Critical Legal Theory and European Private Law', *European Review of Private Law* (2002), vol. 10, no. 1, pp. 1–132; and Christian Joerges and David M. Trubek (eds), *Critical Legal Thought: An American-German Debate* (Baden-Baden: Nomos, 1989).

2 And indeed, as was mentioned earlier, the Universidad de Málaga hosted the First and Second Annual LatCrit Summer Colloquium in 1999 and 2000.

African Americans and Native Americans is more condemnable and less comprehensible. In contrast, with regard to migrants, it is easier to justify less favourable treatment to individuals who presumably migrated freely and autonomously because by coming to Europe, or in the case of many Latinos to the United States, immigrants implicitly or explicitly accepted the conditions existing in the host country. At the same time, similar fears of being swamped by different cultures and languages because of immigration are raised and instrumentalised on both sides of the Atlantic. Often, the same objections and arguments arise in connection with discrimination and racism against Latinos in America and European immigrants. For these reasons, it is interesting to see the way in which LatCrit addresses these common objections while highlighting the racial and exclusionary underpinnings of citizenship[3] as well as of (immigration) policies affecting Latinos,[4] an aspect that is often downplayed if not absent in European analysis of immigration issues.

With regard to ethnicity and related issues, today Latinos have increasingly been viewed and constructed in terms of ethnicity.[5] This trend towards ethnicity is also reflected in the official census, where the category of ethnicity has been increasingly applied to Latinos.[6] In this sense, LatCrit theory works with the broader and more culture-laden term ethnicity but then goes on to link it with racial underpinnings. This in turn provides a more nuanced analysis, which highlights the hybridity and complexity emerging from the combination of race and ethnicity. For these reasons, LatCrit theory could be quite appealing in the European context and provide an interesting starting point for comparison and dialogue.[7]

A third point worth mentioning are the commonalities of Western race thought. In Chapter 3, the focus was on the historical and contextual differences between the United States and Europe. While it is important to understand the local differences and dynamics at play to grasp the historical and conceptual differences behind the terms race and racism, at the same time it may be useful to understand the commonalities in race thought on both sides of the Atlantic Ocean as a means to unite these two continents. Indeed, modern thought on race has been shaped by the same body of anthropologists, scientists, philosophers and historians such as Kant, Locke, or Mills, who have also played a key role in shaping modern thought in other areas. Comte George-Louis Leclerc de Buffon, Johann Friedrich Blumenbach, who introduced the term 'Caucasian' into human classification, Comte Joseph-Arthur de Gobineau, and Houston Stewart Chamberlain, just

3 See e.g. Román, *Citizenship and Its Exclusions.*

4 See e.g. Johnson, 'Race and the Immigration Laws', in Valdes, McCristal Culp and Harris (eds), *Crossroads, Directions, and a New Critical Race Theory*, pp. 187–198.

5 See *Hernandez v. Texas*, 347 U.S. 475 (1954).

6 See e.g. Clara E. Rodríguez, *Changing Race: Latinos, the Census, and the History of Ethnicity in the United States* (New York, London: New York University Press, 2000).

7 In this sense, see Elisabeth Holzleitner, 'Latina and Latino Critical Legal Studies und europäisches Gleichheitsdenken – ein interkultureller Dialog', *juridikum* (2006), no. 2, pp. 88–93.

to name the most 'infamous', are all Europeans who nevertheless have deeply influenced race thought and imagery throughout the Western world, including the United States.[8] It is probably no coincidence that the heyday of scientific or biological racism, which was founded on common pseudo-scientific theories, occurred at the same period in both the United States and Europe. This period has also been described by a leading historian as the time of 'Race is All' (1890–1939).[9] One cannot ignore the fact that anti-Semitism and anti-Black racism share the same ideological matrix. In fact, the American and European colonial settings have influenced each other's thinking on race since the anti-slavery movement in the late 1700s.[10] There is no denying of a common breeding ground, in particular at a theoretical level with the development of a science of race and the rise of nation-states in the mid-1800s. In this context it is not surprising that certainly even today cross-fertilisation between the two continents has occurred regularly, and contemporary European sociologists correctly stress the fact that 'the development of modern racism should be able to provide an explanatory framework that can include both types'[11] and highlight the risks of conceptualising or defining racism as based on only one of these two types.[12] Frequently, images can serve as an excellent means of illustrating a point. Gilroy's seminal book *The Black Atlantic*[13] is possibly the best visual and textual reference to show how much race and racism represent a common thread on both sides of the Atlantic and not just in the United States. Along these same lines, regardless of the different past, the question needs to be directed towards the future and what is yet to come. Some forecasts predict that racism will have a brilliant future due to globalisation and the decline of those political forces to defeat racism in the first place. Racism could therefore become a dominant factor again in the North and South, as well as in the East and in the West.[14]

Once such a common perspective on race and racism is adopted, a glance at continental European legal systems through the lens of CRT does not look completely unreasonable and should at least be given the benefit of doubt against accusations or fears that by (re)introducing race or ethnicity into legal discourse, it may perpetuate racist thought and racial categories. Viewed from this angle, the central CRT arguments challenging mainstream beliefs about racial justice may

8 On the link between race and philosophy: Andrew Valls (ed.), *Race and Racism in Modern Philosophy* (Ithaca: Cornell University Press, 2005), and Julie Ward and Tommy Lott (eds), *Philosophers on Race* (Oxford, Malden: Blackwell Publishers, 2002).

9 Hannaford, *Race. The History of an Idea in the West*, p. 325.

10 Alana Lentin, *Racism and Anti-Racism in Europe* (London, Ann Arbor: Pluto Press, 2004), p. 20.

11 Neil MacMaster, *Racism in Europe* (Basingstoke: Palgrave, 2001), p. 2.

12 Robert Miles, 'The Articulation of Racism and Nationalism: Reflections on European History', in John Wrench and John Solomos (eds), *Racism and Migration in Western Europe* (Oxford, Providence: Berg Publishers, 1993), p. 42.

13 Paul Gilroy, *The Black Atlantic: Modernity and Double Consciousness* (Cambridge, MA: Harvard University Press, 1993).

14 Etienne Balibar, 'La costruzione del razzismo', in Casadei and Re (eds), *Differenza razziale, discriminazione e razzismo nelle società multiculturali*, vol. I, p. 55.

become just as relevant in the European context as in the American one. These mainstream beliefs include: that blindness to race will eliminate racism; that racism is a matter of individuals and not systems; and that one can fight racism without paying attention to sexism, homophobia, economic exploitation, and other forms of oppression and injustice.[15] Moreover, some of the vocabulary and analytical tools, such as 'interest convergence',[16] 'intersectionality',[17] or 'unconscious racism',[18] may, and indeed already have, become helpful instruments to provide new insights and strategies. It has been argued that 'CRT provokes a critical thinking that is not limited to a historical time and place, but confronts law's complicity in the violent perpetuation of a racially defined economic and social order.'[19]

However, before moving on to demonstrate why European CRT is necessary, as well as to describe its appearance and added value, the obstacles, defined as the 'external' conceptual-historical factors related to race, need to be broken down and addressed. This does not mean that the relevance of the other 'internal' obstacles identified in Chapter 3 is discarded; however, it seems that external race issues are most explicit in establishing European CRT. The issues related to legal academia and its rigidity, on the other hand, seem to raise secondary questions which do not necessarily pose the same theoretical conundrums but rather involve practical or functional objections and problems.

4.1.2 Deconstructing narratives on race and racism in mainland Europe

Indeed, we have seen in the previous chapter how in mainland Europe when looking at race, the paradigmatic experience of European racism is that of anti-Semitism and the Holocaust. This focus on the Holocaust and anti-Semitism as the quintessential European kind of racism relies on a series of assumptions that in turn have a number of consequences when analysing the relationship between race and law in Europe. First, it leads to thinking about race and racism in terms of a state-organised policy based on racial hostility. Anything less, such as unconscious, indirect, and structural racism will not be perceived as 'real' racism. Second, it allows for the presentation of these events as exceptional in European history, as the one and only time, in which domestic laws were explicitly racial. Third, it allows those countries that were influenced or occupied by Germany, such as France or Italy, to present these racial laws as being imposed from the outside, as an aberration of their own history rather than part of a broader

15 Valdes, McCristal Culp and Harris (eds), *Crossroads, Directions, and a New Critical Race Theory*, pp. 1 – 2.

16 Bell, '*Brown v. Board of Education* and the Interest Convergence Dilemma', p. 518.

17 Crenshaw, 'Mapping the Margins', pp. 1241–1299.

18 Charles R. Lawrence III, 'The Id, the Ego, and Equal Protection', pp. 317–388.

19 Costas Douzinas and Adam Geary, *Critical Jurisprudence* (Oxford and Portland, Oregon: Hart Publishing 2005), p. 259.

heritage. Fourth, the focus on the Holocaust allows other types of racism, such as colonialism and colonial laws to be forgotten or side-lined. Fifth, even if these laws were taken into account, they are geographically removed because they did not apply throughout Europe, thus strengthening the idea that they did not contribute directly or blatantly to the construction of European racial identity and Whiteness. Sixth, focusing mainly on the Holocaust also reinforces the idea that racism only encompasses biological racism but not necessarily cultural racism. Last but not least, it allows framing post-World War II Europe and its new institutions, new constitutions, and international human rights instruments as a radical break with the past, as a new era. Linking Europe's racial past with its racial present and understanding the dark legacies[20] becomes much more difficult in this context.

Against the backdrop of these divergent rhetorical moves it is challenging to tell a story about race and law in Europe, the ways CRT did and does for racial minorities in the United States. Moreover, they explain why race is perceived differently in the mainland European context and how and why this word has become taboo. They also explain the objections put forward against the use of race and race-conscious measures in this geographical reality.

A first objection is that the continued use of race will perpetuate the idea of the existence of biological races and, by extension, racism. Between 1850 and 1945 especially, race in a biological sense had been used as the basis for many studies in social sciences ranging from anthropology to history. As described earlier, this idea roughly came to an end and fell quickly into disrepute with the end of World War II and the UNESCO declarations, eliminating the issue of race as an object of studies from most if not all scientific endeavours. The acknowledgement that most of the (pseudo-)scientific work done before had been built on a morally and scientifically untenable basis was probably sufficient to argue for the elimination of the term from the research agenda. Today, social scientists working on the issue in mainland Europe must include disclaimers in order not to perpetuate the idea of racial superiority and to deny the existence of biological races. As will be demonstrated below, similar disclaimers appear in legal texts and documents for the same reasons as well.

The fundamental problem with this position is that despite repeated efforts to eliminate any trace of race, during the past fifty years racism has not disappeared. Moreover, this early, rudimentary anti-racist position which can be found, for example, in the first UNESCO 'Statement on Race' of July 1950 is based on shaky foundations, as argued by Pierre-André Taguieff and others. His criticism is because this position creates a 'lexicocentrical' illusion based on primitive cognitive assumptions, according to which the simple removal of race from a language also removes the substantive underlying relationships or interactions. Moreover,

20 Christian Joerges and Navraj Singh Ghaleigh (eds), *Darker Legacies of Law in Europe: The Shadow of National Socialism and Fascism over Europe and its Legal Traditions* (Oxford; Portland, OR: Hart, 2003), in which a number of authors analyse what still lingers with us from the old Nazi and Fascist laws and institutions and how/whether it influenced the construction of Europe.

it creates an additional illusion that racism is only thought about in terms of race and it is sufficient to erase race from the mental space and never utter the word again.[21] We now know that the widespread and general consensus that biological racism is bogus and the silencing of race in various domains has not led to the disappearance of racism. Racial imagery remains visible in society and continues to produce negative effects. It becomes extremely difficult, if not impossible, to address those negative effects, be it through studies or anti-discrimination legislation, when one is prevented from using the word race and addressing precisely the crux of the problem. Hence, rather than thinking about race in biological and objectifying terms, its recognition should occur on a much more pragmatic level, which takes into account its social, cultural, and historical construction as well as its social effects. This move away from biology towards social relevance also has the advantage of showing the dynamic processes involved in constructing the idea of race from different perspectives, including legal, historical, and sociological views, and of showing how similar it is to other socially constructed categories such as 'nation' or 'gender' or 'citizenship' which never raise objections on such a scale when applied in scientific works or legislation.[22]

A second objection to using race posits that other categories such as gender and class, and not race, help explain the lines of subordination, marginalisation or discrimination in the European context. This argument goes back to the strong Marxist and Socialist tradition on the Old Continent, which resulted in a class-based framework of analysis in social sciences in general. Certainly, this argument could be sustained on the basis of perception that in Europe racial laws were and are exceptional and limited to the Nazi regime or the era of colonisation. Nevertheless, we can see elements of the class versus race debate in the United States as well,[23] and in the United Kingdom. Some of the earlier academic writings on CRT also focus on this issue.[24]

The problem with this argument is that it misunderstands and misrepresents what CRT theorists, or other academics who are calling on the incorporation of race, are trying to achieve. Moreover, it uselessly pits race against class, as if they were mutually exclusive. CRT theorists have criticised the absence of race in CLS' analysis of the law and while race did occupy a central space in CRT's analyses, that space was not exclusively occupied by race. Indeed in CRT, other factors such as gender, sexual orientation, and social class do play a role, as demonstrated by intersectionality theory for example. For the same reason, when advocating for a more race-conscious analysis in the European context, this by no means intends

21 Pierre-André Taguieff, 'Du racisme au mot "race": comment les éliminer?', *Mots* (1992), no. 33, pp. 215–239.

22 For a more detailed analysis of how to address the problematic concept of 'race' and Black identities in the French (and also European) context, see Ndiaye, *La condition noire*, pp. 30–47.

23 See e.g. William Julius Wilson, *The Declining Significance of Race: Blacks and Changing American Institutions* (Chicago: University of Chicago Press, 1978) in which the author finds that class more than race is the decisive factor which helps to explain the current social inequalities.

24 See *supra* Chapter 3, part 3.1.3 'Existing CRT transplants'.

to blend out issues related to class or gender. In all likelihood, social class will always remain the main prism of analysis in Europe when trying to explain differences and disadvantages, especially in the legal domain. However, attempts at framing, explaining, and combating issues in terms of race where those issues can clearly be framed, explained and combated predominantly in those terms should not be thwarted due to an alleged exclusion of class analysis or a fear of the return of biological racism.

Given these first two objections, the third one almost follows automatically and mostly revolves around the problem of classifying people along racial lines or collecting data on a similar basis. This objection is more specific to the continental European context, where such classification harks back to the Nazi period. In the United States, on the contrary, the census asks for people's race and ethnicity. This is also the case in the United Kingdom. Therefore, the main tenet of this argument is that by introducing some type of classification or statistical instrument which takes into account race and ethnicity, it actually reproduces, creates, legitimises, and entrenches precisely those racist behaviours and ideas that were intended to be eliminated in the first place. This issue is particularly felt in the French context where a universalising Republican model of citizenship has formed the idea that distinctions between humans are impermissible and where a specific debate has emerged concerning the so-called '*statistiques ethniques*'.[25] The mere idea that people can be classified according to racial and ethnic lines appears odious and impossible to most and is eerily reminiscent of the Nazi period. Hence, any proposal to introduce such classifications or distinctions – such as an assessment of the level of discrimination suffered by European citizens with migrant background – is interpreted as introducing a trend that never existed in Europe at best, or existed under a totalitarian and murderous regime at worse. Last but not least, on the legal level collecting such sensitive data would appear to be contrary to privacy rights and the prohibition to process such sensitive data.[26]

A number of counterarguments can be advanced here. One very strong observation is that France actually collects ethnic and racial data in its overseas territories,[27] thus showing again how the displacement of racial laws to its (former) colonies sustains the national rhetoric of non-racial readings in the French mainland. Beyond this argument, statistics on a person's race or ethnicity are one of the main instruments of proof in social sciences without which it becomes impossible or very difficult to seriously study the phenomena of race discrimination. If it were impossible to request information about race or ethnicity then how would it

25 See e.g. 'Le curieux débat des démographes', *Mouvements* (1999), no. 3, p. 110.

26 See e.g. Article 8(1) of Directive 95/46/EC of the European Parliament and of the Council of 24 October 1995 on the protection of individuals with regard to the processing of personal data and on the free movement of such data, *Official Journal (OJ) L 281* of 23 November 1995, pp. 31–50.

27 'En Nouvelle Calédonie: Des statistiques ethniques tout à fait légales', in Serge Slama (ed.), *Les discriminations selon l'origine* (La documentation française, 2009), pp. 103–104.

be possible to assess the discrimination suffered by visible minorities.[28] As will be shown below, French authorities suggest using proxies such as nationality, birthplace of the parents or the name to substitute for information concerning race or ethnicity. However, they remain imprecise proxies, especially with regard to the increasing number of visible minorities who are first, second, or even third generation Europeans and whose name and parents' place of birth do not indicate their racial and ethnic backgrounds, who nevertheless are victims of racism. This trend illustrates that a more nuanced view on the issue is also required. The parallel with the Nazi racial classifications would only apply to cases in which individuals' names are correlated to their race and ethnicity, thereby establishing some sort of system to officially track one's racial or ethnic origin. What most studies on discrimination collecting racial or ethnic data set out to achieve is to ask respondents, on an anonymous or voluntary basis, to identify their own race or ethnicity. Strictly speaking this does not amount to a really racial classification and the parallel with the Nazi past is invoked wrongly in such cases.[29] But even considering the introduction of some sort of racial or ethnic classification in the census, neither the classification itself nor the data are discriminatory. What can amount to discrimination is the subsequent use of such data.[30] However, once it is clearly stated why individuals are asked, on an anonymous or voluntary basis, to provide such information they would probably also be less reluctant to do so.[31] For example, providing data for better anti-discrimination policies would not be objectionable for most potential respondents. Undoubtedly, from a constructivist point of view, once such classifications are introduced, then something is created. However, classifications are not artificially introduced into a void; they often follow an already underlying, existing type of socially relevant classification. Given the existence of racism and xenophobia towards visible minorities, the introduction of some sort of classification to combat the particular evil is not creating something new. It simply represents the recognition of something that already existed but had not been acknowledged officially. Moreover, some of the most dangerous aspects of such classifications can be tempered by relying on self-identification of individuals rather than by relying on 'forced' official classifications.[32]

The fourth objection follows directly from the third one. Even assuming that in some European countries a classification for anti-discrimination purposes is

28 Patrick Simon, 'Sciences sociales et racisme: où sont les docteurs Folamour?', *Mouvements* (1999), no. 3, p. 113.

29 See on this argument Ndiaye, *La condition noire*, p. 283.

30 Laurent Mucchielli, 'Il n'y a pas de statistique raciste, seulement des interpretations', *Mouvements* (1999), no. 3, p. 115.

31 In this sense again: Ndiaye, *La condition noire*, p. 282.

32 Arguing that self-identification seems to be the preferred and admissible way by authorities to balance between respect for human rights, protection of privacy, and the collection of data on racial and ethnic origins for the purposes of antidiscrimination: Julie Ringelheim and Olivier De Schutter, *Ethnic Monitoring. The Processing of Racial and Ethnic Data in Anti-Discrimination Policies: Reconciling the Promotion of Equality with Privacy Rights* (Brussels: Bruylant, 2010).

allowed or introduced, there is then the possibility of governments misusing such highly sensitive data. In other words, once such data is acquired, there is no guarantee that this information is not misused for other, and perhaps repressive, purposes. Again, here the counterargument is broader and does not necessarily concern data related to race or ethnicity but can also include data about sexual orientation or health for example. Therefore, the same data protection rules that are being established precisely to prevent government, or even private, misuse would also apply in such a case. Clearly this argument presumes that the government will respect and not violate these rules but then most of our Western democracies rely on that presumption and in case of a totalitarian regime there is little to be done anyway.

4.1.3 Anti-White racism

The bias and hypocrisy behind some of the narratives on race in mainland Europe become all the more evident in recent debates in at least two countries, France and Germany, on what has become known as 'anti-White racism'. The slowness and reluctance of institutions, public actors, and the media to call something racism when it involves the victimisation of people of colour is not equalled by slowness and reluctance to frame things in terms of race and racism when the victim belongs to the White/Christian majority. The phenomenon of anti-White racism deserves specific mention here because it highlights some of the problematic assumptions underlying 'Continental European Colourblindness' as well as what effects they may have at the normative level.

Anti-White racism was a term introduced and used in right wing political movements and literature and was initially circumscribed to those limited areas. In France it dates back to the early 1980s,[33] whereas in Germany it has shifted from the right wing position that foreign nations such as France, the United Kingdom, Russia, and the United States were against Germany (*Deutschenfeindlichkeit*) to the idea that now the animosity against Germans comes from inside in the form of Muslim migrants.[34] In both countries these positions recently went mainstream. The trigger for analysing events from that perspective were cases in which White 'French' and 'German' pupils, students, and/or teachers were attacked or at least harassed by other individuals or groups with migrant background.[35] These events have given rise to a debate in which the events are framed in terms of

33 See e.g. in France the early use by Pascal Bruckner, *Le sanglot de l'homme blanc* (Paris: Editions Seuil, 1983) and the explanation that the term was introduced by a right wing Catholic-traditionalist association, AGRIF: Erwan Lecœur (ed.), *Dictionnaire de l'extrême droite* (Paris: Larousse, 2007), pp. 50–52.

34 See in this sense Yasemin Shooman, 'Der Topos "Deutschenfeindlichkeit" in rechtspopulistischen Diskursen', in Bündnis Rechtspopulismus stoppen (eds), *Rechtspopulismus in Berlin* (Berlin, 2011) pp. 45–47, available at: http://rechtspopulismusstoppen.blogsport.de/images/broschuere_rechtspopberlin_web.pdf.

35 On the origins in France, see Luc Bronner, 'Manifestations de lycéens: le spectre des violences

race and racism. Whereas this turn is more explicit in France and has led to an appeal against anti-White bashings by left wing intellectuals and politicians,[36] in Germany this occurred more surreptitiously. In 2008, during regional elections, the Christian Democratic Party (CDP) had already attempted to win votes by asking to deport foreign youths who insulted Germans as 'fucking Germans' ('*Scheiß-Deutsche*') and in that same year Kristina Schröder, a German MP, made the issue one of her topics. It is important to note that it did not fall on fertile ground.

However, *Deutschenfeindlichkeit* reappeared with force in 2010 as a consequence of two separate but related publications. First, an article published in a newspaper on the alleged systematic violence suffered by White, German teachers in schools at the hands of students with migrant backgrounds,[37] which created ripples in the German public debate and prompted critical reactions to framing the issue in terms of racism.[38] Second, an official study on juvenile delinquency (*Jugendkriminalität*) by Germany's Interior Ministry in collaboration with the *Kriminologisches Forschungsinstitut Niedersachsen* (KFN) published in July 2010,[39] contained a specific section referring to hostilities towards Germans (*Feindseligkeit gegenüber Deutschen*). The report explicitly used the term of Germanophobia (*Deutschenfeindlichkeit*) as the functional counterpart to xenophobia,[40] and then statistically evaluated the level of Germanophobia on the basis of different groups of people with migrant backgrounds. The results of the study then led to a public debate in which the step from xenophobia to outright racism against Germans was made. Most prominently, a newspaper article on this study appeared in one of Germany's main daily papers. While the article itself always refers to Germanophobia, it was published under the heading 'Racism' and towards the end of the piece the author states that 'intolerance cannot be rewarded with well intentioned tolerance. Intolerance has to be outlawed, just as racism, which now has to be nicely reduced to "so-called Germanophobia".'[41] These two debates

anti-"Blancs"', *Le Monde*, 16 March 2005, p. 9, and Blandine Grosjean, 'Malaise après un appel contre le "racisme anti-Blancs"', *Libération*, 26 March 2005, pp. 14–15.

36 See Laetitia van Eeckhout, 'Un appel est lancé contre les "ratonnades anti-Blancs"', *Le Monde*, 26 March 2005, p. 10.

37 Andrea Posor and Christian Meyer, 'Deutschenfeindlichkeit in Schulen', *blz*, no. 11/2009, available at: www.gew-berlin.de/1297_1485.php.

38 See e.g. Yasemin Shooman and Evelin Lubig Fohsel, 'Unter Kartoffeln', *taz*, 7 October 2010, available at: www.taz.de/1/debatte/kommentar/artikel/1/unter-kartoffeln/, and Yasemin Shooman, '"Deutschenfeindlichkeit". Zur problematischen Verwendung des Begriffs', *blz – Zeitschrift der GEW Berlin*, no. 12/2010, p. 11, available at: www.gew-berlin.de/1296_1310.php.

39 Dirk Baier, *et al.*, 'Kinder und Jugendliche in Deutschland: Gewalterfahrungen, Integration, Medienkonsum. Zweiter Bericht zum gemeinsamen Forschungsprojekt des Bundesministeriums des Innern und des KFN' (2010), Forschungsbericht Nr. 109, available at: www.kfn.de/versions/kfn/assets/fob109.pdf.

40 *Ibid.*, p. 67.

41 Regina Mönch, 'Das Schweigen der Schulen über Deutschenfeindlichkeit', *Frankfurter Allgemeine Zeitung*, 15 October 2010, p. 31. Translation by the author.

then provided sufficient material for Kristina Schröder, the then Family Minister, to grant the issue a more prominent place in her political agenda and ultimately politically mainstreaming the term *Deutschenfeindlichkeit.*

Anti-White racism in its mainstreamed version shows very clearly how partially colourblind narratives on race function. On the one hand, race and racism are being eliminated whenever it is used in an anti-subordination manner or with the purpose of ameliorating the plight of visible minorities, thus ultimately leaving those minorities at the hands of restrictive and repressive laws and practices and with little effective protection from anti-discrimination legislation. Class analysis instead is invoked as the more acceptable option in order to help those minorities. On the other hand, as soon as the majority sees some sort of hostility or attack on its privileges – namely going about undisturbed, uninsulted, and unthreatened in their daily business – the same class analysis invoked with regard to racial and racialised minorities is tossed aside. What happens to White students or teachers is immediately interpreted almost exclusively in racial terms. All of a sudden race and racism are back in the picture, but ironically only in order to invoke protection of the majority.

The ease and absence of reflection with which this twist occurs shows how little the concern is really about the difficult term race and more about its instrumental use. Moreover, it flattens out the power dimensions existing behind racism. While a minority or even a majority devoid of power in a certain constituency is a potential victim of structural racism, the same cannot be said of a majority, or minority, in power. Racism relies on this power imbalance and is in part constituted by it. Calling something anti-White racism within Europe creates the illusion of an existing symmetry in power and everyday situations. However, being White/Christian-French or White/Christian-German does not amount to the same experiences of social handicap or racial stigmatisation that are exacerbated by legislation and institutions, which is not limited to the private sphere. Similar reflections apply to the more commonly used reference to 'reverse discrimination'. As a consequence, whereas when visible minorities denounce race and racism as occurring to them, class, religion, and citizenship or other narratives as well as narrow definitions and understandings of race and racism are put forward. On the contrary, when the victims of aggression, harassment, and violence are those belonging to the White/Christian-European majority, the reading of such events becomes quickly and almost exclusively racial.

Whereas the debate about anti-White racism has been sociological so far, Kristina Schröder has proposed to expand the legal definition of the crime of sedition (*Volksverhetzung*) so as to include *Deutschenfeindlichkeit.*[42] It is not hard to see how that vision and version will easily be recognised and applied by judges, legislators,

42 See the interview with Kristina Schröder in *Focus*, 17 October 2010, available at: www.focus.de/politik/deutschland/integration-schroeder-fordert-offene-debatte-ueber-rassistische-muslime_aid_562954.html.

and actors involved in the criminal justice sector alike.[43] The arguments of reverse discrimination have worked well already in other contexts. Recent case law by the U.S. Supreme Court on race shows where all claims, except for one, accepted by the court during the last twenty years have involved White people. Moreover, it is not difficult to imagine that judges would have less hesitation about believing the version of the White victim with much more ease and about attributing the aggravating factor of racism to cases of 'anti-White' violence.

4.2 Continental European colourblindness

What I have tried to do so far is show the rhetorical arsenal of arguments, phrases, and stories raised in mainland Europe when addressing race. While there are obvious divergences due to the different histories, it will not have escaped the reader how this resonates with the observations of Bonilla-Silva's *Racism without Races*[44] and his analyses around the subtle forms of discrimination in the post-Civil Rights era, which ultimately helped justify White domination and racial inequalities. Unsurprisingly, Balibar also named the paradox of on-going and perceived racism in the absence of race talk: '*racisme sans races*'.[45] Certain parallels and insights can also be drawn from Goldberg's *The Racial State*, which demonstrates from the perspective of political philosophy and theory how modern nation-states are based on racial distinctions, discrimination, management, and violence.[46] Modern state formation is thus deeply intertwined with racial formation. Both publications are extremely relevant in order to understand some of the broader implications described in this book, which can be seen as integrating or loosely entering into a dialogue with both by looking more closely at the European reality and law's contribution to racism without races and the racial state.

In fact, what is often lacking is a similar account and collection of cases, statutes, decisions, and interpretations that would coherently join them under one unified framework so as to demonstrate how law in mainland European nation-states had its fair share in creating, constructing, and perpetuating race thought, racism, and the racial state. In other words, a European timeline on the history of European racial minorities such as the one provided in Chapter 1 on the history of American racial minorities does not exist as of today. Such a timeline would certainly include the most outrageous and explicit forms of racism and race thought that are found in law and established through law. The most prevalent legal data mapped on this timeline would range from racial legislation against Jews, to colonial legislation, to the legal discrimination against the Roma. Moreover, it would also include less

43 For a doctrinal attempt to broaden the application of Article 130 of the German Criminal Code, see Wolfgang Mitsch, 'Volksverhetzung gegen Deutsche', *Juristische Rundschau* (2011), pp. 380–382.

44 Eduardo Bonilla-Silva, *Racism without Races: Color-Blind Racism and the Persistence of Racial Inequality in America*, 4th edn (Lanham: Rowman & Littlefield, 2013).

45 Etienne Balibar, 'Y-a-t-il un "néo-racisme"?' in Etienne Balibar and Immanuel Wallerstein, *Race, nation, classe* (Paris: Editions La Découverte Syros, 1997), p. 33.

46 Goldberg, *The Racial State* (Oxford: Blackwell, 1993).

explicit and more modern and subtle forms of racism and race discrimination, including Orientalism and Islamophobia as embedded in immigration legislation, citizenship laws, and legislation on the prohibition of headscarves, as well as judicial interpretations of human rights and anti-discrimination legislation.

While such a story is beyond the scope of this book, this section attempts to roughly identify the key legal elements of 'Continental European Colourblindness'. This type of colourblindness can be observed in most continental European systems and is constituted of two different, yet interrelated components that rely heavily on the rhetorical manoeuvres as described above and the representation of race as a taboo: (i) a legally and politically constructed absence of race; and (ii) a legally constructed absence of racists and racism. In particular, the argument is that the removal of race, or any of its traces, from European legislation and jurisprudence in turn establishes a socially, politically, and legally constructed absence of racists and of racism. As a result, racial interpretations in the social and legal domain become almost impossible, especially when they overlap with issues of citizenship or religion.

4.2.1 *The legally and politically constructed absence of race*

On a spectrum of attitudes towards race, it is safe to say that most continental European countries can be classified as racial sceptics. The reason is that most countries in this geographical area, apart from the United Kingdom and Ireland, have in some way or another been influenced, directly or indirectly, by the Nazi regime. In response, owing to modern constitutions and international treaties banning and punishing race thought and racism after World War II, continental Europeans gradually stopped using race as an analytical category in social sciences and refrained from framing social and legal issues in terms of race. For the most part, the Holocaust and its aftermath, which led to the argument of the non-existence of biological race, constitutes the main way of reading race and racism in mainland Europe.

From a policy point of view, this position has played out either by attempting to eliminate any reference to race from legal instruments or by half-heartedly implementing the limited race-conscious provisions. As to the first option, at the international level, during the debate on the General Policy Recommendation No. 7 on national legislation to combat racism and racial discrimination, the European Commission on Racism and Intolerance (ECRI) discussed whether the word race should be removed from the grounds of discrimination.[47] Paragraph 6 of the preamble to the Race Equality Directive (RED)[48] reflects a similar unease with the use of the terms race or racial origins, by providing that '[t]he European Union

47 Giancarlo Cardinale, 'The Preparation of ECRI General Policy Recommendation No. 7', in Jan Niessen and Isabelle Chopin (eds), *The Development of Legal Instruments to Combat Racism in a Diverse Europe* (Leiden: M. Nijhoff, 2004), p. 84 at fn. 7.

48 Directive 2000/43/EC of 29 June 2000.

rejects theories which attempt to determine the existence of separate human races. The use of the term "racial origin" in this Directive does not imply an acceptance of such theories.'[49]

At the national level, one can observe various attempts to either completely eliminate race from public discourse and legislation, or to re-formulate it in the softer terms like ethnicity, ethnic belonging, xenophobia, or racial preference. For instance, in France the debate already dates back to the early 1990s with scholars discussing and proposing various solutions as to whether 'the word "race" is too much in the Constitution'.[50] This later led to various legislative proposals to eliminate race from all legislation,[51] and from the equality principle enshrined in Article 1 of the Constitution[52] on the grounds that since races do not exist, the legal language should not perpetuate the idea of their existence. In Germany, one can observe a similar trend in recent academic proposals to eliminate the word race (*Rasse*) from the grounds of discrimination contained in Article 3 of the German Basic Law (the *Grundgesetz*)[53] and to substitute it with the term 'racial disadvantage' (*rassistische Benachteiligung*).[54] Following the pressure of national non-governmental organisations (NGOs), Austria has already gone one step further by substituting the word race with the expression 'ethnic belonging' (*ethnische Zugehörigkeit*) in part II of the 2004 Federal Equal Treatment Act (*Gleichbehandlungsgesetz*)[55] when implementing the RED.[56] The preparatory works made clear that the replacement is not aimed at limiting the scope of application but merely at eliminating the term *Rasse* with all the negative connotations that this term carries with it in the German language.[57]

49 Similar disclaimers are almost a must for continental European scholars if they do not want to be perceived or accused of being race apologists.
50 This was the question asked to a number of academics during a conference entitled 'Sans distinction de … race' which took place on 27–28 March 1992. The conference papers were published in the journal *Mots* (1992), no. 33.
51 Michel Vaxes, *et al.*, 'Proposition de loi tendant à la suppression du mot "race" de notre législation', No. 623, XIIe Législature (13 mars 2003), available at: www.assemblee-nationale.fr/12/cra/2002-2003/164.asp, and 'Proposition de loi tendant à la suppression du mot "race" de notre législation', No. 218, XIVe Législature (16 May 2013), available at: www.assemblee-nationale.fr/14/ta/ta0139.asp.
52 Victorin Lurel, *et al.*, 'Proposition de Loi constitutionnelle, visant à supprimer le mot "race" de l'article premier de la Constitution', No. 1918, XIIe Législature (14 November 2004), available at: http://lurel.parti-socialiste.fr/files/pion1918.pdf.
53 See e.g. Susanne Baer, 'The Basic Law at 60 – Equality and Difference: A Proposal for the Guest List to the Birthday Party', *German Law Journal* (2010), vol. 11, no. 1, p. 86.
54 Hendrik Cremer, '"… und welcher Rasse gehören Sie an?" Zur Problematik des Begriffs "Rasse" in der Gesetzgebung', *Deutsches Institut für Menschenrechte, Policy Paper No. 10*, November 2009, and Hendrik Cremer, 'Ein Grundgesetz ohne "Rasse". Vorschlag für eine Änderung des Artikels 3 Grundgesetz', *Deutsches Institut für Menschenrechte, Policy Paper No. 16*, April 2010.
55 *Bundesgesetz über die Gleichbehandlung (Gleichbehandlungsgesetz – GlBG)*, 23 June 2004, *BGBl* I, no. 66/2004.
56 Directive 2000/43/EC of 29 June 2000.
57 Willibald Posch, 'Gleichbehandlungsgebot' in Robert Rebhahn (ed.), *Kommentar zum Gleichbehandlungsgesetz* (Wien, New York: Springer, 2005), § 31, pp. 512–513.

However, the racial sceptic position in the legal domain does not only concern the term race as such but also its applications or implementation. For instance, in a decision by the French Constitutional Council (*Conseil constitutionnel*), which will be discussed more in detail in the second part of Chapter 5, the members of the constitutional court declared unconstitutional the use of racial or ethnic origins in legislation authorising studies on discrimination, because they are not deemed to be objective.[58] The memories of how racial and ethnic origins had been used during the Vichy regime in France undoubtedly played a role in deciding this case.[59] Last but not least, a similar reluctance emerged during the implementation of a number of European directives, specifically the RED and the Equal Treatment Framework Directive,[60] where the former has been portrayed as introducing a race-conscious approach into the German legal system.[61] The entry into force of the German Anti-discrimination Act (*Allgemeines Gleichbehandlungsgesetz*, AGG)[62] was viewed as a 'cultural revolution',[63] which threatened to introduce 'American conditions',[64] and to impose 'political correctness as a legal obligation'.[65] It is hard to gauge if these examples could also be the result of a certain bias by European leftist intellectual legal scholars 'against "Uncle Sam" and United States political hegemony',[66] or a general anti-Americanism in legal academia.

What can be gauged and analysed, however, are the consequences of these positions in the legal domain. On the one hand, substituting the legislative use of race with other terms such as ethnicity or ethnic belonging or using xenophobia instead of racism in no way eliminates the social reality and gravity of racism. One of the unintended effects is that it covers up an uncomfortable reality by using cushier terms which are more acceptable for mainstream society. While a positive consequence is that racist behaviour that would otherwise go unsanctioned is punished, it can at the same time leave the victims of racism deprived of a strong

58 Decision CC 2007–557 DC, 15 November, 2007, especially point 29.

59 Esther Duflo, 'Délicates questions ethniques', *Libération*, 26 November 2007, p. 37. The centrality of the memory of Vichy more in general and its effects on French antidiscrimination law has been recently highlighted by Julie Suk, 'Equal By Comparison: Unsettling Assumptions of Antidiscrimination Law', *American Journal of Comparative Law* (2007), vol. 55, p. 295.

60 Directive 2000/78/EC of 27 November 2000 establishing a general framework for equal treatment in employment and occupation, *Official Journal (OJ) L 303* of 2 December 2000, pp. 16–22.

61 See Andrew Geddes and Virginie Guiraudon, 'Britain, France and EU Anti-Discrimination Policy: The Emergence of an EU Policy Paradigm', *West European Politics*, (2004), vol. 27, no. 2, pp. 334–353.

62 *Allgemeines Gleichbehandlungsgesetz (AGG)*, 14 August, 2006, *BGBl.* I, p. 1897.

63 Alexander Wolff, 'Kulturrevolution im Arbeitsrecht', *Arbeit und Arbeitsrecht* (2005), vol. 60, no. 2, pp. 82–85.

64 Dieter Straub, 'Drohen amerikanische Verhältnisse?', *Arbeit und Arbeitsrecht* (2005), vol. 60, no. 2, p. 65.

65 Klaus Adomeit, 'Political correctness – jetzt Rechtspflicht!', *Neue Juristische Wochenschrift* (2006), p. 2169.

66 Ugo Mattei and Anna di Robilant, 'The Art and Science of Critical Legal Scholarship: Postmodernism and International Style in the Legal Architecture of Europe', *Tulane Law Review* (2001), vol. 75, p. 1062.

moral instrument to denounce such crimes and deny them the recognition of their experience of racism. On the other hand, changing the name provides a rosier picture, which amounts to an artificial confirmation, suggesting that we have managed to overcome racism and race thought because it has a different name. Another risk to not talking about race may cause the instruments, put in place to the fight against race discrimination, to loose their bite and their scope of application and enforcement.

The comparison between the United States and Europe also serves to highlight the parallels between this 'Continental European Colourblindness' and its American counterpart. In spite of the differences, both emerged from a 'progressive' anti-racist strategy: the former as a reaction to the persecution of Jews and the latter during the times of segregation. However, what was deemed a progressive and likely well-meant position back then has turned out to have severe negative effects today, by undermining the attempts to introduce an effective anti-discrimination strategy to address these historical injustices. Nonetheless, these traditional approaches to the question of race have become entrenched in the ideology of conservative judges, politicians, and academics alike, and have also negatively impacted short-sighted and undifferentiated positions within left wing circles as well.

Yet, there is one way in which race disappears somewhat differently in Europe than in the United States, which is in large part due to their differing histories of racisms. In the former reality, race tends to disappear behind the veil of religion and citizenship. In fact, certain aspects of anti-Semitism or Islamophobia can be framed in terms of religion or religious freedom rather than in terms of race, racism, or race discrimination. Because of this, the issue no longer becomes one of racism but one of religion or secularism. For instance, the debates on headscarves and burqa bans, which will be analysed below in the case study on Italy, together with anti-Muslim publications and recent debates on male circumcision,[67] are mainly and often interpreted as an issue of religious freedom or of religious differences, without considering any of the potential underlying racial aspects.[68] Another example showing how the overlap between religion and race plays out in Europe comes from a recent United Kingdom Supreme Court case.[69] The issue was whether imposing a criterion for a child to be born by a Jewish mother through the matrilineal test or through conversion in order to be admitted to a Jewish school constituted direct racial discrimination under the Race Relations Act 1976. The problem was that the school rejected the child applicant because the mother did not fulfil the Orthodox criteria of conversion. A majority of five

67 See e.g. the decision by a German Court of Appeals holding that religiously motivated male circumcision of a child is a crime: Landesgericht Köln, Az. 151 Ns 169/11, 7 May 2012.

68 See for an attempt to place religious issues and the study of anti-Semitism and Islamophobia within the fields of race and racism Nasar Meer, 'Racialization and Religion: Race, Culture and Difference in the Study of Antisemitism and Islamophobia', *Ethnic and Racial Studies* (2013), vol. 36, no. 3, pp. 385–398.

69 *R(E) v. Governing Body of JFS* [2009], UKSC 15.

judges held that this constituted direct discrimination on the grounds of race, whereas the two dissenting opinions found that the admission criteria indirectly discriminated on the grounds of race. This was partly possible because the judges distinguished between causation and motive. Regarding the matrilineal requirement that the mother lacked, the court held that race or ethnicity had caused the differential treatment. Whether the motive for doing so was religious was of little relevance. It is clear that this case highlighted the problem caused by the overlap between race and religion and calling the Jewish school racially discriminatory due to the ways the boundaries of Jewish religion and determining Jewishness are defined. This was a good example where racial aspects emerged and it is not a surprise that this case arose in the United Kingdom and was decided in such terms. The question now is whether it would have been possible to do the same thing in Germany, Italy, or France.

Citizenship is the second way in which race and racism disappear behind a legal cloak. This is especially true with regard to colonialism that relied heavily on a geographical separation. This separation was formally upheld by citizenship laws, which often relied on a racial understanding and difference.[70] For example, after the abolition of slavery, France introduced the colonial subject, the *indigène*, who was distinguished from the French citizen. Thus, until 1946, in most French colonies there lived French citizens, French subjects, and French *protégés* with different legal regimes applying to each group.[71] With some exception, the dividing line between these two categories was determined by the colour of their skin.[72] The racial aspects of citizenship laws also came into play at the moment of decolonisation when, for instance, in 1968 the United Kingdom introduced the concept of 'patriality'. This meant that only British citizens, who were born in the United Kingdom or had a parent or grandparent who was a British citizen, could enter the United Kingdom without previous authorisation. In essence this amounted to a racial boundary, according to which White British Africans or White British Indians could come to the United Kingdom without any controls while Black ones from the same areas could not.[73] Later legislation confirmed the concept without explicitly naming it and remains in force today, despite legal challenges being brought before the European Commission of Human Rights (ECommHR)

70 See for the German citizenship law of 1913 Dieter Gosewinkel, 'Rückwirkungen des kolonialen Rasserechts' Deutsche Staatsangehörigkeit zwischen Rassestaat und Rechsstaat', in Sebastian Conrad and Jürgen Osterhammel (eds), *Das Kaiserreich transnational. Deutschland in der Welt 1871–1914*, 2nd edn (Göttingen, Vandenhoeck & Rupprecht, 2006), pp. 236–256.

71 For more details on this, see Emmanuelle Saada, 'Une nationalité par degrés', in Patrick Weil and Stéphane Dufoix (eds), *L'esclavage, la colonisation et après* (Paris: Presses universitaires de France, 2005), pp. 193–226.

72 The *indigène* was introduced by the *Code de l'Indigénat* promulgated by the French government on 28 June 1881 and whose application was extended to all colonies in 1887. It was officially abolished in 1946. For a critical vision of these *Codes*, see Henri Cartier, *Comment la France 'civilise' ses colonies* (Paris: les nuits rouges, 2006).

73 See Christian Joppke, *Selecting by Origin: Ethnic Migration in the Liberal State* (Cambridge, MA: Harvard University Press, 2005), in particular pp. 149–154.

and the ECtHR. In two separate cases, the European judges rejected the race discrimination claims involving British immigration rules finding only a violation of human dignity and gender discrimination for some of the applicants in the former,[74] and one of gender discrimination in the latter.[75] In many ways citizenship guarantees the invisibilisation of racial lines, which are most easily recognised when explicitly stated, such as in the United States until 1965. However, they are less evident when such rules are racially neutralised and framed in more acceptable terms thus ending up having 'only' a disparate racial impact.[76]

Given these precedents and the racial implications and exclusions of many citizenship laws, it should not come as a huge surprise that the RED explicitly states that it:

> does not cover difference of treatment based on nationality and is without prejudice to provisions and conditions relating to the entry into and residence of third-country nationals and stateless persons on the territory of Member States, and to any treatment which arises from the legal status of the third-country nationals and stateless persons concerned.[77]

This ensured that many provisions with a disparate racial impact would not fall under the purview of this legal instrument.

These examples demonstrate the various ways in which race disappears legally in the European context, which gives the impression that the relationship between race and law plays a marginal role in Europe, especially when compared to the United States.

4.2.2 *The legally constructed absence of racism and racists*

The problem illustrated above is compounded further when looking at race scepticism in mainland Europe as illustrated in legal scholarship and instruments. The reluctance to frame objects or situations in terms of race also extends to a reluctance to frame persons as racists or their behaviour in terms of racism. Consequently, a narrow legal definition of racism and a racist under law emerges. In fact, not talking about race has all but eliminated racism in the legal realm.

74 ECommHR, *East African Asians v. the United Kingdom*, nos. 4403/70–4419/70 (and more), 14 December 1973 (finding that singling out a group for differential treatment on racial grounds in immigration policies constitutes a special affront to human dignity and is therefore in violation of Article 3 ECHR, but at the same time limiting the discrimination finding to one of gender discrimination). See also more recently ECHR, *Biao v. Denmark*, no. 38590/10, 25 March, 2014.

75 ECtHR, *Abdulaziz and Others v. the United Kingdom*, nos. 9214/80, 9473/81, 9474/81, 28 May 1985.

76 In this sense, Patrick Weil can find that French citizenship legislation post-World War II avoided the explicitly racial and racist turn because he is comparing it to the explicit racial laws under the Vichy Regime. Patrick Weil, 'Racisme et discrimination dans la politique française de l'immigration 1938–1945/1974–1995', *Vingtième Siècle* (1995), vol. 47, pp. 77–102.

77 Article 3(2), RED.

Europe has put in place provisions penalising racism, racial discrimination and racial hatred mostly through the implementation of international law such as the United Nations' International Convention on the Elimination of All Forms of Racial Discrimination (ICERD), Article 14 of the European Convention on Human Rights (ECHR), and the RED. While these instruments are clearly a step in the right direction they nevertheless demonstrate clear shortcomings which cast some doubt over the real will and intention to apply them effectively throughout Europe.

With regard to the first of these legal instruments, one of the problems with the ICERD is that it demands that states punish individual acts of racial discrimination and racism through criminal law. Since criminal law focuses mostly on acts committed by an individual, this reinforces the idea that racism is merely the product of random actions of irrational individuals or delusional neo-Nazis and fails to address patterns of historical and structural racial discrimination generated by the specific European experience and context of anti-Semitism, Islamophobia, colonialism, and (im)migration. Moreover, the intent requirement of criminal law often prevents certain acts from being characterised as racial discrimination, thereby leading to a patchy and limited application of national legislation implementing the ICERD.

In Italy, for example, the ICERD was ratified by statute in 1975.[78] However, convictions under this statute and its successive amendments were and remain exceptional.[79] This explains the broad public attention to a trial involving the promoters of a political campaign requesting the closure of Roma camps and their removal from Verona's territory by arguing that gypsies are thieves.[80] The promoters were convicted for the dissemination of racially discriminatory ideas and incitement to racially discriminatory acts.[81] The Venice Court of Appeals upheld the conviction but reduced the conviction to dissemination of racially discriminatory ideas while dropping the charges for incitement of racially discriminatory acts.[82] The Italian Supreme Court, the *Corte di Cassazione*, annulled this decision

78 *Legge* No. 654, 13 October 1975, *Gazzetta Ufficiale (GU)* No. 337, 23 December 1975. This statute was amended by the *Legge* No. 205, 25 June 1993, *Gazzetta Ufficiale (GU)* No. 148, 26 June 1993.

79 One of the early cases finding someone guilty for race discrimination under this statutory framework involved a Moroccan and a Tunisian citizen who were denied access to a place in which – ironically – there was an on-going show of African dances. See Tribunale di Torino, Sezione I penale: 13 January 1997, *Questione giustizia* (1997), no. 2, pp. 478–483 with a note by Angelo Caputo, 'Discriminazioni razziali e repressione penale' in the same journal issue at pp. 476–478.

80 The public prosecutor on this case explained that the absence of case law under this statutory framework is caused by the absence of doctrinal comments and general ignorance of it by legal operators. Guido Papalia, 'Efficacia della tutela penale nella repression dei reati di discriminazione razziale: gli strumenti della Legge Mancino', in Ministero per le Pari Opportunità, *Il ruolo della difesa nel contrasto alle discriminazioni razziali ed etniche*, vol. 28 (Roma: Demetra, 2006), p. 71.

81 Tribunale di Verona: Sentenza no. 2203, 2 December 2004, *Diritto, immigrazione e cittadinanza* (2005), no. 2, pp. 191–220, with a note by Lorenzo Picotti, 'La discriminazione razziale e la politica: riflessioni su una recente sentenza del tribunale di Verona', in the same journal pp. 69–92.

82 Corte d'appello di Venezia, Sezione IV: Sentenza 2 April 2007.

and it was remanded to the Venice Court of Appeals, because the appellate court's decision was not detailed enough and not logically convincing.[83] On remand, a different chamber of the Venice Court of Appeals confirmed the first decision but on this occasion the revised reasoning was more complete and convincing.[84] The defendants then decided to petition the Supreme Court but the *Cassazione* rejected the petition, which ultimately put an end to this complex judicial affair.[85] What is important to garner from these legal proceedings was that the sanctions and damage awards were reduced considerably, and the trial did not have any impact on the popularity of the campaign promoters. Indeed, Verona's civil society supported the defendants by protesting during the trial and by electing one of the promoters of this campaign, Flavio Tosi, to become mayor of Verona.[86] It is very telling that it was one of the few decisions on national legislation implementing the ICERD over the last thirty years.[87]

A similar case was recently decided in Portugal under Article 250 of the Portuguese Criminal Code, the national provision implementing the ICERD with regard to racist violence and hatred. In that case the Nationalist Party (*Partido Nacionalista Renovador*) had hung posters from their premises on a Lisbon square stating: 'IMMIGRATION? We say NO! Enough of abuse: open frontiers, dependence benefits, low wages, criminality and multiculturism. Portugal to Portuguese.' In addition to this, a picture showed a white lamb, representing nationals, expelling black lambs, representing immigrants, from the country. José Coelho, the President of the Nationalist Party, who had already been accused of racist statements in other instances, was responsible for the signs. During the trial he argued that he had had no intention of expressing any racist or xenophobic statements and that, in any event, he had the right to freedom of expression. The trial judge dismissed the public prosecutor's accusation that the statements constituted a racist act against immigrants, on the ground that they were only against immigration. The trial judge also held that they were not racist since they did not refer specifically to race or ethnic origin but rather addressed immigration as a

83 Corte di Cassazione, Sezione III penale: Sentenza no. 13234, 13 December 2007, published partially in *Giurisprudenza italiana* (2009), pp. 164–167 with a note by Simone Ferrari, 'Sul concetto di discriminazione razziale penalmente rilevante', in the same journal at pp. 167–171.

84 Corte d'appello di Venezia, Sezione I: Sentenza no. 1553, 20 October 2008.

85 Corte di Cassazione, Sezione IV penale: Sentenza No. 41819, 10 July 2009, published in *Cassazione penale* (2010), No. 6, pp. 2347–2353 with a note by Federica Panizzo, 'Quando la propaganda politica diviene propaganda razzista' in the same journal issue at pp. 2353–2365.

86 See also on the limited moral and political consequences of a conviction for racial slander the case of France's former Interior Minister, Brice Hortefeux, who was convicted for racial slander. Sentenced to a €750 fine and €2000 as damages (Tribunal de Grande Instance de Paris, 17ème Chambre correctionelle, Decision no. 0928108356, 4 June 2010), his conviction neither prevented him from keeping his position as Interior Minister nor from being named special counsel to the French President.

87 For a comment on this decision, see Corrado Caruso, 'Dialettica della libertà di espressione: il "caso Tosi" e la propaganda di idee razziste', in Diletta Tega (ed.), *Le discriminazioni razziali ed etniche* (Roma: Armando Editore, 2011), pp. 133–150.

whole and consequently the judge refused to find the defendant guilty. The Lisbon Court of Appeal confirmed this decision by holding that no explicit reference to racial or ethnic origin was made in the poster and that there was no certainty that racial discrimination against immigrants was being incited or encouraged through the signs.[88] The Italian and the Portuguese cases show the difficulties that courts encounter when applying the provisions deriving from the ICERD. This may be in part due to technical-criminal law related issues. However, suspicion arises that something else might be at play.

On top of criminalising race discrimination and incitement/encouragement of race discrimination pursuant to the ICERD, many European countries such as France, Italy, and Austria also introduced racism or racial hatred as an aggravating factor of a crime. Here again, a look at the scant case law in different countries demonstrates the limits of such provisions. For example, in Milan in 2008 a store owner and his son clubbed an Italian teenager of colour, Abdul Salam Guiebre, to death for stealing some cookies and two bars of chocolate from their store with a group of friends. The two men followed them in a van, attacked and killed one of them, while yelling racial epithets during the murder. They were charged with murder but the public prosecutor only asked for a charge of an aggravated crime for futile motives and not for racist ones. As a result, instead of increasing the penalty by half it was only increased by one third. Moreover, the defendants benefited from general mitigating circumstances because of good behaviour during the trial despite never expressing any apology. Finally, the penalty was reduced by a third because they followed the short track procedure. Thus, the trial court eventually sentenced the two men to 'only' 15 years and 4 months imprisonment and awarded a total of €175,000 compensation to the victim's family.[89] Admittedly, mitigating circumstances or short track procedures are nothing unusual in the Italian judiciary. Moreover, the way in which the aggravating factor is formulated in Article 3 of Statute No. 205/1993, namely requiring that the crime be committed for the *purpose* (*per finalità*) of racial hatred or racism and not just motivated by racial hatred or racism, allows for a very formalistic interpretation and limited application. An interpretation by Italy's Supreme Court, the *Corte di Cassazione*, supports the potential restrictive interpretation of aggravating circumstances. Indeed, in another case the *Cassazione* had already held that the aggravating circumstances of racial hatred applies when the crime is 'motivated *exclusively* by the consideration that the victim belongs to a different race',[90] meaning that as soon as any other motivation for the commission of a crime arises – in this case the reaction to the theft of some biscuits – the racial and racist motivation will not be counted anymore. By itself this interpretation already demonstrates how little the protection of victims of racist crimes matters when translated into law.

88 Tribunal da Relação de Lisboa: Case 59862/08.7TDLSB.L1, 1 February 2011.

89 Tribunale di Milano: Sentenza no. 1586, 16 July 2009.

90 Corte di Cassazione, Sezione V penale: Sentenza no. 38217, 12 June 2008 (italics added). In that case, nevertheless, the Supreme Court had found in favour of the victim.

What is even more interesting and unusual in this case is that the trial court found it necessary to justify the prosecutor's decision not to request aggravating circumstances of a racially motivated crime. Usually, judges are required to address only points addressed by the parties and since neither the prosecutor nor the defence had raised the issue of aggravating circumstances the judges could have simply ignored this point. Instead, they justified its non-application by stating that the murderer's behaviour could be explained by the state of mind of someone who finds himself more afflicted and upset due to the theft and ridicule by foreigners. The court went on to explain that this state of mind reflects a vision towards the conservation of cultural and territorial integrity and is without any underlying theory of discrimination and racial supremacy. Whereas the racial slur of 'dirty niggers' needs to be read like 'shitty Whites' (*bianchi di merda*) or 'shitty Italians' (*italiani di merda*) that were yelled by the victims during the events, the reference to the foreign origins of the thieves constitutes a different type of hostility which is not linked to racial supremacy.[91] We have here a textbook example of how an evidently racist crime, corroborated by witness evidence, is being legally 'whitewashed' by the judges who ultimately side and sympathise with the perpetrator. Not only do we have the symmetrical vision which places the racist insult at the same level as the insults against White Italians,[92] but we also see the restrictive interpretation of what constitutes racism, i.e. only biological racism and racial supremacy. Moreover, the judges' mindset and bias also emerges in their regular references to the youths as 'foreigners', even though Abdul Guiebre was an Italian citizen. The judges do not seem to heed this otherwise legally important detail. On the contrary, when the case eventually reached the Supreme Court, the *Cassazione*, the summary of the events regularly refers to the youths as 'young Moroccans' (*giovani marocchini*), which is more generally an offensive reference to foreign, third country nationals from Africa and is patently wrong because none of the youths involved were Moroccan. What the *Cassazione* also did is to remand the case to the appeals court on the issue of aggravating circumstance for futile motives. It held that the judges on appeal had not sufficiently taken into account the broader circumstances that make these futile circumstances seem less futile, namely that the murderer was of low class and culture, had worked the whole day, was tired and was nevertheless willing to work all night, whereas the foreign youths had stolen from and ridiculed him after partying through the night.[93] Again, the judges more willingly empathised with the version of the White, Italian defendant than with the Black, Italian victim.

A confirmation of this judicial unease, ambiguity, and bias comes from another case in which the Italian *Corte di Cassazione* found that someone addressing a group of Colombian women with the words 'dirty Nigger' (*sporche negre*) and 'what are these Niggers doing here?' (*cosa fanno queste negre qua?*) constituted slander but was

91 Tribunale di Milano: Sentenza no. 1586, 16 July 2009, p. 14.

92 See *supra* on the discussion on anti-White racism.

93 Corte di Cassazione, Sezione I penale: Sentenza no. 31454, 1 August 2012.

not aggravated by racist motives.[94] It later reversed its decision in a very similar case, in which a six-year-old girl of colour who was joining her father was shooed away from a public meeting with the words 'go away from here, dirty Nigger' (*vai via di qua, sporca negra!*).[95] Confirming the later line of cases, the same court held that calling someone 'bastard boar, dirty Arab' (*cinghiale bastardo, sporco arabo*) constituted slander aggravated by racist motives. The interesting aspect here is that the Supreme Court held that the aggravating circumstances applied when it referred 'to a clear prejudice against one race *regardless of the intent of the actor*'.[96] This means that the plaintiff does not need to show the defendant's racial motivations but the mere utterance of the words is sufficient to trigger the application of the aggravating circumstances. Whereas the latter two cases indicate that it is possible to legally interpret Article 3 of Statute 205/1993 in ways that protect the victims of racism – namely avoiding second-guessing the subjective purpose of the actor and instead looking at the intrinsically discriminatory effect on the victim[97] – these cases are just another example of how difficult courts find it to hand down a judgment in seemingly obvious cases.[98]

The importance of the distinction between slander and slander aggravated by racist motives is not only relevant with regards to the severity of the punishment but also has important implications at the procedural level. This is illustrated in a recent case of the Supreme Court. By holding that telling someone, 'African, go back to eat bananas! Monkey!', is characterised as slander aggravated by racist motives, the *Corte di Cassazione* was able to annul a lower court's decision not to pursue a case because the complaint had been withdrawn.[99] Whereas simple slander can be prosecuted only in the presence of a complainant, slander aggravated

94 Corte di Cassazione, Sezione V penale: Sentenza no. 44295, 5 December 2005; excerpts published in *Rivista italiana di diritto e procedura penale* (2007), pp. 1449–1450.

95 Corte di Cassazione, Sezione V penale: Sentenza no. 9381, 20 January 2006; excerpts published in *Rivista italiana di diritto e procedura penale* (2007), pp. 1450–1455. See also Lara Ferla, '"L'applicazione della finalita" di discriminazione razziale in alcune recenti pronounce della Corte di Cassazione', *Rivista italiana di diritto e procedura penale* (2007), pp. 1455–1475.

96 Corte di Cassazione, Sezione V penale: Sentenza no. 38597, 9 July 2009 (emphasis added), *Cassazione penale* (2010), no. 11, pp. 3832–3833 with a note by Maria Teresa Trapasso, 'Il ruolo fondamentale dei "coefficienti soggettivi" nelle fattispecie penali in materia di discriminazione razziale: il caso della circosatanza aggravante della finalita di discriminazione o di odio razziale' in the same journal issue at pp. 3833–3844.

97 This aspect/interpretation has been criticised because it is deemed to be against the black letter law which requires the presence of the subjective and motivational aspects of the crime. *Ibid.* at p. 3844.

98 In another decision the *Cassazione* held that calling someone '*marocchino*' (Moroccan) repeatedly over a longer period of time instead of addressing that person by the name or surname constituted an insult. The judges, however, did not apply the aggravating circumstance of racist motivations here probably because they were not raised by the prosecutors. Corte di Cassazione, Sezione V penale: Sentenza no. 19378, 5 April 2005 with note by Matteo Bellina, 'Sostantivazione dell'aggettivo che riflette la provenienza etnica della persona e delitto di ingiuria: il caso del "marocchino"', *Cassazione penale* (2006), no. 1, pp. 60 –65.

99 Corte di Cassazione, Sezione V penale: Sentenza no. 54694, 26 April 2011.

by racist motives can be prosecuted *ex officio*. Hence, the fact that the victim had withdrawn the complaint could not influence the procedure and the case was remanded to the lower court, which had erred in characterising the case as simple slander.

These examples are necessarily anecdotal but they raise serious questions about the extent of such cases and demonstrate the difficulty or reluctance of judicially establishing the presence of racism and racist motives behind crimes. This observation is confirmed by various reports and academic studies. For instance, the 2006 country report on Italy by the ECRI states that final sentences for racially aggravated offences were only handed down in three cases in 2001, four cases in 2002, two cases in 2003, and none in 2004.[100] Human Rights Watch (HRW) recently found that Germany's response to hate crimes, even if improved, was still insufficient and had a number of flaws.[101] Amnesty International (AI) also denounced widespread non-implementation of criminal law provisions for the protection against racism in the Austrian justice system.[102] Academic studies also seem to indicate that the failure to recognise racism, discrimination, and racist motives is a broader continental European problem. For instance, Michele Grigolo speaks about the ambiguous role the police play in dealing with racially motivated attacks in Barcelona.[103] Scandinavia is also not immune from the phenomenon as demonstrated by a Finnish study. The authors of the study looked at the implementation of Finnish hate crime legislation through an analysis of 107 police reports with racist elements, registered by the Helsinki police in 2006.[104] In none of the thirty-two cases that eventually made it before the court did the prosecutors demand harsher sentencing on the grounds of racial motivations, nor did the judges take the initiative to highlight the racist elements. The authors indicate a number of reasons why crimes with racist elements might be so difficult to encapsulate. First, they identify officials' lack of experience and incompetence in handling the harsher punishment for racially motivated crimes, which was introduced in 2003. Second, a large part of the racist crimes reported to the Finnish police are regarded as being subject to private prosecution and therefore only investigated if the victim so requests. Third, in a number of cases the situation involved mutual assaults in which the sequence of events is hard to establish and

100 European Commission against Racism and Intolerance, 'Third Report on Italy', CRI (2006) 19, p. 8.

101 Human Rights Watch, 'The State Response to "Hate Crimes in Germany"' (2011), available at: www.hrw.org/sites/default/files/related_material/State%20Response%20to%20%27Hate%20Crimes%27%20in%20Germany.pdf.

102 Amnesty International, 'Victim or Suspect: A Question of Colour. Racial Discrimination in the Austrian Justice System' (London: Amnesty International Publications, 2009).

103 Michele Grigolo, 'Human Rights and Cities: the Barcelona Office for Non-Discrimination and its Work for Migrants', *The International Journal of Human Rights* (2010), vol. 14, no. 6, pp. 896–914.

104 Laura Peutere and Juha Kääriänen, 'Racist Crimes in the Finnish Criminal Justice System – Analysis of Cases Reported to the Police in Helsinki in 2006', *European Journal of Crime, Criminal Law and Criminal Justice* (2010), vol. 18, no. 3, pp. 261–279.

the motivation of the parties difficult to assess. Fourth, despite clear racial slurs, often the prosecutors treated them like any other insult rather than as a motivating and aggravating factor.[105] The pattern emerging in this more systematic overview is clear: there is a disconnect between the victim's experience of racism and the legal system's assessment of the criminal situation. This is partly due to the fact that when the reported situation emerged it has often been preceded by a number of single incidents which add up but which the police and criminal justice system fail to analyse as a whole.[106] What the study fails to consider or mention is the conscious or unconscious bias by policemen and other agents in the criminal justice system. This aspect is, however, examined carefully in another sociological study in France. In this study, the authors exclude the charge that the existing differences in criminal sanctions for certain specific crimes between White French and non-White defendants are caused by the judges' bias. Nevertheless, such bias seems to influence the police forces and their decisions to intervene during trials as third party claiming civil damages.[107]

The cases and studies listed here show the widespread problem of judicial actors in the criminal process in dealing with issues of race and race discrimination in hard and easy cases alike. It is highly probable that these examples are only the tip of the iceberg. Situations of 'petty racism' suffered in everyday life by visible minorities in Europe are judicially trivialised and dismissed or interpreted as reactions of over-sensitive individuals.

What emerges from this brief discussion is a very narrow legal definition and understanding of what constitutes racism and therefore also who is deemed a racist or has committed a racially motivated crime. The difficulties of police, judges and institutions to recognise and sanction racially motivated crimes have a number of facets that require deeper reflection and analysis. First, it vastly reduces the phenomenon of racism and the existence of racists, thus making European societies and their statistics on racist crimes look much better than they actually are. Second, in light of the current situation our construction of a racist is extremely narrow and limited to the most evident and outrageous cases. And even in those cases, sometimes one can only wonder what else must be done in order to qualify the crime as racially motivated. This legal construction mirrors and reinforces the social view, which allows racist sentiments and acts while at the same time rejecting any affiliation with racism. Racism and racists in mainland Europe remain limited to openly anti-Semitic statements and acts perpetrated by right wing neo-Nazis, or to the occasional case where a judge finds things have gone too far. Third, given those extremely narrow boundaries within which racism is recognised, anti-racist NGOs are prevented from intervening in the trial

105 *Ibid.* at pp. 278–279.

106 *Ibid.* at p. 273.

107 Fabien Jobard and Sophie Névanen, 'La couleur du jugement. Discriminations dans les décisions judiciaires en matière d'infractions à agents de la force publique', *Revue française de sociologie* (2007), vol. 48, no. 2, pp. 243–272.

thus leaving the victims or their families even more isolated. Fourth, it sends the message to those perpetrating racially motivated crimes that they will go free or at least that the racial motivation will not be recognised as such. Last but not least, the case law sends out a message to those individuals and groups most victimised by racist attacks that the law and the institutions are not with them, are not protecting them in the same way as they do with people who are not prone to that type of attack.

Another area where such an attitude is evident is in the questionably low moral damage awards granted in cases of civil discrimination. This usually means discrimination arising as a tort or from contractual relationships. A couple of cases in Italy serve as an example.[108] In one case, a bar was convicted for civil racial discrimination because it applied higher coffee prices to foreigners than to Italian customers. The judges awarded €100 of non-economic damages for each plaintiff.[109] In another case, a real estate agency was convicted for racial discrimination because it had refused to enter into contracts with third country nationals (*extracomunitari*) of colour. The judge awarded one million Italian lire – the equivalent of €500 – as reparation for the hardship suffered by the plaintiff.[110] These decisions are important also because of their symbolic value. The judge's leniency could be partly explained due to the fact that civil anti-discrimination law had only recently been introduced in Italy, and that up to that legislative change moral damages were only awarded in civil cases as a result of a criminal conviction.[111] However, when considering the fact that racism and race discrimination are always viewed as an odious scourge that needs to be addressed, and considering also the damage to human dignity which these plaintiffs suffered, these moral damage awards certainly do not reflect the gravity of the act.

Taken together, these factors can easily lead to an alienation of law's application as a tool. In this sense, it should not come as a big surprise that many victims actually do not follow up on the investigation and drop the charges in those cases where the prosecution depends on the victim's initiative, as observed in the Finnish study. Moreover, those same victims are frequently immigrants, who are the target of restrictive, repressive, and criminalising immigration legislation. The psychological and also behavioural consequences of such a situation once it becomes engrained are quite easily assessed. In fact, as was stated in an analysis of the effects of past violence towards African Americans on the present violence afflicting African American communities, James W. Clarke states that, 'when human beings are controlled, but unprotected, by law "they come to know

108 For an overview, see Daniele Maffeis, 'Il contratto nella società multietnica: è un atto illecito la determinazione di un prezzo doppio per i clienti extracomunitari', *Giurisprudenza italiana* (2006), pp. 951–962.

109 Tribunale di Padova, Ordinanza 19 May 2005, *Giurisprudenza italiana* (2006), pp. 949–951.

110 Tribunale di Milano, Ordinanza 30 March 2000, *Foro italiano* (2000), part I, cc. 2040–2042.

111 See on this point Luigi Mughini, 'Prime riflessioni a margine dell'ordinanza del Tribunale di Firenze in materia di azione contro la discriminazione razziale', *Diritto, immigrazione e cittadinanza* (2000), no. 1, p. 85.

law only as an enemy, and not as a friend." Any other response is difficult to imagine.'[112] In other words, the combined effect of stricter legal sanctions towards irregular migrants on the basis of their skin colour with the non-acknowledgement of race and racism leading to an absence of protection by the law can only generate a reaction of non-respect for the law with serious psychological and social consequences. This is nothing else but institutional racism and to use Bhikhu Parekh's words:

> [w]hen [the state's] institutions engage in discriminatory behaviour, [it] not only reduces [its] victims to second-class citizens, but also leaves them with no redress. A discriminatory state imposes equal obligations but denies equal rights, and thus forfeits its legitimacy in the eyes of those it treats unequally.[113]

As can be seen, in somehow different ways than in the United States, law nevertheless functions as an instrument of domination of the White, Christian majority at the expense of those who do not belong to that group. In most of the cases of racially motivated crimes, it is the version of the majority that ultimately prevails. It is interesting to see that in Europe, anti-discrimination law is viewed from the 'perpetrator perspective' whereas the 'victim perspective' is silenced and not taken into consideration.[114] This stands in stark contrast with the public rhetoric that we are taking racial discrimination seriously. Policemen, judges, or other actors in the criminal justice system tend to believe the version provided by the defendant or at least question it less than the actual victim's version. One can easily suppose that in a number of these cases we are in the presence of racial bias against those people who are perceived and constructed as being different and culturally not European.

Nevertheless, the picture concerning the ineffectiveness of race discrimination provisions in the continental European context needs to be diversified or nuanced slightly. Indeed, provisions on race discrimination do work in one specific case, namely that of anti-Semitism. As we have seen, pursuant to the Shoah, anti-Semitism has almost become the only paradigmatic prism through which to view race, race discrimination, and racism in Europe. Therefore it is probably true that legal protection against anti-Semitism still works quite effectively. The same cannot be said for anti-Black racism, racism against the Roma, and Islamophobia. For instance, in France some of the actors of the Vichy Republic were held guilty of crimes against humanity. The same penalties did not apply to the events and the acts of torture during the Algerian war however. In other words, French law protected victims of the Holocaust but did not do the same with victims of

112 James W. Clarke, *Race, Violent Crime, and American Culture* (New Brunswick, London: Transaction Publishers, 1998), p. 31, with citation to D.J. Flanigan, *The Criminal Law of Slavery and Freedom, 1800–1868* (New York: Garland, 1987), p. 73.

113 Bhikhu Parekh, *A New Politics of Identity* (Basingstoke, New York: Palgrave Macmillan, 2008) p. 90.

114 Freeman, 'Legitimizing Racial Discrimination Through Anti-Discrimination Law: A Critical Review of Supreme Court Doctrine', pp. 1049–1119.

a gory colonial liberation war.[115] When one looks at European laws prohibiting Holocaust denial or the spread of Nazi ideology, those have been upheld by the ECtHR under Article 17 ECHR instead of under Article 10 (freedom of speech),[116] which goes to show that the issue is framed as a threat to the very basis of European democracies instead of a limitation on freedom of speech. By contrast, when hate speech is at issue there are some indications, for example in the Czech Republic, that judges are more sensitive to anti-Semitic hate speech than anti-Romani speech.[117] Highlighting these differences is not intended to introduce any hierarchies between the different types of racism and their legal treatment. Rather the hope is that by doing so anti-Roma or anti-Black racism will in the future receive the same level of legal protection as that which is currently afforded to anti-Semitism.

Some changes to this picture may happen due to the latest international instrument dealing with racial discrimination, the RED.[118] In fact, the RED represents an important attempt to go beyond ICERD's and the ECHR's approach of sanctioning racial discrimination via criminal law or 'only' if committed by public actors. It manages to overcome some of the issues raised here above. In particular, the concept of indirect discrimination could become helpful in addressing structural and institutional discrimination both at the public and at the private level. However, here again the continental European race sceptic's position and the reluctance to introduce and implement an Anglo American approach, where race is openly addressed in law and politics, mean that there has been resistance against the RED in mainland Europe. The ECJ, today the CJEU, provided a broad interpretation of the RED in the one case which had required a substantive interpretation until this time. The case involved a Belgian company whose manager had publicly declared that they would not hire immigrant employees. The case made it all the way to the ECJ, which held that even though no applicant had been rejected on the grounds of race, this was nevertheless race discrimination.[119] Although it is an important decision, it is insufficient evidence of a strong line of cases from a European legal institution demonstrating a serious and lasting commitment to fighting racial discrimination.[120] Moreover, we have already seen that citizenship is excluded from the application of this instrument and at the

115 For more details, see Stiina Outi Helena Löytömäki, *Committing the Irreparable: Law and Dealing with Past Injustices*, Ph.D. thesis (Florence: European University Institute – Department of Law, 2010).

116 See e.g. ECtHR, *Schimanek v. Austria*, no. 32307/96, 1 February 2000; ECtHR, *Garaudy v. France*, no. 65831/01, 24 June 2003; and ECtHR, *Witzsch v. Germany*, no. 7485/03, 13 December 2005.

117 Uladzislau Belavusau, 'Anti-Roma Hate Speech in the Czech Republic, Hungary and Poland', in Morag Goodwin and Paul De Hert (eds), *European Roma Integration Efforts – A Snapshot* (Brussels: VUB Press, 2013), p. 155.

118 Directive 2000/43/EC of 29 June 2000.

119 ECJ, Case C–54/07, *Centrum voor gelijkheid van kansen en voor racismebestrijding v. Firma Feryn NV* [2008] I–5187.

120 And indeed, in a recent decision, and against the opinion of the Advocate General, the CJEU rejected a Roma discrimination case referred by the Bulgarian non-discrimination authority, on the grounds that it could not be deemed a tribunal or court authorised to do so under EU

EU political level, enthusiasm for non-discrimination is also waning, given that a proposal to revise and harmonise some of the non-discrimination directives has been politically stalled for years.[121] Ultimately, Europe can be characterised both as a place of racism without races and as one of racism without racists. This means that other racial minorities and especially people of colour cannot really rely on the legal system to protect them.

In conclusion, Chapter 4 lays down the rhetorical and legal foundations for a European CRT. Whereas the previous chapter had addressed the differences and obstacles to a transplant of this legal theory from the United States to Europe, here I try to be more constructive, allowing me eventually to outline what I define as the legal aspects of 'Continental European Colourblindness', characterised by an absence/silencing of race coupled with a narrow legal definition of a racist or racism that emerges from case law in many continental European countries. Like American colourblindness, the idea is that despite the different context and history law functions in very similar ways towards racial(ised) minorities in mainland Europe. In other words, this chapter provides the sketch for a general framework within which to read a European CRT before moving on to the more specific case studies where more attention will be given to the national context and histories which lead to variations of 'Continental European Colourblindness'.

law. CJEU, Case C–394/11, *Valeri Hariev Belov v ChEZ Elektro Balgaria AD and ChEZ Raspredelenie Balgaria AD*, 31 January 2013.

121 European Commission, 'Proposal for a Council Directive on Implementing the Principle of Equal Treatment Between Persons Irrespective of Religion or Belief, Disability, Age or Sexual Orientation', COM(2008) 426 final, 2 July 2008.

Chapter 5

Contextualising a European Critical Race Theory

The previous chapter set out the framework and the general context within which to situate a European CRT. This last chapter will offer a more contextualised reading of how race and law interact in a number of different settings in mainland Europe. According to Goldberg's *The Racial State*, just as there is not one single type of racism, there is not one single model of a racial state but many different racial states.[1] Hence, in addition to highlighting the common elements of racism and colourblindness in mainland Europe, this chapter situates them in more specific contexts and realities of their respective racial states. At the same time, this will demonstrate what a European CRT model might look like and counter some of the claims made earlier against CRT, which will enable some additional insights into the overlooked or ignored European (legal) context.

This chapter consists of three separate case studies, which will move from the most blatant instances of discrimination and racism down to the more insidious and sometimes hidden aspects in national and local legislation. The first case study looks at the paradigmatic case of race discrimination against the Roma.[2] Rather than focusing on one country, I look at how law contributes directly and explicitly to the discrimination against individuals of Romani origin. Due to these phenomena they are viewed as a European-wide racial minority par excellence. Simultaneously they are the victims of widespread hostility against a group, which is transcribed into law without the necessity of resorting to colourblindness.

The second case study deals with France's ideology towards colourblindness. Two decisions dealing with race and ethnicity in France show how French colourblindness prevents the adoption of race-conscious measures to eliminate discrimination while at the same time denying the existence of wide-spread racial and ethnic subordination. Hence, in spite of the different historical, social and

1 David Theo Goldberg, *The Racial State* (Malden, Oxford: Blackwell Publishers, 2002), *passim*.

2 The reference to the 'Roma' throughout this book includes individuals and groups as different as the Roma, the Sinti, Travellers, gitanos, or the Jenische and the different names under which they might respectively be known in various European countries (e.g. manouches, Ashkali). While aware of the risk of essentialising by using this overarching term, it reflects the way in which these groups and individuals belonging to them are positioned before and discriminated against by the law in uncannily similar ways.

legal context, French law tends to function in similar ways to U.S. law under the ideology of American colourblindness.

The third case study looks at Italy, where in recent years mayors and town councils, especially in Northern Italy, have adopted an increasing number of municipal ordinances which are legally creating and entrenching the ideal of a White, Christian, Italian identity. Moreover, the combined effect of these ordinances is that individuals with a migrant background are targeted, thus exacerbating racial and ethnic discrimination and harassment. Ordinances like the prohibition on wearing the burqa in public provide a gendered example of how these localised instruments introduced in localities in Northern Italy move up to the national level.

5.1 The legal discrimination of the Roma

5.1.1 *A brief history of persecution against the Roma*

The paradigmatic European-wide case of racism and race discrimination is that of the Roma. The aim of this section is not to provide a coherent history of the Roma which, of and in itself, is problematic because the few existing documents are not written by the Roma.[3] Nevertheless, what can be gleaned from these documents is that from the moment of the Roma's almost mythical arrival to Europe from India, racism and discrimination have been a constant feature in their history. As to their origins and the romanticised vision they sometimes generate,[4] the more traditional hypothesis states that the Roma reached Europe through a number of voluntary migrations between the fifth and the tenth century. Newer hypotheses, however, question this interpretation and instead view the movement as a result of massive military deportations of people from the Ganges valley after the tenth century. This would mean that the Roma have geographical ties only but are actually quite heterogeneous.[5] The first official archival source recording groups of Roma date back to the fourteenth and fifteenth centuries even though it is probable and possible that they have been present in Greece and in the Byzantine Empire as early as the tenth century.[6]

What is unclear is whether the populations arriving in Europe were immediately subject to discrimination, exclusion, criminalisation, and expulsion. One of the main experts in Romani history posits that in the beginning and until the

3 See Emanuela Ignăţoiu-Sora, *La construction d'un régime juridique pour la protection des Roms*, unpublished Ph.D. thesis (Florence: European University Institute, Department of Law, 2010), p. 20.

4 Klaus-Michael Bogdal, '"Dieses schwartz, ungestaltet und wildschweiffige Gesind". Symbolische Codierung und literarische Diskursivierung der "Zigeuner" vor 1800', in Michael Zimmermann (ed.), *Zwischen Erziehung und Vernichtung* (Stuttgart: Franz Steiner Verlag, 2007), pp. 81–84.

5 Elisabeth Clanet dit Lamanit, 'L'objet "origine" et le concept d'un "peuple" dit "rom"', *Lignes* (2011), no. 34, pp. 80–84.

6 Jean-Pierre Liégeois, *Roma in Europe* (Strasbourg: Council of Europe Publishing, 2007), pp. 17–20.

eighteenth century they enjoyed a kind of 'Golden Age'.[7] However, it is telling that one of the first documented traces of Roma in Europe relates to the enslavement of Roma families in Moldavia and Valachia from 1385 onwards.[8] In addition to this, removal of Roma people seems to be a constant feature in their history. For example, a group of Roma were deported to Norway in 1540,[9] and documents show that Roma were sentenced and removed from Scotland to the Americas in the seventeenth and eighteenth centuries.[10] Similarly, France banished the Roma from its territory on numerous occasions.[11]

With the arrival and invention of the nation-state and contemporary racism, those examples of early discrimination were exacerbated and intensified in as much as the Roma were increasingly portrayed as backward. In particular, their mode of nomadic life was considered inappropriate to the concepts of place, boundaries, and territory created by the modern nation-state.[12] Consequently, policies targeting the Roma increased, which included mechanisms to suppress, expel, control, and assimilate this population.

The most outrageous example was their clinical elimination during the Nazi regime, which has been posthumously defined and acknowledged as the Roma Holocaust, or *porrajmos* to use the Romani term for the Holocaust. Approximately 400,000–500,000 Roma and Sinti were killed, exterminated, or starved during that period,[13] even though some historians believe the numbers could be as high as one and a half million.[14] There are indicators that the *porrajmos* did not concern all Roma, especially because of the different existing racial theories concerning the Aryan origins of parts of the Roma.[15] However, there are no doubts that, together with Jews, homosexuals, and political opponents, the Roma were a prime target of Nazi extermination policies to maintain racial supremacy and purity.

Despite this history, European states, and their societies, were reluctant to recognise the status of the Roma as victims of genocide. For example, both Germany and Austria interpreted their restitution legislation for victims of the Holocaust and of forced sterilisations in a restrictive manner.[16] Moreover, discriminatory

7 Henriette Asséo, *Les Tsiganes. Une destinée européenne* (Paris: Gallimard, 1994).
8 Liégeois, *Roma in Europe*, p. 18.
9 *Ibid.* at p. 20.
10 Angus Bancroft, *Roma and Gypsy-Travellers in Europe. Modernity, Race, Space and Exclusion* (Aldershot: Ashgate, 2005), p. 52.
11 Jean-Pierre Liégeois, *Roms et Tsiganes* (Paris: La Découverte, 2009), p. 43.
12 See broadly Bancroft, *Roma and Gypsy-Travellers in Europe.*
13 Liégeois, *Roms et Tsiganes*, p. 54.
14 Ignăţoiu-Sora, *La construction d'un régime juridique pour la protection des Roms*, p. 23, note 50.
15 Michael Zimmermann, 'Jews, Gypsies and Soviet Prisoners of War: Comparing Nazi Persecutions', in Roni Stauber and Raphael Vago (eds), *The Roma. A Minority in Europe* (Budapest: Central European University Press, 2007), in particular pp. 36–40.
16 See for Austria Gerhard Baumgartner and Florian Freund, 'Der Holocaust an den österreichischen Roma und Sinti', in Zimmermann (ed.), *Zwischen Erziehung und Vernichtung*, pp. 220–221, and for Germany Gilad Margalit, 'Zigeunerpolitik und Zigeunerdiskurs im Deutschland der Nachkriegszeit', in *ibid.*, pp. 501–503.

measures continued unabated. Indeed, the atrocities committed against the Roma did not end after World War II, which is often and generally viewed as the cut-off point when Europe supposedly overcame its racial and racist past. Whereas the Nazi genocide represented the most extreme version of controlling the Roma, a second mechanism consisted in forced sterilisations. For example, in Sweden, Romani women were subject to forced sterilisations up until the 1970s.[17] In Slovakia the practice is still on-going,[18] eerily mirroring the forced sterilisations during the Nazi regime in Germany.

Another measure to solve 'the Romani problem' has been through expulsion policies or the prohibition of entry into the territory of a nation-state. What did not correspond with the national image had to be expelled, or was not allowed into the territory in the first place. As we have seen, such expulsions were already practiced in history but with the emergence of nation-states and by extension national identity, which viewed the bourgeois citizen as an underlying unit, those policies became more organised. For example, in Switzerland, between 1906 and 1972 there existed a general prohibition, which denied entry to Gypsies (*Zigeuner*) into Swiss territory and non-Swiss Roma were expelled.[19] Similarly in the Netherlands around 1900, the Justice Department issued several decrees which ordered local authorities to prevent Gypsies from entering the country, and if found inland, it was mandatory to deport them.[20] Another quite original solution in Germany after World War II was the removal of German citizenship from a number of Romani individuals, on the pretext that they allegedly acquired this status illegally.[21]

Due to the lack of feasibility of permanent expulsion, another practiced mechanism to solve the issue, was to separate the Roma from society, put them away or prohibit contact between them and the remainder of society. In fact, the Roma were viewed as a possible threat to the idea and construction of a settled European identity, and therefore one way to eliminate that threat was incarceration through the criminalisation of vagrancy. Another variation of the separation and isolation strategy was segregation, which continues to play out at different levels and in different spaces but is most notorious in education[22] and housing.[23]

17 Bancroft, *Roma and Gypsy-Travellers in Europe*, p. 75.

18 Center for Reproductive Rights and Center for Human and Civil Rights, 'Body and Soul: Forced Sterilization and Other Assaults on Roma Reproductive Freedom in Slovakia' (New York: Center for Reproductive Rights, 2003), also available at: http://reproductiverights.org/sites/crr.civicactions.net/files/documents/bo_slov_part1.pdf.

19 Thomas Meier, 'Zigeunerpolitik und Zigeunerdiskurs in der Schweiz 1850–1970', in Zimmermann (ed.), *Zwischen Erziehung und Vernichtung*, pp. 227–230.

20 Leo Lucassen, 'Gypsy Research and Gypsy Policy in the Netherlands (1850–1970)', in *ibid.* p. 247.

21 Gilad Margalit, 'Zigeunerpolitik und Zigeunerdiskurs im Deutschland der Nachkriegszeit', in *ibid.*, pp. 499–500.

22 See Jack Greenberg, 'Report on Roma Education Today: From Slavery to Segregation and Beyond', *Columbia Law Review* (2010), vol. 110, pp. 919–1001.

23 E.g. in 1999, Usti, a small town in the Czech Republic, built a wall around an apartment block

Another measure to destroy Roma culture and 'fostering' Roma integration was to remove their children and raise them in foster families, institutions, clinics, or orphanages in order to eliminate any cultural and psychological influence on their future development. For example, in Switzerland an action running from 1926 to 1973 by the prestigious private foundation *Pro Juventute*, called 'Hilfswerk für die Kinder der Landstraße' ('Relief Organisation for Children of the Country Road'), systematically took away the children from the *Jenisch* – a Swiss group of travellers – to separate them from their families by placing them into different institutions.[24]

However, solutions like these are not always 'optimal' or 'feasible', therefore attempts at forced assimilation was considered another option. Here again, there were different models or options which were practiced at different times and places. One of the most practiced options was to prevent Roma from travelling and to forcibly settling them, in the hope of eliminating one aspect of Roma culture that contrasted and conflicted with the modern idea of the nation-state, especially administrative control. Thus, Roma people were often settled in peripheral areas of cities, which only added to their marginalisation and segregation. In Italy this decentralised policy emerged in the 1970s and 1980s, which led to the phenomenon known as 'Nomad camps'.[25] France also introduced a similar policy through national legislation which allocated certain areas to the so-called 'gens du voyage'.[26] In addition to this, an older statute required itinerant people to have circulation papers, which need to be renewed every three months.[27]

Coupled with a general picture of recurring violence, usually police violence, against the Roma, the destruction of their homes and general societal prejudice, it is not hard to characterise this picture as outright, century-long societal and institutional racism on a Europe-wide scale. It is only mildly tempered and nuanced from country to country through romanticised notions of the Romani, such as their association with music and circus.

Hence, one would expect that such a history of discrimination would lead to European anti-race discrimination law being particularly effective and sensitive towards the Roma and that today the Roma, similar to the case of the Jewish community, would occupy a particularly protected status in Europe. If one of the

which housed a number of Roma families. On this, see Bancroft, *Roma and Gypsy-Travellers in Europe*, pp. 60–61.

24 Thomas Meier, 'Zigeunerpolitik und Zigeunerdiskurs in der Schweiz 1850–1970', in Zimmermann (ed.), *Zwischen Erziehung und Vernichtung*, pp. 231–233.

25 Tommaso Vitale, 'Governare mediante gli sgomberi e la segregazione dei gruppi zigani', in Salvatore Palidda (ed.), *razzismo democratico* (Milano: Mimesis Edizioni, 2009), pp. 188–189.

26 Loi no. 2000–614, 'relative à l'accueil et à l'habitat des gens du voyage', 5 July, 2000 *Journal Officiel de la République Française (JORF)*, 6 July 2000.

27 Loi no. 69–3, 'relative à l'exercice des activités ambulantes et au regime applicable aux personnes circulant en France sans domicile ni résidence fixe', 3 January 1969, *Journal Officiel de la République Française (JORF)*, 5 January 1969.

moral justifications for anti-discrimination policies is to remedy past injustices, the Roma would certainly have a very strong claim. However, statistics demonstrate that today the Roma remain the most racially discriminated group in Europe.[28] Law has been and continues to be all but an innocent bystander.

5.1.2 *Law's contemporary discriminatory contribution*

Regardless of all the rhetorical efforts by various international and European institutions to address past, racism and hostility toward the Roma, state-tolerated, if not sponsored, discrimination continues almost unabated. Certainly, the most outrageous instances of genocide have ended; however, the policies have changed little and often constitute a historical continuum in their underlying assumptions. A number of examples showing the different levels at which legislation and case law construct and entrench the marginalisation of the Roma in various national European contexts will be provided here. The example of the Roma is particularly interesting because it stands in stark contrast to the image of Europe having overcome its overtly racist past. At the same time, the case of the Roma is so obvious that even lawyers cannot deny the role of law, and some of the first legal analysis on the subject are from a CRT perspective.[29]

Obvious cases of legal discrimination concern the introduction of policies, motivated by anti-Roma sentiments, which directly and repressively target the Roma. Two recent examples from Western European democracies demonstrate how racial discrimination against the Roma is not just a problem in some 'backward' Eastern European countries but is equally structural and problematic in many, if not all, Western European states.

The first, example comes from Italy. Applying as a legal basis legislation to protect civilians against emergencies arising from natural disasters, the Italian government issued a decree declaring a state of emergency in relation to a settlement of nomadic communities in the regions of Campania, Latium, and Lombardy.[30] According to the decree the emergency was caused because 'numerous irregular third-country nationals and nomads have steadily settled in urban areas; that those settlements have caused a situation of serious social alarm, with the potential of severe consequences to public order and security for the local populations; and that the intensity and extent of the phenomenon cannot be tackled with instruments envisaged by ordinary legislation.' The emergency situation was extended temporarily, until 31 December 2010, and spatially, to cover

28 European Union Agency for Fundamental Rights (FRA), 'EU-MIDIS, European Union Minorities and Discrimination Survey: Main Results Report' (Vienna: European Union Agency for Fundamental Rights, 2009), available at: http://fra.europa.eu/fraWebsite/attachments/eumidis_mainreport_conference-edition_en_.pdf.

29 See e.g. Simoni, 'Appunti per una "lettura romanì" del "pacchetto sicurezza"', pp. 217–230.

30 *Decreto Presidente del Consiglio dei ministri (DPCM)*, 21 May 2008, *Gazzetta Ufficiale (GU)*, no. 126, 26 May 2008.

the regions of Veneto and Piedmont.[31] In addition to the first decree, three ordinances for implementation appointed three 'delegate commissioners for the nomad emergency' (the prefects of Rome, Milan and Naples), who were conferred with derogatory powers to adopt a number of measures.[32] Those measures ranged from a number of social and welfare measures in favour of the Roma to the identification and census of people, including minors, in the settlements also by means of fingerprinting, and the use of police force against those individuals deemed irregular and therefore subject to expulsion.

In reality, an earlier piece of emergency legislation passed by Romano Prodi's centre-left government in 2007 had already preceded these three decrees.[33] Following the entry into force of the 2007 legislation, police forces raided a number of Romani settlements. The law decree was not passed into law but its measures were absorbed in the broader 'security package' by the centre-left government, revealing that anti-Romani prejudice was not the exclusive domain of right-wing parties. Moreover, the security package prepared the terrain for further measures by the current right wing government, which has only aggravated and brought anti-Roma feelings to new heights.[34] That the real objective of those measures was repressive became clear shortly after the introduction of the policy when none of the positive measures were adopted, whereas the census and identification started almost immediately. The identification and possible subsequent repressive measures and expulsion targeted individuals with Italian citizenship, regular and irregular foreign residents, and stateless persons. Their only common characteristic was that they were 'nomadic' or were found in 'nomad camps'. The racial and ethnic aspects involved are undeniable.[35]

Unsurprisingly, these measures ignited an international reaction and outrage. The European Parliament adopted a resolution condemning Italy.[36] The European Commission asked for clarifications in order to determine whether there had been an infringement of European Union law both with regard to race discrimination and to the fundamental freedom of movement to which European citizens are entitled. In response, Italy explained that the measures were not

31 *Decreto Presidente del Consiglio dei ministri (DPCM)*, 28 May 2009, *Gazzetta Ufficiale (GU)*, no. 129, 6 June 2009.

32 *Ordinanza del Presidente del Consiglio dei ministri*, no. 3676, 30 May 2008, *Gazzetta Ufficiale (GU)*, no. 127, 31 May 2008; *Ordinanza del Presidente del Consiglio dei ministri*, no. 3677, 30 May 2008, *Gazzetta Ufficiale (GU)*, no. 127, 31 May 2008; and *Ordinanza del Presidente del Consiglio dei ministri*, no. 3678, 30 May 2008, *Gazzetta Ufficiale (GU)*, no. 127, 31 May 2008. All three ordinances are reprinted in *Diritto, immigrazione e cittadinanza* (2008), no. 2, pp. 239–249.

33 *Decreto legge*, no. 181, 1 November 2007, *Gazzetta Ufficiale (GU)*, no. 255, 2 November 2007.

34 Nando Sigona, '"Gypsies out of Italy!"', in Andrea Mammone and Giuseppe A. Veltri (eds), *Italy Today* (London and New York: Routledge, 2010), pp. 143–157.

35 Alessandro Simoni, 'I decreti "emergenza nomadi": il nuovo volto di un vecchio problema', *Diritto, immigrazione e cittadinanza* (2008), no. 3–4, pp. 44–56.

36 European Parliament, 'Resolution of 10 July 2008 on the Census of the Roma on the Basis of Ethnicity in Italy', *P6_TA(2008)0361*, *Official Journal of the European Union (OJEU)*, C 294 E/54, 3 December 2009.

intended to target the Roma only because the reference to nomads also included others who were not ethnically Roma. The European Commission eventually accepted this explanation, meaning that for the purposes of European law, these measures posed no legal problem. At the national level, there were challenges on various grounds with different lawsuits filed either in ordinary or administrative courts. One claim managed to reach the Supreme Administrative Court, the *Consiglio di Stato*, which declared the measures illegal due to the absence of an emergency situation. However, it did not acknowledge the discriminatory character of these measures and did not grant any damages to the victims.[37] In an unusual move, the Italian government appealed against this decision on the grounds that ordinary court judges and not administrative ones can determine when a state of emergency exists. This prompted the *Consiglio di Stato* to suspend parts of its earlier decision.[38] *De facto* segregation and expulsion of Roma in Italy continues unabated,[39] despite a decision by the European Committee of Social Rights (ECSR) which held unanimously that Italy's policies violated various provisions of the Revised European Social Charter.[40] Only recently, five years after the entry into force of the Roma emergency decrees, an Italian court finally declared these provisions racially discriminatory and awarded €8,000 in damages to the plaintiff.[41]

The French situation mirrors Italy's treatment of the Romani.[42] Here, an administrative order by the Ministry of the Interior ordered the dismantlement of any illegal settlement, in particular of those belonging to Romani community, as well as a more efficient expulsion of illegal settlers.[43] Similar to Italy, this led to a major outcry and to preliminary questions before starting an official infringement procedure against France by the European Commission for race discrimination and violation of the freedom of movement of European citizens. This almost caused a diplomatic stalemate between the French government and the European Commission. At the European Council of 16 September 2010, a lively discussion between France's President, Nicolas Sarkozy, and the European Commission President, José Manuel Barroso, took place. On 29 September 2010,

37 Consiglio di Stato, Sezione IV: Sentenza no. 6050, 16 November 2011.

38 Consiglio di Stato, Sezione IV: Ordinanza no. 1760, 9 May 2012.

39 For more information see the brief by the NGO, *Open Society*, to the European Commission entitled 'Roma in Italy: A Continued Emergency', October 2012, available at: www.opensocietyfoundations.org/sites/default/files/italy-briefing-ec-october-10192012.pdf.

40 ECSR, *Centre on Housing Rights and Evictions (COHRE) v. Italy*, Complaint no. 58/2009, 25 June 2010.

41 Tribunale di Roma, Sezione II Civile: Ordinanza in proceeding 49444/2012, 24 May 2013.

42 For a detailed compared analysis of both France and Italy on this issue, see Grégoire Cousin and Francesca Mariani, 'Il passepartout dell'"ordine pubblico". Politica e diritto nelle prassi di allontanamento dei "rumeni detti rom" in Italia e Francia', in Paolo Bonetti, Alessandro Simoni and Tommaso Vitale (eds), *La condizione giuridica di rom e sinti in Italia* (Milano: Giuffré, 2011), pp. 415–454.

43 *Circulaire* du Ministère de l'Intérieur, de l'Outre-mer et des collectivités territoriales, 'Evacuation des campements illicites', 5 August 2010.

the Commission asked the French authorities to provide proof of their respect for European obligations, threatening that if the responses were not satisfactory it would open an infringement procedure against France. The letter by the French government indicated that amendments to a new bill, which would be under discussion in the French parliament in January 2011, would fulfil France's European obligations. On 19 October 2010, the European Commission announced its decision to refrain from opening an infringement procedure against France.[44] In all likelihood, the European Commission was probably satisfied by the fact that, in a move that resembled the Italian case, the Ministry of the Interior had already issued a revised order from which any reference to the Roma was erased.[45] The revised document simply stated that the dissolution of illegal settlements had to continue in respect of the law and 'regardless of the origins of their occupants.'[46] This amendment also convinced France's highest administrative court, the *Conseil d'Etat*, which annulled the first order on the grounds that it violated the Constitution's equality provisions but left the revised order in force because it did not target any specific group.[47]

The *Conseil constitutionnel* also intervened[48] on the January 2011 bill by declaring the unconstitutionality of a framework statute on internal security that, *inter alia*, intended to pursue France's radical policy of forced evacuations of irregular nomadic settlements.[49] Article 90 of that bill would have allowed certain local and departmental state representatives to proceed with forced evacuations of illegal installations whenever they represent a serious risk to the public health, security, or peace through an emergency procedure. The constitutional judges found that the intervention in the name of public security was disproportionate and infringed on the constitutionally enshrined individual rights and freedoms. The judges gave three reasons. First, the emergency procedure could be employed at any moment. Second, the bill did not take into account the personal and familiar circumstances of individuals who do not have decent housing. Third, the possibility of judicial recourse, which would stay the emergency procedure, was an insufficient guarantee for a resolution.[50]

44 See Anastasia Iliopoulou, '"Le temps des gitans": à propos de la libre circulation des Roms dans l'Union', *Europe* (January 2011), no. 1, étude 1, pp. 5–10.

45 See on the EU law aspects of this story Mark Dawson and Elise Muir, 'Individual, Institutional and Collective Vigilance in Protecting Fundamental Rights in the EU: Lessons from the Roma', *Common Market Law Review* (2011), vol. 48, pp. 751–775.

46 *Circulaire* du Ministère de l'Intérieur, de l'Outre-mer et des collectivités territoriales, 'Evacuation des campements illicites', 13 September 2010.

47 Conseil d'Etat, Decision no. 343387, 7 April 2011.

48 Conseil constitutionnel, Decision CC 2011–625 DC, 10 March 2011.

49 'Loi d'orientation et de programmation pour la performance de la sécurité intérieure' (also known as "LOPPSI 2").

50 Conseil constitutionnel, Decision CC 2011–625 DC, 10 March 2011, para. 55. See also an earlier decision by the *Conseil* where it held that the 'ordinary' procedures of forced evacuation established by French legislation as applied to Roma applicants were compatible with the principles of equality and freedom of movement: Decision CC 2010–13 QPC, 9 July 2010.

What was never at issue in practically all these legal challenges to the Italian and French acts was the direct or indirect discriminatory character of these measures. The European Commission ultimately accepted the revisions or explanations provided by Italy and France, even though it was clear that the underlying hostility towards the Roma was only formally removed but substantively remained in place. Moreover, the discriminatory nature of these expulsion measures was only marginally at issue in the litigation that ensued at the internal level, which cannot be defined as a success for the Roma affected.[51] Like in the Italian case, these practices are on-going in France.[52] The only institution to fully acknowledge the discriminatory character of these emergency measures in France was the ECSR, which found a violation of the right to adequate housing and the prohibition of mass expulsions in conjunction with the non-discrimination provisions of the European Charter of Social Rights.[53]

However, bias in the legal system not only happens at the legislative level. The judicial system is also not immune. One Italian case demonstrates how bias and prejudice against the Roma emerge directly from under a judge's gavel. The case involved a 15-year-old Romanian Roma girl, Angelica Varga, who was accused by a woman from Ponticelli of attempting to kidnap her new-born. The girl was almost lynched and the rumour of the event sparked a wave of violence against Roma and Romanian citizens throughout the town.[54] It also led to the adoption of the above-mentioned emergency decrees.[55] Despite serious doubts surrounding the veracity of the story, in January 2009 the Naples Juvenile Court sentenced the girl to three years and eight months in prison. She was denied free legal aid because she allegedly had money in Romania. Moreover, the documents were never translated into a language known by the defendant. In the sentencing, no mitigating circumstances were applied even though she had no previous criminal record. During the trial, the girl was imprisoned as a pre-trial measure, for the alleged risk of repeat offending. In a separate action, her lawyers challenged this pre-trial measure, which was nevertheless confirmed on appeal with the following reasoning:

51 In this sense Costanza Hermanin, '"Counts" on the Italian "Nomad Camps": An Incautious Ethnic Census of Roma?', *Ethnic and Racial Studies* (2011), vol. 34, no. 10, pp. 1731–1750.

52 As proven by the latest interministerial order: *Circulaire interministerielle NOR INTK1233053C*, relative à l'anticipation et à l'accompagnement des operations d'évacuation des campements illicites, 26 August 2012. See Caroline Maillary, 'Diagnostiquer pour mieux trier', *Plein droit* (2013), no. 99, pp. 11–12.

53 ECSR, *Centre on Housing Rights and Evictions (COHRE) v. France*, Complaint no. 63/2010, 28 June 2011. Also see the ECtHR which recently declared that France had violated Article 8 (right to private life) for evictions of French travellers: ECtHR, *Winterstein and Others v. France*, no. 27013/07, 17 October 2013. However, in a recurrent pattern it did not hold that a separate Article 14 violation had occurred.

54 For a detailed account of this story see Miguel Mora, 'Fichado por gitano', *El País (Domingo)*, 1 February 2009, pp. 1–4.

55 See Hermanin, '"Counts" on the Italian "Nomad Camps"', pp. 1731–1750.

> [i]t appears that the appellant is fully integrated into the typical schemes of Roma culture. Precisely that circumstance of being integrated in those life schemes which, absent any concrete analytical processes of her experiences, causes a concrete danger of repeat offences. [...] Indeed, both the placement in a community as well as house detention are inadequate measures also when considering that she adheres to the lifestyle of the Roma which by common experience determines in them an absence for the respect of rules. For these reasons the appeal is rejected.[56]

In other words, the decision confirms the existence of a causal link between belonging to a certain race or ethnicity and the possibility of committing a crime and the danger of recidivism. Coupled with the crime, which reflects an age-old prejudice that the Roma kidnap children, one can see how the whole judicial affair is replete with overt hostility and prejudice and how that prejudice becomes normalised and legally entrenched.

Such a decision could be taken to the ECtHR and challenged for violation of Article 14 in combination with Article 6, para. 1 ECHR. In a similar case, a Bulgarian Roma woman claimed that her custody during trial was based on discriminatory motives. The ECtHR found that there had been a violation of the ECHR.[57] However, even this judicial institution, which has come to be viewed and strategically used as a champion of Roma rights, is not completely immune from some sort of bias. True, in recent years a number of landmark cases especially on race discrimination against Roma segregation in the educational context have been handed down. These decisions have subsequently rattled public and legal opinion as to the continued discrimination suffered by the Roma.[58] However, what is often ignored is that these cases are overshadowed by a much larger number of cases dealing with anti-Romani violence where the ECtHR has only very rarely recognised the racially discriminatory character of such violence, even when perpetrated by police forces.[59] In part, this can be related to the fact the Article 14 ECHR which prohibits discrimination could, until recently, only be invoked in conjunction with the violation of another Convention right.[60] Others

56 Tribunale per i minorenni di Napoli (in sede di appello al riesame), Ordinanza no. 139/09, 29 September 2009 (translation by the author).

57 ECtHR, *Paraskeva Todorova v. Bulgaria*, no. 37193/07, 25 March 2010.

58 ECtHR, *D.H. and Others v. The Czech Republic* (Grand Chamber), no. 57325/00, 13 November 2007; ECtHR, *Sampanis and Others v. Greece*, no. 32526/05, 5 June 2008; ECtHR, *Oršuš and Others v. Croatia* (Grand Chamber), no. 15766/03, 16 March 2010; ECtHR, *Horvath and Kiss v. Hungary*, no. 11146/11, 29 January 2013; and ECtHR, *Lavida and Others v. Greece*, no. 7973/10, 31 May 2013.

59 See for a more detailed discussion and analysis Mathias Möschel, 'Is the European Court of Human Rights' Case Law on Anti-Roma Violence "Beyond Reasonable Doubt"?', *Human Rights Law Review* (2012), vol. 12, no. 3, pp. 479–507.

60 Protocol No. 12 changed this and entered into force in 2005. The ECtHR has handed down its first decision finding a violation of that Protocol in 2009. Not surprisingly, this decision also

have interpreted this reluctance to find Article 14 violations in conjunction with racism as postcolonial denial.[61] Seen through a CRT lens, one could say that discrimination law fails to adopt the perspective of the victim and takes the side of the perpetrator.

What is surprising in these judicial reasonings is that despite most gruesome fact patterns involving death,[62] lynchings,[63] forced sterilisations,[64] and cruel, inhuman, and degrading treatments,[65] the ECtHR only found a full Article 14 violation by a state on two occasions.[66] In all the other cases, while recognising that there had been violations of Article 2 (the right to life) and Article 3 (prohibition of degrading and inhuman treatment) ECHR, the European judges nevertheless consistently held that the defendants had not been able to prove that there had also been an Article 14 violation. Initially, the main legal obstacle in most of these cases was that the judges required the applicants to prove their case 'beyond reasonable doubt'. This self-imposed standard was heavily critiqued by Judge Bonello in a dissenting opinion in *Anguelova*.[67] Hence, the ECtHR's choice to impose that same standard on individual victims of state violence seems arbitrary. It ends up protecting Bulgaria and any other Contracting State whose institutions may be accused of racial discrimination rather than protecting victims of such discrimination. Judge Bonello's dissent provoked some formal changes, in the sense that the ECtHR stopped referring explicitly to this standard of proof in later cases. Nevertheless, when looking at the outcome of the cases in terms of Article 14 violations, little has changed. The fact that racial discrimination forms the basis of the violence and discrimination is judicially silenced.

involved Roma people: *Sejdić and Finci v. Bosnia and Herzegovina* (Grand Chamber), nos. 27996/06 and 34836/06, 22 December 2009.

61 Marie-Bénédicte Dembour, 'In the Name of the Rule of Law: The European Court of Human Rights' Silencing of Racism', in Gurminder K. Bhambra and Robbie Shilliam (eds), *Silencing Human Rights. Critical Engagements with a Contested Project* (Basingstoke, New York: Palgrave, Macmillan, 2009), pp. 184–202 and Marie-Bénédicte Dembour, 'Postcolonial Denial: Why the European Court of Human Rights Finds It So Difficult to Acknowledge Racism', in Kamari Clarke and Mark Goodale (eds), *Mirrors of Justice. Law and Power in the Post-Cold War Era* (Cambridge: Cambridge University Press, 2009), pp. 45–66.

62 E.g. ECtHR, *Anguelova v. Bulgaria*, no. 38361/97, 13 June 2007; ECtHR, *Velikova v. Bulgaria*, no. 41488/98, 18 May 2000; and ECtHR, *Carabulea v. Romania*, no. 45661/99, 13 July 2010.

63 E.g. ECtHR, *Moldovan and Others v. Romania (No.2)*, nos. 41138/98 and 64320/01, 12 July 2005.

64 E.g. ECtHR, *V.C. v. Slovakia*, no. 18968/07, 8 November 2011 and ECtHR, *N.B. v. Slovakia*, no. 29518/10, 12 June 2012.

65 E.g. ECtHR, *Balogh v. Hungary*, no. 47940/99, 20 July 2004 and ECtHR, *Fedorchenko and Lozenko v. Ukraine*, no. 387/03, 20 September 2012.

66 ECtHR, *Stoica v. Romania*, no. 42722/02, 4 March 2008 and ECtHR, *Nachova and Others v. Bulgaria*, nos. 43577/98 and 43579/98, 26 February 2004. However, in the Grand Chamber decision Bulgaria was only *procedurally* held responsible for race discrimination for its failure to investigate the racial background of the violence and death. ECtHR, *Nachova and Others v. Bulgaria* (Grand Chamber), nos. 43577/98 and 43579/98, 6 July 2005.

67 ECtHR, *Anguelova v. Bulgaria* (First Section), Application no. 38361/97, 13 June 2007, dissenting opinion Judge Bonello, para. 10.

Against the institutional and Europe-wide bias and racism sketched here in the first case study, the ERRC and other NGOs have been fighting for many years. But a reoccurring question concerns the limits of framing issues in terms of racial discrimination and solving the Roma issues by strategic litigation in order to create a winning strategy against a reality where the social issues play a central role and pervasive prejudice and hostility against the Roma prevails.[68] Part of the success of such a strategy hinges on how far anti-discrimination law protects the perpetrator or the victim and the extent of the biases existing within the judiciary.[69] However, a broader question concerns the efforts of international NGOs and European institutions, considered a consequence of implicit and explicit neo-liberal politics, which focus on human and civil rights. More often than not, these initiatives are driven by elites, and not (Romani) grassroots organisations, or organic intellectuals, who are more concerned with social justice.[70]

One explanation for the failure can be traced to the state institutions themselves, which are inherently biased against Romani people. This raises the question about the chances of success of court challenges, when and if the judiciary or other state institutions openly or implicitly share biases that led to the actual adoption of legislative or regulatory measures targeting the Roma? How far have prejudices and racial hostility somehow permeated such institutions?

More importantly, from a CRT perspective, what becomes clear is that in a vast number of cases, law functions to the benefit of the non-Roma majority. The majority view can continue to accept as true stereotypes about the Roma, which are reinforced and confirmed by the legal system, while keeping up the appearance that non-discrimination law will actually sanction the nominal cases of race discrimination.

5.2 French colourblindness

A key issue demonstrated by CRT theorists is how seemingly neutral and objective legal reasoning has consistently benefited the White majority in the United States. This has occurred throughout the centuries thus creating, entrenching, and reinforcing the idea of White supremacy. In the U.S. context African American interests were sacrificed so as to (re)establish a White community. Moments of

68 In this sense, see Morag Goodwin, 'Viewing Romani Marginalization Through the Nexus of Race and Poverty', in Dagmar Schiek and Victoria Chege (eds), *European Union Non-Discrimination Law* (London, New York: Routledge-Cavendish, 2009), pp. 137–184 and Emanuela Ignățoiu-Sora, 'The Discrimination Discourse in Relation to the Roma: Its Limits and Benefits', *Ethnic and Racial Studies* (2011), vol. 34, no. 10, pp. 1697–1794.

69 On these two perspectives in anti-discrimination law, see Freeman, 'Legitimizing Racial Discrimination Through Anti-Discrimination Law: A Critical Review of Supreme Court Doctrine', pp. 1049–1119.

70 This critique is mainly raised by a number of contributions in one of the most important recent publications on Romani Politics in Europe, Nando Sigona and Nidhi Trehan (eds), *Romani Politics in Contemporary Europe. Poverty, Ethnic Mobilisation, and the Neoliberal Order* (Basingstoke: Palgrave Macmillan, 2009).

emancipation occurred when White and Black interests converged, only to be abandoned again when those interests no longer converged. Today, especially the doctrine of colourblindness, originally employed in a seemingly progressive sense by Justice Harlan in his dissenting opinion in *Plessy*,[71] has become the main jurisprudential instrument and ideology to functionally continue preventing real, substantive change in the racial hierarchy within the United States. Colourblindness serves as conservatives' justification for the constitutional prohibition of most differentiation or classification in anti-discrimination law based on race, regardless of whether the use of race involves negative stereotyping and discrimination or is intended as an anti-subordination/anti-discriminatory measure.

The question at this point is whether and to what degree Europe's race-blind approach, and its reluctance to use race in legislation, signals that similar tendencies are at play? Does the rhetoric of colourblindness perform an equivalent restrictive, conservative function in legislation and case law in this context? The second case study will look at one specific form of Continental European Colourblindness in France. The aim is to demonstrate that despite the clear historical and contextual differences between American and French colourblindness, both legal systems operate and function in ways which ultimately benefit the White majority.

France is a particularly interesting example for analysis for two reasons. First of all, France used to be one of Europe's main colonial powers. For this reason, it has a relatively long history of people with migrant backgrounds as well as French citizens with perceived different racial and ethnic origins living in its territories. Together with the United Kingdom, it is a prominent example of a European country which has had to deal with the consequences of 'the Empire striking back'[72] and the fact that immigrants are in Europe because European countries colonised, brutalised, and enslaved people in other continents, which later justified intervention to address their cultural and racial inferiority.

The second reason why France makes for an interesting case study is because since the arrival of people from former French colonies and elsewhere, claims for protection against discrimination and racism have increased. But this trend highlights the paradoxes when situating France's notoriously strong colourblind Republican view of nationhood, citizenship, and equality in today's reality. The official rhetoric stemming from the French Revolution in 1789 is that all humans are equal and that classifications and different statuses or castes between people are contrary to the French founding principles and values. Under the Republican ideal, citizenship is one of the few criteria officially allowed to distinguish between human beings. From this perspective, other distinctions in legislation or population census, even with regard to gender or religious affiliation, are considered

71 *Plessy v. Ferguson*, 163 U.S. 537 (1896) (Harlan, J. dissenting).

72 Centre for Contemporary Cultural Studies, *The Empire Strikes Back: Race and Racism in Britain* (London: Hutchinson, 1982).

highly problematic.[73] Race not only conflicts with this Republican ideal, but also serves as a reminder of the events of the 1940s during which the Vichy regime, under German occupation, introduced racial classifications to send mainly French Jews to concentration camps. The strong French Republicanism and the memory of Vichy have led France to frame most problems relating to racism and immigration in socio-economic terms rather than in terms of race and race discrimination. This situation has only changed recently. It also helps explain why anti-discrimination policies based on race are so controversial in France.[74] Clearly, the historical origins of French colourblindness are different to the emergence of American colourblindness. Nevertheless, functionally both colourblindnesses seem to be based on similar assumptions, which are founded on an 'integrationist ideology'.[75] Under this ideology, racism and racial oppression are identified as prejudice and stereotype because of skin colour and progress is seen as transcending racial consciousness. In other words, in order to achieve an enlightened American or French society, it is necessary to eliminate not only White supremacy but also Black nationalist ideology, which ends up placing them both on equal symmetrical levels. In the same way, talking about race in France, and possibly even introducing race or ethnicity conscious measures, feels as if efforts are being made to bring back Vichy or some unenlightened period of France's history. This vision assumes that race-consciousness is indeed part of France's dark history, which has been successfully overcome.

Today, however, this Republican vision is increasingly being questioned and it stands at the centre of an on-going public debate in France over issues on citizenship, immigration, public identity, equality, racism, and positive action. The philosophical-political conflict pits French republicanists against communitarian differentialists. The former plead, in the more benevolent case, for a unitary integrationist state. In the less benevolent case, they call for an outright assimilationist agenda. The latter propose a more pluralistic multicultural view, in which the existence of various groups is openly recognised or even promoted by the state. In this debate, race and ethnicity play an ambiguous role, one that republicanists despise, and one which is uneasily employed by communitarian differentialists.

Around the end of the 1990s, a shift in this broad public debate occurred at two different levels. At the theoretical level, the issue of racism as an independent, special, social problem emerged.[76] Suddenly, it became possible, even if difficult, for researchers and social scientists to mention the word race, to analyse French

73 Dominique Schnapper, 'Statistiques ethniques', *Commentaire* (2007), vol. 30, no. 117, p. 119. For a history of the French census, see Alain Blum, 'Resistance to Identity Categorization in France', in David I. Kertzer and Dominique Arel (eds), *Census and Identity* (Cambridge: Cambridge University Press, 2002), p. 121.

74 See e.g. Suk, 'Equal By Comparison', pp. 295–345.

75 See Peller, 'Race – Consciousness', pp. 758–847.

76 One important publication highlights that change directly in its title: Didier Fassin and Eric Fassin (eds), *De la question sociale à la question raciale* (Paris: Editions La Découverte, 2006).

history or society through a racial prism,[77] or to address certain issues from a moderate identity perspective.[78] Another sign of a shift was that the riots of November 2005 were interpreted as a racial issue in France, something unheard of before then.

The other level at which such a shift occurred was political. Some timid and early indicators of the changing political wind were the establishment of a Discrimination Study Group (*Groupe d'études des discriminations*, GED) launched by the then-Employment and Welfare Minister, Martine Aubry. This led to the publication of an official report in 1999.[79] The issue took political centre stage with the arrival of Nicolas Sarkozy, first as Interior Minister and then as President of the Republic. A son of immigrants, Sarkozy expressed on multiple occasions his preference for positive action, which takes into account race, ethnicity, or religion. In line with this 'multiculturalist approach', on 14 January 2004, while still Interior Minister, he proposed Aïssa Dermouche of Algerian background as *préfet* of the Jura region. When President, he appointed Rachida Dati of Moroccan and Algerian background as Justice Minister and Ramatoulaye Yade of Senegalese background as *Secrétaire d'Etat* under the Foreign Ministry. Without intending to present Nicholas Sarkozy as the symbol of progressive politics in France, his arrival has sparked the debate on such issues and demonstrated the existence of political will and power for the adoption of similar measures.

5.2.1 Legal use of race and ethnicity in an anti-discriminatory mode

The legal world is clearly not impervious or isolated from this public debate. On the contrary courts, and especially the French Constitutional Council (*Conseil constitutionnel*), actively intervene in this discourse, albeit employing their own language, context, constraints, and precedents.

From a constitutional law perspective, the national rhetoric on Republican French citizenship has mostly served to strike down certain distinctions made by the legislator. For instance, in a decision involving a statute on the territorial unit of Corsica,[80] the *Conseil constitutionnel* declared the reference to the 'people of Corsica' as contrary to Article 1 of the Constitution, which contains the principle of equality.[81] The *Conseil* specified that 'the French Constitution only knows the people of France composed of all French citizens without any distinction of

77 See e.g. Carole Reynard-Paligot, *La République raciale (1860–1930)* (Paris: Presses Universitaires de France, 2006).

78 See e.g. Ndiaye, *La condition noire.*

79 See Jean-Michel Belorgey, 'Lutter contre les discriminations' (Paris: La Documentation Française, 1999), also available at: http://lesrapports.ladocumentationfrancaise.fr/BRP/994000631/0000.pdf.

80 *Loi* no. 91–428, 13 May 1991, *Journal Officiel de la Republique Française (JORF)*, 14 May 1991.

81 Decision CC 91–290 DC, 9 May 1991.

origins, race or religion.'[82] The second decision concerned certain provisions of the European Charter for Regional or Minority Languages signed in Budapest on May 7, 1999.[83] In particular, those provisions which intended to encourage the use of regional or minority languages in public life and hence also in the judiciary, administrative bodies, and public services, were deemed to 'undermine the constitutional principles of the indivisibility of the Republic, equality before the law and the unity of the French people',[84] and were therefore declared unconstitutional. While in the Corsica decision the unconstitutionality was limited to the legal recognition of the Corsican people, here the *Conseil* went a step further by declaring the recognition of *any* group of people identified by its origins, culture, language, belief, race, or religion as incompatible with the French Constitution.[85]

Another example of how distinctions between citizens are viewed as problematic from a constitutional, equality and anti-discrimination perspective are the *Conseil*'s decisions on gender quotas in politics.[86] In 1982, the *Conseil* struck down legislation introduced to bar electoral ballots from having more than 75 per cent of their candidates of the same gender in local elections.[87] It argued that such legislation was contrary to the principle of equality, which forbids the division of the electorate or candidates according to categories. In 1999, the *Conseil* invalidated a law which would have introduced a system of strict parity on the electoral ballots for the elections to the Corsican Assembly.[88] Hence, in order to overcome the resistance and this unfavourable case law, the Constitution was modified in 1999 by adding a fourth paragraph to Article 3. The new paragraph states that 'the law shall favour equality among women and men to have access to electoral mandates and hold elective office.'[89] On the back of this amendment, the *Conseil* reversed its precedents and eventually declared gender quota provisions in the electoral context as conforming with the French Constitution. However it limited such quotas to political mandates. In fact it was unwilling to extend the applicability of this new paragraph to elections of the *Conseil supérieur de la magistrature*.[90]

What is relevant about these constitutional decisions, for the limited purposes of this chapter, is that in all cases the unconstitutional classification and distinction of groups in no way aimed at or functioned to stigmatise, subordinate, and discriminate against the group involved. On the contrary, they, especially the

82 *Ibid.*, point 13.

83 Decision CC 99–412 DC, 15 June 1999.

84 *Ibid.*, point 10.

85 Michel Clapié, 'Le français restera la langue de la République', *Les Petites Affiches* (5 January 2000), no. 3, p. 14.

86 See Blanca Rodriguez Ruiz and Ruth Rubio-Marín, 'The Gender of Representation: On Democracy, Equality, and Parity', *International Journal of Constitutional Law* (2008), vol. 6, no. 2, pp. 290–293.

87 Decision CC 82–146 DC, 18 November 1982.

88 Decision CC 98–407 DC, 20 January 1999.

89 *Loi constitutionnelle No. 99–569, relative à l'égalité entre hommes et femmes*, 8 July 1999, *Journal Officiel de la République Française (JORF)*, 9 July 1999.

90 Decision CC 2001–445 DC, 19 June 2001.

proposed statutes, pursued the goal of substantive equality. Nevertheless, the *Conseil* held that these measures contrast with the French Constitution and the equality principle enshrined in it.

This constitutional framework on equality also came into play with regard to racial and ethnic minorities in France as a result of the so-called '*statistiques ethniques*'. These 'ethnic statistics' were initially viewed as a way of collecting data, in which the racial or ethnic origins of a person may appear and/or be asked whenever making studies concerning discrimination, integration, and diversity. What had been a limited scientific discussion between demographers and statisticians until the late 1990s became a broader public debate due to the publication of a number of articles in major national newspapers.[91] Those in favour of this type of statistics argue that they are one of the main instruments of proof in social sciences. Proponents argue that without them it is impossible to seriously study the phenomena of discrimination and by extension to propose political/legal steps to combat them.[92] Moreover, such statistics would have the advantage of providing the victims of discrimination with a sort of social recognition.[93] Because of them, public institutions have also started to acknowledge the day-to-day reality which visible minorities face. The counterarguments are mainly that the introduction of such statistics may serve to reproduce, create, legitimise, and entrench racist behaviour at the national level.[94] Again, the view in France that only citizenship should appear as a legitimate distinction plays a role. The resistance to these ethnic statistics runs so deep that a number of both non-governmental and governmental organisations – SOS Racisme, MRAP, LICAR, GISTI, and the HALDE, France's newly created administrative anti-discrimination authority – are strongly opposed to them.[95] The HALDE subsequently revised its position; such statistics are acceptable as long as sufficient safeguards to individual data protection are guaranteed.[96]

This earlier debate eventually led to a legislative proposal. In fact, Article 63 of the proposed *Loi relative à la maîtrise de l'immigration, à l'intégration et à l'asile*, a piece of legislation that intended to modify existing legislation on immigration, integration, and asylum by introducing the possibility of making a person's ethnic or racial origins appear in studies on discrimination, integration, and diversity of origins, pursuant to an authorisation from the *Commission nationale de l'informatique*

91 'Le curieux débat des démographes', *Mouvements* (1999), no. 3, p. 110.

92 Patrick Simon, 'Sciences sociales et racisme: où sont les docteurs Folamour?', *Mouvements* (1999), no. 3, p. 113.

93 *Ibid.*

94 The response to this argument has been that statistics themselves cannot be racist; only their interpretations are. See Laurent Mucchielli, 'Il n'y a pas de statistique raciste, seulement des interprétations', *Mouvements* (1999), no. 3, p. 115.

95 See e.g. HALDE's decision no. 2006–31, 27 February 2006. This decision is published in HALDE's Annual Report 2006, available at: http://halde.fr/rapportannuel/2006/.

96 See HALDE decision no. 2007–233, 24 September 2007, available at: www.halde.fr/IMG/pdf/Deliberation_du_24_septembre_2007.pdf.

et des libertés (CNIL), France's independent administrative watchdog over privacy matters. This prior authorisation was supposed to substitute the required consent by the interviewed or questioned individual in order to allow the use of sensitive data. Moreover, it would have partially abolished certain provisions of French legislation regulating the treatment of personal data, including a prohibition on any public or private data controller in France to collect data relating to a person's ethnic or racial origins in studies concerning discrimination, integration, and diversity of origins. A group of members of parliament filed a constitutional complaint against this proposed amendment.[97] On 15 November 2007 the *Conseil constitutionnel* declared Article 63 unconstitutional.[98] The *Conseil* based its rejection on procedural reasons, holding that Article 63, which had been introduced as a parliamentary amendment, lacked the necessary logical-legal nexus with the bill under discussion. But in an *obiter dictum* the *Conseil* added:

> Given that, if the processing of data necessary for carrying out studies concerning the diversity of origin of peoples, discrimination and integration can relate to objective data, they cannot be based on ethnicity or race without infringing the principle laid down in Article 1 of the Constitution. [...][99]

In other words, even if the procedure had been correct, such ethnic statistics would have violated Article 1 of the French Constitution. Hence, when fighting racial discrimination against visible minorities, the French legislator cannot use ethnic and racial origins because they are not deemed to be objective data. This distinction between constitutionally permitted objective data and prohibited subjective data is problematic because there is no clear line distinguishing the two. The distinction was blurred even more by a semi-official explanatory comment published in the *Cahiers du conseil constitutionnel*.[100] On the one hand, this commentary explicitly mentions name, geographic origins, or prior citizenship as admissible objective criteria. On the other hand, it dismisses ethnic and racial origins as subjective and thus as unconstitutional. Oddly, the commentary further specifies that the *Conseil* did not hold that data processing can only be based on objective data. The use of subjective data such as those based on an individual's

97 Article 61 of the French Constitution authorises at least sixty members of the *Assemblée nationale* or of the *Sénat* to file constitutional complaints to the *Conseil* before a bill is promulgated and becomes enacted.

98 Decision CC 2007–557 DC, 15 November 2007. For a more detailed description and analysis of this decision and its political background, see Mathias Möschel, '*Race judicata*. The Ban on the Use of Ethnic and Racial Statistics in France', *European Constitutional Law Review* (2009), vol. 5, pp. 197–217.

99 Decision CC 2007–557 DC, 15 November 2007, point 29.

100 *Les Cahiers du Conseil Constitutionnel* (2008), no. 24, p. 13. The 'semi-official' refers to the technique of comments usually written by the Secretary-General of the *Conseil* and published in this law review that is directed by the *Conseil*. While these comments cannot be deemed an authoritative interpretation, the fact that they are written by the *Conseil's* Secretary-General clearly places them in a different league than that of a 'mere' doctrinal comment.

'feeling of belonging' ('*ressenti d'appartenance*') is also permissible. Therefore, there are objective data, and some subjective data, which are constitutionally admissible as legislative criteria. Then there are some other subjective data, like race and ethnic origin, which are not permissible. Without any additional guidance, this distinction between allegedly objective measures and subjective measures is problematic and ultimately highly dependent on subjective assumptions by the *Conseil*, and what it considers objectionable and what it considers unobjectionable.

As a direct, practical outcome and consequence this judgment makes it challenging for researchers in France to assess the extent of discrimination suffered by France's growing number of visible minorities. Two key questions that need to be addressed are: how can one legitimately and legally conduct future studies and polls concerning discrimination, integration, and diversity and to what extent are the questions in existing and on-going studies, such as the TeO (*Trajectoires et Origines*) study by the *Institut national d'études démographiques* (INED) and the *Institut national de statistiques et études économiques* (INSEE) legitimate?[101]

A more indirect consequence concerns the issue of affirmative action contingent on ethnic or racial criteria. In fact, the members of the *Conseil* understood the possible broader implications of allowing ethnic statistics. If widespread discrimination on the basis of people's race and ethnicity could be ascertained by scientific studies, the next step of taking measures against such discrimination follows almost automatically. However, such a move could potentially pave the road towards identity politics and the end of the image that all French citizens are equal and are treated equally. In order to prevent such a scenario, which would test if the abstract image corresponds to the concrete reality, the *Conseil* prefer to pre-emptively block any road leading in the direction of a perceived *communautarisme*. At the same time, the judges have confirmed unequivocally that they will not hesitate to strike down positive action programmes which favour groups identified by their ethnic and racial origin because such identification lacks objectivity.

This decision is interesting because this is the first time when a European constitutional judge decided on the legitimacy of legislative ethnic and racial criteria applied on populations with a migrant background who complained before the courts. It was clear that those criteria were not used in a discriminatory, subordinating, or stereotyping manner but rather they were supposed to help assess racial discrimination towards visible minorities in France. Beyond the procedural issues, colourblindness *à la française* prevented the entry into force of that provision. Somewhat ironically, the *Conseil* was able to use the language of equality, unity, and objectivity to thwart efforts at achieving more equality, and possibly increased unity, by means of a more substantive and thicker concept of citizenship over the formal and thin ideal of French Republican citizenship.

Whereas the *Conseil*'s decision intervened boldly in the broader public and political debate in France on citizenship, immigration, public identity, equality,

101 Laetitia van Eeckhout, 'Données ethniques: perplexité après la décision du Conseil constitutionnel', *Le Monde*, 25–26 November 2007, p. 9.

racism, and positive action, it failed to make any substantial change. In fact, in connection with an overhaul of the French Constitution, Nicholas Sarkozy commissioned a study on the Constitution's Preamble and the question of whether it is advisable to insert new rights and principles. Interestingly, these new rights address 'hot topics', namely equality between men and women, diversity, positive action, and equal opportunity, and the respect of private life and the protection of private data. The expert committee, guided by Simone Veil, produced a public report which concluded that the Constitution's Preamble was not the most direct, efficient, and necessary way to obtain equality and equal opportunity.[102]

The Veil Report was followed by another report, which intervened more directly and explicitly on equality and discrimination. Triggered by President Sarkozy's input,[103] this report on the issue of measuring diversity and discrimination was issued.[104] Following a detailed analysis of the situation, the report made a long list of recommendations. They neither proposed a complete exclusion of references to ethno-racial criteria in studies on diversity and discrimination nor embraced such criteria.[105] Very pragmatically it serves as a reminder on how to work within the current framework, without making any real changes, while carefully avoiding the emergence of anything that could be interpreted as ethno-racial or as positive action or positive discrimination.

5.2.2 *Legal use of race and ethnicity in a repressive mode*

Read by itself, the *Conseil*'s interpretation is not immune from criticism. It looks even more problematic when read in the broader context of French legislation and practice involving the use of race and ethnicity. In fact, the *Conseil*'s prohibition is not consistently applied throughout the system and has continued to problematise race and ethnicity only in their benign use. Ironically, it is in this repressive setting that race and ethnicity have withstood legal challenges so far.

The most egregious example is a little known decision by the Parisian Court of Appeal, *Cour d'appel de Paris*, which established that the division of a prison according to ethnic units did not constitute criminal racial discrimination.[106] The prison, *La Santé*, had an unwritten practice which subdivided four blocks according to

102 Simone Veil, 'Redécouvrir le Préambule de la Constitution – Rapport du Comité présidé par Simone Veil' (Paris: La documentation française, 2008), available at: http://lesrapports.ladocumentationfrancaise.fr/BRP/084000758/0000.pdf.

103 A Presidential speech on diversity: Nicolas Sarkozy, 'Égalité des chances et diversité', Discours de M. Le President de la République à Palaiseau, École polytechnique, 17 December 2008 available at: www.lyceesaintmarc.org/rubriques/gauche/stages/cpge-hk-b-l-1ere-annee/17.12-ecole-polytechnique-palaiseau.pdf.

104 Comité pour la mesure de la diversité et l'évaluation des discriminations (COMEDD), 'Inégalités et discriminations. Pour un usage critique et responsable de l'outil statistique', 5 February 2010, available at: http://lesrapports.ladocumentationfrancaise.fr/BRP/104000077/0000.pdf.

105 *Ibid.*, pp. 212–224.

106 This decision offers an interesting parallel reading to a similar U.S. Supreme Court decision on racial segregation in prisons: *Johnson v. California*, 543 U.S. 499 (2005).

racial/ethnic criteria: Block A, also called 'Little Europe', incarcerated mostly White, European prisoners; Block B housed prisoners of Antillean or sub-Saharan African origins; Block C hosted inmates from the Maghreb; and Block D was designated to other ethnicities and nationalities. It should be noted that this subdivision was not by citizenship but along ethnic/racial lines. In fact, Antilleans, who are French citizens and often dark-skinned, were grouped with sub-Saharan Africans in Block B, whereas French citizens of Algerian background were placed into Block C together with prisoners from the Maghreb but not French citizens. The subdivision itself was also tied to different prison conditions within the separate blocks. It was during renovation works on Block A that the vastly differing incarceration conditions were disclosed. The other blocks were infested by rats and lice and in an advanced stage of disrepair. SOS Racisme, a French anti-racism NGO, initiated criminal proceedings for race discrimination against the prison authorities. Pursuant to Articles 225–1 and 432–7 of the French Criminal Code, racial discrimination is defined as any distinction between natural and legal persons based on certain criteria amongst which are race, ethnicity, or origin. Such distinction is punished by up to five years imprisonment and a €75,000 fine when committed by a public officer in the exercise of a public service whose act interferes with a legal benefit or the normal exercise of an economic activity.

The prison authorities' main defence was that the subdivision and distinction took into consideration the prisoners' common culture and lifestyle and that block allocation was neither automatic nor exclusive. Moreover, they further argued that this type of block allocation had always existed at *La Santé* and was considered a prudent management decision in housing the prison population.[107] Both the trial court[108] and the court of appeal[109] rejected the claim of race discrimination. While both acknowledged that a distinction on the basis of race and ethnicity had taken place, the judges held that no interference of a legal benefit or of a normal economic activity had taken place. They based their decision on the following reasons: (i) no prisoner had brought a claim for racial discrimination; (ii) the differing conditions between the blocks could not be considered an interference with a legal benefit; and (iii) the renovation work was being carried out progressively without any clear indication in the order of renovations or without any deliberate racial or ethnic priority. Accordingly, the second element

107 What the defendants failed to mention (or at least this aspect does not emerge from the available documentation) is that this practice was based on legislative provisions. In fact, Articles D 88 and D 91 FCPC establish that the head of the prison decides personally on the subdivision of inmates and the decision to detain them in common. In such decisions, the guidelines provide that all precautions need to be taken in order to prevent annoying consequences such as promiscuity from arising amongst the inmates and sometimes it might be advisable to ensure the individual imprisonment of some and the *separation by categories* of others (italics added).

108 Tribunal de Grande Instance de Paris, Juge d'Instruction: no. Instruction 243/02/88, 17 July 2003.

109 Cour d'appel de Paris, Première Chambre de l'Instruction: Dossier no. 2003/05865, 10 November 2003.

of the crime of race discrimination was absent and the case was dismissed. SOS Racisme decided to take the case to the French Supreme Court (*Cour de cassation*) even though the public prosecutor had decided to drop the case. Under former Article 575 of the French Criminal Procedure Code (FCPC) this meant that the *Cassation* must dismiss the claim, unless the lower court's decision contained such a fundamental error that the decision must be deemed legally inexistent. A fundamental error would include the absence of legal and logical reasoning or the absence of a response to a brief filed by the aggrieved party. In accordance with Article 575, SOS Racisme argued that the lower court's findings were so contradictory in their legal reasoning that an essential condition of its legal existence was lacking.[110] However, the *Cassation* dismissed the claim, without judging the merits of the case.[111] One could certainly argue that the *Cassation* dismissed the case on purely formal grounds. However, it is telling that the public prosecutors would not find it worthwhile pursuing such a claim or that the trial and appellate judges were unable to characterise the prisoners' differential treatment as interference with a legal benefit. This case demonstrates the narrow limits within which racial discrimination is framed. If a prison can legally subdivide its blocks on the basis of a presumably illegitimate criterion and differentiates living conditions in those blocks, it is difficult to answer what situation or treatment qualifies as racial discrimination in the French context. Despite repeated rhetorical efforts at combating such discrimination, in practice its recognition is limited.

The whole judicial affair received attention from a member of the French parliament and the Minister of Justice. Their questions centred on the subsequent instructions given to the prison management, and whether it was necessary to formally amend applicable legislation and prison regulations in order to end the ethnic separation which violates French constitutional principles and values. The Minister replied that there was no ethnic segregation in French prisons and that the situation at *La Santé* was perfectly in line with the applicable law, as confirmed by the courts. Therefore, according to the Minister, no instructions or changes were necessary.[112] Ultimately, the racial and ethnic status quo of the repressive mechanisms were kept in place, even when it is based on an otherwise unacceptable distinction in French law and society. Moreover, the situation could have easily remained unchanged considering the legal backing from the state's courts and the Minister of Justice, who was in a position to change on a political level such an outrageous judicial decision.

The police and secret service reinforce the picture of how race and ethnicity are used. On the one hand, this happens by means of racial profiling in the context

110 Copy of the brief lodged with the *Cour de cassation* on file with the author.

111 Cour de cassation, Chambre Criminelle: Pourvoi no. G 03–87.649, décision de non-admission, 11 May 2004. It should be mentioned here that Article 575 FCPC was declared unconstitutional by the *Conseil* because it violates the principle of equal access to justice. Decision 2010–15/23 QPC, 23 July 2010.

112 Assemblée nationale, 12ème législature, Question écrite no. 33641, *Journal Officiel de l'Assemblée nationale*, 25 May 2004.

of stops, identity checks, and searches by the police forces. A recent study, which gathered information from over 500 police stops in Paris, showed that Blacks were on average 6 times and Arabs 7.6 times more likely to be stopped by the police than people with White, Western European origins.[113] Racial profiling has already been declared a human rights violation by the UN Human Rights Committee in a case involving Spain.[114] At the national level, the picture is slightly different with the first legal challenges of such practices in France[115] being brought and dismissed only recently.[116] The case involved thirteen applicants who claimed that they had been subject to racial profiling by the police who had performed a number of identity checks on Black and Arab men only. The trial court rejected the claims on the grounds that the plaintiffs' complaint concerned deficiencies in French legislative framework involving identity checks, which goes beyond its competencies. The trial court held that it is up to the legislator, and not the courts, to change the legal framework.[117] In this instance, we see again the racially repressive framework being upheld by the judiciary.

On the other hand, one should also mention the use of police and secret service files, which subdivide suspects according to ethnic and racial groups, even though officially such a practice is held to be unconstitutional. The issue first arose in the early 1990s when a first decree authorised courts to record the racial origins of parties in litigation concerning race discrimination,[118] and a second case allowed French secret services, *renseignements généraux*, to collect information about individuals, in which *inter alia* their ethnic origins could appear as an identification factor.[119] The second decree in particular was viewed as a repressive rather than a protective move. In fact, it allowed the collection and storage of such sensitive data of individuals who threatened public safety or the security of the state, and of those who had direct and non-fortuitous meetings with those people. A third decree published the same day established a separate electronic database, *fichier*, controlled by the secret services of the Interior Minister, in which information

113 Open Society Institute, 'Profiling Minorities: A Study of Stop-and-Search Practices in Paris' (New York: Open Society Institute, 2009), also available at: www.opensocietyfoundations.org/sites/default/files/search_20090630.Web.pdf.

114 HRC, *Rosalind Williams Lecraft v. Spain*, Communication no. 1493/2006, CCPR/C/96/D/1493/2006, 17 August 2009.

115 For a recent case in Germany, see Verwaltungsgericht Koblenz, Az. 5K 1026/11.KO, 28 February 2012 (holding that the identity check of a Black German student for the sole reason of his skin colour constituted only a minor intervention into his civil and political rights and was therefore legitimate). This decision was overturned on appeal: Oberverwaltungsgericht Rheinland-Pfalz, Az. 7A 10532/12.OVG, 28 October 2012.

116 Tribunal de Grande Instance de Paris: Decision no. 12/05884, 2 October 2013.

117 For a comment on this decision, see Axelle Keles, 'La justice française renvoie au législateur le soin de se prononcer sur les contrôles d'identité au faciès', *Lettre "Actualités Droits-Libertés" du CREDOF*, 28 November 2013.

118 *Décret* no. 90–115, 2 February 1990, *Journal Officiel de la République Française (JORF)*, 4 February 1990.

119 *Décret* no. 90–184, 27 February1990, *Journal Officiel de la République Française (JORF)*, 1 March 1990.

concerning individuals suspected of terrorist activities was collected and stored.[120] These decrees led to a public outcry, which forced the government to repudiate the second and third decree. They were substituted with another decree over a year later.[121] Regarding the second decree, it ended the controversy by authorising the collection of data, limited to specific physical, objective, and inalterable signs as identification determinants. It is clear this measure only skirted around the issue formally but did not alter the substance of the matter.[122] In fact, nothing in that formulation prevents the secret services from collecting, classifying, and recording the data of individual suspects on the basis of their skin colour, and by extension their supposed racial or ethnic origins.

The issue arose again in 2006, when a newspaper article described that the French secret services had established a criminal profile for young members of organised gangs; of these members, 87 per cent were of French nationality, and within that group 67 per cent had a Northern African, *maghrébin*, background and 17 per cent an African background.[123] Another article by the same newspaper revealed that the *Gendarmerie nationale*, a branch of the French armed forces in charge of public safety, kept files illegally on Roma people and on *gens du voyage*.[124] It is clear that such classifications and files on French citizens are contrary not only to the idea(l) of formal equality among French citizens but also to constitutional principles.

Clearly, there are certain issues when juxtaposing and comparing a constitutional case with a criminal case and police practices. First of all, criminal law and constitutional law are guided by different principles of interpretation. The former is subject to strict interpretation. Therefore teleological or extensive construction of criminal statutes is out of question. Second, until recently judicial review was only abstract in France, meaning it reviewed legislation only before it entered into force.[125] This means that little overarching constitutional authorities and harmonisation are possible as far as French legislation is concerned. As a result, constitutional law, administrative law, and ordinary legislation follow their own logic and criteria of interpretation. Only the ECtHR has provided some kind of common, unifying principles through its jurisprudence.

In spite of these observations, if one looks at how the legal system works as a whole, some disturbing conclusions can be drawn. One cannot help but notice

120 *Décret* no. 90–185, 27 February 1990, *Journal Officiel de la République Française (JORF)*, 1 March 1990.

121 *Décret* no. 91–1051, 14 October 1991, *Journal Officiel de la République Française (JORF)*, 15 October 1990 and *Décret* no. 91–1052, 14 October 1991, *Journal Officiel de la République Française (JORF)*, 15 October 1990.

122 Danièle Lochak, 'La race: une categorie juridique?', *Mots* (1992), no. 33, pp. 302–303.

123 Piotr Smolar, 'Bandes: la spirale de l'ultra-violence', *Le Monde*, 25 February 2006, p. 3.

124 See Emmanuel Aubin, 'La discrimination à raison de l'origine ethnique', in Félicien Lemaire and Bernard Gauriau (eds), *Les discriminations* (Paris : Editions Cujas, 2011), p. 98.

125 The *Loi constitutionnelle* no. 2008–724, 23 July 2008, *Journal Officiel de la République Française (JORF)*, 24 July 2008 has introduced the possibility of judicial review even after legislation has entered into force.

that when race or ethnic origins are used in a positive, anti-subordination, anti-discriminatory mode, they are automatically viewed as suspect, as contrary to the French Republican model of citizenship, and do not withstand legal challenge. This is especially the case following the *Conseil*'s decision. Colourblindness coupled with the idea(l) of formal equality fulfils the same function as it does in the United States, namely to function to legitimise the status quo by denying rights, or in this case the potential emergence of rights, to racial and ethnic minorities. On the contrary, when the same criteria are deployed in a repressive, criminalising, negative setting, the judges validate them or at least the system does little to challenge them. CRT theorists would highlight how the legal system, including its seemingly neutral provisions – like the equality principle, criminal intent, legal standing or elements of a crime – ultimately benefit the White, French majority, at the expense of France's visible minorities, who are kept in a position of marginalisation and denied equality.

The French case illustrates how far the repressive police practices, prison authorities, and criminal law work formidably, and legally unchallenged, along a racial divide in Europe. Situated under the umbrella of colourblindness, one could even talk about selective colourblindness, where courts and other legal actors turn a blind eye to race and choose to view it very clearly when it is used in an anti-discriminatory fashion.

5.3 Italy's legal construction of a White, Christian, male identity

As described in Chapter 2, besides the critique of American anti-discrimination law, CRT scholars have also been prominent in demonstrating the fundamental role law played in constructing racial identities. Historically, law was constitutive in determining racial privilege and racial subordination, and who belongs and does not belong to an imagined national community. As we have also seen, law's role in the European context has been less visible, or less explicit. With the exception of colonial legislation, and cases of the Roma and Jews, in Europe legal racial and ethnic subordination ran and runs along slightly different fault lines that remain hidden and blurred by the concepts of citizenship and/or religion, and are often couched in the colonial past. However, every now and then those fault lines emerge.

This third case study will look more closely at the Italian context. Through an examination of local regulations and their effects on national legislation in particular, I will attempt to unearth the racial, ethnic, and gendered fault lines that lie at the basis of several provisions adopted. Whereas often these fault lines remain invisible or subject to speculation, when they emerge they cast an eerie light on the remaining framework. This case study also demonstrates how law builds on those fault lines and incorporates them, thus contributing to the construction of a White, male, Christian, Italian (European) identity as the neutral, invisible reference model.

The Italian example provides a particularly interesting case study in this domain for several reasons. On the one hand, Italy is a country which has only passed from being a country of emigrants to one receiving immigrants in recent decades. Therefore it is interesting to see how institutions react to this apparent change. On the other hand, Italy has recently undergone a constitutional reform in a federalist sense. Under the previous system, the competences of the regions were listed and anything else was the competence of the central state. Following the constitutional reform of Article 117 in the Italian Constitution, it now expressly lists the competences of the central state. By default, the remaining competences fall under regional/local competence.[126] Provinces and municipalities were also recognised by the Constitution as autonomous actors in this revised framework.[127] The reform can be attributed to the pressure of the Northern League, *Lega Nord*, a populist political party, which, since its inception, demanded more independence from the central government for the rich Northern regions. Becoming part of the government in the early 1990s those demands were finally heard and transformed Italy into a more federal state. Importantly, local authorities ranging from regional and provincial councils and governments down to mayors and local councils of cities and towns, in particular those located in Northern Italy and governed by the Northern League, have interpreted this reform as giving them free rein on a number of key issues. In particular, they have adopted a number of measures whose direct or indirect targets are the Roma, migrants, or people with a migrant background. Moreover, these mayors are now better coordinated and institutionally linked. During conventions assembling mayors belonging to the Northern League, they ensure that ideas for ordinances can circulate easily, be assessed as to their legal validity, and obtain confirmation at higher political levels.[128]

This last case study looks at the combined effect of these local and national provisions, the racist and xenophobic sentiments they draw upon, and how they eventually create and enforce the image of a Christian, male, White-Italian (European) identity at the exclusion of anyone not fitting the category. More specifically, this section first looks at a number of council deliberations and municipal ordinances targeting migrants directly and indirectly and how the legal system deals with neutralising these measures at the constitutional, administrative, and ordinary court level. The specific case of ordinances dealing with the prohibition of the burqa demonstrate the religious and gender dimensions of such a legal construction at the hands of local ordinances and proposed national legislation. Moreover, the focus on the local and micro-level shows how the populist discourse permeates local regulations, which are then legally challenged. This localised process functions like a laboratory for legal argumentation, before entering the more visible national domain. Finally, two very specific local measures in the small towns of Morazzone and Coccaglio unveil the racial and ethnic fault lines, or the 'racial

126 Article 117 of the Italian Constitution.

127 Articles 114 and 118 of the Italian Constitution.

128 See e.g. the first convention of Northern League mayors on 24 October 2009 in Milan.

knowledge',[129] underlying many of the local provisions involving racial minorities. Ultimately, local legislation and regulations also construct who is Italian, the make-up of an Italian appearance, Italian cultural belonging, and when an individual or group gains access to membership of the national community.[130]

Moreover, it is impossible to understand the normative picture drawn here without briefly mentioning the social context, in which these measures are adopted: cities building walls to isolate neighbourhoods with high immigration levels,[131] parents taking their children out of schools with a high percentage of Roma children,[132] hunting parties organised against alleged irregular migrants and Roma,[133] just to name some of the most outrageous actions reported in Italian newspapers. Even the press contributes to these sentiments and 'Othering' with reports that often only reflect the racist attitudes observable by the public.[134] In that context, one can only imagine the daily, everyday racism which migrants, people of colour, Muslims, and Roma must experience, which is rarely reported. On top of all this comes the additional layer of legal discrimination with the already demonstrated difficulties to challenge such racism in court.

5.3.1 Local (and national) measures targeting migrants

During the past fifteen years, Italy's media has been filled with news from regional legislators, mayors, and local councils adopting measures that either directly or indirectly target migrants or the Roma, mainly on the assumption that (irregular) immigration equates criminality.[135]

In the first category of provisions that directly target and distinguish people of migrant origins, mostly third country nationals, two areas have been particularly prominent: (i) residency requirements imposing additional criteria for third country nationals and (ii) local welfare/social security benefits granted on the basis of

129 David Theo Goldberg, *Racist Culture: Philosophy and the Politics of Meaning* (Oxford: Blackwell 1993).

130 For a slightly different overview and classification of such local measures, see Maurizio Ambrosini, '"We are Against a Multi-Ethnic Society": Policies of Exclusion at the Urban Level in Italy', *Ethnic and Racial Studies* (2013), vol. 36, no. 1, pp. 136–155.

131 See e.g. in Padova. For more details on this, see Francesca Musiani, 'Walls Built Up, Walls Written Down: Of Symbolic Value, Material Effectiveness and Media Representations of Barriers in Padua, Italy', in John Holten and Line Simenstadt Madsen (eds), *You are Here: Europa Today* (Berlin: Broken Dimanche Press, 2009), pp. 39–61.

132 http://torino.repubblica.it/cronaca/2013/09/10/news/troppi_bambini_rom_a_scuola_i_genitori_italiani_ritirano_i_loro_figli-66265446/.

133 http://romanolil.blog.tiscali.it/2007/09/18/scene_di_caccia__ai_rom__in_bassa_padania_1801146-shtml/.

134 On the role and contribution by the Italian press, see Chris Hanretty and Costanza Hermanin, 'Nominalization as Racialization in the Italian Press', *Bulletin of Italian Politics* (2010), vol. 2, no. 2, pp. 75–94.

135 According to a general trend, mayors have become very 'creative' with their regulatory powers issuing ordinances on virtually any issue. See Sergio Bontempelli, '"Ordinanza pazza". I sindaci e il versante grottesco del razzismo', in Lunaria (ed.), *Libro bianco sul razzismo* (Roma: Lunaria, 2009), pp. 75–82. See also the website: http://ordinanzapazza.wordpress.com/.

Italian citizenship only or imposing additional criteria for third country nationals. As to the first category, a number of ordinances in different localities in Northern Italy have attempted to make it particularly onerous for immigrants to establish residency in their municipality. Their ways of doing so have differed. For example, the mayor of Alessandria required that third country nationals seeking registration, *iscrizione anagrafica*, in the town's registrar provide: (i) a residence permit; (ii) a rental agreement; (iii) an employment contract; (iv) a certificate of healthy and robust constitution; and (v) their criminal record.[136] Similarly, the mayor of Cittadella passed an ordinance that required all foreigners, including EU citizens, to demonstrate that they earned a minimum income of €5,061 annually.[137] The mayor of Mirano went further by requiring a certain number of square metres per person in addition to income requirements to obtain registration in the town's registrar.[138] Under those criteria, many Italians already living in this location would not have qualified for registration or residency. The mayor of Ospitaletto tried to limit the influx of foreigner residents by means of two ordinances which required a five-year permanent residence in Italy in order to register or, if that was not possible, an original or certified copy of the criminal record from the country of origin.[139]

The local registrar's strict administrative registration requirements lead to the second category of cases of direct discrimination against individuals with migrant backgrounds: the granting of local social security or welfare benefits. In many towns once residency is obtained, one is entitled to certain local welfare and social benefits such as public housing. Following this logic, efforts to make it hard for non-Italians, or individuals who became naturalised Italians, to obtain residence act as a double 'benefit': first, they keep the town Christian/Italian and second, they prevent migrants and their children from accessing the welfare system. Once the first barrier of residence has proved to be ineffective, mayors, and local and/or regional authorities simply try to deny the benefits directly, mostly on the basis of citizenship. One of the most notorious examples involved Lombardy's regional statutory regulation, then implemented by Milan, which established that only disabled Italian citizens could benefit from free regional public transportation.[140] In that same region, in accordance with another regional statute,[141] Milan conferred five additional points to Italian citizens in the assignment of public housing. Functionally and formally this amounts to an explicit affirmative action quota for

136 Alessandria, Ordinanza del Sindaco, no. 19, 25 January 1999, *Questione giustizia* (1999), no. 2, pp. 351–352.

137 Cittadella, Ordinanza no. 258, prot. 50875, 16 November 2007.

138 Mirano, Ordinanza no. 145, 28 November 2008.

139 Ospitaletto, Ordinanza, 11 February 2009 and 8 March 2009.

140 See Article 8, para. 2, *Legge regionale Lombardia*, no. 1, 12 January 2002, *Bollettino Ufficiale della Regione Lombardia*, no. 3, 15 January 2002, as amended by Article 7 of *Legge regionale Lombardia*, no. 25, 9 December 2003, *Bollettino Ufficiale della Regione Lombardia*, no. 50, 12 December 2003, and implemented by decision of the Giunta regionale Lombardia, *Delibera* no. 7/16747, 12 March 2004.

141 See Article 10, *Legge regionale Lombardia*, no. 28, 4 May 1990, *Bollettino Ufficiale della Regione Lombardia*, no. 19, 7 May 1990.

Italians. One can only imagine the public outcry had a similar quota been established for migrants, Roma, or other minorities. Many of the cases in the Italian context concern the granting of child subsidies at various levels. One example is the deliberation taken by the local council of Brescia,[142] which granted a child subsidy of €1,000 to resident Italian families only. Following a judicial decision, which held that the nature of those criteria was discriminatory, the local legislator decided not to grant the child subsidy to anyone.[143] The examples given above are only the proverbial tip of the iceberg and there are many other examples that do not make it into the news or before Italy's courts.[144]

To complete the picture of local provisions directly targeting migrants, other municipalities have created imaginative manoeuvres as a means to adopt directly discriminatory measures. This is the case of Lucca in Tuscany. In a regulation introducing new rules on the sale of food and beverages, Lucca's local council prohibited the additional grant of licenses to restaurants selling ethnic food.[145] Some municipalities have imposed the use of the Italian language in public meetings or assemblies which are held on the territory.[146] Other municipalities have issued an ordinance establishing an area of protection of 15 metres around sacred Christian sites in order to safeguard Christian values from contamination by other religions and based on reciprocity that other countries prohibit the access to certain areas to non-believers of a certain religion.[147]

This localised discourse directly targets migrants. In these examples of local measures similar situations can be found at the national, legislative level as well.[148] For example, the Budget Act, *legge finanziaria*, for the year 2001 limited family subsidy to families with Italian and EU citizenship with a minimum of three children.[149] The Italian Budget Act for 2006 determined that a subsidy for infants born in 2006, the so-called '*bonus bebè*', would be granted to Italian or EU citizens only.[150] More recent legislation introduced a card for the most economically disadvantaged classes to acquire goods and services and limited it to residents with

142 Brescia, *Deliberazione del Consiglio comunale* no. 1062/52053, 21 November 2008.

143 Brescia, *Deliberazione del Consiglio comunale* no. 46, 30 January 2009.

144 See e.g. the local executive's deliberation of Brignano Gera d'Adda, which decided to grant families a subsidy for certain medical visits of their children but then required that *inter alia* those children needed to be Italian citizens. Brignano Gera d'Adda, *Deliberazione* no. 75, 14 June 2008.

145 Lucca, *Regolamento* sugli esercizi di somministrazione di alimenti e bevande, 22 January 2009.

146 Trenzano, Ordinanza no. 312, 5 December 2009.

147 Rovato, Ordinanza del Sindaco no. 86, prot. 22916, 21 November 2000, *Diritto, immigrazione e cittadinanza* (2000), no. 4, p. 224. This ordinance was annulled by the *prefetto* for radical voidness. See Alessandra Algostino, 'L'ordinanza del sindaco di Rovato e il pericolo di "contaminazione" dei valori cristiani. Nota a margine di un atto "considerato radicalmente nullo"', *Diritto, immigrazione e cittadinanza* (2001), no. 2, pp. 84–91.

148 For more information on this national legislation, see Cecilia Corsi, 'Prestazione assistenziali e cittadinanza', *Diritto, immigrazione e cittadinanza* (2009), no. 2, pp. 30–47.

149 Article 80, para. 5 of *Legge* 23 December 2000, no. 388, *Gazzetta Ufficiale (GU)* no. 302, 29 December 2000.

150 Article 1, para. 333 of *Legge* 23 December 2005, no. 266, *Gazzetta Ufficiale (GU)* no. 302, 29 December 2005.

Italian citizenship[151] or reserved the reimbursement of expenses for artificial milk and diapers for new-borns up to the age of three months to the most economically disadvantaged Italian citizens.[152]

The second broader category of municipal ordinances or local legislation targets migrants indirectly. These local provisions, while facially neutral, have or had a disproportionate impact on migrants or third country nationals. For instance, in 2007 the mayor of Florence issued three ordinances which explicitly prohibited and punished the activity of window-washers, *lavavetri*, on Florentine traffic lights.[153] This activity was predominantly exercised by people belonging to the Roma minority. Another example is in the city of Vicenza, where a local ordinance prohibits parking with campers or house trailers in a limited area of town.[154] In addition to criminal sanctions, there is a penalty fine of €350–€500 for non-observance of the order. Again, this, like the other local legislation, mostly affects the Roma minority. In addition to this, a number of mayors have moved to issue ordinances concerning street prostitution and begging.[155] Even here, the intended targets of such ordinances are the Roma minority, foreigners, and migrants.[156] Another classical example of indirectly discriminatory provisions concerns the condition of having a prolonged residence before being allowed to access certain social or welfare benefits. This was the case of a regional statute of Lombardy which, in order to obtain public housing, demanded five years of residence or professional activity in the region of Lombardy.[157] Residence requirements also emerged in another contested and debated matter this time at the national level. Indeed, one of the right wing government's first actions in 2008 was the abolishment of the so-called '*assegno sociale*', a subsidy of €395 per month for people over 65 years and living in very poor social conditions, which does not require any type of prior contributions. In Italy, about 800,000 people had the right to this subsidy, of which 1.8 per cent were foreigners. The right-holders had to be resident in Italy and either Italian citizens, EU citizens, or third country nationals with a permanent residence permit. A statutory amendment proposed by the government changed these conditions. In the first proposal, the bill to obtain the subsidy, starting from 1 January 2009, required that the recipient

151 Article 81, para. 32 of *Legge* no. 133, 6 August 2008, *Gazzetta Ufficiale (GU)* no. 195, 21 August 2008.

152 Article 19, para. 18 of *Legge* no. 2, 28 January 2009, *Gazzetta Ufficiale (GU)* no. 22, 28 January 2009.

153 Firenze, Ordinanza no. 774, 25 August 25 2007; Ordinanza no. 883, 11 September 2007 and Ordinanza no. 975, 15 October 2007.

154 Vicenza, Ordinanza del Sindaco no. 43291, 5 August 2008.

155 See Roma, Ordinanza no. 242, 16 September 2008; Milano, Ordinanza del Sindaco no. 29, 4 November 2008. Excerpts are published in Marco Gasparini, 'Criminalità e degrado urbano: la battaglia è a colpi di ordinanze', *Guida al Diritto – Il Sole 24 Ore* (6 December 2008), no. 48, p. 20.

156 Nazzarena Zorzella, 'I nuovi poteri dei sindaci nel "pacchetto sicurezza" e la loro ricaduta sugli stranieri', *Diritto, immigrazione e cittadinanza* (2008), no. 3–4, p. 71.

157 Article 1, a) *Legge regionale Lombardia*, 8 February 2005, no. 7, *Bollettino Ufficiale della Regione Lombardia*, 10 February 2005, no. 6.

must have continuously resided in Italy and worked for a sum at least equal to the amount of the subsidy for a minimum of ten years. The objective was to exclude migrants from having access to such benefits. However, public outcry resulted from this first proposal since it became clear that under these conditions many older Italian women would also be excluded. Since many women did not have ten years of employment at even the minimal amount, because they would have cared for their families without receiving any salary, they would have been excluded. Moreover, the argument was made that this amendment would prevent Italians residing abroad to be able to benefit from this subsidy. In the final text, the reference to income was eliminated, whereas the residence requirement of minimum ten years was maintained.[158] With the inclusion of Italian women, this ended the public outcry, even though many migrants who previously benefited from the *assegno sociale* were excluded.

So far, the legal challenges brought against these provisions in the Italian legal system have been relatively successful. It should be noted that pursuant to the Italian Constitution only acts having force of law, such as statutes, regional statutes, and delegated legislation in the form of decrees – *decreti legge* – and legislative decrees – *decreti legislativi* – are subject to judicial review.[159] But even regarding these acts, direct judicial review is only applicable when they are challenged due to competence conflicts between institutions. Otherwise the review is often subsidiary or indirect, meaning such legislation only makes it to the Italian Constitutional Court, the *Corte costituzionale*, in the context of underlying litigation. Other types of legal provisions such as ordinances or deliberations by regional, provincial, or local governments, however, cannot be constitutionally tested. Their review is therefore 'only' based on principles of common or administrative law.

Hence, in this part I will look at how the above described measures were challenged in Italian courts, first with regard to the constitutionality of acts having force of law and second with regard to the common or administrative legality of local measures.

As far as the constitutionality of legislative measures is concerned, a number of decisions need to be mentioned. Most of these cases focus on the issue whether statutory distinctions between citizens and foreigners, or between citizens and foreigners with long-term/short-term residence permits, violate the equality principle enshrined in Article 3 of the Italian Constitution. For example, in 2005 the *Corte costituzionale* declared that the Lombardy regional statute, which excluded disabled foreigners from the benefit of free regional public transportation, violated Article 3.[160] In particular, the judges applied the reasonableness test, by holding that the criterion of citizenship was completely unrelated to the scope of the

158 Article 20, para. 10, *Legge* 6 August 2008 no. 133, *Gazzetta Ufficiale (GU)* no. 195, 21 August 2008.

159 See Article 1, *Legge costituzionale*, 9 February 1948 no. 1, *Gazzetta Ufficiale (GU)* no. 43, 20 February 1948.

160 Corte costituzionale: Sentenza no. 432/2005, 28 November 2005.

benefit and that the only reason for the distinction was to discriminate against foreigners as such. On this basis, the legislator's distinction was contrary to the principle of equality.

In other decisions the constitutional court struck down legislative provisions that conditioned the award of certain disability benefits on possession of a long-term residence permit. Since obtaining such a residence permit requires that a person demonstrate he or she is in regular employment and this is precisely what a disabled person often does not have, such provisions automatically excluded foreign citizens from being able to take advantage of such benefits. Again the legislator's choice was deemed unreasonable and therefore the *Corte costituzionale* declared the unconstitutionality of these provisions because they violated the equality principle.[161] Unreasonableness was also the reason why the same court declared unconstitutional some revised provisions of the regional statute of Friuli, which established that certain social services were available to Italian citizens or EU citizens only after 36 months of residence in the region.[162]

These decisions, however, do not address the issue of whether the distinction between a long-term resident foreigner and a short-term resident foreigner – in order to determine whether to grant or withhold certain social benefits – is reasonable and compatible with the equality principle and the Italian Constitution. This constitutionality issue has been raised by a trial court.[163] The outcome is not clear and it really depends on what the *Corte costituzionale* deems to be reasonable or unreasonable, which is highly indeterminate and contingent on the underlying political situation. For instance the constitutional court held that a Lombardy regional statute, which subordinated the assignment of public housing to a five-year residence or employment in the region, did not violate the Italian Constitution.[164] The ECJ has already declared unconstitutional residency requirements for accessing social benefits because they violate the principle of non-discrimination on the grounds of nationality under EU law.[165] The question ultimately comes down to the duration of the residency in order to ascertain if certain or all social benefits are available. The longer the residency requirement, the more suspicious it will be with regard to discriminatory intent or effect.[166]

As far as the review of local measures whose constitutionality cannot be raised is concerned, they can be annulled nevertheless in three different ways: through

161 Corte costituzionale: Sentenza no. 306/2008, 28 July 2008 and Corte costituzionale: Sentenza no. 11/2009, 24 January 2009.

162 Corte costituzionale: Sentenza no. 40, 7 February 2011.

163 Tribunale di Brescia: Ordinanza no. 615, 15 January 2007, *Diritto, immigrazione e cittadinanza* (2007), no. 4, pp. 106–111.

164 Corte costituzionale: Sentenza no. 32, 21 February 2008.

165 See e.g. ECJ, Case C–57/96, *Meints v. Minister van Landbouw, Natuurbeheer en Visserij* [1997] ECR I–6689; ECJ, Case C–337/97, *CPM Meeusen v. Hoofdirectie van de IBG* [1999] ECR I–3289; ECJ, Case C–299/01, *Commission v. Luxemburg,* [2002] ECR I–5899.

166 See Cecilia Corsi, 'Prestazione assistenziali e cittadinanza', *Diritto, immigrazione e cittadinanza* (2009), no. 2, pp. 30–47.

common law principles in ordinary courts,[167] administratively in administrative courts, or hierarchically by the administrative superior. With regard to the first option, the 'easier' cases are represented by ordinances containing direct discrimination, mostly based on nationality. Some courts[168] annulled these provisions on the basis of Article 43 of the Italian Immigration Code,[169] and in some cases on the basis of the legislative decree 215/2003 implementing the RED.[170] The main difference between these two pieces of legislation is that Article 43 protects against nationality discrimination amongst other grounds of discrimination, whereas the Legislative decree 215/2003 protects against discrimination on the grounds of race and ethnicity but excludes discrimination on grounds of nationality. In Italy this has led to a partial overlap, and in most discrimination cases the violation and the remedies of either are being claimed in parallel. This occurred, for instance, in a recent decision by the Milan tribunal confirming a lower court's decision,[171] which struck down a local citizenship-based limitation on child subsidies, '*bonus bebé*',[172] due to its discriminatory nature by applying and referring to both legislative provisions as well as to the principle of equality enshrined in Article 3 of the Italian Constitution.[173]

An even more interesting judicial ruling is represented by the case of Brescia's child subsidies granted to parents of children residing in the city. In the first decision, the Brescia tribunal declared the discriminatory nature of the deliberation and a violation of Article 43 of the Immigration Code, which contains a non-discrimination clause on the grounds of race, ethnicity, nationality, or religion.[174] When the city of Brescia decided to cancel the child subsidy *tout court,* rather than extending it to everyone, the plaintiffs took the case to court again, arguing that the revocation of the subsidy for everyone had a retaliatory and discriminatory impact. The court agreed with the plaintiffs' arguments.[175] Other judges found

167 See Annamaria Casadonte and Alberto Guariso, 'L'azione civile contro la discriminazione per motive etnico-razziali e religiosi', *Questione giustizia* (2010), no. 4, pp. 179–191.

168 See e.g. Tribunale di Milano: Sentenza 21 March 2002, *Foro italiano* (2003), part I, columns 3179–3184, ordering the city of Milan to eliminate the discriminatory aspects of its decision in the assignment of public housing mentioned above. See also Alessandro Simoni, 'La discriminazione razziale alla vigilia dell'attuazione della direttiva 43/2000: considerazioni a partire da alcune recenti pronunce giurisprudenziali', *Diritto, immigrazione e cittadinanza* (2002), no. 4, pp. 81–90. See also Tribunale di Brescia: Ordinanza no. 3071, 11 December 2009 annulling the ordinances of Ospitaletto mentioned in this section.

169 *Decreto legislativo* no. 286, 25 July 1998, *Gazzetta Ufficiale (GU)* no. 191, 18 August 1998.

170 *Decreto legislativo* no. 215, 9 July 2003, *Gazzetta Ufficiale (GU)* no. 186, 12 August 2003.

171 Tribunale di Milano, Sezione Lavoro: Ordinanza no. 2909, 29 September 2010.

172 Tradate had decided to introduce a child subsidy of €500 limitedly to families where both parents are Italian and resident in the town for at least five years. See Tradate, *Verbale di deliberazione del Consiglio comunale* no. 55, 28 September 2007.

173 Giuseppe Tucci, 'Principio di eguaglianza e discriminazione per nazionalità e cittadinanza: "bonus bebè" e razzismo "padano"', *Rivista critica del diritto privato* (2010), no. 4, pp. 677–699.

174 Tribunale di Brescia: Ordinanza no. 335, 26 January 2009, *Diritto, immigrazione e cittadinanza* (2009), no 2, pp. 163–166.

175 Tribunale di Brescia: Ordinanza 12 March 2009, *Diritto, immigrazione e cittadinanza* (2009), no. 3,

that the distinction between citizens and non-citizens violated Article 2 of the Italian Immigration Code, which establishes the principle of equal treatment between citizens and foreigners with a residence permit with duration of more than a year as far as their civil rights are concerned.[176]

With regard to the administrative challenges brought in the Italian legal system, they mainly involve municipal ordinances adopted by mayors, and their cancellation because the mayors have exceeded their statutory powers.[177] Under Italian law, mayors have a double function, which determines the exercise of their powers. On the one hand, mayors have a political function as representatives of the local electorate. In the limited context of the local competences granted to municipalities they have full powers to adopt ordinances. On the other hand, mayors also have an administrative, state function. In this role, the mayor is simply a representative of the state and the exercise of his powers is subject to review by hierarchical superiors, the *prefetto*, and at the very top the Interior Minister, the *Ministro degli Interni*. In this context the mayor adopts ordinary ordinances implementing state policies in specific areas, laid down in law. An exception to these ordinary ordinances is in the case of public necessity and urgency whenever there is grave danger to the safety of Italian citizens. In such cases, the mayor has full competences to adopt any necessary measures to prevent harm to the citizens on the municipalities' territory. This means that these exceptional ordinances do not have a statutorily predetermined content and they can be adopted with simplified procedures. They have to be limited in time however.[178] Moreover some areas, such as criminal law, are constitutionally reserved to the legislator, meaning that mayors as a matter of principle cannot adopt criminal law provisions or interpretations by ordinance.

One of the above-mentioned ordinances, namely that of Cittadella, where the mayor single-handedly changed the residence requirements by imposing more stringent conditions on non-citizens and instituted a municipal commission to determine the social danger of residence registration applicants, led to criminal

pp. 170–181 and in *Rivista italiana di diritto del lavoro* (2010), part II, pp. 198–211 with a note by Andrea Lassandri, 'Agli italiani o a nessuno: i c.d. bonus bebè e la ritorsione discriminatoria' in the same journal issue at pp. 198–201. See also Tribunale di Brescia, Sezione Lavoro: Ordinanza 22 July 2010, *Questione giustizia* (2010), no. 4, pp. 192–194.

176 See Tribunale di Biella: Ordinanza 2 January 2007 (declaring the discriminatory character of a statutory provision denying the child subsidy to foreign citizens with a long-term residence permit), *Diritto, immigrazione e cittadinanza* (2007), no. 1, pp. 116–126. For an additional analysis of similar cases, see Stefano Rossi, '*Law in Action*: Diritto antidiscriminatorio e politiche locali', *Responsabilità civile e previdenza* (2010), no. 12, pp. 2541–2660.

177 See e.g. the *prefetto* of Alessandria who annulled the ordinance imposed by the mayor mentioned *supra* in this section because of its discriminatory character. See Prefetto di Alessandria: Provvedimento 6 February 1999, *Questione giustizia* (1999), no. 2, p. 353.

178 Nazzarena Zorzella, 'I nuovi poteri dei sindaci nel "pacchetto sicurezza" e la loro ricaduta sugli stranieri', *Diritto, immigrazione e cittadinanza* (2008), no. 3–4, pp. 59–60.

charges against him for usurping his public functions.[179] Indeed, according to the attribution of competences, residence requirements are determined at the national level and mayors simply supervise their implementation. Nevertheless, criminal charges against the mayor for usurpation of powers are the most drastic and exceptional measure. In most cases the adopted measures themselves are simply suspended or annulled. For instance, in the wake of Cittadella and following the publicity it generated, a number of other Northern Italian municipalities – Lecco, Desio, Seregno, Lissone, Biassono, Lesmo, Cogliate, and Lazzate – had adopted this 'worst practice' in their own territories. The competent Regional Administrative Tribunal of Lombardy, the *Tribunale Amministrativo Regionale* (TAR), suspended the execution of a few of these ordinances,[180] finding they represented an irregular and illegitimate use of the mayors' powers, while also holding that they seemed null and void because of the suspicion of discriminatory intent.[181]

Another example, where the mayor exceeded his powers, was in the case of Florence and the ordinance providing that window cleaning at traffic lights would be punishable pursuant to Article 650 of the Italian Criminal Code. This article sanctions the non-observance for reasons of justice, public security, and order or hygiene, when non-observance does not constitute a more serious criminal offence.[182] The Florentine ordinance made reference to a municipal police regulation which granted authorisation for all kinds of vagrant professions, and that window cleaners had never obtained such an authorisation. Pursuant to this ordinance, the police pressed charges against a window cleaner and the public prosecutor made a request to dismiss the case. The judge agreed by holding that Article 650 was not applicable because it punishes individual non-observance of an authority's order and not the non-observance of provisions, which may apply to an indeterminate number of people.[183] Moreover, in another similar case involving window-cleaners and Article 650, Italy's Supreme Court found that window-cleaning, and other vagrant professions, had been exonerated from the authorisation requirement for public security reasons in 2001 by a presidential decree.[184] For this reason, the *Cassazione* held that mayors cannot pass an ordinance to reintroduce the criminalisation of an action that had been statutorily

179 Carlo Ruga Riva, 'Il lavavetri, la donna col burqa e il sindaco. Prove atecniche di "diritto penale municipale"', *Rivista italiana di diritto e procedura penale* (2008), no. 1, p. 142.

180 Seregno, Ordinanza del Sindaco no. 563, 12 December 2007; Biassono, Ordinanza del Sindaco no. 107, 6 December 2007; Lecco, Ordinanza del Sindaco no. 355, 31 December 2007.

181 T.A.R. Milano (Lombardia), Sezione III: *Ordinanze* no. 701, no. 702 and no. 717, 8 May 2008.

182 Article 650 c.p. *Chiunque non osserva un provvedimento legalmente dato dall'autorità per ragione di giustizia o di sicurezza pubblica o d'ordine pubblico o d'igiene, è punito, se il fatto non costituisce un più grave reato, con l'arresto fino a tre mesi o con l'ammenda fino a euro 206.*

183 Tribunale di Firenze: Decreto no. 10834/07, 20 September 2007, *Diritto, immigrazione e cittadinanza* (2007), no. 3, pp. 195–198 with a note by Fausto Giunta and Alessandro Simoni, 'Il diritto e i lavavetri: due prospettive sulle "ordinanze fiorentine"' in the same journal at pp. 81–91.

184 Article 6 of *Decreto del Presidente della Repubblica (DPR)* no. 311, 28 May 2001, *Gazzetta Ufficiale (GU)* no. 178, 2 August 2001.

de-criminalised and thereby exceeded their powers.[185] Following these principles, the only possible sanctions that can be imposed for this type of behaviour are administrative. And not surprisingly, this is precisely what the mayor of Florence did in the third ordinance[186] by threatening administrative sanctions of €75–€500 to individuals who approach drivers offering to clean windows and headlamps.[187]

One of the latest examples of when the courts annulled a mayor's ordinance concerns the requirement to hold public meetings in Italian. In this case, the competent TAR found that the mayor had exceeded his powers because decisions limiting the freedom of assembly can only be taken by the *prefetto* and not by the mayor. This remains the case even under the increased competences attributed recently to mayors, which will be explained in more detail in the section below concerning the burqa.[188]

5.3.2 *The Italian version of burqa bans in public spaces*

The issue of mayors exceeding their powers has become the core issue in a number of ordinances involving the burqa. The debate on the burqa ban is not limited to Italy,[189] and currently the ECtHR is reviewing the legitimacy of French legislation prohibiting the wearing of the veil in public.[190] However, whereas in other European states the debate has arisen at the national level, Italy has what could be defined a local laboratory in which to test the legal system with regards to burqa bans in public spaces at the local level.

The first of such municipal ordinances to reach widespread public attention was issued in 2007 by the mayor of Azzano Decimo, a small town in North Eastern Italy.[191] He ordered citizens to comply with two provisions: (i) Article 85 of the Public Security Code,[192] a Fascist relic, which prohibits covering your face in public; and (ii) Article 5 of the Public Order Protection Act (POPA).[193] The latter article prohibits the unjustified wearing of protective helmets or any other means intended to make the identification of a person difficult in public or spaces open to the public. In any case, such use is prohibited during public events or during events open to the public, except for sports' events where similar gear

185 Corte di cassazione, Sezione I penale: Sentenza no. 37112, 2 October 2002.

186 Comune di Firenze, Ordinanza no. 975, 15 October 2007.

187 For more details on the Florentine ordinances, see Carlo Ruga Riva, 'Il lavavetri, la donna col burqa e il sindaco. Prove atecniche di "diritto penale municipale"', *Rivista italiana di diritto e procedura penale* (2008), no. 1, pp. 133–148.

188 T.A.R. Brescia (Lombardia), Sezione II: Sentenza no. 19, 15 January 2010.

189 See David Koussens and Olivier Roy (eds), *Quand la burqa passé à l'ouest* (Rennes: Presses universitaires de Rennes, 2013).

190 ECtHR, *S.A.S. v. France*, no. 43835/11.

191 Azzano Decimo, Ordinanza del Sindaco no. 24, 27 July 2004.

192 *Regio decreto* no. 773, 18 June 1931, *Gazzetta Ufficiale (GU)* no. 146, 26 June 1931.

193 *Legge* no. 152, 22 May 1975, *Gazzetta Ufficiale (GU)* no. 136, 24 May 1975. For a comment on this law and its history in relation to the burqa bans, see Giancarlo Scarpari, 'La legge Reale, il burqa e il "comune sentire del popolo"', *Diritto, immigrazione e cittadinanza* (2006), no. 1, p. 78.

is required. Violations are punished with imprisonment for one–two years and a fine of €1,000–€2,000 with the possibility to proceed with a warrantless arrest. This provision introduces two different types of prohibition. First, a general prohibition against wearing clothing that is intended to make the identification of a person difficult in the case of public events, with the exception of certain sports events. Second, a more limited prohibition in the case of public spaces, which depends on the intent of the person wearing the item that makes the identification of such person difficult and which is unjustified. What the ordinance did is to explicitly include the veil, which covers the face, amongst those 'means which may render the identification of a person difficult in public spaces or spaces open to the public'. The person's intent and justification for wearing the veil are disregarded.

This municipal ordinance was cancelled at the administrative level by the mayor's competent hierarchical superior, the *prefetto*,[194] following an Advisory Opinion by the Interior Ministry[195] recommending its annulment. The mayor disagreed with this decision and took the case to the TAR against both the *prefetto*'s decision and the Interior Minister's opinion. The mayor's main argument was that he had acted according to his functions and competences as the local political elected representative and not on the basis of the administrative competences attributed to him as an Italian government official. As was already explained, only in the latter case is the *prefetto* deemed to be the mayor's hierarchical superior with powers to annul ordinances. The TAR did not agree with the mayor's arguments. Instead, the TAR determined that the *prefetto* had acted within his competences in annulling the ordinance. The TAR further established that a general criminal prohibition on wearing such kinds of clothing in public can only derive from legislation, specifying such a prohibition, which would also be in line with the political implications of a similar decision.[196] Azzano Decimo's mayor then appealed to the Supreme Administrative Court, the *Consiglio di Stato* (CdS). In what became a landmark decision on the allocation of powers and competences between mayors and the state, the CdS confirmed the lower court's decision.[197] The administrative judges first analysed the nature of the adopted provision and observed that the mayor's ordinance was not an exercise of his powers as representative of the local polity but an attempted exercise of general competence in public security. These competences in public security are exercised in a coordinated and dependent manner with the state authorities. Hence, in this case the *prefetto* was the mayor's hierarchical superior. In order to ensure a unitary direction and coordination of

194 *Decreto del Prefetto della Provincia di Pordenone* prot. no. 11202/669/Area I, 9 September 2004.

195 *Parere del Ministero degli Interni* no. 11001/65, 23 August 2004.

196 T.A.R. Trieste (Friuli Venezia Giulia), Sentenza no. 645, 16 October 2006, *Diritto e Giustizia* (2006), no. 44, pp. 111–113; also published in *Giurisprudenza di merito* (2007), no. 9, pp. 2423–2425, with a note by Vincenzo Greco 'Il divieto di indossare il velo islamico: tutela della sicurezza o strumento di lotta politica? Quando il sindaco eccede i suoi poteri', in the same journal issue at pp. 2426–2431.

197 Consiglio di Stato, Sezione VI: Decisione no. 3076, 19 June 2008.

the public security officials and agents within the provincial territory or to eliminate illegitimate provisions, the *prefetto* is entitled to annul ordinances. Therefore the annulment was held to be legitimate.

Having answered the issue of whether the annulment of the ordinance had been *ultra vires*, the CdS then went on to analyse the substantive issues raised, namely the interpretation of the prohibition of covered faces in public. The CdS held that far from being an application of statutory law, the ordinance provided an innovative interpretation of criminal legislation. As such, neither the reference to Article 85 of the Public Security Code nor to Article 5 of the POPA was correct or legal. Regarding Article 85, which prohibits appearing masked in public, the CdS held that a burqa is not a mask but is considered a traditional, even religious, item of clothing. Article 5 only establishes the prohibition to appear with covered faces in the case of public events. Otherwise, in public it is permitted to cover one's face if there is a reasonable justification for it and the disguise is not to avoid recognition. Applying Article 5 to a woman wearing the burqa, the CdS determined that religious and cultural motives are sufficient justification to cover one's face in public and that in any case there is no intention to prevent recognition. The requirements of public security are satisfied by the prohibition of wearing such means during protests and by the obligation of such persons to identify themselves and to remove the veil, when necessary. Nevertheless, the CdS continued, this interpretation does not exclude the possibility that in certain places or in specific instances, behavioural rules may be prescribed by administrative means, as long as they are reasonable and justified on the basis of a specific necessity.

In another case, the local police of Treviso reported a woman of Moroccan background with a veil covering her whole face on the basis of a municipal ordinance containing the same prohibition. Here, rather than an administrative challenge, the case was solved at the criminal law level because during the preliminary hearings the public prosecutor asked the judge to dismiss the case.[198] He argued that the woman was not wearing the veil so as to avoid identification or to make such identification difficult but for reasons related to religious tradition. Hence, one of the elements of the crime, namely the woman's *mens rea*, was absent. Wearing the veil for religious purposes certainly qualified as one of the justified motives for which one could cover one's face in public and, coupled with that, the police forces had no problem identifying the person. The judge agreed with the public prosecutor's arguments and ordered the charges to be dropped.[199]

This last case also highlights another problematic aspect characteristic of wearing the veil under Article 5 of the POPA. How little the application of these ordinances corresponds with the purported aim to guarantee public order and security, arising from the risk of attack by unidentifiable women walking in public,

198 Procura della Repubblica presso il tribunale di Treviso, Richiesta di archiviazione, 19 November 2004, *Diritto, immigrazione e cittadinanza* (2006), no. 1, pp. 176–177.

199 Tribunale di Treviso: Decreto di archiviazione, 3 March 2005, *Diritto, immigrazione e cittadinanza* (2006), no. 1, p. 177.

is best demonstrated by the example of another municipal ordinance adopted by the mayor of Drezzo, a small town in North Western Italy.[200] Again, the ordinance included the veil amongst those 'means which may render the identification of a person difficult in public spaces or spaces open to the public'. The competent *prefetto* annulled the ordinance on 9 September 2004. However, prior to that annulment, Sabrina Varroni, born and raised in Drezzo, was fined twice pursuant to that ordinance. She had married a Tunisian man, whereupon she converted to Islam and decided to wear the veil. Upset because she had also received insulting correspondence in addition to the fines, she sought legal assistance and sent an open letter to the former President of the Republic, Carlo Azeglio Ciampi, who answered by stating that in Italy there is freedom of religion and that the *prefetto* had already proceeded to annul the ordinance.[201] The story of this ordinance clearly shows how little these instruments actually have to do with public order and security or with the fact that the woman was wearing the veil in order to avoid identification. In fact, Varroni was the only veiled woman in Drezzo and everyone knew her, including the policeman administering the fines, who had even attended school with her. Moreover, it was clear that she was wearing the veil for religious reasons, and was certainly not attempting to avoid identification so as to commit a crime or a terrorist act.

From a positive perspective, the Italian legal system has until now worked in neutralising these ordinances. As illustrated, all these cases were ultimately decided in favour of the women wearing the veil, either because they were annulled at the administrative, hierarchical level or because the courts intervened. However, the case law contains some troublesome implications for the future. In fact, two main obstacles to mayors adopting municipal ordinances based on Article 5 of the POPA emerge from the cases and arguments. On the one hand, from an administrative law perspective, mayors do not have the powers and/or competences to regulate certain broad security related issues because this falls within the competence of the state. On the other hand, from a criminal law perspective, interpretation by analogy or extensive interpretations in criminal law are impermissible. Due to constitutional requirements, criminal laws have to be introduced

200 Drezzo, Ordinanza del Sindaco no. 8, 12 July 2004. See Matteo Gnes, 'L'annullamento prefettizio delle ordinanze del sindaco quale ufficiale del governo', *Giornale di diritto amministrativo* (2009), no. 1, p. 46 at fn. 10. Other ordinances have also been adopted during that same time period in other small towns such as Biassono and Caloziocorte (Biassono, Ordinanza del Sindaco, 10 August 2004 and Calolziocorte, Ordinanza del Sindaco, 22 September 2004). The former ordinance was annulled by the Prefect of Milan. See Giuseppe Guastella, 'Il prefetto stoppa il sindaco: non può vietare il velo', *Corriere della Sera*, 4 September 2004, p. 12. On the latter ordinance, see Angelo Panzero, 'Velo a Calolziocorte, parola al prefetto', *Corriere della Sera*, 5 October 2004, p. 52.

201 'Multata perche portava il burqa. E ora Sabrina scrive a Ciampi', *La Repubblica*, 26 September 2004, available at: www.repubblica.it/2004/i/sezioni/cronaca/chapis/drezzo/drezzo.html and 'Il Quirinale alla donna col burqa "In Italia c'è libertà di culto"', *La Repubblica*, 13 October 2004, available at: www.repubblica.it/2004/i/sezioni/cronaca/chapis/ciampiscrive/ciampiscrive.html.

and amended by the legislator only. Hence, if anyone can modify the POPA so as to include wearing the veil in public amongst the prohibited pieces of clothing, it is only the Italian Parliament, and not the mayorly ordinance. A judge confirmed this requirement in a different case which involved a woman wearing the burqa, who had been charged with the violation of Article 5 of the POPA for entering a courthouse to assist a trial for terrorism involving one of her relatives. When entering, she was asked to identify herself, which she duly did in front of female police officers. Notwithstanding her compliance, she was accused of rendering her identification difficult and was in turn sued. The judge acquitted the case, in part on the grounds that there is no explicit statutory provision criminalising such behaviour.[202] Nevertheless, both the administrative decision as well as the acquittal leave it open to the legislator to decide whether to include the wearing of a veil under such restrictive public security legislation.[203]

In order to overcome these obstacles two strategies are possible: increase the powers of the mayors when they act as government officials to maintain public order and security at the local level, or have the Italian legislator intervene to amend Article 5 of the POPA. Both strategies were pursued, meaning that the aim and vision embodied, created, and constructed in those local ordinances in Northern Italy moved up to the national arena.

As to the first strategic move in 2008, concerning the so-called security package legislation, the Italian executive introduced a decree increasing the mayors' powers.[204] Shortly thereafter this decree was converted into ordinary legislation.[205] The most important provision in this context is Article 6 of the decree, which specifically increased the powers of the mayor relating to matters of public order and security. This amendment responded to demands by mayors and local entities to have increased powers to address issues of public order and security and to provide a legal basis for other types of very creative municipal ordinances that have mushroomed in Italy over the past years.[206] Following this amendment, mayors have kept their extraordinary powers to issue ordinances on the basis of necessity and urgency in any matter relating to the safety of citizens. The most

202 Tribunale di Cremona: Sentenza 27 November 2008, *Il Corriere del Merito* (2009), no. 3, pp. 294–295, with a note by Natalina Folla, 'L'uso del *burqa* non integra reato in assenza di una previsione normativa espressa', published in the same journal issue at pp. 295–302. See also the more critical analysis disagreeing with the decision, mainly because holding that the burqa or the niqab fall under the security legislation, of Simona Paola Bracchi, 'La "burqa" nelle aule di giustizia', *Famiglia, Persone e Successioni* (2009), no. 11, pp. 912–914.

203 In this sense for the administrative decision by the T.A.R. Friuli Venezia Giulia, see Massimo Minniti and Francesco Minniti, 'Tra libertà religiosa e ordine pubblico Sindaco ko alla guerra del velo islamico', *Diritto e Giustizia* (2006), no. 44, p. 110; also in this sense for the Cremona case, see Natalina Folla, 'L'uso del *burqa* non integra reato in assenza di una previsione normativa espressa', *Il Corriere del Merito* (2009), no. 3, p. 300.

204 *Decreto legge* no. 92, 23 May 2008, *Gazzetta Ufficiale (GU)* no. 122, 26 May 2008.

205 *Legge* no. 125, 24 July 2008, *Gazzetta Ufficiale (GU)* no. 173, 25 July 2008.

206 On this point Gnes, 'L'annullamento prefettizio delle ordinanze del sindaco quale ufficiale del governo', pp. 49–50.

important aspect is that their ordinary powers have been increased to protect public safety, *incolumità pubblica*, and urban security, *sicurezza urbana*, also in the absence of situations of necessity and urgency. Now, mayors are competent to issue ordinances that concern public safety and urban security, provided that they previously inform the *prefetto* of the planned actions. It is clear that the concepts of 'public safety' and 'urban security' can be subject to very broad interpretations and indeed most of the creative municipal ordinances adopted during the past years were justified by referring to broadly analogous concepts.

Hence, the Interior Minister by decree[207] defined what is intended by 'public safety' and 'urban security' in Article 1: the first term stands for the physical integrity of the population, whereas the second term indicates a public good that needs to be protected by means of activities aimed at defending the respect for provisions that regulate civil life, better living conditions in urban centres, and social cohesion in the local community. Article 2 of the same decree identifies a number of typical situations in which the mayor is authorised to intervene. Nevertheless, the impression is that the definitions are still vague and leave considerable room for discretion and interpretation on what public integrity and urban security actually mean when viewed from a public order and security perspective.[208]

This renewed regulatory framework has the following chracteristics; first, it grants increased powers to mayors; second, it is vague; and third, Italy's then Interior Minister, Roberto Maroni, was from the Northern League – the political party of most mayors issuing these ordinances on the veil as well as the others described above. The combination of these factors may have initiated a new round of municipal veil ordinances. A survey shows that from August 2008, when the reform entered into force, until August 2009, mayors adopted 788 ordinances on the basis of these new powers.[209] Local and national newspapers in 2009 and 2010 kept reporting that other towns in Northern and Central Italy such as Alassio,[210] Varallo Sesia,[211] Codognè,[212] Novara,[213] and

207 *Decreto del ministro dell'Interno*, 5 August 2008, *Gazzetta Ufficiale (GU)* no. 186, 9 August 2008.

208 For a more detailed evaluation of mayors' increased powers, see Simona Calcagnini, 'I nuovi poteri del sindaco in materia di sicurezza', *Studium iuris* (2009), no. 5, pp. 502–509.

209 Cittalia – Fondazione Anci ricerche, 'Oltre le ordinanze. I sindaci e la sicurezza urbana', 2nd edn, September 2009, p. 13, available at: www.cittalia.it/images/file/oltre-le-ordinanze09.pdf?php MyAdmin=95af31fc7e586d80e7d664a36f07b8b6&phpMyAdmin=3dc56f06dc02f3f7ac2bf9bdd4ec9b2f.

210 Alassio, Ordinanza del sindaco no. 444, 1 October 2008.

211 Varallo, Ordinanza del sindaco no. 99, 19 August 2010 and Ordinanza del sindaco no. 100, 21 August 2010. The former ordinance prohibits the wearing of the so-called burkini, swimming clothing designed for Muslim women and covering most parts of the female body. The irony of such an ordinance issued in a little Alpine town where the bathing space is a river which few kilometers upstream springs from a glacier, cannot escape anyone. The latter ordinance prohibits the wearing of the burqa.

212 Codognè, Ordinanza del sindaco no. 6, 19 March 2010.

213 Novara, Ordinanza del sindaco no. 917, 15 December 2009, substituted later by Ordinanza del sindaco no. 36, 29 January 2010.

Cossato[214] adopted anti-burqa ordinances on the basis of the new directions from Rome and the Interior Ministry. Surprisingly, however, in the case of Fermignano, the answer given by these authorities was negative. While respecting the decision, the mayor Cancellieri nevertheless gave instructions to local police to ask for the identification of women wearing a burqa. Following this authorised harassment of five women in the town, none remained in the city or ventured out again.[215] It should be noted that, as opposed to some of the earlier veil ordinances, which attempted to sanction the women on the basis of an extensive interpretation of Article 5 of the POPA and therefore as a criminal law matter, these latest cases are based on the mayors' new powers in matters of public safety and security which enables them to issue administrative sanctions of up to €500. In light of recent developments, it is only a matter of time before criminal sanctions can be legally applied as well. This last point relates to the elimination of the second obstacle to the prohibition of veils in public: the fact that criminal law can only be amended by the legislator, which would also apply to Article 5 of the POPA.

Regarding the second strategic move to amend the POPA by introducing the criminal prohibition to wear the veil in public, a first step in that direction was taken in 2005. The fine established under Article 5(2) of the POPA was increased from imprisonment of six months to one year to imprisonment of one to two years and a fine of €1,000–€2,000. This amendment was introduced by a decree establishing new rules on personal identification.[216] That decree was transformed into statutory law by the Act on Urgent Measures to Combat International Terrorism.[217] Even though the political representatives of the Northern League tried to specifically mention the burqa or chador as clothing forbidden by the statute, this first amendment of the POPA only introduced stricter sanctions but did not specify which garments. With the escalation of these trends throughout Italy, the risk was that the xenophobic political propaganda targeting Muslims would not go unheeded and would eventually influence judges and legislators alike.[218]

The answer came quickly: a total of thirteen bills aimed at modifying Article 5 of the POPA and proposed by different political parties were proposed to the lower and upper houses of the Italian Parliament.[219] All of these bills, except for

214 Cossato, Ordinanza del sindaco no. 77, 26 May 2010.

215 Paolo Stefanini, *Avanti Po: la Lega Nord alla riscossa nelle regioni rosse* (Milano, il Saggiatore, 2010), pp. 235–236.

216 Article 10, para. 4-*bis*, *Decreto legge* no. 144, 27 July 2005, *Gazzetta Ufficiale (GU)* no. 173, 27 July 2005.

217 *Legge* no. 155, 31 July 2005, *Gazzetta Ufficiale (GU)* no. 177, 1 August 2005.

218 In this sense, see Giancarlo Scarpari, 'La legge Reale, il burqa e il "comune sentire del popolo"', *Diritto, immigrazione e cittadinanza* (2006), no. 1, p. 80.

219 All were proposed during the XVIth legislature. For the lower house they were: Binetti, *et al.*, Proposta di legge no. 627, 30 April 2008; Sbai and Contento, Proposta di legge no. 2422, 6 May 2009; Cota, *et al.*, Proposta di legge no. 2769, 2 October 2009; Mantini and Tassone, Proposta di legge no. 3018, 3 December 2009; Amici, *et al.*, Proposta di legge no. 3020, 4 December 2009; Lanzillotta, Proposta di legge no. 3183, 8 February 2010; Vassallo, *et al.*, Proposta di legge no.

one,[220] had the purpose to explicitly include the Muslim veil under the prohibited means of covering one's face in public. The techniques of doing so, however, varied. Restrictive proposals bluntly added a sentence to Article 5(1) of the POPA, which explicitly prohibits the use of female clothing, named burqa and niqab, worn by Muslim women.[221] Other bills were even more restrictive and basically introduced a general prohibition not to be unidentifiable in public under any circumstance, including for religious reasons. The only permissible exceptions were protective helmets, explicitly required by legislation for traffic safety or for certain sports.[222] Seemingly more liberal are those bills which tried to strike a different balance between freedom of religion and the public security. While approving certain clothing in public for religious, cultural, or ethnic motives under specific justifications with regard to Article 5 of the POPA, such clothing nevertheless needed to keep the person's face free and identifiable.[223] As opposed to all the other bills, the most lenient and progressive proposal maintained the original Article 5 of POPA distinction between public events and public spaces in general. Moreover, it established that clothing worn in public for religious, cultural, or ethnic reasons was a justification with regard to Article 5 of the POPA and that, upon request by a public official when specific grounds and motives of public security exist, that person must give consent and show his or her face so as to allow for temporary identification.[224]

The reasons and justifications for introducing these bills vary slightly. Public security reasons and the fight against terrorism, with specific references to the terrorist attacks in the United Kingdom on 7 and 21 July 2005, are mentioned as primary reasons in some proposals. Freedom of religion is never mentioned in these proposals.[225] Other proposals make some attempt to address religious freedom, only to justify its restriction by broadly referring to the dignity of women.[226] According to such proposals, the burqa or niqab are symbols of submission and for this reason cannot be tolerated in civil societies based on the rule of law.[227] They further argue that these types of veil are not really required by the Muslim faith and are only the result of radical, cultural, misogynist tendencies leading to female segregation in civil and social life.[228] These justifications allow them

3205, 11 February 2010; Vaccaro *et al.*, Proposta di legge no. 3368, 7 April 2010; Reguzzoni *et al.*, Proposta di legge no. 3715, 17 September 2010; Garagnani, Proposta di legge no. 3719, 21 September 2011; and Bertolini, Proposta di legge no. 3760, 11 October 2011. For the upper house: Baio *et al.*, Disegno di legge no. 1543, 8 May 2007 and Spadoni Urbani, Disegno di legge no. 2343, 20 September 2010. Hereinafter all bills are referred to by their number only.

220 3205.

221 627, 2422, 3018, 3760 and 2343.

222 2769, 3368 and 3715.

223 3020 and 1543.

224 3205.

225 2422 and 2769.

226 3020.

227 In particular, 3018.

228 3183 and 3018.

to reject the argument that freedom of religion might be at stake. According to this reasoning, since the burqa is not required by the Qur'an, it is unnecessary to invoke freedom of religion. In other words, there is no violation of Article 19 of the Italian Constitution or Article 9 ECHR.[229] The more moderate proposals simply find that, in balancing necessities of public security and religious freedom, it is a reasonable compromise to require that the face be made visible.[230] Last but not least, one of the proposals also mentions the need to clarify the original meaning of Article 5 of the POPA. This would also include a harmonisation of the non-homogeneous, but mostly restrictive, judicial decisions, in order to clarify the scope of this provision on the national territory.[231]

Two of these bills were criticised during parliamentary hearings, which started before the later bills were proposed and were subsequently amalgamated.[232] These critiques were voiced by university professors. They pointed to the fact that there was never an incident in Italy or Europe where the veil was used for terrorist purposes.[233] Another point that was raised is that a criminal statute, which developed in a specific historical context and had a certain specific public order function, is not the best and most sensitive instrument to deal with more complex topics presented by the Muslim veil.[234] In addition, both bills risk violating the equality principle in the Italian Constitution, because both clearly refer to the Muslim religion.[235] There are then other, more specific, critiques which can be applied to each individual bill. For example, the explicit reference only to Muslim women runs the risk of a challenge of unconstitutionality because of its discriminatory nature. Moreover, the explicit naming of two types of Muslim clothing, such as the burqa and the niqab, opens the possibility for women to argue that they are wearing other clothing, giving it a different name, which would evade the application of the provision.[236] A similar problem is raised by a study of the Italian Parliament's Constitutional Affairs Committee, which highlights how the use of foreign terms such as burqa and niqab in legislation may lead to interpretative uncertainties and inconsistencies. This is particularly problematic in provisions of criminal law when the terms can be used with partially different meanings according to the geographical location and the specific context.[237] Other critiques concern the radical elimination of any reference to a justified motive for covering

229 3018.

230 627 and 3020.

231 2769.

232 2422 and 2769.

233 See Roberta Aluffi, intervention before Camera dei Deputati – Commissione I, Affari Costituzionali, della Presidenza del Consiglio e Interni, *Resoconto Stenografico*, 10 November 2009, at p. 4.

234 See Roberto Mazzola, intervention before Camera dei Deputati – Commissione I, Affari Costituzionali, della Presidenza del Consiglio e Interni, *Resoconto Stenografico*, 10 November 2009, at p. 12.

235 *Ibid.* at p. 11.

236 See Aluffi, *Resoconto Stenografico*, 10 November 2009, at pp. 4–5.

237 Camera dei deputati (Servizio Studi, Dipartimento Istituzioni), 'Divieto di indossare gli indumenti

one's face in public. As noted already the only permissible justification for face covering in public spaces is when it is required by traffic safety or sport events. This is an overly broad prohibition and means that many everyday situations in which people cover their faces or heads, for example skiing helmets for adults, sanitary masks, or carnival masks, would fall under that criminal provision.[238] Other broader critiques are raised, which are advanced in the bill that stands out in this panorama.[239] Ultimately, this exceptional bill rejected the proposals contained in the other bills because such measures risked increasing the segregation of precisely those women whose dignity the legislation purports to protect. These measures also risked being interpreted as a form of religious discrimination, thus only feeding precisely the radical tendencies which the bills sought to repress. Moreover, the bill argued that it was not up to the legal system to verify what a community's religious obligation is and whether a certain interpretation corresponds to the correct interpretation of a text. Any religion, including Western religious beliefs, have evolved over time and incorporated different practices, rules, and rites. Last but not least, the proponents of this bill reject the security argument. They argue that a burqa or niqab would be an unlikely item to wear in public if an individual wanted to commit a crime or act of terrorism.

The interesting point, which all these bills share, except for the more progressive one,[240] is that the veil continues to be interpreted in the limited framework of criminal law sanctions related to security concerns and terrorism. It never really steps out of this logic or proposes a broader framework of analysis and problem-solving. Any reform is limited to a simple amendment to criminal law.[241] In a final step, all these bills were amalgamated and merged into one single bill in July 2011, which was a combination of the most restrictive and repressive solutions contained in the bills.[242] Nevertheless, with the end of the legislature on 22 December 2012, this proposal failed because it had not been voted on. The bill will not be voted upon unless it is re-proposed in the new term of legislature, which has not been the case so far. In the absence of any progressive and sensitive interventions and in light of the broader picture regarding the domestic treatment of migrants and individuals with migrant backgrounds, the question remains as to whether these rules are concerned with public security and the dignity of women wearing the veil. When trying to answer this question it is important to bear in mind that there has not been one single instance involving veiled women terrorists in Italy

denominati *burqa* e *niqab*', A.C. no. 2422, 30 September 2009, available at: http://documenti.camera.it/leg16/dossier/Testi/ac0378_0.htm.

238 Aluffi, *Resoconto Stenografico*, 10 November 2009, at p. 5.

239 3205.

240 *Ibid.*

241 See Marco Ventura, intervention before Camera dei Deputati – Commissione I, Affari Costituzionali, della Presidenza del Consiglio e Interni, *Resoconto Stenografico*, 10 November 2009, at pp. 17–18.

242 See http://leg16.camera.it/824?tipo=A&anno=2011&mese= 07&giorno=13&view=&commissione=01#data.20110713.com01.allegati.all00030.

or any Western country. Another significant point not to be ignored in the Italian context is that there are a small number of veiled women in Italy.

What is important for the purposes of this case study is that when read in conjunction with the other measures targeting migrants or visible minorities and local ordinances regulating the veil, these legislative proposals take on a very different character. Indeed, they become the expression of widespread xenophobia, Islamophobia, and racism hidden behind the pretext of public security or the protection of female dignity. For this reason, the Italian example on the prohibition of the veil should be read as a specific example in which a bottom-up racist and xenophobic approach has worked itself into the national sphere. Mayors, belonging to the Northern League mainly, have managed to place the issue on the legislative agenda. Their political colleagues in the Italian Parliament and in the Italian government have managed to influence national legislative proposals. This does not bode well for the future of Muslim women in Italy, who the law frames and constructs as a danger to public order and security. At a broader level, the case of the veil in Italy also illustrates how the local level functions as a sort of legal laboratory, where future measures are tested and their legislative limits identified. This subsequently permits a broader strategy to eliminate those limits – in the current case to amend criminal legislation through the legislator and to increase the powers of mayors – through intervention at the national level. Simultaneously, the local discourses on Muslim women or migrants are reinforced at the national level, thus completing the legal construction of those individuals as 'Others' not only in society but in the legal context as well.

5.3.3 *The overtly racial and ethnic aspect of local measures on migrants*

The examples of local and national measures provided above demonstrate how these ordinances create, construct and enforce the image of a uniformly Christian, Western European Italy at the local level by appealing to public order and state security. The 'Other' is identified not on the basis of some imminent danger to the society and public order but for the simple fact that the individual looks different, or behaves differently, speaks differently, or has a different religion, culture, or ethnic background. This can go so far that even when a woman who is known to everyone in her community decides to wear a veil, it can be considered a threat under Italian law. While the Italian courts have annulled measures in several instances and at various levels, the harm such provisions cause cannot be ignored. First of all, the denial of residency, welfare rights and social benefits, and freedom of association and of movement affects some of Italy's most disadvantaged members. Even in those few cases when justice is done, it comes slowly. Moreover, for every challenge to one legal provision, it is highly likely that a larger number of people have been unable to lead a decent life or do not have the means or knowledge to challenge the discriminatory measures.

Second, all these cases illustrate that these measures discriminate on the basis of race and ethnicity. As mentioned at the beginning of the case study, in most cases the racial and ethnic fault lines are buried under layers of citizenship, residence, or religion. Sceptical observers might find that while many of these provisions are legally problematic, which courts recognised and annulled, there is nothing explicitly racial or ethnic involved. Nevertheless, like the earth's fault lines which usually run invisibly under the crust, every now and then they crack and show that underneath there is something else at work. In fact, in two cases, those fine and implicit dividing lines between White, Christian Europeans or Italians and the formerly colonised, non-White and/or Muslim were made quite explicit.

The first case concerned a mechanism of direct exclusion of migrants on the local level at the hands of the municipal executive, *giunta comunale*, of Morazzone, another little town in Italy's North West.[243] The local executive decided to grant a €500 subsidy to families residing in the municipality for any additional child after their first, born after 1 December 2005. The explicit intent was to 'support families who contribute to the growth of our community and thus reduce the demographic disequilibrium to protect European culture.' However, the deliberation further established that one parent had to be an Italian citizen and the other parent had to be either an Italian citizen by birth *ab initio*, or an EU citizen, or a Swiss citizen. By these criteria the municipality ensured that the bonus would not be granted to second-born children of non-Italian parents, those with naturalised Italian parents, or to families where even only one parent is a naturalised Italian. The effect of such an ordinance is to exclude families of immigrants from the 'imagined' community along a line that is clearly ethnic and racial. Italian citizenship of one of the parents is not sufficient. It must be genetic or by descent, and cannot be acquired.[244] How much European Whiteness is important is further highlighted by including Swiss citizens in addition to the legitimacy of EU citizens. Certainly, the proximity of the Swiss border from Morazzone, which is about five minutes away by car, and therefore gives rise to a number of mixed Italian-Swiss families in Morazzone, explains the explicit reference to Swiss citizens. The other explanation for the inclusion is that the Swiss do not represent a danger to European culture, which the measure intends to protect. The border that is relevant here is certainly not the Swiss–Italian one but a completely different one where White, Christian Europeanness is the relevant demarcation line. Thus, the former colonial, ethnic, and racial line is to some extent revived and reconstituted within the local legal system of a small town in Northern Italy. By referring to demographic disequilibrium, the ordinance further appeals to the claim that Europe is being overrun and outnumbered by foreigners who have more children. According to this claim, this is a reason why it is necessary to incentivise the birth

243 Morazzone, *Delibera della giunta comunale* no. 176, 19 December 2005, then confirmed by *Delibera della giunta comunale* no. 16, 13 February 2006.

244 There are clearly cases in which an Italian-born parent may not be White due to adoption or birth in Italy. However, those cases are still the exception and with the formulation of its deliberation the municipality made sure to target most of the cases it wanted to exclude.

of autochthonous, Christian, White Europeans to counter the flood of invading Muslims or non-European cultures.[245]

The second case where the racial aspects of local legislation became evident, and not just an implicit understanding in municipal and regional provisions, comes from another Northern Italian town in Lombardy. On 25 October 2009, Coccaglio's town council launched an initiative dubbed 'White Christmas', which ran until 25 December that year. As part of the initiative, city officials visited about 400 homes of the town's 1,500 foreigners,[246] to check their immigration papers. The initiative targeted immigrants whose resident permit had expired six months earlier, and who should have started the administrative steps for renewal. If they had not done so, their residency would be cancelled automatically. In a sample of 150 inspections already carried out, roughly 50 per cent found that the person no longer had a right to reside in Italy.[247] As in all other examples provided in this case study, the town council was controlled by three members of Prime Minister Silvio Berlusconi's conservative People of Freedom Party (*Partito della Libertà*) and four members of the right wing and anti-immigrant Northern League, including mayor Franco Claretti. The city official in charge of security and a member of the Northern League, Claudio Abiendi, stated that for him Christmas was not about the celebration of hospitality but of Christian tradition and identity.[248] This initiative best represents the central objective of these ordinances: literally and physically whitewashing Italian's towns as much as possible, through the elimination other identities not belonging to the Italian identity and the Christian tradition. Two other towns, Castelcovati and Castrezzato, copied the initiative.[249] To add insult to injury, the name chosen for the initiative was 'White Christmas', a reference to Bing Crosby's song.[250] It made clear that the first target of the initiative was the non-Christian community, namely Muslims. The second target were non-White Christians, who, irrespective of their sense of belonging to Coccaglio, learned they did not. With two seemingly innocent words

245 One should note that these deliberations became subject to lengthy litigation which ended by decision of the Tribunale di Roma, Ordinanza 4 December 2008, *Diritto, immigrazione e cittadinanza* (2009), no. 3, pp. 162–164, with a note by Giuseppe delle Vergini in the same journal issue at pp. 164–166. The Roman court did not enter into the merits of the matter and whether the municipal deliberation was discriminatory because Morazzone's executive had eliminated the requirement of Italian citizenship 'by birth' through another decision, the *Delibera della giunta comunale* no. 82, 12 June 2006.

246 Between April 1998 and April 2009 the number of resident foreigners had risen from 177 to 1,583. See Sandro De Riccardis, 'Viaggio nel paese di White Christmas. "I nostri figli hanno troppi amici neri"', *La Repubblica*, 20 November 2009, p. 26.

247 Sandro De Riccardis, '"A Natale via i clandestini" nel Bresciano si festeggia così', *La Repubblica*, 18 November 2009, p. 21.

248 *Ibid.*

249 *Ibid.*

250 It nevertheless strikes as somewhat odd that the name of this initiative is in English, especially when 'Silent Night' in Italian is called 'Bianco Natale', i.e. White Christmas.

the town council highlighted the racial and ethnic lines underlying current immigration legislation and policies in Italy and throughout Europe.

The reactions to this ordinance were strong. Some city officials tried to defend the action as a population census with a poorly chosen title. The mayor himself conceded that the name for the operation might have been ill-fitting but then justified it by stating that the initiative ended on Christmas day. Umberto Bossi, founder of the Northern League, defended the municipality's initiative but conceded that there was no need to call the initiative 'White Christmas' and suggested that it could just have been called 'Christmas Regularity Control'.[251] Most surprising and worrisome is that such initiative is legal, since mayors with their increased powers and competency have the authority to verify the registration of the population.

The initiative's name simply underscores a *de facto* reality, something that everyone is aware of and that is read between the lines in several local, and increasingly in national, actions in Italy. In a continent which prides itself on combatting racism ever since the end of World War II, which has managed to keep its segregation lines in the colonies via immigration and citizenship measures, and which has inscribed a non-racial reading of many phenomena, the explicit emergence of what is believed to be part of the past in a collective amnesia is indeed unsettling.[252] Clearly, these actions need to be condemned through civil and political outcry. However, the public protest is also part of another aspect, which is slightly more disturbing – amnesia concerning race thought and racism. It undermines the tacit agreement that as long as things like race, racism, and racial discrimination are not called by their names, so as to leave these societal phenomena present between the lines, we can happily live under the belief that Europe has overcome the worst type of racism. If it does in fact emerge on these rare occasions then it is only the result of misguided individuals or isolated actions and not a structural aspect of society or law.

The detailed overview and description provided here attempts to highlight how far those assumptions are indefensible and need revision. Even though legislation on race in European Member States has not been as explicit as in American law, law's functional participation in constructing identities is very similar. What Italian local measures, especially in the North, demonstrate is how far that identity is based on and creates the idea(l) of a male, Christian, White Italian, and more broadly European. True, the legal system has been able to erase a number of these instances but the example of the burqa ordinances, and legislation in other European countries, demonstrates that even here it is only a matter of time before things change at the national level and the legal obstacles are eliminated. As

251 Sandro De Riccardis, 'Viaggio nel paese di White Christmas. "I nostri figli hanno troppi amici neri"', *La Repubblica*, 20 November 2009, p. 26.

252 The reference here is to Emile Durkheim's term of 'collective consciousness' by which he intends the shared beliefs and moral attitudes which operate as a unifying force within society. Collective amnesia in some ways functions in similar ways in that it fosters unification but by a shared omission of certain (shameful) events of a country's history.

CLS scholars have demonstrated, law and rights are indeterminate and strongly depend on the underlying political climate and power structures. In Italy, and many other European countries, these have shifted dramatically to the racist right, or rather the racist arguments are mainstream and are found amongst the left wing as illustrated in the case of the burqa. Hence, it becomes all the more important to unveil those aspects and to show how race, gender, and religion overlap in peculiar ways in the Italian and European legal context. This could be yet another of the important ways in which a European CRT could contribute to analyse law from a new perspective.

Conclusions

In this book I demonstrated how law contributes to the construction and subordination of individuals and groups along racial and ethnic lines in the continental European context. In many ways, my observations are similar to views of critical race theorists in the United States. CRT, thus, was a helpful prism through which to analyse the European experience of race with the necessary precautions and contextual adaptations. Even though the task of highlighting the link between race and law was more obvious and direct in the American context, the same cannot be said for Europe, where law's discriminatory role is seen as less evident, often cloaked behind religious and citizenship laws, and where racial prejudice and hostility are harder to detect. In turn, this makes it easier to defend the position that in Europe, except for exceptional periods like the colonialism era or Nazism that now belong to a shameful past, race and racism play a marginal role in law and legal analysis today and should not play any role in the future.

This book challenges this position on three different levels. The first level concerns the *historical* extent and demonstrates how race did not disappear from continental Europe with the end of World War II and the arrival of modern constitutions and international treaties or conventions. The case study of the Roma is the perfect example; the historical continuity of the discriminatory measures adopted against them in all European democracies is incredible. That same case study also addresses the second level; the *geographical* extent. Indeed, with this book I argue that the relationship between race and law involves all European democracies on the Old Continent and not just the new democracies in Eastern Europe. But even when race and ethnicity are not explicitly mentioned, they often play a role in the unspoken, underlying assumptions in legal provisions and decisions as the Italian case study demonstrated. Here I move to the third level, which is the extent of the *subject matter*. Indeed, as I have endeavoured to show, it is not just in the most obvious areas where this type of discrimination takes place – immigration law, asylum law, criminal law and criminal procedure, administrative law – but also in exactly that area of law which is supposed to protect against racism and race discrimination, namely anti-discrimination law. Here the broader setting of the European context and what I defined as 'Continental European Colourblindness', together with the specific French case study, are particularly revealing and helpful in understanding the operation of law and how ultimately the European position is as problematic as American colourblindness and reflects the position of the majority society.

Whereas these findings are probably not big news for visible minorities and people of colour in Europe, who daily experience different types of institutional and societal racism, for many continental European legal scholars steeped in the traditional legal dogmatic analysis and who, owing to their skin colour, religion, nationality, and gender, do not share that same experience, this book may come as an unpleasant surprise. It may even come as a surprise for those scholars who have suspected or been aware of this trend but never guessed the extent of the phenomenon.

Ultimately, with this book I hope to open up and broaden a debate which is already present in some rudimentary form in mainland European scholarship and which critiques its limits both from a substantive point of view as well as from a methodological point of view. In fact, the analysis I provided here would not have been possible with traditional, mainstream doctrinal, continental European legal analysis. Too sociological, too philosophical, not pragmatic, not useful, not applicable by courts, and just purely and simply not legal are some of the critiques 'traditional' lawyers may levy. Nevertheless, lawyers should be as interested in the intricacies of legal doctrine and reasoning as in the effects those produce in people's lives. And here I am highlighting a very uncomfortable effect on a broader scale, one that we purport to prevent but which we are fighting at best rhetorically so far.

Bibliography

Books, book chapters, dictionaries, encyclopedias and theses

ARNULL, ANTHONY 'The Americanization of EU Law Scholarship', in ANTHONY ARNULL, PIET EECKHOUT and TAKIS TRIDIMAS (eds) *Continuity and Change in EU Law* (Oxford: Oxford University Press, 2007)

ASSÉO, HENRIETTE *Les Tsiganes. Une destinée européenne* (Paris: Gallimard, 1994)

AUBIN, EMMANUEL 'La discrimination à raison de l'origine ethnique', in FELICIEN LEMAIRE and BERNARD GAURIAU (eds), *Les discriminations* (Paris: Editions Cujas, 2011)

AYLWARD, CAROL A. *Canadian Critical Race Theory* (Halifax: Fernwood Publishing, 1999)

BAL, MIEKE *Travelling Concepts in the Humanities: A Rough Guide* (Toronto: Toronto University Press, 2002)

BALIBAR, ETIENNE 'Y-a-t-il un "néo-racisme"?' in ETIENNE BALIBAR and IMMANUEL WALLERSTEIN, *Race, nation, classe* (Paris: Editions La Découverte Syros, 1997)

'La costruzione del razzismo', in THOMAS CASADEI and LUCIA RE (eds), *Differenza razziale, discriminazione e razzismo nelle società multiculturali*, Vol. I (Reggio Emilia: Diabasis, 2007)

BANCROFT, ANGUS *Roma and Gypsy-Travellers in Europe. Modernity, Race, Space and Exclusion* (Aldershot: Ashgate, 2005)

BAUMGARTNER, GERHARD and FREUND, FLORIAN 'Der Holocaust an den österreichischen Roma und Sinti', in MICHAEL ZIMMERMANN (ed.) *Zwischen Erziehung und Vernichtung* (Stuttgart: Franz Steiner Verlag, 2007)

BELAVUSAU, ULADZISLAU *Freedom of Speech. Importing European and US Constitutional Models in Transitional Democracies* (London, New York: Routledge, 2013)

'Anti-Roma Hate Speech in the Czech Republic, Hungary and Poland', in MORAG GOODWIN and PAUL DE HERT (eds), *European Roma Integration Efforts – A Snapshot* (Brussels: Brussels University Press, 2013)

BELL, DERRICK A., JR. *Faces at the Bottom of the Well. The Permanence of Racism* (New York: Basic Books, 1992)

Race, Racism, and American Law, 5th edn (New York: Aspen Publishers, 2004)

BELL, MARK *Anti-Discrimination Law and the European Union* (Oxford: Oxford University Press, 2002)

BENTOUHAMI, HOURYA '*Critical Race Theory* ou comment la "race" compte', in HOURYA BENTOUHAMI, *et al.* (eds) *Le souci du droit : Où en est la théorie critique?* (Paris: Sens & Tonka, 2010)

BLUM, ALAIN 'Resistance to Identity Categorization in France', in DAVID I. KERTZER and DOMINIQUE AREL (eds) *Census and Identity* (Cambridge: Cambridge University Press, 2002)

BOGDAL, KLAUS-MICHAEL '"Dieses schwartz, ungestaltet und wildschweiffige Gesind". Symbolische Codierung und literarische Diskursivierung der "Zigeuner" vor 1800', in MICHAEL ZIMMERMANN *Zwischen Erziehung und Vernichtung* (Stuttgart: Franz Steiner Verlag, 2007)

BONILLA-SILVA, EDUARDO *Racism without Races: Color-Blind Racism and the Persistence of Racial Inequality in America*, 4th edn (Lanham: Rowman & Littlefield, 2013)

BONTEMPELLI, SERGIO '"Ordinanza pazza". I sindaci e il versante grottesco del razzismo', in Lunaria (ed.) *Libro bianco sul razzismo* (Roma: Lunaria, 2009)

BRUCKNER, PASCAL *Le sanglot de l'homme blanc* (Paris: Editions Seuil, 1983)

CAPPELLETTI, MAURO *Judicial Review in the Contemporary World* (Indianapolis: Bobbs-Merrill, 1971)

'"Constitutional Justice" and the Overcoming of the Antithesis "Equity-Law" and "Natural-Positive Law"', in *Conflict and Integration: Comparative Law in the World Today* (Tokyo: Chuo University Press, 1988)

CARBADO, DEVON and GULATI, MITU *Acting White? Rethinking Race in Post-Racial America* (New York: Oxford University Press, 2013)

CARBONNIER, JEAN *Droit et passion du droit sous la Ve République* (Paris: Flammarion, 1996)

CARDINALE, Giancarlo 'The Preparation of ECRI General Policy Recommendation No. 7', in JAN NIESSEN and ISABELLE CHOPIN (eds) *The Development of Legal Instruments to Combat Racism in a Diverse Europe* (Leiden: M. Nijhoff, 2004)

CARTIER, HENRI *Comment la France 'civilise' ses colonies* (Paris: les nuits rouges, 2006)

CARUSO, CORRADO 'Dialettica della libertà di espressione: il "caso Tosi" e la propaganda di idee razziste', in DILETTA TEGA (ed.) *Le discriminazioni razziali ed etniche* (Roma: Armando Editore, 2011)

CASADEI, THOMAS and RE, LUCIA (eds) *Differenza razziale, discriminazione e razzismo nelle società multiculturali*, Vols I and II (Reggio Emilia: Diabasis, 2007)

CENTRE FOR CONTEMPORARY CULTURAL STUDIES *The Empire Strikes Back: Race and Racism in Britain* (London: Hutchinson, 1982)

CHALMERS, DAMIAN 'The Mistakes of the Good European?', in SANDRA FREDMAN (ed.) *Discrimination and Human Rights. The Case of Racism* (Oxford: Oxford University Press, 2001)

CHILDS, PETER and WILLIAMS, PATRICK *An Introduction to Post-Colonial Theory* (Essex: Pearson Education Limited, 1997)

CLARKE, JAMES W. *The Lineaments of Wrath. Race, Violent Crime, and American Culture* (New Brunswick, London: Transaction Publishers, 1998)

CLIFFORD, JAMES 'Travelling Cultures', in LAWRENCE GROSSBERG, CARY NELSON and PAULA TREICHLER (eds) *Cultural Studies* (New York, London: Routledge, 1992)

COCCOPALMERIO, DOMENICO *Francesco Carnelutti. Il 'realismo giuridico italiano'* (Napoli: Edizioni Scientifiche Italiane, 1989)

CONZE, WERNER 'Rasse', in OTTO BRUNNER, WERNER CONZE and REINHART KOSELLECK *Geschichtliche Grundbegriffe* (Stuttgart: Klett-Cotta, 1984), Band 5, Pro – Soz

COUSIN, GRÉGOIRE and MARIANI, FRANCESCA 'Il passepartout dell'"ordine pubblico". Politica e diritto nelle prassi di allontanamento dei "rumeni detti rom" in Italia e Francia', in PAOLO BONETTI, ALESSANDRO SIMONI and TOMMASO VITALE (eds) *La condizione giuridica di rom e sinti in Italia* (Milano: Giuffré, 2011), pp. 415–454

CRENSHAW, KIMBERLÉ W., *et al.* (eds) *Critical Race Theory: The Key Writings that Formed the Movement* (New York: The New Press, 1995)

DAVID, RENÉ 'Sources of Law', in RENÉ DAVID (ed.), *International Encyclopedia of Comparative Law* (Tübingen: Mohr; The Hague, Boston, London: Martinus Nijhoff Publishers, 1984), Vol. II, Chapter 3

DAVID, RENÉ and JAUFFRET-SPINOSI, CAMILLE *Les grands systèmes de droit contemporains*, 11th edn (Paris: Dalloz, 2002)

DE JONG, MARTIN, MAMADOUH, VIRGINIE and LALENIS, KONSTANTINOS 'Drawing Lessons About Lesson Drawing. What the case reports tell us about institutional transplantations', in MARTIN DE JONG, KONSTANTINOS LALENIS and VIRGINIE MAMADOUH (eds) *The Theory and Practice of Institutional Transplantation* (Dordrecht, Boston, London: Kluwer Academic Publishers, 2002)

DE TOCQUEVILLE, ALEXIS *Democracy in America* [1835], GEORGE LAWRENCE (trans.), J.P. Mayer (ed.), 12th edn (London: Fontana Press, 1994)

DELEUZE, GILLES and GUATTARI, FELIX *A Thousand Plateaus: Capitalism and Schizophrenia* [1980], BRIAN MASSUMI (trans.), 1st edn (Minneapolis: University of Minnesota Press, 1987)

DELGADO, RICHARD *The Rodrigo Chronicles: Conversations About America and Race* (New York, London: New York University Press, 1995)

DELGADO, RICHARD and STEFANCIC, JEAN (eds) *Critical White Studies: Looking Behind the Mirror* (Philadelphia: Temple University Press, 1997)

(eds) *Critical Race Theory: The Cutting Edge* (Philadelphia: Temple University Press, 2000)

Critical Race Theory: An Introduction (New York: New York University Press, 2001)

DEMBOUR, MARIE-BÉNÉDICTE *Who Believes in Human Rights: Reflections on the European Convention* (Cambridge, New York: Cambridge University Press, 2006)

'In the Name of the Rule of Law: The European Court of Human Rights' Silencing of Racism', in GURMINDER K. BHAMBRA and ROBBIE SHILLIAM (eds) *Silencing Human Rights. Critical Engagements with a Contested Project* (Basingstoke, New York: Palgrave, Macmillan, 2009)

'Postcolonial Denial: Why the European Court of Human Rights Finds It So Difficult to Acknowledge Racism', in KAMARI CLARKE and MARK GOODALE (eds) *Mirrors of Justice. Law and Power in the Post-Cold War Era* (Cambridge: Cambridge University Press, 2009)

DIOUF, ANNA SYLVIANE *Dreams of Africa in Alabama: The Slave Ship Clotilda and the Story of the Last Africans Brought to America* (New York: Oxford University Press, 2007)

DIXSON, ADRIENNE D. and ROUSSEAU, CELIA K. *Critical Race Theory in Education* (New York, London: Routledge, 2006)

DOUZINAS, COSTAS and GEARY, ADAM *Critical Jurisprudence* (Oxford and Portland, Oregon: Hart Publishing, 2005)

DU BOIS, W.E.B. *The Souls of Black Folk* [1903] (New York: The Modern Library, 2003)

DUDZIAK, MARY L. *Cold War Civil Rights: Race and the Image of American Democracy* (Princeton: Princeton University Press, 2001)

DULITZKY, ARIEL E. 'A Region in Denial: Racial Discrimination and Racism in Latin America', in ANANI DZIDZIENYO and SUZANNE OBOLER (eds) *Neither Enemies Nor Friends: Latinos, Blacks, Afro-Latinos* (New York: Palgrave Macmillan, 2005)

DUXBURY, NEIL *Patterns of American Jurisprudence* (Oxford: Clarendon Press, 1995)

EGGERS, MAUREEN MAISHA, *et al.* (eds) *Mythen, Masken und Subjekte: kritische Weissseinsforschung in Deutschland* (Münster: Unrast, 2005)

EIDE, ASBJØRN 'Racial and Ethnic Discrimination in Europe: Past, Present and Future', in DANIÈLE JOLY (ed.) *Scapegoats and Social Actors: The Exclusion and Integration of Minorities in Western and Eastern Europe* (Basingstoke: Macmillan, 1998)

EL TAYEB, FATIMA *Schwarze Deutsche: der Diskurs um "Rasse" und nationale Identität 1890–1933* (Frankfurt a. Main/New York: Campus-Verlag, 2001)

ESSED, PHILOMENA 'Foreword', in DARLENE CLARK HINE, TRICA DANIELLE KEATON and STEPHEN SMALL (eds) *Black Europe and the African Diaspora* (Urbana, Chicago: University of Illinois Press, 2009)

FANON, FRANTZ *Peau noire, masques blancs* [1952] (Paris: Seuil, 1971)

Les damnés de la terre [1961] (Paris: La Découverte, 2002)

FARBER, DANIEL A. and SHERRY, SUZANNA *Beyond All Reason. The Radical Assault on Truth in American Law* (New York: Oxford University Press, 1997)

FASSIN, DIDIER and FASSIN, ERIC (eds) *De la question sociale à la question raciale* (Paris: Editions La Découverte, 2006)

FELDMAN, STEPHEN M. *American Legal Thought from Premodernism to Postmodernism* (New York: Oxford University Press, 2000)

FREDMAN, SANDRA 'Beyond the Dichotomy of Formal and Substantive Equality: Towards a New Definition of Equal Rights', in Ineke Boerefijn, *et al.* (eds) *Temporary Special Measures: Accelerating De Facto Equality of Women under Article 4(1) UN Convention on the Elimination of All Forms of Discrimination Against Women* (Antwerp: Intersentia, 2005), pp. 111–118

FULLER, LON *The Morality of Law* (New Haven: Yale University Press, 1977)

GAMBARO, ANTONIO and SACCO, RODOLFO *Sistemi giuridici comparati*, 1st edn (Torino: UTET, 1996)

GARCÍA, JUAN RAMÓN *Operation Wetback: The Mass Deportation of Mexican Undocumented Workers in 1954* (Westport, CT: Greenwood Press, 1980)

GEULEN, CHRISTIAN *Geschichte des Rassismus* (München: C.H. Beck, 2007)

GILMORE, GRANT *The Ages of American Law* (New Haven and London: Yale University Press, 1977)

GILROY, PAUL *The Black Atlantic: Modernity and Double Consciousness* (Cambridge, MA: Harvard University Press, 1993)

GOLDBERG, DAVID THEO *The Racial State* (Oxford: Blackwell, 2002)

Racist Culture: Philosophy and the Politics of Meaning (Oxford: Blackwell, 1993)

GOLDBERG, DAVID THEO and ESSED, PHILOMENA 'Introduction: From Racial Demarcations to Multiple Identifications', in DAVID THEO GOLDBERG and PHILOMENA ESSED (eds) *Race Critical Theories* (Oxford: Blackwell, 2002)

GOODWIN, MORAG 'Viewing Romani Marginalization Through the Nexus of Race and Poverty', in DAGMAR SCHIEK and VICTORIA CHEGE (eds) *European Union Non-Discrimination Law* (London, New York: Routledge-Cavendish, 2009)

GOSEWINKEL, DIETER 'Rückwirkungen des kolonialen Rasserechts? Deutsche Staatsangehörigkeit zwischen Rassestaat und Rechsstaat', in SEBASTIAN CONRAD and JÜRGEN OSTERHAMMEL (eds) *Das Kaiserreich transnational. Deutschland in der Welt 1871–1914*, 2nd edn (Göttingen, Vandenhoeck & Rupprecht, 2006)

GREWE, CONSTANCE and FABRI, HÉLÈNE RUIZ *Droits constitutionnels européens* (Paris: Presses Universitaires de France, 1995)

HANEY LÓPEZ, IAN F. *White by Law*, revised 10th anniversary edn (New York: New York University Press, 2006)

HANNAFORD, IVAN *Race. The History of an Idea in the West* (Washington, DC: Woodrow Wilson Center Press, 1996)

HARRIS, ANGELA P. *Race and Equality Law* (Farnham, Burlington: Ashgate, 2013)

HAYWOOD BURNS, W. 'Law and Race in Early America', in DAVID KAIRYS (ed.), *The Politics of Law: A Progressive Critique*, 3rd edn (New York: Basic Books, 1998)

HAZARD, ANTHONY Q., JR. *Postwar Anti-Racism. The United States, UNESCO and 'Race', 1945–1968* (New York: Palgrave Macmillan, 2012)

HIGGINBOTHAM, A. LEON, JR. *In the Matter of Color: Race and the American Legal Process: The Colonial Period* (New York: Oxford University Press, 1978)

HINE, DARLENE CLARK, KEATON, TRICA DANIELLE and SMALL, STEPHEN (eds) *Black Europe and the African Diaspora* (Urbana, Chicago: University of Illinois Press, 2009)

HORWITZ, MORTON J. *The Transformation of American Law 1780–1860* (Cambridge, MA: Harvard University Press, 1977)

HUBER-KOLLER, ROSE-MARIE 'Schwarze Deutsche: Zwischen "Ethnos" und "Demos" im historischen Spannungsfeld unterschiedlicher Legitimationsgrundlagen und Techniken politischer Herrschaft', in FRANZ F. MÜLLER, *et al.* (eds) *Vom Ausländer zum Bürger: Problemanzeigen im Ausländer-, Asyl-, und Staatsangehörigkeitsrecht* (Baden-Baden: Nomos, 1994)

HYLTON, KEVIN *'Race' and Sport. Critical Race Theory* (London, New York: Routledge, 2009)

IGNĂȚOIU-SORA, EMANUELA *La construction d'un régime juridique pour la protection des Roms*, Ph.D. thesis (Florence: European University Institute – Department of Law, 2010)

JACKSON, VICKI C. and TUSHNET, MARK *Comparative Constitutional Law*, 1st edn (New York: Foundation Press, 1999)

JOERGES, CHRISTIAN 'On the Context of German-American Debates on Sociological Jurisprudence and Legal Criticism: A History of Transatlantic Misunderstandings and Missed Opportunities', in ALBERTO FEBBRAJO and DAVID NELKEN (eds) *European Yearbook in the Sociology of Law 1993* (Milano: Giuffrè, 1994)

JOERGES, CHRISTIAN and GHALEIGH, NAVRAJ SINGH (eds) *Darker Legacies of Law in Europe: The Shadow of National Socialism and Fascism over Europe and its Legal Traditions* (Oxford, Portland: Hart, 2003)

JOERGES, CHRISTIAN and TRUBEK, DAVID M. (eds) *Critical Legal Thought: An American-German Debate* (Baden-Baden: Nomos, 1989)

JOHNSON, KEVIN 'Race and the Immigration Laws: The Need for Critical Inquiry', in FRANCISCO VALDES, JEROME MCCRISTAL CULP and ANGELA HARRIS (eds) *Crossroads, Directions, and a New Critical Race Theory* (Philadelphia: Temple University Press, 2002)

JOPPKE, CHRISTIAN *Selecting by Origin: Ethnic Migration in the Liberal State* (Cambridge, MA: Harvard University Press, 2005)

KEATON, TRICA DANIELLE, SHARPLEY WHITING, T. DENEAN and STOVALL, TYLER (eds), *Black France/France Noire: The History and Politics of Blackness* (Durham: Duke University Press, 2012)

KELSEN, HANS *Pure Theory of Law* [1960, 2nd edn], MAX KNIGHT (trans.), (Gloucester, MA: Peter Smith, 1989)

KOUSSENS, DAVID and ROY, OLIVIER (eds) *Quand la burqa passé à l'ouest* (Rennes: Presses universitaires de Rennes, 2013)

KRISZAN, ANDREA, SKJEIE, HEGE and SQUIRES, JUDITH (eds) *Institutionalizing Intersectionality. The Changing Nature of European Equality Regimes* (Basingstoke: Palgrave Macmillan, 2012)

LACEY, NICOLA 'Feminist Legal Theory and the Rights of Women', in KAREN KNOPP (ed.) *Gender and Human Rights* (Oxford: Oxford University Press, 2004)

LAWRENCE, CHARLES R. III, 'Foreword. Who Are We? And Why Are We Here? Doing Critical Race Theory in Hard Times', in FRANCISCO VALDES, JEROME MCCRISTAL CULP and ANGELA HARRIS (eds) *Crossroads, Directions, and a New Critical Race Theory* (Philadelphia: Temple University Press, 2002)

LECŒUR, ERWAN (ed.) *Dictionnaire de l'extrême droite* (Paris: Larousse, 2007)

LEGRAND, PIERRE 'What "Legal Transplants"?', in DAVID NELKEN and JOHANNES FEEST (eds) *Adapting Legal Cultures* (Oxford: Hart Publishing, 2001)

LEITER, BRIAN 'American Legal Realism', in MARTIN P. GOLDING and WILLIAM A. EDMUNDSON (eds) *The Blackwell Guide to the Philosophy of Law and Legal Theory* (Malden: Blackwell Publishing, 2005)

LENTIN, ALANA *Racism and Anti-Racism in Europe* (London, Ann Arbor: Pluto Press, 2004)

LIÉGEOIS, JEAN-PIERRE *Roma in Europe* (Strasbourg: Council of Europe Publishing, 2007)

Roms et Tsiga nes (Paris: La Découverte, 2009)

LLEWELLYN, KARL N. *The Common Law Tradition: Deciding Appeals* (Boston: Little, Brown and Co., 1960)

LORDE, AUDRE *Sister Outsider* [1984] (Berkeley, CA: Ten Speed Press, 2007)

LORENZ, CHRIS 'An Introduction to Conceptual History' in STEFAN BERGER and CHRIS LORENZ (eds) *The Contested Nation: Ethnicity, Class, Religion and Gender in National Histories* (London: Palgrave, 2008)

LÖYTÖMÄKI, STIINA OUTI HELENA *Committing the Irreparable: Law and Dealing with Past Injustices*, Ph.D. thesis (Florence: European University Institute – Department of Law, 2010)

LUCASSEN, LEO 'Gypsy Research and Gypsy Policy in the Netherlands (1850–1970)', in MICHAEL ZIMMERMANN (ed.) *Zwischen Erziehung und Vernichtung* (Stuttgart: Franz Steiner Verlag, 2007)

MACMASTER, NEIL *Racism in Europe* (Basingstoke: Palgrave, 2001)

MALMINEN, TONI 'The Effects of Scandinavian Legal Realism on Finnish Legal Studies, 1929–1965', in VANESSA DUSS, *et al.* (eds) *Rechtstransfer in der Geschichte* (München: Martin Meidenbauer, 2006)

MARCHETTI, SABRINA 'Intersezionalità. Pensare la differenza', in CATERINA BOTTI (ed.) *Etiche della diversità culturale* (Firenze: Le Lettere, 2013), pp. 133–148

MARCHETTONI, LEONARDO '*Razza* e cultura. Un confronto', in THOMAS CASADEI and LUCIA RE (eds) *Differenza razziale, discriminazione e razzismo nelle società multiculturali*, Vol. I (Reggio Emilia: Diabasis, 2007)

MARGALIT, GILAD 'Zigeunerpolitik und Zigeunerdiskurs im Deutschland der Nachkriegszeit', in MICHAEL ZIMMERMANN (ed.) *Zwischen Erziehung und Vernichtung* (Stuttgart: Franz Steiner Verlag, 2007)

MARTIN, MICHAEL *Legal Realism. American and Scandinavian* (New York: Peter Lang, 1997)

MATSUDA, MARI J., *et al.* (eds) *Words That Wound: Critical Race Theory, Assaultive Speech and the First Amendment* (Boulder: Westview Press, 1993)

MATTEI, UGO *Comparative Law and Economics* (Ann Arbor: University of Michigan Press, 1997)

MAYERI, SERENA *Reasoning from Race: Feminism, Law, and the Civil Rights Revolution* (Cambridge, MA: Harvard University Press, 2011)

MEIER, THOMAS 'Zigeunerpolitik und Zigeunerdiskurs in der Schweiz 1850–1970', in MICHAEL ZIMMERMANN (ed.) *Zwischen Erziehung und Vernichtung* (Stuttgart: Franz Steiner Verlag, 2007)

MEZZADRA, SANDRO and RIGO, ENRICA 'Diritti d'Europa. Una prospettiva postcoloniale sul diritto coloniale', in ALDO MAZZACANE (ed.) *Oltremare. Diritto e istituzioni dal Colonialismo all'età postcoloniale* (Napoli: CUEN, 2006)

MILES, ROBERT 'The Articulation of Racism and Nationalism: Reflections on European History', in JOHN WRENCH and JOHN SOLOMOS (eds) *Racism and Migration in Western Europe* (Oxford, Providence: Berg Publishers, 1993)

MINDA, GARY *Postmodern Legal Movements* (New York, London: New York University Press, 1995)

Teorie postmoderne del diritto [1995], MAURO BARBERIS (trans.) (Bologna: il Mulino, 2001)

MODOOD, TARIQ '"Black", Racial Equality and Asian Identity', in MARCO MARTINIELLO and JAN RATH (eds) *Selected Studies in International Migration and Immigrant Incorporation* (Amsterdam: Amsterdam University Press, 2010)

MORRISON, TONI 'Playing in the Dark: Whiteness and the Literary Imagination', in RICHARD DELGADO and JEAN STEFANCIC (eds) *Critical White Studies: Looking Behind the Mirror* (Philadelphia: Temple University Press, 1997)

MUSIANI, FRANCESCA 'Walls Built Up, Walls Written Down: Of Symbolic Value, Material Effectiveness and Media Representations of Barriers in Padua, Italy', in JOHN HOLTEN and LINE SIMENSTADT MADSEN (eds) *You are Here: Europa Today* (Berlin: Broken Dimanche Press, 2009)

NÄF, KASPAR 'Die nationale Autonomie Karl Renners als Vorbild für die jüdische Kulturautonomie in Litauen und Lettland während der Zwischenkriegszeit', in VANESSA DUSS, *et al.* (eds) *Rechtstransfer in der Geschichte* (München: Martin Meidenbauer, 2006)

NDIAYE, PAP *La condition noire* (Paris: Calmann-Lévy, 2008)

NIMAKO, KWAME and SMALL, STEPHEN 'Theorizing Black Europe and the African Diaspora: Implications for Citizenship, Nativism, and Xenophobia', in DARLENE CLARK HINE, TRICA DANIELLE KEATON and STEPHEN SMALL (eds) *Black*

Europe and the African Diaspora (Urbana, Chicago: University of Illinois Press, 2009), pp. 212–237

OGUNTOYE, KATARINA, OPITZ, MAY and SCHULTZ, DAGMAR (eds) *Farbe Bekennen: Afro-deutsche Frauen auf den Spuren ihrer Geschichte* (Berlin: Orlanda Verlag, 1986)

PAPALIA, GUIDO 'Efficacia della tutela penale nella repression dei reati di discriminazione razziale: gli strumenti della Legge Mancino', in MINISTERO PER LE PARI OPPORTUNITÀ, *Il ruolo della difesa nel contrasto alle discriminazioni razziali ed etniche*, Vol. 28 (Roma: Demetra, 2006)

PARDOLESI, ROBERTO and TASSONE, BRUNO *I giudici e l'analisi economica del diritto privato* (Bologna: il Mulino, 2003)

PAREKH, BHIKHU *A New Politics of Identity* (Basingstoke, New York: Palgrave Macmillan, 2008)

PARKER, LAURENCE, DEYHLE, DONNA and VILLENAS, SOFIA (eds) *Race Is … Race Isn't: Critical Race Theory and Qualitative Studies in Education* (Boulder: Westview Press, 1999)

PARKS, GREGORY S., JONES, SHAYNE and CARDI, W. JONATHAN (eds) *Critical Race Realism* (New York: The New Press, 2008)

POSCH, WILLIBALD 'Gleichbehandlungsgebot', in ROBERT REBHAHN (ed.) *Kommentar zum Gleichbehandlungsgesetz* (Wien, New York: Springer, 2005)

POSNER, RICHARD A. *Overcoming Law* (Cambridge, MA: Harvard University Press, 1995)

RÄTHZEL, NORA 'Developments in Theories of Racism', in THE EVENS FOUNDATION (ed.) *Europe's New Racism. Causes, Manifestations, and Solutions* (New York: Berghahn Books, 2002)

REYNARD-PALIGOT, CAROLE *La République raciale (1860–1930)* (Paris: Presses Universitaires de France, 2006)

RINGELHEIM, JULIE and DE SCHUTTER, OLIVIER *Ethnic Monitoring. The Processing of Racial and Ethnic Data in Anti-Discrimination Policies: Reconciling the Promotion of Equality with Privacy Rights* (Brussels: Bruylant, 2010)

RODRÍGUEZ, CLARA E. *Changing Race: Latinos, the Census, and the History of Ethnicity in the United States* (New York, London: New York University Press, 2000)

ROMÁN, EDIBERTO *Citizenship and Its Exclusions* (New York, London: New York University Press, 2010)

ROMANY, CELINA 'Critical Race Theory in Global Context', in FRANCISCO VALDES, JEROME MCCRISTAL CULP and ANGELA P. HARRIS (eds), *Crossroads, Directions, and a New Critical Race Theory* (Philadelphia: Temple University Press, 2002)

SAADA, EMMANUELLE 'Une nationalité par degré', in PATRICK WEIL and STÉPHANE DUFOIX (eds) *L'esclavage, la colonisation et après* (Paris: Presses Universitaires de France, 2005)

SAID, EDWARD W. *Reflections on Exile* (Cambridge, MA: Harvard University Press, 2001)

SCHIEK, DAGMAR and CHEGE, VICTORIA (eds) *European Union Non-Discrimination Law – Comparative Perspectives on Multidimensional Equality Law* (London, New York: Routledge-Cavendish, 2009)

SCHIEK, DAGMAR and LAWSON, ANNA (eds) *European Non-Discrimination Law and Intersectionality: Investigating the Triangle of Racial, Gender and Disability Discrimination* (Farnham: Ashgate, 2011)

SIGONA, NANDO and TREHAN, NIDHI (eds) *Romani Politics in Contemporary Europe. Poverty, Ethnic Mobilisation, and the Neoliberal Order* (Basingstoke: Palgrave Macmillan, 2009)

SIGONA, NANDO 'Gypsies out of Italy!', in ANDREA MAMMONE and GIUSEPPE A. VELTRI (eds) *Italy Today* (London and New York: Routledge, 2010)

SIMPSON, JOHN and WEINER, EDMUND (prepared by) *The Oxford English Dictionary*, 2nd edn (Oxford: Clarendon Press, 1989)

SOLANKE, IYIOLA *Making Anti-Racial Discrimination Law. A Comparative History of Social Action and Anti-Racial Discrimination Law* (London, New York: Routledge, 2009)

SOWELL, THOMAS *Civil Rights: Rhetoric or Reality* (New York: William Morrow & Co., 1984)

SPIJKERBOER, THOMAS *Gender and Refugee Status* (Aldershot: Ashgate, 2000)

SPIJKERBOER, THOMAS and VAN WALSUM, SARAH (eds) *Women and Immigration Law: New Variations on Classical Feminist Themes* (Abingdon, New York: Routledge-Cavendish, 2007)

STEFANINI, PAOLO *Avanti Po: la Lega Nord alla riscossa nelle regioni rosse* (Milano: il Saggiatore, 2010)

STRAZŻARI, DAVIDE *Discriminazione razziale e diritto* (Padova: CEDAM, 2008)

TAGUIEFF, PIERRE-ANDRÉ *La force du préjugé. Essai sur le racisme et ses doubles* (Paris: La Decouverte, 1988)

TAYLOR, CHARLES 'The Politics of Recognition' in CHARLES TAYLOR and AMY GUTMAN (eds) *Multiculturalism: Examining the Politics of Recognition* (Princeton, NJ: Princeton University Press, 1994)

TAYLOR, ED, GILLBORN, DAVID and LADSON-BILLINGS, GLORIA (eds) *Foundations of Critical Race Theory in Education* (New York, London: Routledge, 2009)

THOMAS, KENDALL and ZANETTI, GIANFRANCESCO (eds) *Legge, razza e diritti. La Critical Race Theory negli Stati Uniti* (Reggio Emilia: Diabasis, 2005)

TISSBERGER, MARTINA, *et al.* (eds) *Weiss, Weisssein, Whiteness: kritische Studien zu Gender und Rassismus* (Frankfurt am Main, New York: P. Lang, 2006)

TUSHNET, MARK *The NAACP's Legal Strategy Against Segregated Education, 1925–1950*, 2nd edn (Chapel Hill: University of North Carolina Press, 2005)

VALDES, FRANCISCO, MCCRISTAL, CULP JEROME and HARRIS, ANGELA (eds) *Crossroads, Directions, and a New Critical Race Theory* (Philadelphia: Temple University Press, 2002)

VALLS, ANDREW (ed.) *Race and Racism in Modern Philosophy* (Ithaca: Cornell University Press, 2005)

VAN CLEVE, GEORGE WILLIAM *A Slaveholder's Union: Slavery, Politics and the Constitution in the Early American Republic* (Chicago, London: University of Chicago Press, 2010)

VAN DIJK, TEUN A. 'Denying Racism: Elite Discourse and Racism', in JOHN WRENCH and JOHN SOLOMOS (eds) *Racism and Migration in Western Europe* (Oxford, Providence: Berg Publishers, 1993)

VERKUYTEN, MAYKEL and TER WAL, JESSICA 'Introduction: Racism in a Comparative Perspective', in MAYKEL VERKUYTEN and JESSICA TER WAL (eds) *Comparative Perspectives on Racism* (Aldershot: Ashgate, 2000)

VITALE, TOMMASO 'Governare mediante gli sgomberi e la segregazione dei gruppi zigani', in SALVATORE PALIDDA (ed.) *razzismo democratico* (Milano: Mimesis Edizioni, 2009)

WARD, JULIE and LOTT, TOMMY (eds) *Philosophers on Race* (Oxford, Malden: Blackwell Publishers, 2002)

WATSON, ALAN *The Nature of Law* (Edinburgh: Edinburgh University Press, 1977)

Legal Transplants: An Approach to Comparative Law, 2nd edn (Athens, GA: University of Georgia Press, 1993)

Society and Legal Change (Edinburgh: Scottish Academic Press, 1997)

WILKINSON, CHARLES *American Indians, Time, and the Law: Native Societies in a Modern Constitutional Democracy* (New Haven: Yale University Press, 1987)

WILLIAMS, PATRICIA *The Alchemy of Rights* (Cambridge, MA: Harvard University Press, 1991)

WILLIAMS, ROBERT A., JR. *Like a Loaded Weapon: The Rehnquist Court, Indian Rights, and the Legal History of Racism in America* (Minneapolis, London: University of Minnesota Press, 2005)

WILSON, WILLIAM JULIUS *The Declining Significance of Race: Blacks and Changing American Institutions* (Chicago: University of Chicago Press, 1978)

WING, ADRIEN KATHERINE (ed.) *Global Critical Race Feminism* (New York: New York University Press, 2000)

WOODWARD, C. VANN *The Strange Career of Jim Crow* (New York: Oxford University Press, 1955)

YAMAMOTO, ERIC K., *et al.* (eds) *Race, Rights, and Reparation: Law of the Japanese-American Internment* (New York: Aspen Publishers, 2001)

ZIMMERMANN, MICHAEL 'Jews, Gypsies and Soviet Prisoners of War: Comparing Nazi Persecutions', in RONI STAUBER and RAPHAEL VAGO (eds) *The Roma. A Minority in Europe* (Budapest: Central European University Press, 2007)

ZWEIGERT, KONRAD and KÖTZ, HEIN *An Introduction to Comparative Law*, 3rd edn (Oxford, New York: Oxford University Press, 1998)

Journal articles and journal issues

'Colloquy – Responses to Randall Kennedy's Racial Critiques of Legal Academia', *Harvard Law Review* (1990), Vol. 103, No. 8, pp. 1844–1886

'Critical Race Theory and International Law', *Villanova Law Review* (2000), Vol. 45, No. 5, pp. 827–1220

'Critical Race Theory: History, Evolution and New Frontiers', *American University Law Review* (2004), Vol. 53, No. 6, pp. 1187–1472

'Critical Race Theory: The Next Frontier', *Washington and Lee Law Review* (2004), Vol. 61, No. 4, pp. 1485–1799

'Going Back to Class? The Reemergence of Class in Critical Race Theory', *Michigan Journal of Race and Law* (2005), Vol. 11, No. 1, pp. 1–273

'Le curieux débat des démographes', *Mouvements* (1999), No. 3, p. 110

'Nanook of the Nomos: A Symposium on Critical Race Praxis', *Michigan Journal of Race and Law* (1999), Vol. 5, pp. 31–237

'Re-defining Critical Race Theory: The Future of the Movement', *Iowa Law Journal* (2009), Vol. 94, No. 5, pp. 1497–1649

'Special Issue on Critical Legal Theory and European Private Law', *European Review of Private Law* (2002), Vol. 10, No. 1, pp. 1–132

'The First Annual LatCrit Summer Colloquium: Spain, the Americas and Latino/as:

International and Comparative Law in Triangular Perspective', *University of Miami International and Comparative Law Review* (2001–2001), Vol. 9, pp. 1–224

'Theorizing the Connections Among Systems of Subordination', *UMKC Law Review* (2002), Vol. 71, No. 2, pp. 227–527

'Unconscious Discrimination Twenty Years Later: Application and Evolution', *Connecticut Law Review* (2007–2008), Vol. 40, No. 4, pp. 927–1235

ABRAMS, KATHRYN 'Hearing the Call of Stories', *California Law Review* (1991), Vol. 79, pp. 971–1052

ADOMEIT, KLAUS 'Political Correctness – jetzt Rechtspflicht!', *Neue Juristische Wochenschrift* (2006), pp. 2169–2171

ALGOSTINO, ALESSANDRA 'L'ordinanza del sindaco di Rovato e il pericolo di "contaminazione" dei valori cristiani. Nota a margine di un atto "considerato radicalmente nullo"', *Diritto, immigrazione e cittadinanza* (2001), No. 2, pp. 84–91

AMBROSINI, MAURIZIO '"We are Against a Multi-Ethnic Society": Policies of Exclusion at the Urban Level in Italy', *Ethnic and Racial Studies* (2013), Vol. 36, No. 1, pp. 136–155

APPLEMAN, LAURA I. 'The Rise of the Modern American Law School: How Professionalization, German Scholarship, and Legal Reform Shaped Our System of Legal Education', *New England Law Review* (2005), Vol. 39, pp. 251–306

ARENDT, HANNAH 'Race-Thinking before Racism', *The Review of Politics* (1944), Vol. 6, pp. 36–73

AUSTIN, REGINA 'Sapphire Bound!', *Wisconsin Law Review* (1989), Vol. 1989, pp. 539–578

BAER, SUSANNE 'The Basic Law at 60 – Equality and Difference: A Proposal for the Guest List to the Birthday Party', *German Law Journal* (2010), Vol. 11, No. 1, pp. 67–87

BARCELLONA, MARIO 'La scienza giuridica italiana e il marxismo (prima e dopo l'"uso alternativo del diritto")' *Rivista critica di diritto privato* (2000), Vol. 18, No. 4, pp. 715–739

BARNES, MARIO L., CHEMERINSKY, ERWIN and JONES, TRINA 'A Post-Race Equal Protection?', *Georgetown Law Journal* (2010), Vol. 98, pp. 967–1004

BARSKANMAZ, CENGIZ 'Rassismus, Postkolonialismus und Recht – Zu einer deutschen *Critical Race Theory*?', *Kritische Justiz* (2008), Vol. 41, pp. 296–301

BELL, DERRICK A., JR. 'Serving Two Masters: Integration Ideals and Client Interests in School Desegregation Litigation', *Yale Law Journal* (1976), Vol. 85, pp. 470–516

'*Brown v. Board of Education* and the Interest Convergence Dilemma', *Harvard Law Review* (1980), Vol. 93, pp. 518–533

BELLEAU, MARIE-CLAIRE 'The "Juristes Inquiets": Legal Classicism and Criticism in Early Twentieth-Century France', *Utah Law Review* (1997), Vol. 1997, pp. 379–424

BENEDÍ LAHUERTA, SARA 'Race Equality and TCNs, or How to Fight Discrimination with A Discriminatory Law', *European Law Journal* (2009), Vol. 15, No. 6, pp. 738–756

BEYER, JONATHAN A. 'Second Line: Reconstructing the Jazz Metaphor in Critical Race Theory', *Georgetown Law Journal* (2000), Vol. 88, pp. 537–563

BLASI, GARY 'Advocacy against the Stereotype: Lessons from Cognitive Social Psychology', *UCLA Law Review* (2002), Vol. 49, pp. 1241–1281

BLAUNER, ERIC 'Internal Colonialism and Ghetto Revolt', *Social Problems* (1969), Vol. 16, pp. 393–408

BRACCHI, SIMONA PAOLA 'La "burqa" nelle aule di giustizia', *Famiglia, Persone e Successioni* (2009), No. 11, pp. 912–914

BREST, PAUL 'Plus Ça Change', *Michigan Law Review* (1993), Vol. 91, pp. 1946–1952

BREWER, SCOTT 'Introduction: Choosing Sides in the Racial Critiques Debate', *Harvard Law Review* (1990), Vol. 103, pp. 1844–1854

BROWN, DOROTHY A. 'Pensions, Risk, and Race', *Washington and Lee Law Review* (2004), Vol. 61, pp. 1501–1539

BROWN, ELEANOR MARIE 'The Tower of Babel: Bridging the Divide Between Critical Race Theory and "Mainstream" Civil Rights Scholarship', *Yale Law Journal* (1995), Vol. 105, pp. 513–547

BRUCE-JONES, EDDIE 'Race, Space and the Nation-State: Racial Recognition and the Prospects for Substantive Equality Under Anti-Discrimination Law in France and Germany', *Columbia Human Rights Law Review* (2008), Vol. 39, pp. 423–470

BUGARIC, BOJAN 'Courts as Policy Makers: Lessons from Transition', *Harvard International Law Journal* (2001), Vol. 42, pp. 247–288

CALCAGNINI, SIMONA 'I nuovi poteri del sindaco in materia di sicurezza', *Studium iuris* (2009), No. 5, pp. 502–509

CALMORE, JOHN O. 'Exploring The Significance of Race and Class in Representing the Black Poor', *Oregon Law Review* (1982), Vol. 61, pp. 201–244

'Critical Race Theory, Archie Shepp, and Fire Music: Securing an Authentic Intellectual Life in a Multicultural World', *Southern California Law Review* (1992), Vol. 65, pp. 2129–2230

CARBADO, DEVON 'Afterword. Critical What What?', *Connecticut Law Review* (2011), Vol. 43, pp. 1595–1643

CARBADO, DEVON and GULATI, MITU 'The Law and Economics of Critical Race Theory', *Yale Law Journal* (2003), Vol. 112, pp. 1757–1828

CARBIN MARIA and EDENHEIM SARA 'The Intersectional Turn in Feminist Theory: A Dream of a Common Language', *European Journal of Women's Studies* (2013), Vol. 20, No. 3, pp. 233–248

CARBIN MARIA and TORNHILL, SOFIE 'Intersektionalitet – ett oanvändbart begrepp?', *Kvinnovetenskaplig Tidskrift* (2004), Vol. 25, No. 3, pp. 111–114

CARTER, STEPHEN L. 'Academic Tenure and "White Male" Standards: Some Lessons from the Patent Law', *Yale Law Journal* (1991), Vol. 100, pp. 2065–2085

CASADONTE, ANNAMARIA and GUARISO, ALBERTO 'L'azione civile contro la discriminazione per motive etnico-razziali e religiosi', *Questione giustizia* (2010), No. 4, pp. 179–191

CHO, SUMI 'Post-Racialism', *Iowa Law Review* (2009), Vol. 94, pp. 1589–1650

CHO, SUMI and WESTLEY, ROBERT 'Critical Race Coalitions: Key Movements that Performed the Theory', *UC Davis Law Review* (2000), Vol. 33, pp. 1377–1427

CLANET DIT LAMANIT, ELISABETH, 'L'objet "origine" et le concept d'un "peuple" dit "rom"', *Lignes* (2011), No. 34, pp. 79–88

CLAPIÉ, MICHEL 'Le français restera la langue de la République', *Les Petites Affiches* (5 January, 2000), No. 3, pp. 14–18

COLE, MIKE 'Critical Race Theory Comes to the UK: A Marxist Response', *Ethnicities* (2009), Vol. 9, pp. 246–269

'A Response to Charles Mills', *Ethnicities* (2009), Vol. 9, pp. 281–284

'The Color-Line and the Class Struggle: A Marxist Response to Critical Race Theory in

Education as it Arrives in the United Kingdom', *Power and Education* (2009), Vol. 1, pp. 111–124

'On "White Supremacy" and Caricaturing, Misrepresenting and Dismissing Marx and Marxism: A Response to David Gillborn's "Who's Afraid of Critical Race Theory in Education?"', *Journal for Critical Education Policy Studies* (2009), Vol. 7, pp. 29–49

CORSI, CECILIA 'Prestazione assistenziali e cittadinanza', *Diritto, immigrazione e cittadinanza* (2009), No. 2, pp. 30–47

COUGHLIN, ANNE M. 'Regulating the Self: Autobiographical Performances in Outsider Scholarship', *Virginia Law Review* (1995), Vol. 81, pp. 1229–1340

CREMER, HENDRIK '" ... und welcher Rasse gehören Sie an?" Zur Problematik des Begriffs "Rasse" in der Gesetzgebung', *Deutsches Institut für Menschenrechte, Policy Paper No. 10* (November 2009)

'Ein Grundgesetz ohne "Rasse". Vorschlag für eine Änderung des Artikels 3 Grundgesetz', *Deutsches Institut für Menschenrechte, Policy Paper No. 16* (April 2010)

CRENSHAW, KIMBERLÉ W. 'Race, Reform, and Retrenchment: Transformation and Legitimation in Anti-Discrimination Law', *Harvard Law Review* (1988), Vol. 101, pp. 1331–1387

'Demarginalizing the Intersection of Race and Sex', *University of Chicago Legal Forum* (1989), Vol. 1989, pp. 139–167

'Mapping the Margins: Intersectionality, Identity Politics, and Violence Against Women of Color', *Stanford Law Review* (1991), Vol. 43, pp. 1241–1299

'The First Decade: Critical Reflections, or "A Foot in the Closing Door"', *UCLA Law Review* (2002), Vol. 49, pp. 1343–1394

'Twenty Years of Critical Race Theory. Looking Back to Move Forward', *Connecticut Law Review* (2011), Vol. 43, pp. 1253–1354

DALTON, HARLON L. 'The Clouded Prism', *Harvard Civil Rights – Civil Liberties Law Review* (1987), Vol. 22, pp. 435–447

DAVIS, KATHY 'Intersectionality as Buzzword: A Sociology of Science Perspective on What Makes a Feminist Theory Successful', *Feminist Theory* (2008), Vol. 9, pp. 67–85

DAWSON, MARK and MUIR, ELISE 'Individual, Institutional and Collective Vigilance in Protecting Fundamental Rights in the EU: Lessons from the Roma', *Common Market Law Review* (2011), Vol. 48, pp. 751–775

DE BÉCHILLON, DENYS 'La structure des normes juridiques à l'épreuve de la postmodernité', *Revue interdisciplinaire d'études juridiques* (1999), No. 43, pp. 1–25

DE HAAN, WILLEM; SILVIS, JOS and THOMAS, PHILIP A. 'Democracy, Rule of Law and Critical Legal Theory in Germany', *Journal of Law and Society* (1991), Vol. 18, pp. 347–352

DELGADO, RICHARD 'Words That Wound: A Tort Action For Racial Insults, Epithets and Name Calling', *Harvard Civil Rights – Civil Liberties Law Review* (1982), Vol. 17, pp. 133–181

'The Imperial Scholar: Reflections on a Review of Civil Rights Literature', *University of Pennsylvania Law Review* (1984), Vol. 132, pp. 561–578

'The Imperial Scholar Revisited: How to Marginalize Outside Writing, Ten Years Later', *University of Pennsylvania Law Review* (1992), Vol. 140, pp. 1349–1372

'Rodrigo's Chronicle', *Yale Law Journal* (1992), Vol. 101, pp. 1363–1383

'Rodrigo's Tenth Chronicle: Merit and Affirmative Action', *Georgetown Law Journal* (1995), Vol. 83, pp. 1711–1748

'Coughlin's Complaint: How to Disparage Outsider Writing, One Year Later', *Virginia Law Review* (1996), Vol. 82, pp. 95–109

'Official Elitism or Institutional Self-Interest? 10 Reasons Why UC Davis Should Abandon the LSAT (and Why Other Good Law Schools Should Follow Suit)', *UC Davis Law Review* (2001), Vol. 34, pp. 593–614

'Crossroads and Blind Alleys: A Critical Examination of Recent Writings About Race, Crossroads, Directions, and a New Critical Race Theory', *Texas Law Review* (2003), Vol. 82, pp. 121–152

'Liberal McCarthyism and the Origins of Critical Race Theory', *Iowa Law Review* (2009), Vol. 94, pp. 1505–1545

'The Law of the Noose: A History of Latino Lynching', *Harvard Civil Rights – Civil Liberties Law Review* (2009), Vol. 44, pp. 297–312

DELGADO, RICHARD and STEFANCIC, JEAN 'Critical Race Theory, An Annotated Bibliography', *Virginia Law Review* (1993), Vol. 79, pp. 461–516

'Critical Race Theory, An Annotated Bibliography 1993, A Year of Transition', *University of Colorado Law Review* (1995), Vol. 66, pp. 159–193

DICKERSON, A. MECHELE 'Race Matters in Bankruptcy', *Washington and Lee Law Review* (2004), Vol. 61, pp. 1725–1776

DUDZIAK, MARY L. 'Desegregation as a Cold War Imperative', *Stanford Law Review* (1988), Vol. 41, pp. 61–120

ESPINOZA, LESLIE and HARRIS, ANGELA P. 'Embracing the Tar-Baby – LatCrit Theory and the Sticky Mess of Race', *California Law Review* (1997), Vol. 85, pp. 1585–1645

ESSED, PHILOMENA and TRIENEKENS, SANDRA, 'Who Wants to Feel White? Race, Dutch Culture and Contested Identities', *Ethnic and Racial Studies* (2008), Vol. 31, No. 1, pp. 52–72

EWALD, WILLIAM 'American Revolution and the Evolution of Law', *American Journal of Comparative Law Supplement* (1994), Vol. 42, pp. 1–14

FARALLI, CARLA 'La ricezione del realismo giuridico nei paesi latini', *Materiali per una storia della cultura giuridica* (2000), Year 30, No. 2, pp. 427–448

FARBER, DANIEL A. and SHERRY, SUZANNA 'Telling Stories Out of School: An Essay on Legal Narratives', *Stanford Law Review* (1993), Vol. 45, pp. 807–855

'Is the Radical Critique of Merit Anti-Semitic?', *California Law Review* (1995), Vol. 83, pp. 853–884

FERLA, LARA '"L'applicazione della finalita" di discriminazione razziale in alcune recenti pronounce della Corte di cassazione', *Rivista italiana di diritto e procedura penale* (2007), No. 4, pp. 1455–1475

FLAGG, BARBARA J. '"Was Blind, But Now I See": White Race Consciousness and the Requirement of Discriminatory Intent', *Michigan Law Review* (1993), Vol. 91, pp. 953–1017

FOLLA, NATALINA 'L'uso del burqa non integra reato in assenza di una previsione normative espressa', *Il Corriere del Merito* (2009), No. 3, pp. 294–302

FREEMAN, ALAN DAVID 'Legitimizing Racial Discrimination Through Anti-Discrimination Law: A Critical Review of Supreme Court Doctrine', *Minnesota Law Review* (1978), Vol. 62, pp. 1049–1119

GARCÍA-VILLEGAS, MAURICIO 'Comparative Sociology of Law: Legal Fields, Legal Scholarships, and Social Sciences in Europe and the United States', *Law & Social Inquiry* (2006), Vol. 31, No. 2, pp. 343–382

GASPARINI, MARCO 'Criminalità e degrado urbano: la battaglia è a colpi di ordinanze', *Guida al Diritto – Il Sole 24 Ore* (December 6, 2008), No. 48, pp. 18–23

GAUDREAULT-DESBIENS, JEAN-FRANÇOIS 'La *Critical Race Theory* ou le droit étatique comme outil utile, mais imparfait, de changement social', *Droit et Société* (2001), Vol. 48, pp. 581–612

GEDDES, ANDREW and GUIRAUDON, VIRGINIE 'Britain, France and EU Anti-Discrimination Policy: The Emergence of an EU Policy Paradigm', *West European Politics* (2004), Vol. 27, No. 2, pp. 334–353

GILLBORN, DAVID 'Who's Afraid of Critical Race Theory in Education? A Reply to Mike Cole's "The Color-Line and the Class Struggle"', *Power and Education* (2009), Vol. 1, pp. 125–131

GNES, MATTEO 'L'annullamento prefettizio delle ordinanze del sindaco quale ufficiale del governo', *Giornale di diritto amministrativo* (2009), No. 1, pp. 44–50

GOLDBERG, SUZANNE B. 'Equality without Tiers', *Southern California Law Review* (2003–2004), Vol. 77, pp. 481–582

GOLDONI, MARCO 'Costituzionalismo americano e razza. La lezione della *Critical Race Theory*', *Politica del diritto* (2006), No. 3, pp. 475–495

'Profiles of Discrimination: A Critical Argument Against Racial Profiling', *Sortuz. Oñati Journal of Emergent Socio-Legal Studies* (2013), Vol. 5, No. 1, pp. 19–35

GORDON, LEWIS B. 'A Short History of the "Critical" in Critical Race Theory', *The APA Newsletter on Philosophy and the Black Experience* (Spring 1999), Vol. 98, No. 2, pp. 23–26

GOTANDA, NEIL 'A Critique of "Our Constitution Is Colorblind"', *Stanford Law Review* (1991), Vol. 44, pp. 1–68

GRECHENIG, KRISTOFFEL R. and GELTER, MARTIN 'The Transatlantic Divergence in Legal Thought: American Law and Economics vs. German Doctrinalism', *Hastings International and Comparative Law Review* (2008), Vol. 31, pp. 295–360

GREENBERG, JACK 'Report on Roma Education Today: From Slavery to Segregation and Beyond', *Columbia Law Review* (2010), Vol. 110, pp. 919–1001

GRIGOLO, MICHELE 'Human Rights and Cities: the Barcelona Office for Non-Discrimination and its Work for Migrants', *The International Journal of Human Rights* (2010), Vol. 14, No. 6, pp. 896–914

HANEY-LÓPEZ, IAN F. 'The Social Construction of Race: Some Observations on Illusion, Fabrication, and Choice', *Harvard Civil Rights – Civil Liberties Law Review* (1994), Vol. 29, pp. 1–62

'Race, Ethnicity, Erasure: The Salience of Race to LatCrit Theory', *California Law Review* (1997), Vol. 85, pp. 1143–1211

'Post-Racial Racism: Racial Stratification and Mass Incarceration in the Age of Obama', *California Law Review* (2010), Vol. 98, pp. 1023–1073

HANRETTY, CHRIS and HERMANIN, COSTANZA 'Nominalization as Racialization in the Italian Press', *Bulletin of Italian Politics* (2010), Vol. 2, No. 2, pp. 75–94

HARRIS, ANGELA P. 'Race and Essentialism in Feminist Legal Theory', *Stanford Law Review* (1992), Vol. 42, pp. 581–616

'Foreword: The Jurisprudence of Reconstruction', *California Law Review* (1994), Vol. 82, pp. 741–785

'Beyond Equality: Power and the Possibility of Freedom in the Republic of Choice', *Cornell Law Review* (2000), Vol. 85, pp. 1181–1193

'From Color Line to Color Chart? Racism and Colorism in the New Century', *Berkeley Journal of African-American Law & Policy* (2008), Vol. 10, pp. 52–69

HARRIS, CHERYL I. 'Whiteness as Property', *Harvard Law Review* (1993), Vol. 106, pp. 1707–1791

HARRIS, CHERYL I. and WEST-FAULCON, KIMBERLY 'Reading *Ricci*: Whitening Discrimination, Racing Test Fairness', *UCLA Law Review* (2010), Vol. 58, pp. 73–165

HERMANIN, COSTANZA '"Counts" on the Italian "Nomad Camps": An Incautious Ethnic Census of Roma?', *Ethnic and Racial Studies* (2011), Vol. 34, No. 10, pp. 1731–1750

HERNANDEZ, TANYA KATERÌ 'The Value of Intersectional Comparative Analysis to the "Post-Racial" Future of Critical Race Theory: A Brazil–U.S. Comparative Study', *Connecticut Law Review* (2011), Vol. 43, pp. 1407–1438

HOLZLEITNER, ELISABETH 'Latina and Latino Critical Legal Studies und europäisches Gleichheitsdenken – ein interkultureller Dialog', *juridikum* (2006), No. 2, pp. 88–93

HUTCHINSON, DARREN LENARD 'Ignoring the Sexualization of Race: Heteronormativity, Critical Race Theory, and Anti-Racist Politics', *Buffalo Law Review* (1999), Vol. 47, pp. 1–116

'Identity Crisis: "Intersectionality", "Multidimensionality", and the Development of an Adequate Theory of Subordination', *Michigan Journal of Race and Law* (2001), Vol. 6, pp. 285–317

'Critical Race Histories: In and Out', *American University Law Review* (2004), Vol. 53, pp. 1187–1215

'Racial Exhaustion', *Washington University Law Review* (2009), Vol. 86, pp. 917–974

HYLTON, KEVIN, 'How a Turn to Critical Race Theory can Contribute to our Understanding of "Race", Racism and Anti-Racism in Sports', *International Review for the Sociology of Sport* (2010), Vol. 45, No. 3, pp. 335–354

HYMAN, DAVID A. 'Lies, Damned Lies, and Narrative', *Indiana Law Journal* (1998), Vol. 73, pp. 797–865

IGNĂȚOIU-SORA, EMANUELA 'The Discrimination Discourse in Relation to the Roma: Its Limits and Benefits', *Ethnic and Racial Studies* (2011), Vol. 34, No. 10, pp. 1697–1794

IKEMOTO, LISA C. 'The Code of Perfect Pregnancy: At the Intersection of the Ideology of Motherhood, the Practice of Defaulting to Science, and the Interventionist Mindset of Law', *Ohio State Law Journal* (1992), Vol. 53, pp. 1205–1306

ILIOPOULOU, ANASTASIA '"Le temps des gitans" : à propos de la libre circulation des Roms dans l'Union', *Europe* (January 2011), No. 1, Étude 1, pp. 5–10

ISAKSEN, JUDY L. 'From Critical Race Theory to Composition Studies: Pedagogy and Theory Building', *Legal Studies Forum* (2000), Vol. 24, pp. 695–710

JAUNAIT, ALEXANDRE and CHAUVIN, SÉBASTIEN, 'Les théories de l'intersectionnalité à l'épreuve des sciences sociales', *Revue française des sciences politiques* (2012), Vol. 62, No. 1, pp. 5–20

JOBARD, FABIEN and NEVANEN, SOPHIE 'La couleur du jugement. Discriminations dans les décisions judiciaires en matière d'infractions à agents de la force publique', *Revue française de sociologie* (2007), Vol. 48, No. 2, pp. 243–272

JOHNSON, ALEX 'The New Voice of Color', *Yale Law Journal* (1991), Vol. 100, pp. 2007–2063

JOHNSON, KEVIN R. 'An Essay on Immigration Politics, Popular Democracy, and

California's Proposition 187: The Political Relevance and Legal Irrelevance of Race', *Washington Law Review* (1995), Vol. 70, pp. 629–667

'The Last Twenty-Five Years of Affirmative Action?', *Constitutional Commentary* (2004), Vol. 21, pp. 171–190

'A Case Study of Color-Blindness: The Racially Disparate Impacts of Arizona's SB 1070 and the Failure of Comprehensive Immigration Reform', *UC Irvine Law Review* (2012), Vol. 2, pp. 313–358

JONES, BERNIE D. 'Critical Race Theory: New Strategies for Civil Rights in the New Millennium', *Harvard Blackletter Journal* (2002), Vol. 18, pp. 1–90

KELES, AXELLE 'La justice française renvoie au législateur le soin de se prononcer sur les contrôles d'identité au faciès', *Lettre 'Actualités Droits-Libertés' du CREDOF*, 28 November 2013

KANTOLA, JOHANNA and NOUSIAINEN, KEVÄT, 'Institutionalizing Intersectionality', *International Feminist Journal of Politics* (2009), Vol. 11, No. 4, pp. 459–477

KELMAN, MARK G. 'Trashing', *Stanford Law Review* (1984), Vol. 36, pp. 293–348

KELSEN, HANS 'Judicial Review of Legislation, A Comparative Study of the Austrian and the American Constitution', *The Journal of Politics* (1942), Vol. 4, pp. 183–200

KENNEDY, DUNCAN 'The Structure of Blackstone's Commentaries', *The Buffalo Law Review* (1979), Vol. 28, pp. 209–321

'Freedom and Constraint in Adjudication: A Critical Phenomenology', *Journal of Legal Education* (1986), Vol. 36, pp. 518–562

KENNEDY, RANDALL L. 'Racial Critiques of Legal Academia', *Harvard Law Review* (1989), Vol. 102, pp. 1745–1819

KLEIN, CHRISTINE A. 'Treaties of Conquest: Property Rights, Indian Treaties and the Treaty of Guadalupe Hidalgo', *New Mexico Law Review* (1991), Vol. 26, pp. 201–256

KNAPP, GUDRUN-AXELI 'Race, Class, Gender: Reclaiming Baggage in Fast Travelling Theories', *European Journal of Women's Studies* (2005), Vol. 12, No. 3, pp. 249–265

KÜNNE, JOHANNA 'Critical Race Theory. Eine andere Sichtweise im Deutschen Recht', *ForumRecht* (2008), No. 3, pp. 92–94

LADSON-BILLINGS, GLORIA and TATE, WILLIAM F. IV 'Toward a Critical Race Theory of Education', *Teachers College Record* (1995), Vol. 97, No. 1, pp. 47–68

LAWRENCE, CHARLES R. III 'The Id, the Ego, and Equal Protection: Reckoning with Unconscious Racism', *Stanford Law Review* (1987), Vol. 39, pp. 317–388

'Doing the "James Brown" at Harvard: Derrick Bell as Liberationist Teacher', *Harvard Blackletter Journal* (1991), Vol. 8, pp. 263–273

'The Word and the River: Pedagogy as Scholarship as Struggle', *Southern California Law Review* (1992), Vol. 65, pp. 2231–2298

LEVIT, NANCY 'Critical of Race Theory: Race, Reason, Merit, and Civility', *Georgetown Law Journal* (1999), Vol. 87, pp. 795–822

LEWIS, GAIL 'Celebrating Intersectionality? Debates on a Multi-Faceted Concept in Gender Studies: Themes from a Conference', *European Journal of Women's Studies* (2009), Vol. 16, pp. 203–210

LITOWITZ, DOUGLAS E. 'Some Critical Thoughts on Critical Race Theory', *Notre Dame Law Review* (1996–1997), Vol. 72, pp. 503–529

LOCHAK, DANIÈLE 'La race : une categorie juridique?', *Mots* (1992), No. 33, pp. 291–303

LÓPEZ, GERARDO R. 'The (Racially Neutral) Politics of Education: A Critical Race Theory Perspective', *Educational Administration Quarterly* (2003), Vol. 39, No. 1, pp. 68–94

LOSANO, MARIO G. 'La legge e la zappa. Origini e sviluppo del diritto alternativo in Europa e in Sudamerica', *Materiali per una storia della cultura giuridica* (2000), Year 30, No. 1, pp. 109–151

LYNN, MARVIN 'Toward a Critical Race Pedagogy', *Urban Education* (1999), Vol. 33, No. 5, pp. 606–626

MACKINNON, CATHERINE 'Feminism, Marxism, Method, and the State: An Agenda for Theory', *Signs: Journal of Women in Culture and Society* (1982), Vol. 7, No. 3, pp. 515–544

MAFFEIS, DANIELE 'Il contratto nella società multietnica: è un atto illecito la determinazione di un prezzo doppio per i clienti extracomunitari', *Giurisprudenza italiana* (2006), pp. 951–962

MAILLARY, CAROLINE 'Diagnostiquer pour mieux trier', *Plein droit* (2013), No. 99, pp. 11–12.

MALLON, RON '"Race": Normative, Not Metaphysical or Semantic', *Ethics* (2006), Vol. 116, pp. 525–551

MARKHARD, NORA 'Die andere Frage stellen: Intersektionalität als Analysekategorie im Recht', *Kritische Justiz* (2009), Vol. 42, pp. 353–364

MARSHALL, THURGOOD 'Reflections on the Bicentennial of the United States Constitution', *Harvard Law Review* (1987), Vol. 101, pp. 1–5

MATSUDA, MARI J. 'Looking to the Bottom: Critical Legal Studies and Reparations', *Harvard Civil Rights – Civil Liberties Law Review* (1987), Vol. 22, pp. 323–399

'Affirmative Action and Legal Knowledge: Planting Seeds in Plowed-Up Ground', *Harvard Women's Law Journal* (1988), Vol. 11, pp. 1–17

'Public Response to Racist Speech: Considering the Victim's Story', *Michigan Law Review* (1989), Vol. 87, pp. 2320–2381

MATTEI, UGO 'Why the Wind Changed: Intellectual Leadership in Western Law', *American Journal of Comparative Law* (1994), Vol. 42, pp. 195–218

'Efficiency in Legal Transplants. An Essay in Comparative Law and Economics', *International Review of Law and Economics* (1994), Vol. 14, pp. 3–19

MATTEI, UGO and DI ROBILANT, ANNA 'The Art and Science of Critical Legal Scholarship: Postmodernism and International Style in the Legal Architecture of Europe', *Tulane Law Review* (2001), Vol. 75, pp. 1053–1092

MEER, NASAR 'Racialization and Religion: Race, Culture and Difference in the Study of Antisemitism and Islamophobia', *Ethnic and Racial Studies* (2013), Vol. 36, No. 3, pp. 385–398

MILLS, CHARLES W. 'Critical Race Theory: A Reply to Mike Cole', *Ethnicities* (2009), Vol. 9, pp. 270–281

MINNITI, MASSIMO and MINNITI, FRANCESCO 'Tra libertà religiosa e ordine pubblico Sindaco ko alla guerra del velo islamico', *Diritto e Giustiza* (2006), No. 44, pp. 108–111

MINOW, MARTHA 'Law Turning Outward', *Telos* (1986), Vol. 73, pp. 79–100

MITSCH, WOLFGANG 'Volksverhetzung gegen Deutsche', *Juristische Rundschau* (2011), pp. 380–382

MÖSCHEL, MATHIAS 'L'assenza della *Critical Race Theory* nei paesi di civil law', *Rivista trimestrale di scienza dell'amministrazione* (2007), No. 4, pp. 109–123

'Color Blindness or Total Blindness? The Absence of Critical Race Theory in Europe', *Rutgers Race and Law Review* (2007), Vol. 9, pp. 57–128

'*Race judicata*. The Ban on the Use of Ethnic and Racial Statistics in France', *European Constitutional Law Review* (2009), Vol. 5, pp. 197–217

'Is the European Court of Human Rights' Case Law on Anti-Roma Violence "Beyond Reasonable Doubt"?', *Human Rights Law Review* (2012), Vol. 12, No. 3, pp. 479–507

MUCCHIELLI, LAURENT 'Il n'y a pas de statistique raciste, seulement des interpretations', *Mouvements* (1999), No. 3, pp. 115–117

MUGHINI, LUIGI 'Prime riflessioni a margine dell'ordinanza del Tribunale di Firenze in materia di azione contro la discriminazione razziale', *Diritto, immigrazione e cittadinanza* (2000), No. 1, pp. 82–85

MUIR WATT, HORATIA 'La fonction subversive du droit comparé', *Revue internationale de droit comparé* (2000), Vol. 52, No. 3, pp. 503–527

MURPHY, TIM 'BritCrits: Subversion and Submission, Past, Present and Future', *Law and Critique* (1999), Vol. 10, pp. 237–278

MUTUA, ATHENA D. 'The Rise, Development and Future Directions of Critical Race Theory and Related Scholarship', *Denver University Law Review* (2006), Vol. 84, pp. 329–394

NARULA, SMITA 'Equal By Law, Unequal By Caste: The "Untouchable" Condition in Critical Race Perspective', *Wisconsin International Law Journal* (2008), Vol. 26, pp. 255–343

ONWUACHI-WILLIG ANGELA and BARNES MARIO L. 'The Obama Effect: Understanding Emerging Meanings of "Obama" in Anti-Discrimination Law', *Indiana Law Journal* (2012), Vol. 87, pp. 325–348

OSTERTAG, JUERGEN R. 'Legal Education in Germany and the United States – A Structural Comparison', *Vanderbildt Journal of Transnational Law* (1993), Vol. 26, pp. 301–340

PAPADOPOULOS, IOANNIS S. 'Guerre et paix en droit et littérature', *Revue interdisciplinaire d'études juridiques* (1999), No. 42, pp. 181–196

PELLER, GARY 'The Metaphysics of American Law', *California Law Review* (1985), Vol. 73, pp. 1151–1290

'Race Consciousness', *Duke Law Journal* (1990), Vol. 1990, pp. 758–847

'The Discourse of Constitutional Degradation', *Georgetown Law Journal* (1992), Vol. 81, pp. 313–341

PEREA, JUAN F. 'The Black/White Binary Paradigm of Race: The "Normal Science" of American Racial Thought', *California Law Review* (1997), Vol. 85, pp. 1213–1258

PEUTERE, LAURA and KÄÄRIÄNEN, JUHA 'Racist Crimes in the Finnish Criminal Justice System – Analysis of Cases Reported to the Police in Helsinki in 2006', *European Journal of Crime, Criminal Law and Criminal Justice* (2010), Vol. 18, No. 3, pp. 261–279

PHILLIPS, STEPHANIE 'The Convergence of the Critical Race Theory Workshop with LatCrit Theory: A History', *University of Miami Law Review* (1999), Vol. 53, pp. 1247–1472

RAMIREZ, STEVEN A. 'Games CEOs Play and Interest Convergence Theory: Why Diversity Lags in America's Boardrooms and What To Do About It', *Washington and Lee Law Review* (2004), Vol. 61, pp. 1583–1613

RIVA, NICOLA 'Differenza "razziale" ed eguaglianza di opportunità', *Materiali per una storia della cultura giuridica* (2008), Year 38, No. 2, pp. 553–560

RODRIGUEZ RUIZ, BLANCA and RUBIO-MARÍN, RUTH 'The Gender of

Representation: On Democracy, Equality, and Parity', *International Journal of Constitutional Law* (2008), Vol. 6, No. 2, pp. 287–316

ROSSI, STEFANO '*Law in Action*: Diritto antidiscriminatorio e politiche locali', *Responsabilità civile e previdenza* (2010), No. 12, pp. 2541–2660

RUBIN, EDWARD L. 'On Beyond Truth: A Theory Evaluating Legal Scholarship', *California Law Review* (1992), Vol. 80, pp. 889–963

'Book Review: Jews, Truth, and Critical Race Theory', *Northwestern University Law Review* (1999), Vol. 93, pp. 525–545

RUGA RIVA, CARLO 'Il lavavetri, la donna col burqa e il sindaco. Prove atecniche di "diritto penale municipale"', *Rivista italiana di diritto e procedura penale* (2008), No. 1, pp. 133–148

SAGERS, CHRISTOPHER L. 'Postmodern Legal Movements: Law and Jurisprudence at Century's End – Book Review', *Michigan Law Review* (1997), Vol. 95, pp. 1938–1942

SAID, EDWARD W. 'Travelling Theory', *Raritan: A Quarterly Review* (1982), Vol. 1, No. 3, pp. 41–67

SCARPARI, GIANCARLO 'La legge Reale, il burqa e il "comune sentire del popolo"', *Diritto, immigrazione e cittadinanza* (2006), No. 1, pp. 78–80

SCHNAPPER, DOMINIQUE 'Statistiques ethniques', *Commentaire* (2007), Vol. 30, No. 117, pp. 119–121

SHAPIRO, FRED and PEARSE, MICHELLE 'The Most Cited Law Review Articles of All Time', *Michigan Law Review* (2012), Vol. 110, pp. 1483–1520

SHELBY, TOMMY 'Foundations of Black Solidarity: Collective Identity or Common Oppression?', *Ethics* (2002), Vol. 112, pp. 231–266

SIEGEL, REVA 'The Rule of Love: Wife Beating as Prerogative and Privacy', *Yale Law Journal* (1996), Vol. 105, pp. 2117–2208

SIMON, PATRICK 'Sciences sociales et racisme: où sont les docteurs Folamour?', *Mouvements* (1999), No. 3, pp. 111–114

SIMONI, ALESSANDRO 'La discriminazione razziale alla vigilia dell'attuazione della direttiva 43/2000: considerazioni a partire da alcune recenti pronunce giurisprudenziali', *Diritto, immigrazione e cittadinanza* (2002), No. 4, pp. 81–90

'I decreti "emergenza nomadi": il nuovo volto di un vecchio problema', *Diritto, immigrazione e cittadinanza* (2008), No. 3–4, pp. 44–56

'Appunti per una "lettura romanì" del "pacchetto sicurezza"', *Diritto, immigrazione e cittadinanza* (2009), No. 4, pp. 217–230

SKEEL, DAVID A., JR. 'Racial Dimensions of Credit and Bankruptcy', *Washington and Lee Law Review* (2004), Vol. 61, pp. 1695–1724

SOLANKE, IYIOLA 'Diversity and Independence in the European Court of Justice', *Columbia Journal of European Law* (2008), Vol. 15, pp. 89–121

'Putting Race and Gender Together: A New Approach to Intersectionality', *Modern Law Review* (2009), Vol. 72, No. 5, pp. 723–749

SOLORZANO, DANIEL G. 'Images and Words that Wound: Critical Race Theory, Racial Stereotyping, and Teacher Education', *Teacher Education Quarterly* (1997), Vol. 24, No. 3, pp. 5–20

SOMEK, ALEXANDER 'From Kennedy to Balkin: Introducing Critical Legal Studies from a Continental Perspective', *University of Kansas Law Review* (1994), Vol. 42, pp. 759–783

SPANN, GIRARDEAU A. 'Pure Politics', *Michigan Law Review* (1990), Vol. 88, pp. 1971–2033

'The Dark Side of Grutter', *Constitutional Commentary* (2004), Vol. 21, pp. 221–250

'Disparate Impact', *Georgetown Law Journal* (2010), Vol. 98, pp. 1133–1164

STEFANCIC, JEAN 'Latino and Latina Critical Theory: An Annotated Bibliography', *California Law Review* (1997), Vol. 85, pp. 1509–1584

STRAUB, DIETER 'Drohen amerikanische Verhältnisse?', *Arbeit und Arbeitsrecht* (2005), Vol. 60, No. 2, p. 65

STRICKLAND, RENNARD 'Genocide-at-Law: An Historic and Contemporary View of the Native American Experience', *University of Kansas Law Review* (1986), Vol. 34, pp. 713–756

SUK, JULIE 'Equal By Comparison: Unsettling Assumptions of Antidiscrimination Law', *American Journal of Comparative Law* (2007), Vol. 55, pp. 295–345

SUNSTEIN, CASS 'Lochner's Legacy', *Columbia Law Review* (1987), Vol. 87, pp. 873–919

TAGUIEFF, PIERRE-ANDRE 'Du racisme au mot "race": comment les eliminer ?', *Mots* (1992), No. 33, pp. 215–239

THOMAS, KENDALL 'The Political Economy of Recognition: Affirmative Action Discourse and Constitutional Equality in Germany and the U.S.A.', *Columbia Journal of European Law* (1998–1999), Vol. 5, pp. 329–364

'Legge, Razza e Diritti: "Critical Race Theory" e politica del diritto negli Stati Uniti', *Filosofia politica* (2003), No. 3, pp. 447–466

TRELOGAN, THOMAS, MAZURANA, STEVE and HODAPP, PAUL 'Can't We Enlarge the Blanket and the Bed? A Comparative Analysis of Positive Action in the European Court of Justice and the United States Supreme Court', *Hastings International and Comparative Law Review* (2004), Vol. 28, pp. 39–93

TUCCI, GIUSEPPE 'Principio di eguaglianza e discriminazione per nazionalità e cittadinanza: "bonus bebè" e razzismo "padano"', *Rivista critica del diritto privato* (2010), No. 4, pp. 677–699

TUSHNET, MARK 'An Essay on Rights', *Texas Law Review* (1984), Vol. 62, pp. 1363–1403

'Critical Legal Studies: A Political History', *Yale Law Journal* (1991), Vol. 100, pp. 1515–1544

'The Degradation of Constitutional Discourse', *Georgetown Law Journal* (1992), Vol. 81, pp. 251–311

'Reply', *Georgetown Law Journal* (1992), Vol. 81, pp. 343–350

TWINING, WILLIAM 'Have Concepts, Will Travel: Analytical Jurisprudence in a Global Context', *International Journal of Law in Context* (2005), Vol. 1, pp. 5–40

VALDES, FRANCISCO 'Sex and Race in Queer Legal Culture: Ruminations on Identities and Inter-Connectivities', *Southern California Review of Law and Women's Studies* (1995), Vol. 5, pp. 25–71

WATSON, ALAN 'Legal Change: Sources of Law and Legal Culture', *University of Pennsylvania Law Review* (1983), Vol. 131, pp. 1121–1157

WECHSLER, HERBERT 'Toward Neutral Principles of Constitutional Law', *Harvard Law Review* (1959), Vol. 73, pp. 1–35

WEIL, PATRICK 'Racisme et discrimination dans la politique française de l'immigration 1938–1945/1974–1995', *Vingtième Siècle* (1995), Vol. 47, pp. 77–102

WHITE, G. EDWARD 'From Realism to Critical Legal Studies: A Truncated Intellectual History', *Southwestern Law Journal* (1986), Vol. 40, pp. 819–843

WILLIAMS, PATRICIA 'Minority Critique of CLS: Alchemical Notes: Reconstructing Ideals from Deconstructed Rights', *Harvard Civil Rights – Civil Liberties Law Review* (1987), Vol. 22, pp. 401–433

WING, ADRIEN KATHERINE 'A Critical Race Feminist Conceptualization of Violence: South African and Palestinian Women', *Albany Law Review* (1997), Vol. 60, pp. 943–976

WING, ADRIEN KATHERINE and SMITH, MONICA NIGH 'Critical Race Feminism Lifts the Veil? Muslim Women, France, and the Headscarf Ban', *UC Davis Law Review* (2006), Vol. 39, pp. 743–785

WISE, EDWARD M. 'The Transplant of Legal Patterns', *American Journal of Comparative Law Supplement* (1990), Vol. 38, pp. 1–22

WOLFF, ALEXANDER 'Kulturrevolution im Arbeitsrecht', *Arbeit und Arbeitsrecht* (2005), Vol. 60, No. 2, pp. 82–85

YAMAMOTO, ERIC 'Critical Race Praxis: Race Theory and Political Lawyering Practice in Post-Civil Rights America', *Michigan Law Review* (1997), Vol. 95, pp. 821–900

ZORZELLA, NAZZARENA 'I nuovi poteri dei sindaci nel "pacchetto sicurezza" e la loro ricaduta sugli stranieri', *Diritto, immigrazione e cittadinanza* (2008), No. 3–4, pp. 57–73

Miscellaneous sources

Official reports, studies, decisions, parliamentary debates/hearings/questions, speeches, and press releases

ALUFFI, ROBERTA intervention before Camera dei Deputati – Commissione I, Affari Costituzionali, della Presidenza del Consiglio e Interni, *Resoconto Stenografico*, 10 November 2009

AMNESTY INTERNATIONAL 'Victim or Suspect: A Question of Colour. Racial Discrimination in the Austrian Justice System' (London: Amnesty International Publications, 2009)

ASSEMBLEE NATIONALE '12ème législature, Question écrite no. 33641', *Journal Officiel de l'Assemblée nationale*, 25 May 2004

BAIER, DIRK, *et al.* 'Kinder und Jugendliche in Deutschland: Gewalterfahrungen, Integration, Medienkonsum. Zweiter Bericht zum gemeinsamen Forschungsprojekt des Bundesministeriums des Innern und des KFN', Forschungsbericht Nr. 109, 2010, available at: www.kfn.de/versions/kfn/assets/fob109.pdf

BELORGEY, JEAN-MICHEL 'Lutter contre les discriminations' (Paris: La Documentation Française, 1999), available at: http://lesrapports.ladocumentationfrancaise.fr/BRP/994000631/0000.pdf

CAMERA DEI DEPUTATI (Servizio Studi, Dipartimento Istituzioni) 'Divieto di indossare gli indumenti denominati *burqa* e *niqab*', A.C. no. 2422, 30 September 2009, available at: http://documenti.camera.it/leg16/dossier/Testi/ac0378_0.htm

CENTER FOR REPRODUCTIVE RIGHTS AND CENTER FOR HUMAN AND CIVIL RIGHTS 'Body and Soul: Forced Sterilization and Other Assaults on Roma Reproductive Freedom in Slovakia' (New York: Center for Reproductive Rights, 2003), available at: http://reproductiverights.org/sites/crr.civicactions.net/files/documents/bo_slov_part1.pdf

CITTALIA – FONDAZIONE ANCI RICERCHE 'Oltre le ordinanze. I sindaci e la sicurezza urbana', 2nd edn, September 2009, available at: www.cittalia.it/images/file/oltre-le-ordinanze09.pdf?phpMyAdmin=95af31fc7e586d80e7d664a36f07b8b6&phpMyAdmin=3dc56f06dc02f3f7ac2bf9bdd4ec9b2f

COMITÉ POUR LA MESURE DE LA DIVERSITÉ ET L'ÉVALUATION DES DISCRIMINATIONS (COMEDD) 'Inégalités et discriminations. Pour un usage critique et responsable de l'outil statistique', 5 February 2010, available at: http://lesrapports.ladocumentationfrancaise.fr/BRP/104000077/0000.pdf

'En Nouvelle Calédonie: Des statistiques ethniques tout à fait légales', in SERGE SLAMA (ed.), *Les discriminations selon l'origine* (La documentation française, 2009), pp. 103–104

EUROPEAN COMMISSION 'Tackling Multiple Discriminations – Practices, Policies and Law' (Luxembourg: Office of the Official Publications of the European Communities, 2007), available at: http://ec.europa.eu/social/main.jsp?catId=738&langId=en&pubId=51&type=2&furtherPubs=no

EUROPEAN COMMISSION AGAINST RACISM AND INTOLERANCE 'Third Report on Italy', CRI (2006) 19, available at: http://hudoc.ecri.coe.int/XMLEcri/ENGLISH/Cycle_03/03_CbC_eng/ITA-CbC-III-2006-19-ENG.pdf

EUROPEAN COMMISSION AGAINST RACISM AND INTOLERANCE (ECRI) 'Annual Report on ECRI's Activities covering the period from 1 January to 31 December 2009', CRI (2010) 20, available at: www.coe.int/t/dghl/monitoring/ecri/activities/Annual_Reports/Annual%20report%202009.pdf

EUROPEAN UNION AGENCY FOR FUNDAMENTAL RIGHTS (FRA) 'EU-MIDIS, European Union Minorities and Discrimination Survey: Main Results Report' (Vienna: European Union Agency for Fundamental Rights, 2009), available at: http://fra.europa.eu/fraWebsite/attachments/eumidis_mainreport_conference-edition_en_.pdf

HALDE, decision No. 2006–31, 27 February 2006, available at: http://halde.fr/rapport annuel/2006/

HALDE, decision No. 2007–233, 24 September 2007, available at: www.halde.fr/IMG/pdf/Deliberation_du_24_septembre_2007.pdf

HUMAN RIGHTS WATCH 'The State Response to "Hate Crimes in Germany"', (2011), available at: www.hrw.org/sites/default/files/related_material/State%20Response%20to%20%27Hate%20Crimes%27%20in%20Germany.pdf

MAZZOLA, ROBERTO intervention before Camera dei Deputati – Commissione I, Affari Costituzionali, della Presidenza del Consiglio e Interni, *Resoconto Stenografico*, 10 November 2009

OPEN SOCIETY INSTITUTE 'Profiling Minorities: A Study of Stop-and-Search Practices in Paris' (New York: Open Society Institute, 2009), available at: www.opensocietyfoundations.org/sites/default/files/search_20090630.Web.pdf

SARKOZY, NICHOLAS Conférence de presse, 8 January 2008, in *La Semaine Juridique, JCP G* (2008), Actualités, 43, p. 5

'Égalité des chances et diversité', Discours de M. Le Président de la République à Palaiseau, École polytechnique, 17 December 2008, available at: www.lyceesaintmarc.org/rubriques/gauche/stages/cpge-hk-b-l-1ere-annee/17.12-ecole-polytechnique-palaiseau.pdf

VEIL, SIMONE 'Redécouvrir le Préambule de la Constitution – Rapport du Comité présidé par Simone Veil' (Paris: La documentation française, 2008), available at: http://lesrapports.ladocumentationfrancaise.fr/BRP/084000758/0000.pdf

VENTURA, MARCO intervention before Camera dei Deputati – Commissione I, Affari Costituzionali, della Presidenza del Consiglio e Interni, *Resoconto Stenografico*, 10 November 2009

News articles

BELL, DERRICK A., JR. 'Letter to the Editor', *New York Times*, 26 January 1990, p. A30, col. 6

BOHLEN, CELESTINE 'Italians Contemplate Beauty in a Caribbean Brow', *New York Times*, 10 September 1996, p. A3

BRONNER, LUC 'Manifestations de lycéens: le spectre des violences anti-"Blancs"', *Le Monde*, 16 March 2005, p. 9

CLEAVER, ELDRIDGE 'The Land Question', *Ramparts*, May 1968, No. 6, p. 51

DE RICCARDIS, SANDRO '"A Natale via i clandestini" nel Bresciano si festeggia così', *La Repubblica*, 18 November 2009, p. 21

'Viaggio nel paese di White Christmas. "I nostri figli hanno troppi amici neri"', *La Repubblica*, 20 November 2009, p. 26

DUFLO, ESTHER 'Délicates questions ethniques', *Libération*, 26 November 2007, p. 37

GROSJEAN, BLANDINE 'Malaise après un appel contre le "racisme anti-Blancs"', *Libération*, 26 March 2005, pp. 14–15

GUASTELLA, GIUSEPPE 'Il prefetto stoppa il sindaco: non può vietare il velo', *Corriere della Sera*, 4 September 2004, p. 12

MÖNCH, REGINA 'Das Schweigen der Schulen über Deutschenfeindlichkeit', *Frankfurter Allgemeine Zeitung*, 15 October 2010, p. 31

MORA, MIGUEL 'Fichado por gitano', *El País (Domingo)*, 1 February 2009, pp. 1–4

PANZERO, ANGELO 'Velo a Calolziocorte, parola al prefetto', *Corriere della Sera*, 5 October 2004, p. 52

POSNER, RICHARD A. 'The Skin Trade', *The New Republic*, 13 October 1997, p. 40.

POSOR, ANDREA and MEYER, CHRISTIAN 'Deutschenfeindlichkeit in Schulen', *blz*, No. 11/2009, available at: www.gew-berlin.de/1297_1485.php

ROSEN, JEFFERY 'The Bloods and the Crits', *The New Republic*, 9 December 1996, p. 27

SHOOMAN, YASEMIN and LUBIG FOHSEL, EVELIN 'Unter Kartoffeln', *taz*, 7 October 2010, available at: www.taz.de/1/debatte/kommentar/artikel/1/unter-kartoffeln/

SHOOMAN, YASEMIN '"Deutschenfeindlichkeit". Zur problematischen Verwendung des Begriffs', *blz – Zeitschrift der GEW Berlin*, No. 12/2010, p. 11, available at: www.gew-berlin.de/1296_1310.php

SHOOMAN, YASEMIN 'Der Topos "Deutschenfeindlichkeit" in rechtspopulistischen Diskursen', in Bündnis Rechtspopulismus stoppen (eds), *Rechtspopulismus in Berlin* (Berlin, 2011), pp. 45–47, available at: http://rechtspopulismusstoppen.blogsport.de/images/broschuere_rechtspopberlin_web.pdf

SMOLAR, PIOTR 'Bandes: la spirale de l'ultra-violence', *Le Monde*, 25 February 2006, p. 3

VAN EECKHOUT, LAETITIA 'Un appel est lancé contre les "ratonnades anti-Blancs"', *Le Monde*, 26 March 2005, p. 10

'Données ethniques: perplexité après la décision du Conseil constitutionnel', *Le Monde*, 25–26 November 2007, p. 9

WIENER, JON 'Law Profs Fight the Power', *The Nation*, September 4/11, 1989, pp. 246–248

Table of cases

National cases

France

Conseil constitutionnel: Decision CC 82–146 DC, 18 November 1982
Conseil constitutionnel: Decision CC 91–290 DC, 9 May 1991
Conseil constitutionnel: Decision CC 98–407 DC, 20 January 1999
Conseil constitutionnel: Decision CC 99–412 DC, 15 June 1999
Conseil constitutionnel: Decision CC 2001–445 DC, 19 June 2001
Tribunal de Grande Instance de Paris, Juge d'Instruction: No. Instruction 243/02/88, 17 July 2003
Cour d'appel de Paris, Première Chambre de l'Instruction: Dossier No. 2003/05865, 10 November 2003
Cour de cassation, Chambre Criminelle: Pourvoi No. G 03–87.649, décision de non-admission, 11 May 2004
Conseil constitutionnel: Decision CC 2007–557 DC, 15 November 2007
Tribunal de Grande Instance de Paris, 17eme Chambre correctionelle: Decision No. 0928108356, 4 June 2010
Conseil constitutionnel: Decision 2010–13 QPC, 9 July 2010
Conseil constitutionnel: Decision 2010–15/23 QPC, 23 July 2010
Conseil constitutionnel: Decision CC 2011–625 DC, 10 March 2011
Conseil d'Etat: Decision No. 343387, 7 April 2011
Tribunal de Grande Instance de Paris: Decision No. 12/05884, 2 October 2013

Germany

Verwaltungsgericht Koblenz: Az. 5K 1026/11.KO, 28 February 2012
Landesgericht Köln: Az. 151 Ns 169/11, 7 May 2012
Oberverwaltungsgericht Rheinland-Pfalz: Az. 7A 10532/12.OVG, 28 October 2012

Italy

Tribunale di Torino, Sezione I penale: 13 January 1997
Prefetto di Alessandria: Provvedimento 6 February 1999
Tribunale di Milano: Ordinanza 30 March 2000

Tribunale di Milano: Sentenza 21 March 2002
Corte di cassazione, Sezione I penale: Sentenza No. 37112, 2 October 2002
Procura della Repubblica presso il tribunale di Treviso: Richiesta di archiviazione, 19 November 2004
Tribunale di Verona: Sentenza No. 2203, 2 December 2004
Tribunale di Treviso: Decreto di archiviazione, 3 March 2005
Corte di cassazione, Sezione V penale: Sentenza No. 19378, 5 April 2005
Tribunale di Padova: Ordinanza 19 May 2005
Corte di cassazione, Sezione V penale: Sentenza No. 44295, 5 December 2005
Corte costituzionale: Sentenza No. 432/2005, 28 November 2005
Corte di cassazione, Sezione V penale: Sentenza No. 9381, 20 January 2006
T.A.R. Trieste (Friuli Venezia Giulia): Sentenza No. 645, 16 October 2006
Tribunale di Biella: Ordinanza 2 January 2007
Tribunale di Brescia: Ordinanza No. 615, 15 January 2007
Corte d'appello di Venezia, Sezione IV: Sentenza 2 April 2007
Tribunale di Firenze: Decreto in case no. 10834/07, 20 September 2007
Corte di cassazione, Sezione III penale: Sentenza No. 13234, 13 December 2007
Corte costituzionale: Sentenza No. 32/2008, 21 February 2008
T.A.R. Milano (Lombardia), Sezione III: Ordinanza No. 701, 8 May 2008
T.A.R. Milano (Lombardia), Sezione III: Ordinanza No. 702, 8 May 2008
T.A.R. Milano (Lombardia), Sezione III: Ordinanza No. 717, 8 May 2008
Corte di cassazione, Sezione V penale: Sentenza No. 38217, 12 June 2008
Consiglio di Stato, Sezione VI: Decisione No. 3076, 19 June 2008
Corte costituzionale: Sentenza No. 306/2008, 28 July 2008
Corte d'appello di Venezia, Sezione I: Sentenza No. 1553, 20 October 2008
Tribunale di Cremona: Sentenza 27 November 2008
Tribunale di Roma: Ordinanza 4 December 2008
Corte costituzionale: Sentenza No. 11/2009, 24 January 2009
Tribunale di Brescia: Ordinanza No. 335, 26 January 2009
Tribunale di Brescia: Ordinanza 12 March 2009
T.A.R. Roma (Lazio), Sezione I: Sentenza No. 6352, 1 July 2009
Corte di cassazione, Sezione V penale: Sentenza No. 38597, 9 July 2009
Corte di cassazione, Sezione IV penale: Sentenza No. 41819, 10 July 2009
Tribunale di Milano: Sentenza No. 1586, 16 July 2009
Tribunale per i minorenni di Napoli: Ordinanza No. 139/09, 29 September 2009
Tribunale di Brescia: Ordinanza No. 3071, 11 December 2009
T.A.R. Brescia (Lombardia), Sezione II: Sentenza No. 19, 15 January 2010
Tribunale di Brescia, Sezione Lavoro: Ordinanza 22 July 2010
Tribunale di Milano, Sezione Lavoro: Ordinanza No. 2909, 29 September 2010
Tribunale di Brescia: Ordinanza No. 2798, 29 November 2010
Corte costituzionale: Sentenza No. 40, 7 February 2011
Corte di cassazione, Sezione V penale: Sentenza No. 54694, 26 April 2011
Consiglio di Stato, Sezione IV: Sentenza No. 6050, 16 November 2011
Consiglio di Stato, Sezione IV: Ordinanza No. 1760, 9 May 2012
Corte di cassazione, Sezione I penale: Sentenza No. 31454, 1 August 2012
Tribunale di Roma, Sezione II Civile: Ordinanza in proceeding 49444/2012, 24 May 2013

Portugal

Tribunal da Relação de Lisboa: Case 59862/08.7TDLSB.L1, 1 February 2011

United Kingdom

R(E) v. Governing Body of JFS [2009], UKSC 15

United States

Supreme Court: *Marbury v. Madison*, 5 U.S. (1 Cranch) 137 (1803)
Supreme Court: *Johnson v. M'Intosh*, 21 U.S. (8 Wheat.) 543 (1823)
Supreme Court: *Cherokee Nation v. Georgia*, 30 U.S. (5 Pet.) 1 (1831)
Supreme Court: *Worcester v. Georgia*, 31 U.S. (6 Pet.) 515 (1832)
Supreme Court: *Swift v. Tyson*, 41 U.S. (16 Pet.) 1 (1842)
Supreme Court: *Prigg v. Pennsylvania*, 41 U.S. (16 Pet.) 539 (1842)
Supreme Court: *Dred Scott v. Sanford*, 60 U.S. (19 How.) 393 (1857)
Supreme Court: *The Slaughter House Cases*, 83 U.S. (16 Wall.) 36 (1873)
Supreme Court: *United States v. Cruikshank*, 92 U.S. 542 (1876)
Circuit Court for the District of California: *In re Ah Yup*, 1 F.Cas. 223 (C.C.D. Cal. 1878)
Supreme Court: *Strauder v. West Virginia*, 100 U.S. (10 Otto) 303 (1880)
Supreme Court: *United States v. Harris*, 106 U.S. 629 (1882)
Supreme Court: *The Civil Rights Cases*, 109 U.S. 3 (1883)
Supreme Court: *Ex parte Crow Dog*, 109 U.S. 556 (1883)
Supreme Court: *Elk v. Wilkins*, 112 U.S. 94 (1884)
Supreme Court: *Yick Wo v. Hopkins*, 118 U.S. 356 (1886)
Supreme Court: *United States v. Kagama*, 118 U.S. 375 (1886)
Supreme Court: *Chae Chan Ping v. United States*, 130 U.S. 581 (1889)
Supreme Court: *Plessy v. Ferguson*, 163 U.S. 537 (1896)
District Court, Western District of Texas: *In re Rodriguez*, 81 F. 337 (W.D. Tex. 1897)
Supreme Court: *De Lima v. Bidwell*, 182 U.S. 1 (1901)
Supreme Court: *Downes v. Bidwell*, 182 U.S. 244 (1901)
Supreme Court: *Dorr v. United States*, 195 U.S. 138 (1904)
Supreme Court: *Lochner v. New York*, 198 U.S. 45 (1905)
Supreme Court: *Coppage v. Kansas*, 236 U.S. 1 (1915)
Supreme Court: *Balzac v. Porto Rico*, 258 U.S. 298 (1922)
Supreme Court: *Ozawa v. United States*, 260 U.S. 178 (1922)
Supreme Court: *United States v. Thind*, 261 U.S. 204 (1922)
Supreme Court: *Terrace v. Thompson*, 263 U.S. 197 (1923)
Supreme Court: *Porterfield v. Webb*, 263 U.S. 225 (1923)
Supreme Court: *Gong Lum v. Rice*, 275 U.S. 78 (1927)
Supreme Court: *Hirabayashi v. United States*, 320 U.S. 81 (1943)
Supreme Court: *Korematsu v. United States*, 323 U.S. 214 (1944)
Supreme Court: *Ex parte Endo*, 323 U.S. 283 (1944)
Supreme Court: *Morgan v. Virginia*, 328 U.S. 373 (1946)
Supreme Court: *Oyama v. California*, 332 U.S. 633 (1947)
Supreme Court: *McLaurin v. Oklahoma State Regents*, 339 U.S. 637 (1950)
Supreme Court: *Sweatt v. Painter*, 339 U.S. 629 (1950)

Supreme Court: *Beauharnais v. Illinois*, 343 U.S. 250 (1952)
Supreme Court: *Hernandez v. Texas*, 347 U.S. 475 (1954)
Supreme Court: *Brown v. Board of Education (Brown I)*, 347 U.S. 483 (1954)
Supreme Court: *Brown v. Board of Education (Brown II)*, 349 U.S. 294 (1955)
Supreme Court: *Bradley et al. v. School Board of City of Richmond*, 382 U.S. 103 (1965) (*per curiam*)
Supreme Court: *Brandenburg v. Ohio*, 395 U.S. 444 (1969)
Supreme Court: *Washington v. Davis*, 426 U.S. 229 (1976)
Supreme Court: *National Socialist Party of America v. Village of Skokie*, 432 U.S. 43 (1977)
Supreme Court: *Regents of the University of California v. Bakke*, 438 U.S. 265 (1978)
Supreme Court: *United States v. Sioux Nation of Indians*, 448 U.S. 371 (1980)
District Court, Northern District of California: *Korematsu v. United States*, 584 F. Supp. 1406 (N.D. Cal. 1984)
Supreme Court: *City of Richmond v. J.A. Croson Co.*, 488 U.S. 469 (1989)
Supreme Court: *Metro Broadcasting, Inc. v. FCC*, 497 U.S. 547 (1990)
Supreme Court: *R.A.V. v. City of St. Paul*, 505 U.S. 377 (1992)
Court of Appeals, 9th Circuit: *Lam v. University of Hawaii*, 40 F.3d 1551, 1562 (9th Cir. 1994)
Supreme Court: *Adarand Constructors, Inc. v. Peña*, 515 U.S. 200 (1995)
District Court, District of Massachusetts: *America v. Leviner*, 31 F. Supp. 2d 23 (D. Mass. 1998)
Supreme Court of New Jersey: *Taylor v. Metzger*, 706 A.2d 685 (N.J. 1998)
Supreme Court of Minnesota: *State v. Buggs*, 581 N.W.2d 329, (Minn. 1998)
Supreme Court: *Saenz v. Roe*, 526 U.S. 489 (1999)
Supreme Court: *Gratz v. Bollinger*, 539 U.S. 244 (2003)
Supreme Court: *Grutter v. Bollinger*, 539 U.S. 306 (2003)
Supreme Court: *Johnson v. California*, 543 U.S. 499 (2005)
District Court, District of Connecticut: *Ricci v. DeStefano*, 554 F. Supp. 2d 142 (D. Conn. 2006)
Supreme Court: *Parents Involved in Community Schools v. Seattle School District No. 1*, 551 U.S. 701 (2007)
Court of Appeals, 2nd Circuit: *Ricci v. DeStefano*, 530 F.3d 87 (2d Cir. 2008) (*per curiam*)
Supreme Court: *Ricci v. DeStefano*, 557 U.S. 557 (2009)
Supreme Court: *Arizona v. United States*, 132 S.Ct. 2492, 567 U.S. _(2012)
Supreme Court: *Fisher v. University of Texas*, 133 S.Ct. 2411, 570 U.S. _(2013)
Supreme Court: *Shelby County v. Holder*, 133 S.Ct. 2612, 570 U.S. _(2013)

International cases

ECommHR: *East African Asians v. the United Kingdom*, Applications Nos. 4403/70–4419/70 (and more), 14 December 1973
ECtHR: *Ireland v. the United Kingdom* (Plenary), Application No. 5310/71, 18 January 1978
ECtHR: *Abdulaziz and Others v. the United Kingdom*, Application Nos. 9214/80, 9473/81, 9474/81, 28 May 1985
ECJ: Case C–57/96, *Meints v. Minister van Landbouw, Natuurbeheer en Visserij* [1997] ECR I–6689
ECJ: Case C–337/97, *CPM Meeusen v. Hoofdirectie van de IBG* [1999] ECR I–3289

ECtHR: *Schimanek v. Austria*, Application No. 32307/96, 1 February 2000
ECtHR: *Velikova v. Bulgaria*, Application No. 41488/98, 18 May 2000
ECtHR: *Anguelova v. Bulgaria*, Application No. 38361/97, 13 June 2002
ECJ: Case C–299/01, *Commission v. Luxemburg* [2002] ECR I–5899
ECtHR: *Garaudy v. France*, Application No. 65831/01, 24 June 2003
ECtHR: *Nachova and Others v. Bulgaria*, Application Nos. 43577/98 and 43579/98, 26 February 2004
ECtHR: *Balogh v. Hungary*, Application No. 47940/99, 20 July 2004
ECtHR: *Nachova and Others v. Bulgaria* (Grand Chamber), Application Nos. 43577/98 and 43579/98, 6 July 2005
ECtHR: *Moldovan and Others v. Romania (No.2)*, Application Nos. 41138/98 and 64320/01, 12 July 2005
ECtHR: *Witzsch v. Germany*, Application No. 7485/03, 13 December 2005
ECtHR: *D.H. and Others v. The Czech Republic* (Grand Chamber), Application No. 57325/00, 13 November 2007
ECtHR: *Stoica v. Romania*, Application No. 42722/02, 4 March 2008
ECtHR: *Sampanis and Others v. Greece*, Application No. 32526/05, 5 June 2008
ECJ: Case C–54/07, *Centrum voor gelijkheid van kansen en voor racismebestrijding v. Firma Feryn NV* [2008] ECR I–5187
HRC: *Rosalind Williams Lecraft v. Spain*, Communication No. 1493/2006, CCPR/C/96/D/1493/2006, 17 August 2009
ECtHR: *Sejdić and Finci v. Bosnia and Herzegovina* (Grand Chamber), Application Nos. 27996/06 and 34836/06, 22 December 2009
ECtHR: *Sashov and Others v. Bulgaria*, Application No. 14383/03, 7 January 2010
ECtHR: *Oršuš and Others v. Croatia* (Grand Chamber), Application No. 15766/03, 16 March 2010
ECtHR: *Paraskeva Todorova v. Bulgaria* , Application No. 37193/07, 25 March 2010
ECSR: *Centre on Housing Rights and Evictions (COHRE) v. Italy*, Complaint No. 58/2009, 25 June 2010
ECtHR: *Carabulea v. Romania*, Application No. 45661/99, 13 July 2010
ECtHR: *Soare and Others v. Romania*, Application No. 24329/02, 22 February 2011
ECSR: *Centre on Housing Rights and Evictions (COHRE) v. France*, Complaint No. 63/2010, 28 June 2011
ECtHR: *V.C. v. Slovakia*, Application No. 18968/07, 8 November 2011
ECtHR: *N.B. v. Slovakia*, Application No. 29518/10, 12 June 2012
ECtHR: *Fedorchenko and Lozenko v. Ukraine*, Application No. 387/03, 20 September 2012
ECtHR: *Horvath and Kiss v. Hungary*, Application No. 11146/11, 29 January 2013
CJEU: *Valeri Hariev Belov v ChEZ Elektro Balgaria AD and ChEZ Raspredelenie Balgaria AD*, Case C–394/11, 31 January 2013
ECtHR: *Lavida and Others v. Greece*, Application No. 7973/10, 31 May 2013
ECtHR: *Winterstein and Others v. France*, Application No. 27013/07, 17 October 2013
ECtHR: *S.A.S. v. France*, Application No. 43835/11, 27 November 2013
ECtHR: *Biao v. Denmark*, Application No. 38590/10, 25 March 2014

Index